Subnational Politics and Democratization in Mexico

U.S.–Mexico Contemporary Perspectives Series, 13
Center for U.S.–Mexican Studies
University of California, San Diego

Contributors

Kathleen Bruhn
Tomás Calvillo Unna
Wayne A. Cornelius
Todd A. Eisenstadt
Víctor Alejandro Espinoza Valle
Neil Harvey
Luis Hernández Navarro
Jane Hindley
Jean-François Prud'homme
Jeffrey W. Rubin
David Shirk
Richard Snyder
Ligia Tavera-Fenollosa
Gabriel Torres

Subnational Politics and Democratization in Mexico

edited by

WAYNE A. CORNELIUS,

TODD A. EISENSTADT &

JANE HINDLEY

LA JOLLA

CENTER FOR U.S.–MEXICAN STUDIES

UNIVERSITY OF CALIFORNIA, SAN DIEGO

Printed in the United States of America

Library of Congress Cataloging-in-Publication Data

Subnational politics and democratization in Mexico / edited by Wayne
    A. Cornelius, Todd A. Eisenstadt & Jane Hindley.
        p.   cm. -- (U.S.-Mexico contemporary perspectives series ; 13)
        Includes bibliographical references (p.   ).
        ISBN 1-878367-39-0 (pbk.)
        1. Local government--Mexico.   2. Democratization--Mexico.
    3. Political parties--Mexico--States--Case studies.   4. Political
participation--Mexico--States--Case Studies.   I. Cornelius, Wayne
A., 1945- .   II. Eisenstadt, Todd A.   III. Hindley, Jane, 1963- .
IV. Series.
JS2117.A2S83 1999   98-5480?
320.972′09′049--dc21   CIP

Contents

Preface

This volume is the culmination of a four-year research project on the role of subnational political actors in Mexico's democratization process, based in the Center for U.S.–Mexican Studies at the University of California, San Diego. Begun in the fall of 1994, the project eventually involved over thirty anthropologists, sociologists, historians, and political scientists, as well as nonacademic political practitioners from Mexico, Cuba, the United States, and the United Kingdom.

In its initial year, the project brought together a core group of researchers in residence at the Center for U.S.–Mexican Studies, including project director Wayne Cornelius, Center director Kevin Middlebrook, and four visiting research fellows—Tomás Calvillo, Haroldo Dilla, Todd Eisenstadt, and Jane Hindley. This core research group met on a weekly basis to discuss the major conceptual and empirical issues raised by Mexico's protracted and spatially uneven transition to a democratic system, comparing the Mexican experience (especially from President Luis Echeverría's political opening in the 1970s through the administration of President Carlos Salinas de Gortari, 1988–1994) with transitions from authoritarian rule in other postrevolutionary regimes in Latin America. The group also discussed fieldwork-based case studies of specific subnational political transformations or resistance to political change, several of which were selected for in-depth analysis.

In February 1996, the core group convened a three-day research workshop in Mexico City, which was hosted by the Instituto de Estudios Sociales of the Universidad Nacional Autónoma de México (UNAM), directed by Pablo González Casanova. This workshop brought together leading scholars of democratization, representatives of political parties and nongovernmental organizations, and social movement activists to discuss first drafts of the case studies appearing in this volume. We would like to make special mention of the contribution by workshop commentator Sabino Estrada Guadalupe, then president of the Consejo Guerrerense de Quinientos Años de Resistencia Indígena. His untimely death in a car accident in September 1996 constitutes a significant loss for democratic forces in the state of Guerrero and for the national indigenous rights movement. In April 1997, revised drafts of several of the Mexico City workshop papers were presented at a panel session on "The 'New Federalism' and Political Conflict Resolution in Mexico," at the XX International Congress of the Latin American Studies Association in Guadalajara.

Principal funding for this project was generously provided by the Ford Foundation (New York and Mexico City offices). Jane Hindley wishes to thank the Department of Sociology, University of Essex, for a Fuller Fund travel grant for final editing. We are also indebted to the Center for U.S.–Mexican Studies for administrative support, and especially to the Center's editor, Sandra del Castillo.

Wayne Cornelius
Todd Eisenstadt
Jane Hindley

La Jolla, California
México, D.F.
Colchester, U.K.
January 1999

PART I

Introduction

1

Subnational Politics and Democratization: Tensions between Center and Periphery in the Mexican Political System

Wayne A. Cornelius

This volume highlights the growing disjuncture between Mexico's recently accelerated transition to democracy at the national level and what is occurring at the state and local levels in many parts of the country. Subnational political regimes controlled by hard-line antidemocratic elements linked to the Institutional Revolutionary Party (PRI) remain important in late twentieth-century Mexico, even in an era of much-intensified interparty competition. The survival and even strengthening of subnational authoritarian enclaves in states like Puebla, Tabasco, Guerrero, Chiapas, Oaxaca, Campeche, and Yucatán raises major theoretical and policy issues: What, specifically, has been the role of opposition party–controlled state and local governments and autonomous popular movements in promoting democratization in Mexico? What is the potential contribution of democratizing agents operating at subnational levels to the national-level democratic transition? To what extent will failure to democratize in subnational political spaces where little or no change has yet occurred constrain or disrupt the national democratization process? How can fiscal and administrative decentralization—a key dimension of democratization

I am indebted to Federico Estévez and Jeffrey Weldon for insightful and provocative comments. Useful suggestions for revision were also made by participants in research seminars at the Latin American Centre at Oxford University, the David Rockefeller Center for Latin American Studies at Harvard University, and the Mexico Study Group of the Pacific Council on International Policy, where earlier drafts of this chapter were presented. I bear full responsibility for the conclusions.

in what has been a highly centralized, authoritarian-presidentialist system—proceed without strengthening authoritarian elites in the periphery? To what extent is the increasingly uneven, patchwork character of democratization in Mexico an obstacle to completing the process in an expeditious and low-conflict manner? These are the key questions suggested by the contributions to this volume, based on recent fieldwork conducted in ten different Mexican states.

Conceptualizing Center-Periphery Relations in Mexican Politics

The conventional model of center-periphery relations in the Mexican political system, developed in the 1960s through fieldwork in such places as Jalapa, Veracruz (Fagen and Tuohy 1972), stressed the pervasive importance of tight, centralized, top-down control, exercised mainly through the presidency and the corporatist structures established in the 1930s, which kept the system "in equilibrium" at almost all times. In this model, political actors at the state and local levels were dependably tied to the center through clientelistic and family ties, economic incentives, partisan loyalties, and coercion. The political subordinates' need to avoid embarrassing their higher-level patrons within the PRI-government apparatus—for example, by highly visible authoritarian excesses or spectacular corruption—clearly had an inhibiting effect. Direct intervention by the president was an ever-present possibility that served to preemptively discipline potential "troublemakers"—be they state governors, congressmen, labor or peasant organization bosses, or local caciques. There was a credible threat that any breach of discipline would be severely and summarily punished, effectively nullifying one's prospects for upward mobility within the system.

By the late 1980s, some historians and political scientists were forcefully reminding us that the centralized, top-down controls were never really as tight, nor as spatially uniform, as the conventional wisdom would have it. Rather, a "Swiss-cheese" conception of political control in Mexico was more consistent with the historical evidence, as well as with contemporary Mexican political dynamics (Meyer 1986; Knight 1990; Fox 1992; Rubin 1990, 1997).[1] Today, there

---

[1] Renewed attention to regional variations and center-periphery conflicts in Mexico was also a by-product of the resurgence of historical research on specific regions and localities since 1980. This vast and continually growing body of literature has illuminated many subnational differences in economic development and political organization. In general, local and regional studies by historians have been effective in demonstrating the impact of national and international developments on "the provinces" and in documenting the modes of resistance by local communities and sub-

can be little doubt that centralized presidential control, and discipline within the ruling party and the government-affiliated sectoral organizations, are breaking down, throughout the system.

This breakdown began under President Carlos Salinas de Gortari (1988–1994) and accelerated under his successor, Ernesto Zedillo (1994–2000). It was evident by the late 1980s that central control of the PRI apparatus, its "mass" sectoral organizations, and even local caciques, was weakening. Lower-echelon PRI leaders were no longer aligning themselves automatically with dictates from the center. During the first three years of Salinas's term, he was challenged openly by the state-level PRI machines in Baja California (1989), Guanajuato (1991), and San Luis Potosí (1991), which had been defeated or suffered major reverses in gubernatorial elections and sought to prevent opposition party takeovers of the state governments. Salinas snuffed out these challenges through various tactics and, in doing so, won points in international media, financial, and governmental circles for his "democratizing" actions.[2] But in 1994, Salinas's successor adopted a policy of strict nonintervention in electoral disputes as well as in matters of internal PRI governance. Ernesto Zedillo publicly declared that he would maintain a *sana distancia* (healthy distance) between his government and the PRI apparatus. To some observers, this abdication of the president's traditional role as official party leader and power broker was just a reflection of Zedillo's personal distaste for, and inexperience in, partisan politics. Others saw it as a gambit for making quicker progress in multiparty talks on electoral system reform, by preserving an "honest broker" status for himself. The obvious risk is that subnational actors not sharing Zedillo's political reform objectives would take him at his word.

Whatever their previous validity, 1960s–vintage models of center-periphery relations in Mexican politics are unhelpful in an era when the incumbent president takes a "hands-off" approach to subnational political conflicts (except those that provoke violence serious enough to command national and international media attention); when the president has voluntarily surrendered his most potent, metaconstitu-

---

national political actors to centralizing forces. They have been much less concerned with elucidating the influence of subnational political phenomena on national-level political structures and elite behavior. See the perceptive review of this literature in Knight 1997.

[2] In Baja California, the overwhelming victory of the PANista gubernatorial candidate, Ernesto Ruffo, was quickly recognized by the national head of the PRI and President Salinas; in Guanajuato and San Luis Potosí, the elected PRI governors were pressured by Salinas to resign, as opposition party protests and foreign media criticism of election irregularities mounted. In Guanajuato, a PANista serving as mayor of the city of León was appointed as interim governor; in San Luis Potosí, a PRIista was named interim governor. Both of these appointments were orchestrated by the Salinas government.

tional power—that of choosing his own successor by dictating the PRI's presidential nominee; when substantial devolution of financial resources from the federal to the state and municipal governments is occurring, under the banner of "the new federalism"; when political control has already been ceded to opposition party governments governing between 55 and 60 percent of the total population; when scores of municipal governments are now controlled by a party that is different from that which controls the state in which the municipality is located; and when divided governments have emerged in several key states and, since June 1997, at the federal level, with the PRI's loss of majority control in the federal Chamber of Deputies.

Challenges from the Periphery

Under such conditions, it could have been expected that tensions between center and periphery within the system would rise. Indeed, since 1994 we have witnessed some truly extraordinary breaches of political discipline, amounting in some cases to open defiance of the center by subnational political actors. The most blatant case is the successful rebellion of PRIista governor Roberto Madrazo of Tabasco against President Zedillo—a rebellion that was supported by the entire PRIista bloc in the Tabasco state legislature (see Eisenstadt, this volume). Zedillo had made a widely reported agreement with the opposition Party of the Democratic Revolution (PRD) to force Madrazo out of office, as evidence of Zedillo's commitment to deeper electoral reforms, and as a quid pro quo for the PRD's future cooperation with the government in Congress on a wide range of sensitive issues. According to documents that surfaced several months after his election, Governor Madrazo spent somewhere between U.S.$39 and $76 million on his campaign. (The upper end of that range would be about seventy times the amount allowed under state and federal election laws.) Nevertheless, Madrazo was able to induce powerful allies in the national PRI leadership to support his cause, and his local supporters threatened to block any opposition party takeover of the Tabasco government. After a standoff lasting nearly two months, Zedillo caved in, and today Madrazo no longer seems to be a target for removal. For the first time since the 1930s, a sitting state governor has openly defied the president and survived in office. Indeed, since 1997 Madrazo has been an undeclared candidate for the PRI's presidential nomination, using his political allies in the Southeast and anti-reform elements in the national PRI elite to promote his candidacy. Meanwhile, the state of Tabasco continues to seethe with long-unresolved labor disputes, takeovers of oil wells by Indian groups seeking environmental indemnities from PEMEX (the national petroleum company), and other conflicts that the governor seems incapable of resolving.

Another kind of challenge to Zedillo was posed by the PRI governor of Guerrero, Rubén Figueroa. For three years, Figueroa presided over a systematic, brutal, highly visible repression of dissident campesinos and opposition party militants in his state. A state-level prosecutor had absolved Figueroa of all responsibility for the premeditated massacre of seventeen unarmed peasants at Aguas Blancas, Guerrero, in August 1995. After months of dithering, Zedillo asked the Supreme Court to conduct its own investigation of the massacre. The Court determined that Figueroa had falsified evidence in order to cover up the massacre, even though the justices could find no direct evidence that he had ordered it. Eventually, Figueroa was forced to resign, but only after a huge "smoking gun" was handed to Zedillo, in the form of a video showing how the peasant massacre really occurred. The video surfaced on national television and was soon shown around the world. Up to that point, Zedillo had insisted unconvincingly that his "new federalism" doctrine precluded any kind of presidential intervention. Figueroa remains an influential figure in Guerrero politics, leading a faction of the PRI whose candidate won the party's nomination for the February 1999 gubernatorial election.

Still another type of defiance from the provinces is exemplified by Mario Villanueva, governor of the state of Quintana Roo, which in recent years has become one of the key transshipment points for cocaine destined for the United States. Various federal government investigations found Villanueva to be deeply implicated in the drug-smuggling operations in his state. In the era of traditional *presidencialismo*, a state governor accused of nonpolitical criminal activity potentially embarrassing to the regime was likely to be forced from office, under direct presidential pressure. But Governor Villanueva launched a counteroffensive, demanding that federal authorities produce the evidence gathered against him and accusing national PRI leaders of fomenting opposition to him in Quintana Roo (Dillon and Golden 1998). President Zedillo might have lent his support to an effort in the federal Congress to impeach Villanueva, thereby paving the way for criminal charges to be filed against him, but he declined to do so. Villanueva governs his state in a highly authoritarian manner, keeping the state legislature, the law enforcement system, and the media under tight control. He appears likely to remain in office until his term ends in April 1999. Such cases may multiply in the future, as alleged "*narco-políticos*" like Villanueva and other state and local politicians with ties to organized crime test the resolve and capacity of federal officials to bring them to justice.

In many ways, Manuel Bartlett, governor of the state of Puebla (1993–1999), has been the most consistently effective and politically ingenious challenger of central authority during the Zedillo *sexenio*. Bartlett is a prominent leader of the PRI's old guard and a former hard-line interior minister (under President Miguel de la Madrid, 1982–1988) who gained a reputation as a master manipulator of election results. In the 1994 national elections, as a state governor, he was accused of setting up a secret, computerized vote tabulation system in Puebla that supposedly operated independently of the Federal Electoral Institute's system. In November 1995 he orchestrated the reversal of local election results in a small but economically strategic municipality called Huejotzingo. The original result favored the National Action Party (PAN) by 907 votes, but after the state electoral court— dominated by Governor Bartlett—reviewed the count, the PRI was declared the winner by 28 votes. Arguing that the federal government had allowed the state electoral tribunal to validate a clear case of vote fraud, the national-level PAN leadership used this as a pretext for abandoning multiparty talks on further political reforms, which went on without the PANistas for nearly four months. The PAN ended its boycott only when the PRIista whose election as municipal president in Huejotzingo in 1995 was recognized by the state government was forced to resign, apparently under pressure from President Zedillo, and was replaced by a PANista. Thus the resolution was a Carlos Salinas–style presidential intervention to reverse an embarrassing, politically inconvenient election result. Manuel Bartlett's shenanigans clearly caused major problems for Zedillo, but he never seemed to be in danger of losing his job.

In late 1997, Bartlett publicly declared that he wanted to be the PRI's next presidential nominee, thereby issuing another direct challenge to Zedillo and the technocratic wing of the party. Throughout 1998, Bartlett ran openly for the presidency. To strengthen his PRI machine in Puebla for the November 1998 gubernatorial and municipal elections (and indirectly, to boost his own presidential campaign), Bartlett crafted a state law enabling him to divert the lion's share of increased revenue-sharing funds approved by Congress in the 1998 federal budget, from cities controlled by the opposition PAN to rural areas where the PRI is stronger.[3] "Bartlett's Law" was quickly copied by PRIista governors in several other states, and it remains available as a legal mechanism for shoring up the PRI's base, pending the outcome of a Supreme Court challenge lodged by the PAN. Zedillo's Ministry of Finance initially criticized "Bartlett's Law" but soon caved

---

[3] Bartlett's official rationale was that the allocation of federal funds among municipalities within his state should be based on poverty levels rather than on population size. The effect of this formula is to skew the distribution toward the poorer rural areas from which the PRI harvests most of its votes.

in and reaffirmed its constitutionality. This type of state-level legislation not only penalizes opposition party–controlled governments in urban areas; it gives state governors greater power over tax revenues collected by the federal government, and it complicates relations between the president and the opposition parties at the national level. If the president cannot deliver on revenue-sharing commitments made with the opposition parties (as Zedillo did in his negotiations with the PAN to gain its approval for the 1998 federal budget), why should these parties have any confidence in his pledges during future budget battles or on nonbudgetary issues?

What is the pattern here? Three elements need to be highlighted. First, the Zedillo government has been extremely reluctant to take any action that would undermine key state-level PRI leaders, so long as they retain their personal power base within their domains. That reluctance seems to apply even to politicians whose abuses of authority are egregious, by the traditional standard. Only when the abuses become too sensational to ignore is remedial action taken. Second, there is no consistent presidential strategy for dealing with such cases. During the first half of Zedillo's term, his preference was to dump the mess into the federal judiciary and expect Supreme Court justices to "separate the autocrats from the democrats," as a PANista member of the Senate put it in 1996. Sometimes that strategy has backfired, as it did in the Madrazo case. Third, the way in which major conflicts of interest between the central government and subnational political actors have been handled under Zedillo is a measure of the loss of presidential control over the state governors and the PRI apparatus. Unlike his predecessors, and especially Salinas,[4] this president clearly has not possessed the power to remove strong PRI governors, especially for purely political reasons.

During his 1994 campaign for the presidency, Zedillo pledged to maintain a "healthy distance" between himself as president and the PRI, not intervening in the party's nomination process nor other aspects of its internal affairs. In practice, the healthy distance doctrine clearly backfired. The PRI leadership, at both the national and state levels, apparently took it as an invitation to dictate political strategy, while Zedillo occupied himself with macroeconomic policy issues. On political matters, the president seemed to be going with the flow, rather than the PRI disciplining itself to presidential interests.

As a consequence of this reversal of traditional roles, subnational conflicts over issues ranging from electoral fraud and unfair terms of interparty competition to human rights violations, environmental threats, and labor disputes festered for many months or even years—

---

[4] Salinas forced the resignations of at least eleven state governors and governors-elect during his presidency, for offenses ranging from embezzlement to highly disruptive election irregularities.

often with serious national and even international political ramifications. As of this writing, the standoff with Governor Roberto Madrazo has been going on for nearly four years. The electoral dispute between the PRI and the PAN in Huejotzingo, Puebla, lasted for seven months and paralyzed the electoral reform negotiations for much of that period. The rebellion in Chiapas is now in its fifth year, and the December 1997 massacre of forty-five Zapatista sympathizers by paramilitary elements protected and apparently financed by the local and state-level PRI apparatus demonstrates that the profound economic, cultural, and political conflict in that state has only acquired dangerous new layers of complexity (see Harvey 1998).

What is certain is that, under a president who seems increasingly less capable of controlling what happens in subnational political spaces (even if he has the will to do so), state and local political actors are exercising greater autonomy within their domains than at perhaps any time since the 1920s and early 1930s. Some of these subnational actors have democratic proclivities; others are frankly authoritarian in their designs and are aggressively pursuing their own agendas and interests. As Jesús Silva-Herzog Márquez has observed, "With traditional [political] discipline having been shattered, political bosses, barons, and paramilitary squads are sprouting like mushrooms on the damp soil of the transition" (1998: 2).

It is indisputable that, prior to the recent breakdown of centralized controls, some of Mexico's subnational political actors behaved with considerable autonomy, if not impunity. State governors, in particular, have traditionally enjoyed considerable latitude in using their financial and manpower resources and their coercive powers. But it was all done within generally recognized limits, set by central authorities. Today, it is increasingly difficult to see where the limits are drawn. What mechanisms of centralized political control are still operating? What demands can subnational actors make upon the center, without fear of retribution? We used to know the answers to all these questions—or at least we thought we did.

Subnational Politics as a Constraint on Democratization

What happens at subnational levels—especially resistance to democratic change—has been largely neglected in the literatures on democratic transition and consolidation, apart from some passing references by scholars like Guillermo O'Donnell to "gaps" or "blind spots" in the democratization process (O'Donnell 1992). "Bottom-up" and "top-down" theories of democratization have seldom been concerned with explaining what happens at the intersection of local and national-level democratizing processes, and how these two processes reinforce or constrain each other (see, for example, Przeworski 1992; Linz and Stepan 1996). Neither does the huge literature on popular movements with a local or regional base help us very much to understand this dynamic; it tends to focus on the conditions under which such movements develop, the strategic choices they make, and their ability to remain autonomous in agenda setting (see Cook 1996: chap. 2; Escobar and Álvarez 1992; Foweraker and Craig 1990; Haber 1994).

A working hypothesis for the Mexican case, supported by much of the field research reported in this volume, is that during the present phase of the country's political evolution, the subnational political arena will be the principal source of inertia and resistance to democratization, rather than the prime breeding ground for democratic advances. This hypothesis runs contrary to the expectations of numerous Mexican and U.S. political analysts during the 1980s and early 1990s, who saw democracy advancing inexorably from the periphery to the center, through the steady accumulation of subnational conquests by opposition parties: "*la vía centrípeta a la democracia*" (see Mizrahi 1997, 1998).

In retrospect, there was ample reason for skepticism that this scenario could ever be viable in the Mexican context. The scenario assumed two conditions: (1) a relatively high level of cohesion and discipline within the national PRI elite; and (2) a continuation of strong presidential leadership, including leadership of the PRI. The first of these conditions (high elite cohesion and discipline) has not obtained since the mid–1980s; and the second condition (strong presidential leadership) has not been met under Zedillo.

We can still expect democratizing pressures on national-level political actors and institutions to emanate from subnational political spaces controlled by the opposition parties, nongovernmental organizations (NGOs), or truly independent popular movements—assuming that these subnational agents of democratization have succeeded in neutralizing the influence of authoritarian elements within their domains. Opposition politicians like Vicente Fox of Guanajuato can legitimately claim to be "making a [democratic] transition in the provinces" (quoted by Bruhn, this volume). But only under extraordinary circumstances are such transformations of subnational spaces, per se, likely to achieve major democratic advances at the national level.

Moreover, a countervailing influence will be operating in the periphery, so long as anti-democratic forces at the state and local levels can operate with relative impunity. Indeed, in those subnational spaces where entrenched, hard-line PRIista leaders continue to hold sway, we can anticipate even greater impunity and more rigid authoritarian control, including freer recourse to official violence.

These leaders—especially the anti-reform PRIista state governors—
have been growing stronger over time, not weaker. In recent years,
PRIista leaders have shown that they are still capable of manipulating
results in elections for state legislature seats and municipal offices,
through their control of state-level electoral tribunals (see Eisenstadt
1998: chap. 3). The most egregious of these manipulated outcomes
(for example, in the states of Puebla, México, and Yucatán) were subsequently reversed by the Federal Electoral Tribunal or through
presidential intervention, but only after protracted and highly visible
resistance by recalcitrant PRIista state governors.

With the major advances in enhancing the transparency and competitiveness of national elections and the independence of federal
electoral authorities that have been made since 1990, it seems unlikely
at this juncture that Mexico will suffer any significant retrogression in
the democratization of its national-level political institutions. The
pace of still-needed reforms in areas like campaign finance and media
access may be less than optimal, especially if the presidency remains
in the PRI's hands after the 2000 elections. In the foreseeable future,
however, setbacks to democratization are more likely to result from
"shocks" and challenges to central authority engineered by anti-
democratic forces operating in the states and localities than from ir-
resolvable conflicts among national-level actors.

In the current context of greatly weakened presidential rule and
disintegrating PRI discipline—an imploding center—the "new federalism" being implemented in Mexico (Rodríguez 1997; Ward and
Rodríguez 1999) is very much a double-edged sword. The obvious
danger is that, rather than establishing the bases of a broad and irreversible democratic transition, at all levels, the end result of the dispersion of power now under way in Mexico could be a fragmentation
of the traditional, centralized, presidentialist system into a highly
variegated mosaic: a "crazy quilt" of increasingly competitive, plural-
istic political spaces where pro-democracy forces have consolidated
themselves, juxtaposed with hardened authoritarian enclaves in
which the surviving "*dinosaurios*" of the PRI-government apparatus
are able to resist not only local pressures for democratization but also
external pressure.[5]

Both the PAN and the PRD have been pushing for much larger
transfers of funds from the federal to the state and municipal treasur-
ies. At the outset of the 1998 budget negotiations, for example, the
opposition bloc in the Chamber of Deputies demanded a U.S.$50 bil-
lion devolution (they got $15 billion). What will be the ultimate con-

---

[5] It is also possible, as Spalding (1998: 33) has argued, that one of the PRI's future survival strategies may be deliberately to increase the autonomy of state and local party
apparatuses that remain electorally successful, even if their tactics include criticizing
national-level party leaders and government policies.

sequences of placing significantly greater federal resources, and authority to raise more revenues locally, in the hands of some of the most retrograde elements of the system—politicians whose links and perceived obligations to the center are increasingly tenuous? Some clues can be gleaned from a recently published study of the impacts of World Bank loans to Mexico during the last ten years on local governance. Most of the Bank's loans were made under the banner of promoting decentralization and "pro-accountability governance reforms," in World Bank parlance. Based on their analysis of municipal-level data for the state of Oaxaca, Fox and Aranda (1996: 50) conclude:

> It is often assumed that decentralization necessarily encourages more accountable governance. [But] the impact of decentralization on accountability depends on how representative local government was before receiving additional external resources. At least in Mexico, there is no evidence that increased external funding for municipalities ... increases local-level accountability.... These conclusions suggest, therefore, that increased funding without institutional change is likely [only] to reinforce the existing institutional structure.

This is exactly the kind of outcome that some opposition party and popular movement leaders have feared—that is, that Zedillo's "new federalism" is tantamount to impunity for PRIista state governors and local politicians who are no longer being held accountable by the national PRI leadership, nor by the president. Which is worse? The traditional system, whereby officials were answerable only to their superiors within the PRI-government apparatus? Or a situation in which they are accountable, essentially, to no one but themselves?

Subnational Authoritarian Enclaves and the Decentering of Mexican Politics

Some Mexican political analysts have argued that at this stage of Mexico's democratization process, it may be better to put up with a few subnational caudillos than to have an all-powerful center, as in the past. After all, growing electoral competition and transparency "inevitably" creates new *espacios de participación* at the state and local levels, which will gradually undermine the authoritarian enclaves that remain. Nevertheless, there is reason to doubt that a coherent, national-level democratization project can go forward, with an archipelago of deeply entrenched, well-protected subnational authoritarian enclaves still in place, even within a much more competitive electoral system. More vigorous electoral competition per se clearly is not enough to eliminate these enclaves; otherwise, we would have seen considerably greater political change in states like Oaxaca and Yucatán, among others where PRIista governors and local caciques have used government resources to rebuild clientelistic networks while continuing to sanction localized electoral abuses (see Spalding 1998). Interparty competition should therefore be seen as a necessary but not a sufficient condition for undermining subnational authoritarian enclaves.

Since the late 1980s, at least, it is been apparent that a key factor accounting for the persistence of authoritarian practices in many states and localities is unreformed PRI organizations. Would-be reformers within the PRI apparatus remain highly vulnerable—not just in the "politically primitive" and economically underdeveloped South, but in such "modern" states as San Luis Potosí, Michoacán, and Puebla. For example, efforts to democratize the state PRI in San Luis Potosí in the early 1990s failed completely because of weak-to-nonexistent support from the national party leadership; the reformist state party chairman was purged. In the future, how much support and pressure for reforming state and local-level PRI organizations will be forthcoming from the center? It is difficult to envision much progress in this vital area under a politically laissez-faire presidency like that of Zedillo.

Except for unreconstructed PRI *dinosaurios*, there is no significant constituency in Mexico for a resurrection of old-style, highly centralized presidential rule. Indeed, Ernesto Zedillo has already dismantled enough of traditional *presidencialismo* and the opposition-controlled Congress has begun to exert enough checks on executive authority to make such a restoration impossible. On the other hand, the record to date suggests that pell-mell deconcentration of power—without credible mechanisms for enforcing party discipline and assuring that state and local officials can be held accountable—is just as likely to cause political decay as it is to set the stage for a durable and comprehensive democratic breakthrough (cf. Willis et al. 1998). If so, serious risks attach to Zedillo's attempt to end *presidencialismo* as we have known it and simultaneously to implement federalism as we have never known it in the Mexican context. The challenge remains: how to engineer a deconcentration of political power and a fiscal decentralization that do not simply strengthen authoritarian elites in the periphery. Committed and skillful political architects—not just effective firemen—are still needed at this stage of Mexico's democratic transition.

References

Cook, Maria Lorena. 1996. *Organizing Dissent: Unions, the State, and the Democratic Teachers' Movement in Mexico.* University Park: Pennsylvania State University Press.

Dillon, Sam, and Tim Golden. 1998. "Drug Inquiry Into a Governor Tests Mexico's New Politics," *New York Times*, November 26.

Eisenstadt, Todd A. 1998. "Courting Democracy in Mexico: Party Strategies, Electoral Institution-Building, and Political Opening." Ph.D. dissertation, University of California, San Diego.

Escobar, Arturo, and Sonia E. Álvarez, eds. 1992. *The Making of Social Movements in Latin America: Identity, Strategy, and Democracy.* Boulder, Colo.: Westview.

Fagen, Richard R., and William S. Tuohy. 1972. *Power and Privilege in a Mexican City.* Stanford, Calif.: Stanford University Press.

Foweraker, Joe, and Ann L. Craig, eds. 1990. *Popular Movements and Political Change in Mexico.* Boulder, Colo.: Lynne Rienner, in association with the Center for U.S.–Mexican Studies, University of California, San Diego.

Fox, Jonathan. 1992. *The Politics of Food in Mexico: State Power and Social Mobilization.* Ithaca, N.Y.: Cornell University Press.

Fox, Jonathan, and Josefina Aranda. 1996. *Decentralization and Rural Development in Mexico: Community Participation in Oaxaca's Municipal Funds Program.* Monograph Series, no. 42. La Jolla: Center for U.S.–Mexican Studies, University of California, San Diego.

Haber, Paul L. 1994. "The Art and Implications of Political Restructuring in Mexico: The Case of Urban Popular Movements." In *The Politics of Economic Restructuring: State-Society Relations and Regime Change in Mexico*, edited by Maria Lorena Cook, Kevin J. Middlebrook, and Juan Molinar Horcasitas. La Jolla: Center for U.S.–Mexican Studies, University of California, San Diego.

Harvey, Neil. 1998. *The Chiapas Rebellion: The Struggle for Land and Democracy.* Durham, N.C.: Duke University Press.

Knight, Alan. 1990. "Historical Continuities in Social Movements." In *Popular Movements and Political Change in Mexico*, edited by Joe Foweraker and Ann L. Craig. Boulder, Colo.: Lynne Rienner.

———. 1997. "Latin America: An Historiographical Overview." In *Companion to Historiography*, edited by Michael Bentley. London: Routledge.

Linz, Juan J., and Alfred Stepan. 1996. *Problems of Democratic Transition and Consolidation: Southern Europe, South America, and Post-Communist Europe.* Baltimore, Md.: Johns Hopkins University Press.

Meyer, Lorenzo. 1986. "Un tema añejo siempre actual." In *Descentralización y democracia en México*, edited by Blanca Torres. Mexico City: El Colegio de México.

Mizrahi, Yemile. 1997. "Pressuring the Center: Opposition Governments and Federalism in Mexico." Documentos de Trabajo, 71. División de Estudios Políticos, Centro de Investigación y Docencia Económicas.

———. 1998. "Voto retrospectivo y desempeño gubernamental: las elecciones en Chihuahua." Paper presented at the XXI International Congress of the Latin American Studies Association, Chicago, Ill., September 24–26.

O'Donnell, Guillermo. 1992. "Transitions, Continuities, and Paradoxes." In *Issues in Democratic Consolidation: The New South American Democracies in Comparative Perspective*, edited by Scott Mainwaring, Guillermo O'Donnell, and J. Samuel Valenzuela. Notre Dame, Ind.: University of Notre Dame Press.

Przeworski, Adam. 1992. "The Games of Transition." In *Issues in Democratic Consolidation: The New South American Democracies in Comparative Perspective*, edited by Scott Mainwaring, Guillermo O'Donnell, and J. Samuel Valenzuela. Notre Dame, Ind.: University of Notre Dame Press.

Rodríguez, Victoria E. 1997. *Decentralization in Mexico: From Reforma Municipal to Solidaridad to Nuevo Federalismo*. Boulder, Colo.: Westview.

Rubin, Jeffrey W. 1990. "Popular Mobilization and the Myth of State Corporatism." In *Popular Movements and Political Change in Mexico*, edited by Joe Foweraker and Ann L. Craig. Boulder, Colo.: Lynne Rienner.

————. 1997. *Decentering the Regime: Ethnicity, Radicalism, and Democracy in Juchitán, Mexico*. Durham, N.C.: Duke University Press.

Silva Herzog-Márquez, Jesús. 1998. "Mexico's Political Institutions." Paper presented at the January 12 session of the Study Group on the Future of Mexico, Pacific Council on International Policy, Los Angeles, California.

Spalding, Rose J. 1998. "Political Parties in Yucatán: Regionalism, Strategy, and Prospects for the PRI." Paper presented at the XXI International Congress of the Latin American Studies Association, Chicago, Ill., September 24–26.

Ward, Peter M., and Victoria E. Rodríguez. 1999. *Bringing the States Back In: New Federalism and State Government in Mexico*. U.S.–Mexico Policy Studies Monograph Series. Austin: Lyndon B. Johnson School of Public Affairs, University of Texas at Austin.

Willis, Eliza, Christopher da C.B. Garman, and Stephan Haggard. 1998. "The Politics of Decentralization in Latin America," *Latin American Research Review* 34 (1): 7–56.

PART II

Subnational Party Organizations and Democratization

2

PRD Local Governments in Michoacán: Implications for Mexico's Democratization Process

Kathleen Bruhn

"Democracy from the provinces: and why not?" asked Vicente Fox Quesada, the newly elected National Action Party governor of Guanajuato, in a 1995 conference on political transition in Mexico. Indeed, while prospects for democracy were being debated in the center, said Fox, "we *are making* a transition in the province." Though supporting national dialogue to reform electoral law and the state, Fox argued that the most immediate problem was not constitutional reform but "management": on the basis of citizen organization and existing laws, it was already possible—and Guanajuato would "give the example"—to build true federalism and democracy in Mexico.

At the same table, Cuauhtémoc Cárdenas, two-time presidential candidate of the Left, presented a rather different vision of democratic transition, as a product of political struggle resulting in "a substantive pact among the representative forces to change the regime." Warning that such a transition would be difficult because of the regime's capacity to adapt to challenges and to use the media for "ideological cooptation," Cárdenas argued that "every transition implies a certain level of coercion." Thus "the power of the transforming alliance is key." It was the task of the leftist Party of the Democratic Revolution (PRD) to construct this alliance "capable of imposing a democratic transition on an unwilling regime." Implicit in this formulation is an understanding of democratization as fundamentally constructed at the national rather than the local level, and as a product of mobilization rather than the exercise of power.

In these two approaches to democratic transition, some would argue, lies one of the keys to the explanation of the different political fortunes of the conservative National Action Party (PAN) and the PRD since the shattering events of 1988, which stripped the ruling Institutional Revolutionary Party (PRI) of its aura of invincibility. While the leftist authors of the PRI's near defeat in the 1988 presidential election lost much of their electoral support and failed to capture even one state government, the PAN steadily accumulated a track record of governing, not only in major cities but also in a growing number of states. In Mexico's 1994 presidential election, the PAN emphasized its experience in states like Baja California as a reason to trust its leadership, contrasting its own responsible record with the strident performance of Cárdenas, who had only governed when still a member of the PRI, who had cordial meetings with the guerrilla rebel leader Subcomandante Marcos, and who loudly predicted popular rebellion if the PRI tampered with electoral results.

The PRD, from this perspective, had foolishly neglected the potential of local government as a path to power and as a method of democratization. Relatively few national figures in the PRD had chosen to run for state office—Heberto Castillo (in Veracruz) and Porfirio Muñoz Ledo (in Guanajuato) being something of an exception—while prominent state leaders like Andrés Manuel López Obrador (in Tabasco) and Cristóbal Árias (in Michoacán) seemed uninterested in positions below the level of governor. The decision of Cárdenas to run—successfully—for mayor of Mexico City in 1997 reflects in part the national significance of the position and in part his own marginalization following his second electoral defeat, in the 1994 presidential campaign. Mexico City, despite being technically a local government, is immediately a national position in a way that Baja California or Chihuahua never were.

Yet the PRD did win municipal elections. From 1988 to 1991, the PRD governed nearly three times as many municipalities (*municipios*) as the PAN, though most PRD municipalities were smaller and nearly all were located in the rural state of Michoacán (Ureña 1991). Moreover, within the PRD, significant constituencies supported such a bottom-up path to democratization. One top national leader remarked in a 1991 interview that:

> In the PRD, there are two main hypotheses: that of those who think that [PRI recovery] is a wave that must be blocked with social mobilization, insistence on our principles, distancing ourselves from the government ... and waiting until 1994 so that, betting on a social and economic crisis, the personality of Cárdenas will rise again.... Many of us do not agree. I think that the only possible bet now is steadily to capture spaces of real power—municipalities,

> state governments. To the degree that we win these spaces of real power, we will give the opposition credentials as an option of government. It is a more modest road, but there is no other.... We must fight for governorships, fight for municipalities, and gradually diminish the spaces of fraud, increasing our credibility before the people, *even if* in 1994 we expect a conjuncture similar to that of 1988.

In this way, the "municipalists" hoped to bind the PRI with a thousand cords, each weak alone but strong together, much as the tiny Lilliputians bound the giant Gulliver.

The PRD's failure to convert its numerous local victories into repeat voting for the party in the municipalities it governed, let alone into a more effective constraint on the PRI, raises profound questions about the potential of this Lilliputian path. Why did PRD local governments fail? What did the PRD's larger difficulties have to do with its experience of local government? Does a focus on local and state elections build party strength, or does it scatter party resources? More broadly, under what conditions is alternation in power at the local level a viable path toward national regime change? And finally, what conclusions can we draw from this about the contribution of local parties to democratization?

In addressing these questions, the present analysis relies primarily on an examination of the PRD's experience in Michoacán, with some references to contrasts with the PAN. Based on this analysis, it is argued that the PRD experience shows that the exercise of municipal government in centralized systems does not necessarily improve prospects for national democratic change—and may in fact help defuse it. All municipal governments face severe constraints in their autonomy and ability to carry out alternative programs or introduce major innovations. With the exception of only a few principal cities, municipal governments can do relatively little to limit the control of the PRI over national policy. National changes—in overall support for opposition parties, in the behavior of the PRI, and in institutional reform—tend to reflect national shocks or demonstration effects from the capture of symbolically significant state and municipal governments rather than the direct experience of local opposition administration.

Moreover, most of the variation in local outcomes between the PAN and PRD reflects national differences between the parties. Constraints tighten for parties that present a bigger threat to the party that dominates the central government. From its foundation in 1989 until 1994, the PRD faced much greater hostility from the PRI, based on Cárdenas's demonstrated ability to pose a national electoral threat to the PRI's own social bases (unlike the PAN), on the PRD's opposition to the economic program of President Carlos Salinas de Gortari

(1988–1994) (unlike the PAN), and on its stubborn refusal to negotiate with the "usurper" government (again, unlike the PAN, which cooperated extensively with the PRI during Salinas's administration). Second, as members of a new party, PRD municipal presidents tended to have less opposition experience and a much less consolidated party organization than the PAN. Third, the more affluent urban social base of the PAN helped it win important and symbolically salient municipalities with relatively engaged and organized populations, while until 1996 the largest city governed by the leftist and more agrarian-based PRD was Morelia—strategic in neither location, size, nor economic significance.[1] The economic and social structure of the PRD's stronghold, Michoacán, left municipal governments there relatively more vulnerable to manipulation. In the smallest, rural municipalities—the ones most likely to be won by the PRD—fiscal constraints loomed particularly large, though the relative unimportance of the stakes also gave these municipalities more freedom from interference. In larger municipalities, where the opposition tended to have more independent resources, the PRI also made more extensive efforts to undermine the PRD.

Finally, in centralized systems like Mexico, it is extremely difficult to govern successfully at the local level by depending on the resources of local government alone. Winning an election is only the first step. Long-term effectiveness requires frustrating and unromantic efforts to build local party organization and construct alliances with social movements. Even with such efforts, local government only contributes to national regime change indirectly. Nevertheless, successful local democratization enhances the likelihood of smooth transition and stable consolidation. If it does not *require* alternation in power, transition must pose that possibility. This prospect will produce less anxiety and pose less risk if opposition parties have trained administrators and disciplined activists. Or, as Vicente Fox warned in the Mexico City conference, "if a party wants to exercise government it should not wait to be in it in order to develop militants."

Local Government and Democratization

Five basic hypotheses emerge from an analysis of the causal effects of local opposition government on national democratization, referred to here as addition, exponentialism, multiplication, subtraction, and di-

---

[1] According to data from the 1990 census, Morelia is not even among the twenty largest cities in the country. With fewer than 500,000 inhabitants, Morelia ranks lower than many of the key cities held by the PAN in recent years, including León (867,920), Tijuana (747,381), Guadalajara (1,650,205), Ciudad Juárez (789,522), and even Mérida, Yucatán (556,819) (INEGI 1992: 8, 1991: 110; Wilkie 1995: 128).

vision. In formulating these hypotheses, the author assumes that local government occurs in the context of a centralized national regime, defined as a regime that concentrates resources and authority at the central level and exercises domination through vertical, authoritative linkages with local government. It is likely that the relationship between local government and democratization will differ depending on the degree of centralization of the national state, but testing this assumption would require a cross-national study that cannot be undertaken here. In Mexico, a single ruling party has controlled the central government and used its resources to preserve its electoral position. Any incumbent party would use its partial and temporary control of state resources in the same way, but the PRI's monopoly enhanced the effect.

Democratization is defined here as the expansion of opportunities for citizens to participate in and/or influence collective decisions. This definition accepts that local democratization (expanded participation or influence) may occur in the absence of alternation in power, though this possibility is not directly examined. It also separates local opposition government from the dependent variable of national democratization. Local alternation in power does not necessarily expand opportunities for citizens to influence decisions that affect them if local governments have little power, nor does the accumulation of local governments necessarily improve people's ability to influence decisions made at the national level. One cannot assume that local opposition government *must* constitute an advance toward national democratization. These are, rather, empirical questions that this chapter attempts to analyze.

Local Government as Addition

In this first hypothesis, local governments appear in a Lilliputian sense as small toeholds which, when added together, tip the balance for national regime change. Local government gives resources and credibility to opponents of the regime. By adding local bases together, one might tie down the giant central government, one municipality at a time. Thus, if a national government tries to buy off the opposition by doling out some local victories, it may find eventually that it has given away too many bases of strength to hang on to national power. This hypothesis does not require local governments to be democratic themselves, but it benefits from association with the second, "multiplication," hypothesis, which finds local government an ideal site for democratization.

Direct evidence of addition at work would include patterns of electoral support in which victories at higher levels follow from and build upon victories at lower levels. In addition, democratic reforms should reflect loss of control by the dominant regime at the local level. Reforms might focus first on issues affecting local government or involve negotiations with local leaders. At the very least, the spread of local opposition bases should have some impact on calculations at the level where reforms occur.

Local Government as Exponentialism

The additive process differs slightly from a demonstration effect (here called "exponentialism" to keep the mathematical tone), in which successful opposition efforts in one state or a few municipalities encourage opposition in other states by example rather than by either experience or the accumulation of local strength. Referring to national regime change, Huntington (1991: 100) classifies this effect as an external shock that "encourages democratization in other countries, either because they seem to face similar problems, or because successful democratization elsewhere suggests that democratization might be a cure for their problems ... or because the country that has democratized is powerful and/or is viewed as a political and cultural model." The clustering of democratization in rapid sequence in a wide variety of states with little connection might indicate the presence of a demonstration effect, though simultaneous external shock (such as an economic crisis) may also explain clustering in time. However, any exponential effect influences national regime change through its impact on external audiences (like voters in other states), which depends critically on the ability to control image and on the saliency of the particular local government won. It differs logically from the slow accumulation of real local capacities. This is called an "exponential" effect of local alternation in power because it is neither proportional nor additive.

Local Government as Multiplication

The third hypothesis proposes that increased competition at the local level multiplies the opportunities for democratic participation in a system. This hypothesis makes no direct claims about the impact of local opposition government on broader political processes, but it dovetails nicely with an addition hypothesis because local administrations are more likely to add up to national change if they offer real opportunities for parties to differentiate themselves and create democratic linkages between parties and society.

From this point of view, democratization does not simply occur at the local level because alternation in power is more likely with lower stakes, but also because democratic participation is easier in the smaller local environment. At the local level, information about decisions and decision makers becomes relatively cheaper. The smaller size of the polis may also make broader participation feasible, though in larger cities, such as Mexico City, this would require further decentralization of administrative units. And popular movements are most effectively organized at the local level and around local issues.

The two most important assumptions of the multiplication hypothesis in the case of Mexico are that: (1) even when local governments face resource limitations, these advantages make it possible for them to be more effective democratizers than the national government; and (2) opposition parties in local government seek to expand participation. However, proponents also favor transferring responsibility to local government. Thus local governments are a good thing, and local governments with authority are even better.

Evidence supporting this hypothesis would include marked variations among local governments in budget allocations, institutional innovations permitting more local access and input into government policies, and competition for local offices. Each is a sufficient but not necessary element to show democratization. Variation in local budgets should occur if local people have real influence, since preferences are unlikely to be identical across towns. Institutional innovations that create opportunities for participation in the design and implementation of social policy are democratic by this definition. Competition for local office is a straightforward measure of the viability of choice, though it is a limited measure of the quality of participation.[2]

Local Government as Subtraction

A more pessimistic view of local government points out the potential for central governments to defuse political competition by dispersing it to the local level. In essence, local government fools the opposition into subtracting from its scarce total resources whatever time, energy, and assets a local opposition spends, in the mistaken belief that it is contributing to national regime change. Thus, other things being equal (such as the performance of the central government), local government should tend to distract and divide political opposition. For

---

[2] One should distinguish as separate any measures of greater efficiency of outcomes, such as lower levels of corruption, improved social service provision, or more public works for the same amount of money. While efficiency may result from democratization, as competing candidates and parties hold each other to higher standards and bid for popular support, it may also result from authoritarian micro-management of urban problems by units subordinated to the central government.

example, the Congress Party in India regularly lost regional elections to different local oppositions but dominated at the national level, winning over half the seats in the Congress for virtually all of India's postcolonial history.[3] By allowing regional opposition parties to take power, the Congress Party discouraged them from joining in an anti-Congress coalition capable of winning at the national level.

In addition, localizing opposition parties allows a strong national party to compete on a more favorable basis, using its control of national resources to shape the conditions for competition. As a result, according to Schulz (1979: 3):

> Local offices are not a good base for extending opposition party strength into the national political arena. In fact, local authority diminishes the ability of opposition parties to compete nationally. India's two communist parties ... participated in governing at the local and state levels, but ... unable to implement effective programs without support from the center, local leftist officials have appeared to the voters as ineffectual and lacking commitment to social reforms.[4]

This pattern has a particularly anti-democratic effect when regional and local governments exist within a strongly centralized system that maximizes the imbalance between local and national power. In some cases, one might make a good argument that subtraction effects coexist with multiplication effects, in true federalist fashion. In Mexico, so much power was concentrated at the central level and in the hands of an incumbent party that subtraction effects were not adequately compensated for by genuine local autonomy. Under such conditions, the dispersion of opposition results in its harmless dissipation, like a dye diluted in too much water. Local governments have too little power to serve as effective democratic instruments, but they do entice the opposition to scatter its efforts. Even if frustration with limited opportunities leads local politicians to demand change, they may find it more rewarding (and attainable) to demand decentralization than national democratization.

This argument requires demonstrating both the existence of strong centralization and its employment to marginalize and weaken opposition local governments. A further step would link the experience of local government to division among opposition forces at a national level. Local government should not lead, as in the addition hypothe-

---

[3] The principal exceptions were 1977 and the post–1989 period.

[4] Schulz also notes that similar patterns of domination by dispersion appear in the dominant party systems of Italy and Japan, as well as South Africa, France, and Mexico.

sis, to success at higher levels or in other states. Any "demonstration effect" should be negative, discouraging others from following the same path. Local governments, once captured, should not remain solidly in the hands of the opposition or they would more easily serve as building blocks. At the same time, counterintuitively, complete destruction of opposition competitiveness after one local government would make this approach an unstable way to disperse opposition, as its appeal would vanish once the lure of local power disappeared. Thus one should observe repeated and costly efforts to capture local government that seldom lead to permanent consolidated bases or bigger substantive victories.

Local Government as Division

According to the final hypothesis, local government may serve as a method of dividing up stubborn and complex problems and removing them from the national political agenda. Rather than tackling the issue of health care at a national level, for example, governments might turn over its provision to local governments in the hope that local government will take the blame for any failures and sustain the brunt of conflict over policy. By dividing up stubborn problems, local government can help bolster national stability and the legitimacy of authoritarian rulers.

This hypothesis also points out that decentralization may conceal a logic of division. Nickson's (1995: 24) "uneasy domestic coalition" in favor of decentralization includes: "neoliberals, who viewed decentralization as an essential part of a wider strategy for reducing the role of the public sector,... radical reformers, who saw decentralization as a progressive measure designed to overcome ... inegalitarian and undemocratic social structures,... [and] technocrats, who viewed decentralization primarily as a means to improve the overall efficiency of service delivery through better coordination at the local level." In addition, confronted with the need to make drastic budget cuts, many governments found it attractive to palm off responsibilities to the local level. As a result, according to Reilly (1995: 2), "another unanticipated outcome of economic crisis, structural adjustment, and austerity may be the revival of city and local government." However, since the point of decentralization was to relieve central governments of budgetary responsibility, devolution of resources may not accompany the devolution of authority.

Thus, even if central governments delegate decision-making authority, two chief dangers remain for local opposition governments. First, the state may pass on the responsibility for a problem without passing on the resources or training to deal with it. This shallow de-

PRD than to strengthen and build it. Gaps between the responsibilities and resources of local government inhibited democratic resolution of problems. Finally, there were few signs that alternation in power created significant new opportunities for popular participation.

Centralization and Limits to the Potential of Local Government

Mexico "has a particularly centralist system of government, even by Latin American standards" (Nickson 1995: 200). In 1984 the Mexican national government controlled 84 percent of public revenue and 89 percent of public spending (comparable figures for the United States are 51 percent of revenue and 56 percent of spending, according to Bailey 1994: 105).[5] Municipal governments in Mexico also face legal limitations on their autonomy and authority, despite 1983 reforms to Article 115 of the Mexican Constitution, intended to improve municipal autonomy. Among other things, these reforms turned over some financial resources to municipalities and extended proportional representation to municipal elections, making it easier for opposition parties to compete.[6] The reforms also defined a set of common responsibilities of municipal government, including police and regulatory powers. Many of these responsibilities were new, especially for smaller municipalities. However, the reforms left Mexican municipalities far behind municipal governments in comparable countries. Most important, the reassignment of property taxes to municipalities fell short of meeting existing needs, let alone new responsibilities. All but the largest municipalities remain dependent on federal contributions (from taxes collected by the national state) for between 60 and 80 percent of their income.[7] Most municipalities do not have the institutional capacity to collect fees efficiently or to update the census of property values on which the property tax is based. Municipal employment is "low by Latin American standards," at about 2.6 percent of total public-sector employment (Nickson 1995: 203). As a result, state governments usually collect taxes, keeping an often substantial portion of the tax as a fee. Without new resources and training, the

---

[5] Of seven countries analyzed (Australia, Brazil, Canada, Chile, Mexico, the United States, and Argentina), only Chile had a higher fiscal concentration. Chile, unlike Mexico, does not have a formal federal system.

[6] The reforms assigned income from local property taxes and fees for services to municipal governments. They also gave "losing" parties control of minority positions on the town council, including the *síndico*, who countersigns executive measures. For summaries of these reforms, see Nickson 1995; Beltrán and Portilla 1986; also Mexico 1994: Article 115.

[7] Based on an analysis of eight municipal budgets for 1991 in Michoacán, collected by the author.

majority of municipal governments are unlikely to develop the capacity to take over this function. By assigning local governments more responsibilities without guaranteed funding, the reforms to Article 115 suggest an attempt at "division" of problems, as in our fifth hypothesis.

Moreover, municipalities still face significant restrictions on their independence. Even after reforms, the 1994 Mexican Constitution gave state legislatures the right to oust municipal governments on a two-thirds vote and designate new officers from among residents of the community, with no specification that they come from the same parties that won the election.[8] State governments decide what share of federal contributions each municipality receives, though the Constitution mandates that states must distribute to municipalities 20 percent of total income they receive from the federal government. State governments establish rates of taxation on property, and municipal governments are expressly forbidden to establish "exemptions or subsidies with respect to the mentioned taxes [property tax and fees for municipal services]." Governors "command the police forces in the municipalities where they habitually or temporarily reside." And state legislatures approve and audit all municipal budgets (on the income side); municipal governments must then approve spending "on the basis of their available income." Municipal governments exercise only about 4 percent of total public-sector expenditure in Mexico (Nickson 1995: 204).

The municipal governments' weak financial base and tightly bounded legislative authority make them safe to hand over to the opposition—and limit what the opposition can do with a local victory. The most fundamental constraint is financial. While some municipal governments improve their resource base significantly, they do so at a political cost. For example, the PRD government in Morelia, Michoacán, decided to raise fees for water service between 100 and 300 percent, in order to manage a heavy debt incurred by a previous administration of the water district. Essentially, the fee increase amounted to a reduction in the subsidy of this service. Nevertheless, since it was not accompanied by any real improvement in service, the increase led to popular protests, which the PRI exploited and helped organize. The PRD's image suffered (Ávila García 1991: 253). Similarly, the PRD government of Morelia put considerable effort into updating its property census and increasing the efficiency of tax collection. They increased municipal income. Yet the practical impact of more efficient tax collection is higher perceived taxes—not exactly a

---

[8] This two-thirds majority did represent an improvement from the majority previously required. The Constitution also allows the legislature to hold new elections or permit the functionaries' *suplentes* to take office, but it does not require either procedure.

popular outcome. Local government has little authority to escape such income caps.

Partly as a result of these constraints, a comparison of eight municipal budgets in Michoacán failed to demonstrate consistent differences by party in the share of budget for staffing, debt payments, or electricity provision, despite complaints from PRD municipal presidents that they were charged more for such services by the state (Bruhn and Yanner 1995: 124). A broader quantitative and longitudinal study of variation in municipal budgets might clear up whether the differences that do exist resulted from idiosyncratic factors in one year or one municipality. However, fiscal constraints seem to impose some uniformity of outcome on local governments. Services and employee salaries ate up most available funds. This finding contradicts the expectations of the multiplication hypothesis (see table 2.2).

TABLE 2.2
MUNICIPAL EXPENDITURES, 1991

Budget share of:	Small Municipios (pop. 1–15,000)		Midsized Municipios (pop. 15,001–30,000)	
	PRI	PRD	PRI	PRD
Personnel	NA	32%	26%	NA[a]
Public works	20%	10%	25%	NA[a]
Light/electricity	10%	11%	8%	15%
Public debt	none	none	7%	NA[a]

Budget share of:	Large Municipios (pop. 30,001–100,000)		Super-large Municipios (pop. over 100,000)	
	PRI[b]	PRD	PRI	PRD
Personnel	30%	39%	50%	30%
Public works	19%	9%	11%	17%
Light/electricity	NA	NA	14%[c]	14%[c]
Public debt	3%	15%	6%	10%

[a] This budget was too disaggregated to place accurately in comparable categories.
[b] This budget was missing figures for November. It is impossible to say whether this would have affected percentage figures, calculated on the basis of the available months.
[c] This figure for both cities represents General Services—light plus garbage service, etc.
Sources: Eight municipal budgets for 1991, collected by the author from annual reports or directly from municipal treasury books.

Use of National Resources to Marginalize Local Opposition

Michoacán also provides evidence confirming expectations of both the subtraction and division hypotheses that the central government can exploit gaps between local capabilities and responsibilities to undermine local opposition strength. While an examination of municipal income found no evidence that the state systematically discriminated against PRD municipalities in the assignment of mandated federal funds (Bruhn and Yanner 1995: 121),[9] fiscal constraints on municipal governments left them dependent on federal and state governments for extra help to accomplish more than minimum service provision. A hostile central government could deny access to these additional funds to make particular local governments look bad.

During the Salinas administration, this extra help came mostly through the National Solidarity Program (PRONASOL), a social spending program that aimed to share responsibility for welfare and public works projects with state and local governments as well as civil society. Though they constituted only 7.7 percent of total social spending in 1992, Solidarity funds accounted for "nearly half of all public investment in social development" (Bennett and Contreras 1994: 282). While Solidarity projected a decentralizing image by requiring the formation of local "solidarity committees" to propose and oversee projects, "Solidarity's operating logic is one of deconcentration, not decentralization.... [It] operates to reinforce executive dominance" (Bailey 1994: 103).[10] Final proposal approval rested with field officers of the National Solidarity Program, run by the central (PRI) government.[11] Solidarity funds went into a checking account separate from municipal funds. Municipal officials who administered projects had to prepare monthly reports (quarterly after 1993) for the Solidarity

---

[9] Differences in federal contributions reflected the size of the community much more strongly than the partisan identification of its government.

[10] Students of public administration contrast *deconcentration*—"delegating some degree of decision-making authority from the federal ministries *to their own field offices*"—with *decentralization*—"the devolution of decision-making authority to constitutionally authorized bodies separate from the central government line ministries that operate under presidential authority" (Bailey 1994: 102).

[11] Bailey demonstrates, for example, that in the Fondos Municipales program, the central government limited how municipal governments could spend money (1994: 113–16). National bureaucrats in negotiation with governors determined the overall budget and identified municipalities to get funding. Municipal officials could not pick project proposals to go to the federal level except through a "municipal solidarity council" which also had state representatives. This council could forward for approval only budgets that spent most money outside the municipal seat, avoided "agrarian problems," and guaranteed project completion within a fiscal year. The municipal seat could spend more money if two-thirds of its population lived there, but it was limited to less than 50 percent of the total.

field office. The state field office of the federal comptroller did a final audit. Bailey concluded that "Fondos Municipales, like all PRONASOL programs, comes in a grant-in-aid package, densely wrapped in red tape and thoroughly tied up in procedural strings that ultimately reach Mexico City" (1994: 116). While municipal officials in interviews often reported feeling they had some effect on projects selected, Solidarity generally did not give them discretionary funds to establish their own priorities.

In awarding such funds, the PRI–controlled central government had no reason to make PRD governments look good. Government refusal to release Solidarity budgets disaggregated to the municipal level made direct comparison of Solidarity expenditures in PRD versus PRI municipalities impossible. Local officials from both parties reported in interviews that they did not even know how much Solidarity money had been spent in their municipality. The only hint might lie in the fact that the share of public works in municipal budgets was higher for the PRI in three of the pairs available, possibly an indirect measure of Solidarity expenditures, which often require contributions from municipal budgets.

In interviews, local officials reported only limited participation. According to these officials, the principal Solidarity programs in the municipalities were Escuela Digna (repair and maintenance of schools), Niños de Solidaridad (scholarships and food baskets), and Apoyo a la Producción (production credits to farmers with marginal land). Some PRD officials complained that they simply received lists of names; others (from smaller municipalities) said they participated in selecting beneficiaries, but follow-up questions suggest this meant they participated in ratification of lists.

Perhaps more importantly, the use of a national program to channel social welfare funds tended to identify social expenditure with the PRI, independent of the contribution of local opposition governments. PRD officials strenuously protested that even when they could get Solidarity money, the program robbed them of public credit for their ideas and hard work. Media efforts to link Solidarity to the PRI, including the use of PRI colors in the program logo, reinforced this impression. Thus, as one PRD official put it, "they stick us with the cost of distribution, but we don't get the credit" (confidential author interview, July 1992).

Less subtle efforts to discredit opposition municipal governments involved PRI control of Mexican unions. In the capital city of Morelia, for example, PRI–affiliated garbage workers went on strike shortly after the inauguration of a PRD municipal president. As the garbage mounted, local and even national media started to refer to Morelia as a dirty city and criticized the PRD for failing to resolve the crisis.[12] In

---

[12] Garbage strikes and garbage dumping seem common, perhaps because suspension of

contrast to PRI officials, most PRD officials in larger cities reported persistent problems with municipal employees and popular organizations. Morelia is again a case in point. Because it is the state capital, its police force is state run. PRD officials charged that state police allowed disturbances of public order if they cast the PRD government in a bad light. For example, the police allowed vandals to dump nearly a ton of garbage in the public square despite advance warnings, and they refused to dislodge a local PRI–affiliated organization of street vendors that occupied city hall for some weeks, forcing the PRD municipal president to set up office in a tent in the public square. Negotiations between the municipal president and the organization failed to resolve the conflict until the day before the scheduled gubernatorial election in July 1992, when the governor finally intervened and negotiated a peaceful withdrawal. The clear message: only the PRI could ensure public order and social peace. These efforts seemed particularly directed at large municipalities, where the loss of PRI control had more significant implications.

Not content to let voters draw their own conclusions, however, the PRI took advantage of its control over the media to identify the PRD with incompetence, confrontation, and violence. In the 1992 gubernatorial campaign in Michoacán, the PRI candidate spent much of his time painting the PRD as a violent party. Local newspapers did their part by publishing predictions that the PRD had prepared provocations to disrupt the elections. The PRI governor even called in the army to protect *michoacanos* from the PRD. In addition, local newspapers slanted their coverage of the parties to favor the PRI. One survey of coverage during the three months prior to the election found the PRI candidate on the front page 180 times, versus 37 for the PRD candidate; as a party, the PRI appeared 419 times, to 150 for the PRD (Alemán Alemán and Cuéllar 1992). The PRD's few appearances were a mixed blessing: many condemned a PRD action or predicted PRD violence. Articles reminded readers of the shortcomings of PRD governments, especially in large municipalities, which the PRI wanted most to recover. Thus, even if voters did not hold the PRD government responsible for failures, the media reminded them that there were costs involved in voting for the opposition. It took a PRI municipal president to establish a cooperative, productive relationship with state and federal authorities.

Last but not least, Michoacán became the site of numerous episodes of political violence, at least half of them associated with municipal elections or directed against PRD municipal officials and candidates. Of the sixty-eight PRD activists killed in Michoacán between

---

service has few dangerous effects, but it quickly becomes a public nuisance. See, for example, Martínez Assad 1985.

1988 and March 1994, 25 percent were PRD municipal officials or municipal candidates at the time of their murder, and an additional 25 percent died in confrontations involving protest about municipal electoral fraud.[13] The PRD also lists "illegal" detentions of over fifty activists, including the well-documented case of the PRD municipal president of Aguililla, jailed on false charges of involvement in drug trafficking and released on the recommendation of the Mexican National Commission on Human Rights after he had spent over six months in prison.

Local Government as a Source of Internal Party Divisions

Local government did not help resolve persistent problems of internal division within the PRD. Though one might expect the availability of resources, influence, and positions to help cement party loyalties (as it has often done in the PRI), neither the size of the stakes nor the rules governing their distribution favored such use of local patronage for party building. Instead, existing divisions in the PRD were reflected within municipal government, as well as between the government and the party. Municipal officials often saw themselves more as public servants than as party servants, with an independent basis of legitimacy in the vote. Thus they were among the least likely activists to accept party discipline. At the same time, party activists often attributed electoral victories to the party's hard work or identity rather than to the popularity of the municipal president. When they were not rewarded, they felt insulted and betrayed. This exacerbated some conflicts.

In addition, municipal officials had to engage in constant dialogue with the PRI–state in order to get any resources. This caused conflicts with party leaders who shared a profound suspicion of the PRI, along with concern that dialogue only bolstered the political position of their enemies. PRD members often supported the "legitimate right" of a PRD municipal president to negotiate with the PRI–state, as a "necessity" and "a natural part of his duty" (author interview with Roberto Robles Garnica, 1991). In practice, however, many activists suspected that PRD municipal presidents who got along "too well" with the PRI must have sold out.[14] This resulted, ironically, in suspi-

---

[13] In fact, according to PRD investigations, nearly all of these cases (fourteen of seventeen) were actually municipal officials or persons who died in the course of ambushes, including two wives of PRD municipal presidents. Based on accounts in PRD 1994.

[14] For instance, in conversation with the author, an activist stated that she would never trust a certain municipal president because he dined with Salinas and called him "Mr. President" publicly. She felt that this implied recognition of Salinas as the legitimate president of Mexico and therefore betrayed Cárdenas.

cion of the very municipal presidents who had most success in getting Solidarity money. Party statutes maximized this separation by prohibiting municipal presidents from belonging to municipal committees (PRD 1990: 55).

New Left parties in other centralized political systems suffered from similar problems, even in a context of nationally democratic institutions. The first local governments of the Brazilian Workers' Party (PT), especially in important cities like Diadema, São Paulo, and Fortaleza, "did not enjoy a sympathetic national press; there was extensive reporting of intraparty conflict and of the PT's mistakes in Diadema, and very little coverage of successful efforts" (Keck 1992: 199). Further, "internal factors"—including a "lack of prior programmatic consensus within the local party on priorities for municipal policy," intraparty struggles, and conflicts between party and administration—kept the PT from using its municipal victory to showcase its skills. The administration's denial of party authority over appointments to posts in the government and its refusal to submit administrative decisions to the PT delegation for approval also sparked conflicts (Keck 1992: 204, 211–12). As in the case of the PRD, the PT's problems seemed most severe in large cities (with more diverse town councils and more significance to elites) and in early victories, before the PT accumulated experience and moved toward pragmatism.

PRD Electoral Support in Michoacán

Several aspects of patterns of electoral support in Michoacán support the hypothesis that local government may serve as a surrogate for national democratization, rather than adding together many local bases. First, communities with PRD governments did not build on their success or even, in many cases, repeat it. In 1991 congressional elections, for example, the PRD lost in nearly half the municipalities where it governed.[15] It also lost the 1992 gubernatorial race despite governing 52 of 113 municipalities at the time. At the municipal level, the PRD suffered demoralizing reverses in the December 1992 elections, losing all the major cities it had held since 1989, including Morelia, Pátzcuaro, and Lázaro Cárdenas. From 1992 to 1995, the PRD controlled only 39 municipalities, down from 52 (Ávalos and Alfaro 1993). There is even some statistical evidence that experience of a PRD government significantly enhanced support for the PRI in later elections (see tables 2.3 and 2.4). This hardly looks like an additive

---

[15] Congressional districts do not coincide with municipal boundaries. However, the PRD disaggregated these figures in order to plan electoral strategy for 1992. The author relies on these figures with some confidence, as they were intended for practical use and internal consumption. See PRD 1992.

pattern of local democratization, with previous successes building into future ones, enhancing democratic competition at higher levels. On the contrary, the PRD lost ground, and electoral competition weakened. Although PRI losses are not necessarily equivalent to democratization, weaker electoral competition is one indicator of the viability of choice, while the PRI's methods of regaining support (including Solidarity) do not appear to involve nearly as much popular participation as the PRI would like to suggest.

Table 2.3
Congressional Vote in Michoacán, by Municipio, 1991[a]

	PRD Vote	PRI Vote
Agricultural population	.08	-.01
Illiteracy	.22***	-.16**
Municipal population	-.16*	.02
PRD government	.64***	-.61***
R-squared	.52	.39
Adjusted R-squared	.51	.37

[a] Each cell reports Beta coefficient, N= 109
Significance levels: * = < .10, ** = < .05, *** = < .01
Sources: PRD, *Tablas comparativas*, 1992; *Michoacán: Resultados definitivos*, 1991.
Note: These results should be viewed with caution: due to lack of municipal-level data on some variables (especially income per capita, abstention, and Solidarity expenditures), the models may be misspecified and the significance of individual variables could change. Still, they pose tantalizing questions about how governmental performance might affect electoral success, and they are included in that spirit.

TABLE 2.4
VOTE SWING, 1989–1991

	PRD Loss	PRI Gain
Agricultural population	.01	-.01
Illiteracy	.09	-.17*
Municipal population	.31***	.41***
PRD government	.11	.27***
R-squared	.10	.33
Adjusted R-squared	.06	.31

[a] Each cell reports Beta coefficient, N= 109
Significance levels: ** = < .05, *** = < .01
Sources: PRD, *Tablas comparativas*, 1992; *Michoacán: Resultados definitivos*, 1991.

At the same time, experience of a PRD government did not necessarily lead to fewer votes in absolute numbers. Rather, PRD votes in Michoacán changed relatively less than votes for either the PRI or the PAN.[16] The PRD still lost elections, since the PRI was making strong and successful efforts to mobilize new voters; but because it *was* keeping voters, it did not lose hope of recapturing municipal governments it had lost or of winning state races. This led to repeated and costly efforts to capture local governments which led neither to consolidated bases of support nor to expansion of competition, exactly as a subtraction hypothesis would suggest.

Finally, trends in PRD support reflect national developments more than local track records. First, the national problems of the PRD affected its local image. Its reputation for internal conflict, disruptive protests, and aversion to compromise was replicated faithfully in local politics. Divisions between factions of the state party led at times to violent clashes and public accusations of everything from fraud to secret dealings with the PRI. Second, the national problems of the PRI powerfully affected the electoral fortunes of the opposition in Michoacán. Despite no change (except for the worse) in its image or local effectiveness,[17] the PRD made significant advances in the 1995 municipal elections in Michoacán, winning fifty-four municipalities, against forty-three for the PRI (*La Voz de Michoacán*, December 22, 1995, p. 38). This increase in local competition has everything to do with the national economic crisis and corruption scandals that have so discredited the PRI, and virtually nothing to do with local government in Michoacán. At the same time and for similar reasons, the PAN made significant electoral advances. This pattern is most consistent with a national shock affecting local voters, not an addition hypothesis or even a demonstration effect (exponential growth).

---

[16] For example, the PRD lost 2,587 votes between 1991 (congressional vote) and 1992 (gubernatorial vote), compared to 17,586 lost by the PAN and 88,561 lost by the PRI. See Alemán Alemán and Cuéllar 1992.

[17] In 1995, the two main party factions in Michoacán engaged in bitter public confrontations and even some violent attacks. Each claimed victory in the primary election to nominate a gubernatorial candidate. The loser (Robles Garnica) accused the winner (Árias) of fraud. The National Executive Committee eventually supported the nomination of Árias, despite "irregularities" in the primary, for the eminently pragmatic reason that it was too late to hold another primary. Robles continued to speak against Árias publicly. The conflict greatly discredited the PRD on the eve of its most viable opportunity to win its first governorship, and it may well explain its narrow defeat in the November election.

PRD Governments and Local Participation

Nor do PRD local governments confirm a multiplication hypothesis. In contrast to the Brazilian Workers' Party, which set up popular councils to promote co-participation in public works, the PRD introduced few institutional innovations in its early municipal governments. PRD municipal presidents in two cities set up "urban councils" for citizens to propose solutions to urban problems, but they later dissolved them, claiming that apathy and disorganization made the councils ineffective or that "PRIistas" on the council tried to "usurp government functions." Solidarity committees linked to the central government may have preempted PT–style experiments. Solidarity could offer more resources than could any local government to attract participation.

Nevertheless, many PRD administrations did not try. The organizational problems of the PRD had something to do with this. Lack of party discipline made the PRD an unreliable coalition partner. Internal divisions threatened to infect popular organizations or turn them into prizes for which party factions would compete. Curiously, however, complaints about a municipal president's "authoritarian" attitudes seemed less related to his cooperation with movements or his construction of institutional channels for participation than to his willingness to take party considerations into account and to allow easy personal access. The two Michoacán municipal presidents most accused of authoritarianism were the same ones who set up urban councils. Moreover, only one of the four PRD governments in our budget sample reported replacing PRIista employees with PRD activists. This municipality also had better party-administration relations, and it was the only one that the PRD won in 1991. PRD officials said in interviews—sometimes without being asked—that they constantly had problems with PRD activists who wanted them to fire PRIistas and hire them, or who expected special treatment, such as preference in contracts, because of their party affiliation. The officials had trouble honoring such requests. Some saw nonpartisan administration as a moral rejection of old PRI practices. More practically, most municipal employees in large municipalities belong to PRI unions and are hard to fire. Further, PRD governments face constant scrutiny. Some have been audited more than once. Special treatment for PRD partisans would certainly be used to discredit the party.

Personal access to the municipal president might resolve some perceptions of authoritarianism. The most successful PRD government also published detailed accounts of municipal finance and kept open lines of communication. This might be a cheap way to improve evaluations of opposition government.[18] The result of later elections in PRD towns suggests that good performance in technical terms alone does not consolidate party loyalty. In Morelia, the local government significantly improved efficiency and services by many standards. Yet PRD support deteriorated to the point where the party lost not only to the PRI but also to the PAN. The key to converting government into electoral success may go through stronger party-government links, not performance per se.

The Generalizability of Michoacán

For practical reasons, this chapter holds constant a number of potentially significant variables. Most importantly, it focuses on one state, one party, and one time period. All three factors may have contributed to the depressing results. Michoacán is not a wealthy or strategically central state. In the neoliberal agenda, states with industrial potential take precedence. In such states, opposition parties might have more leverage. However, these states are the support base of the PAN, not the PRD. Second, the PRD has a different ideology, problems, and strategies than other opposition parties. This had some impact on the results. Even if the PRD is exceptional, it must be argued that its experience alone demonstrates that local government does not *necessarily* lead to democratizing outcomes—and may, indeed, lead to negative ones. Still, the PRD was so new in the period studied that it may be premature to generalize about its problems, for example, as it faces the challenge of governing Mexico City. Political learning could make PRD municipal governments more effective. Third, the PRD governments studied here had the "misfortune" to govern in a rare period of economic recovery. Under different national economic conditions, the ruling party's ability to undermine opposition governments may weaken.

In addition, there are two major sources of disconfirming evidence for the hypotheses of subtraction and division, which the Michoacán cases alone tend to confirm. First, the PAN followed a strategy centered on demonstrating competence in local government, and it has experienced more electoral success. While this chapter cannot deal at length with the PAN, there are four points to be made about this supposed relationship. First, the model of managerial government assumed to have contributed to positive evaluations of the PAN was in fact not unique to this party (see, for example, the cases examined in

---

[18] A similar style of openness by the PAN administration of Mérida, Yucatán, including public postings of monthly municipal expenditures, may have contributed to the consolidation of PAN support there.

Rodríguez and Ward 1992; Ward 1995; Rodríguez 1995; Cabrero Mendoza, García del Castillo, and Gutiérrez Mendoza 1995). The PRD government of Morelia boasted many experienced administrators who talked openly about efficiency as their basic goal and who succeeded in improving tax collection and garbage service in their city. More significant differences lay in relative levels of PRI hostility toward each party, relative tolerance for confrontation, and internal divisions. These differences largely reflected national disputes between each party and the PRI, as well as differences in the character of the parties. Strong centralization means that even an effective local government may fail without outside support. Thus adoption of a managerial model by a party under siege can actually *decrease* its conversion of local government into lasting support. It may be more useful for such parties to focus on goals within the individual capacity of local governments, such as providing opportunities for participation.

Second, patterns of electoral gain for the PAN provide even stronger evidence for a "demonstration effect" than does Michoacán. The PAN's victories in one state improved its chances of victory in other states with little or no direct experience of PAN government, and victories came bunched in time. This effect may have been magnified by the fact that PAN victories often occurred in highly visible and economically advanced states. This pattern is more consistent with an exponential growth hypothesis than an addition hypothesis. This does not make local elections unimportant, but it does make effective local government less central to the causal process leading from local to national democratization.

Third, national rather than local events precipitated the PAN onto center stage. The PRI's tolerance of PAN governments (and the PAN's corresponding willingness to cooperate with the PRI) played a significant role in converting the PAN into the choice of anti–PRI protest voters. The PRI would accept defeat at the hands of the PAN but not at the hands of the PRD. Thus, to whip the PRI, one should vote for the PAN. As a result, the December 1994 peso crash, economic crisis, and popular protest against the PRI initially benefited the PAN (which supported PRI economic policies) rather than the PRD (which did not). The change in this position may reflect PRI perceptions that the PAN presented a greater threat to the ruling party's control of Congress in 1997; this could account, for example, for the PRI's decision to exclude the PAN from a televised debate among Mexico City mayoral candidates.

Finally, PAN municipal presidents did better at parlaying local success into national prominence, hinting at different patterns of recruitment and advancement. Most PRD municipal presidents from 1989 to 1992 either dropped out of politics or were marginalized, having accumulated internal enemies and lost their reputations after failures in government. However, it takes time for leaders who start at the local level to win national fame, and not all will succeed. The apparent lack of local-to-national trajectories in the PRD may thus correct itself over time. As of this writing, the individual elected president of the PRD in July 1996—Andrés Manuel López Obrador— won his reputation as a local party leader in the state of Tabasco, though he had no opposition government experience. Moreover, because the PRD is new, most members entered the party laterally from other organizations, and career patterns remain unstable. It may still be too early to test this proposal through a comparison of career paths in the PAN and PRD.

The second source of disconfirming evidence comes from analyses of innovation in local government. These cases demonstrate that more is possible—even in Mexico—than most PRD governments have attempted. However, they also suggest several common threads. First, successful municipal presidents often managed to dramatically increase municipal income, usually by attracting significantly greater resources from the central system. The municipality of Xico, Veracruz, for instance, increased its Solidarity funding from 481,968 pesos in the first year of an opposition administration to 3,665,262 pesos in its final year. In Atoyac de Álvarez, Guerrero, municipal income increased over 75 percent during the opposition administration, mainly in the "outside income" category, which included PRONASOL money. Investments in Santiago Maravatío went from 964,095 new pesos in 1991 to 8,291,363 in 1994 (Cabrero Mendoza, García del Castillo, and Gutiérrez Mendoza 1995: 146, 183, 257). Their example may not be generalizable, as resources are not infinitely expandable.

Second, it is suggestive that successful municipal presidents in the cases available often exaggerated their distance from the PRD, even when they generally fit on the left of the political spectrum. The Coalition of Workers, Peasants, and Students of the Isthmus (COCEI) in Juchitán consistently stresses its origins in civil society and frequently criticizes its PRD "partners." In Atoyac de Álvarez, Guerrero, the "PRD" municipal president "openly declared [she was] not a member of that political organization." In Xico, Veracruz, the PRD municipal president worked very closely with Solidarity and drew heavily on "traditional forms of social organization," as opposed to party structures. And in the PRD strongholds of the *meseta purépecha* in Michoacán, one regional conflict resolution initiative (the Brigada Mixta de Conciliación y Concertación Agraria) survived largely by working outside the structures of municipal government, through the Ministry of Agrarian Reform (SRA) and the National Indigenous Institute (INI). Finally, these "creative" governments relied on ties with popular movements or traditional communitarian structures. It is hard to innovate in Mexico through party structures alone.

Conclusions

The evidence examined in this chapter suggests that in centralized authoritarian regimes, alternation in power at the local level can serve more as a diversion than as a path to either local democratization or national regime change. The relative simultaneity of the disintegration of PRI support in areas as diverse as Chiapas and Mexico City suggests that the string of opposition victories in local elections has been fundamentally a national process, with demonstration effects as the chief mechanism translating local opposition gains into national change. One could think of this as a feedback effect, in which local victories of both the PAN and the PRD, while basically a *symptom* rather than a cause of national change, nevertheless magnified and spread opposition to the PRI. Some apparent "waves" of local opposition victory result directly from a single external shock—economic crisis—which affects many regions at once, and which owes little or nothing to experiences of local government and party building.

Nor does the construction of genuine local democracy result automatically or easily from local opposition victory. The PRD had trouble building new opportunities for participation due to the lack of a strong civil society, the dominance the PRI exercises on organizational life, the limitations of local government, and its own organizational failures.

Finally, in contrast to the broad alliance that opposed Augusto Pinochet in Chile, Mexican opposition parties largely failed to cooperate even on limited goals like the fight for electoral and institutional reform during the Salinas period. Differential expectations of local electoral success may have played a role in encouraging the parties to believe they could go it alone. The fundamental ideological incompatibility of the PRD and the PAN does limit prospects for cooperation. Nevertheless, if parties could not win local elections, they would have no means of demonstrating their superiority as an alternative to the PRI, and they would thus be forced to consider limited cooperation even with the devil himself.

The mitigation or removal of several key constraints—particularly limits on local resources and authority, hostility from a strong central government, and the lack of effective civil society partners—might produce different results. Local governments with resources and autonomy would give opposition parties a chance to demonstrate their effectiveness as alternatives to the PRI, even without PRI tolerance. An organizationally dense civil society should give parties more opportunities and incentives for effective collaboration. The ongoing process of electoral and state reform, therefore, should affect the potential of local government to contribute to national change.

Moreover, even under the present difficult circumstances, alternation at the local level contributes to the consolidation of an eventual democracy by giving parties opportunities to acquire experience and incentives to make responsible promises. Local opposition victories may encourage some change in relations between a state and the central government, along with more limited changes in relations between state and municipal governments or branches of government. These changes seem as much practical as legal, and they reflect the readiness of opposition governors, municipal presidents, and legislators to negotiate aggressively. More independent PRIistas could accomplish the same effect. In addition, the ability of the PRD and PAN to mobilize local protests helped limit electoral fraud, though party building had more impact than local government per se. Both major opposition parties mobilized poll watchers in areas where they had little electoral success. Better party organization would certainly enhance this effect.

Indeed, the most crucial short circuit between local and national politics may involve political party organization. With the exception of organizations that focus on national political change, such as Alianza Cívica, the concerns of most civil society organizations reflect primarily local problems. It is irrational to expect such movements to invest scarce resources in developing a national presence, especially if the central state proves willing to meet their demands without it. Parties, in contrast, have a vital interest in national democratization and political reform. Ideally, national party leaders would like to turn on local mobilization to increase the pressure when negotiations stall and turn it off when concessions are made. Thus it is the breakdown in *party* communication—national leaderships that do not respond to the direction of local parties, and local parties that do not accept the authority of national leaderships to negotiate on their behalf—that makes it so difficult for national democratizers to use whatever local organization may develop through local government to press for national democratic change.

The evidence from Michoacán suggests that local opposition government does not necessarily create the will, capacity, or leadership to build more strongly linked party organizations. Indeed, a centralized regime with a dominant party can make it functional for local opposition parties to insulate their electoral victories from projects for national democratic reform, and irrational for them to develop strong organizational ties that would subject them to decisions by the national party. Local municipal governments require such extensive cooperation with higher levels of the state that a close association with organizations that actively promote state reform may negatively affect their ability to perform their duties. Both local and national leaders have some interest in allowing this dissociation. The many PRD candidates that distance themselves from the party after or during elections cannot be dismissed simply as an aberration of a new and unformed party.

Nor will the financial resources for constructing party organizations come from local government. Local governments do not offer sufficient resources to build an effective clientelist network to attract the interest of national sponsors or to win the loyalty of local constituents. And unless local experience leads to national prominence, national leaders have little incentive to focus on local government; while local leaders will resist putting their political capital at the disposal of national coordinators. To the extent that parties and local leaders gain more from demonstration effects than from addition effects, they should focus on capturing the larger, more economically developed cities, though this is a high-risk strategy if the PRI tries harder to undermine opposition in such cities.

In conclusion, democratization seems more likely to result from national pressures, events, and personalities that focus disorganized discontent than to result from local political experience. Progress toward democracy will continue to depend heavily on the favorability of the national context for the PRI. In 1996 and 1997, the PRI faced strong national rejection of the consequences of economic crisis and spreading corruption scandals. This helped propel the opposition into an increasing number of important local governments, including most recently the government of Mexico City. The PRD's victory in Mexico City, and in the large municipality of Nezahuacoyotl, in 1996 gave the party control over the largest municipalities it has ever had the opportunity to govern.

Yet in meeting these challenges, at least some of the lessons of Michoacán seem likely to apply. First, salient local elections can boost national opposition support. The PRD rode Cuauhtémoc Cárdenas's coattails into 25 percent of the new national Congress. If Cárdenas is effective as mayor of Mexico City, he could help his party—and himself—considerably in 2000. Second, local governments face constraints in meeting popular expectations. Cárdenas is likely to confirm this sooner than he would like as he takes responsibility for the many serious problems of Mexico City, including crime, pollution, unemployment, and service gaps. The flip side of saliency is that poor performance can have effects far beyond the original local government. Finally, building party-government connections and strengthening popular participation will probably be key factors in any hypothetical success. If Cárdenas can offer citizens a new sense that the local administration belongs to them, is accountable to them, and gives them unusually open access, he may win some forgiveness for his inevitable failure to solve all of Mexico City's pressing problems.

References

Alemán Alemán, Ricardo, and Mireya Cuéllar. 1992. "El caso de Michoacán hace indispensable una profunda reforma electoral en el país," *La Jornada*, July 31.

Ávalos, Bernardo, and J. Alfaro. 1993. *Cuadernos de Nexos* 182 (February): 10–11.

Ávila García, Patricia. 1991. "Estudio preliminar sobre el deterioro socio-ambiental en la ciudad de Morelia: el caso del agua." In *Urbanización y desarrollo en Michoacán*, edited by Gustavo López Castro. Zamora: El Colegio de Michoacán.

Bailey, John. 1994. "Centralism and Political Change in Mexico: The Case of National Solidarity." In *Transforming State-Society Relations in Mexico: The National Solidarity Strategy*, edited by Wayne A. Cornelius, Ann L. Craig, and Jonathan Fox. La Jolla: Center for U.S.–Mexican Studies, University of California, San Diego.

Beltrán, Ulises, and Santiago Portilla. 1986. "El proyecto de descentralización del gobierno mexicano (1983–1984)." In *Descentralización y democracia en México*, edited by Blanca Torres. Mexico City: El Colegio de México.

Bennett, Vivienne, and Oscar Contreras. 1994. "National Solidarity in the Northern Borderlands: Social Participation and Community Leadership." In *Transforming State-Society Relations in Mexico: The National Solidarity Strategy*, edited by Wayne A. Cornelius, Ann L. Craig, and Jonathan Fox. La Jolla: Center for U.S.–Mexican Studies, University of California, San Diego.

Bruhn, Kathleen, and Keith Yanner. 1995. "Governing under the Enemy." In *Opposition Government in Mexico*, edited by Victoria Rodríguez and Peter Ward. Albuquerque: University of New Mexico Press.

Cabrero Mendoza, Enrique, Rodolfo García del Castillo, and Martha Gutiérrez Mendoza. 1995. *La nueva gestión municipal en México: análisis de experiencias innovadoras en gobiernos locales*. Mexico City: Centro de Investigación y Docencia Económicas.

González Casanova, Pablo. 1970. *Democracy in Mexico*. London: Oxford University Press.

Huntington, Samuel. 1991. *The Third Wave*. Norman, Ok.: University of Oklahoma Press.

INEGI (Instituto Nacional de Estadística, Geografía e Informática). 1991. *Michoacán: resultados definitivos, datos por localidad; XI Censo general de población y vivienda, 1990*. Mexico City: INEGI.

———. 1992. *Perfil sociodemográfico: XI Censo general de población y vivienda, 1990*. Mexico City: INEGI.

Keck, Margaret. 1992. *The Workers' Party and Democratization in Brazil*. New Haven, Conn.: Yale University Press.

Martínez Assad, Carlos, ed. 1985. *Municipios en conflicto*. Mexico City: Universidad Nacional Autónoma de México.

Mexico. 1994. *Constitución Política de los Estados Unidos Mexicanos*. Mexico City: Berbera.

Nickson, R. Andrew. 1995. *Local Government in Latin America*. Boulder, Colo.: Lynne Rienner.

PRD (Partido de la Revolución Democrática). 1990. *Documentos básicos*. Mexico City: PRD.

————. 1992. *Tablas comparativas de los resultados electorales*. Mexico City: Secretaría de Defensa del Voto, PRD.

————. 1994. *En defensa de los derechos humanos: un sexenio de violencia política.* Mexico City: Secretaría de Derechos Humanos, Grupo Parliamentario, PRD.

Reilly, Charles. 1995. "Public Policy and Citizenship." In *New Paths to Democratic Development in Latin America: The Rise of NGO–Municipal Collaboration*, edited by Charles Reilly. Boulder, Colo.: Lynne Rienner.

Rodríguez, Victoria. 1995. "Municipal Autonomy and the Politics of Intergovernmental Finance." In *Opposition Government in Mexico*, edited by Victoria Rodríguez and Peter Ward. Albuquerque: University of New Mexico Press.

Rodríguez, Victoria, and Peter Ward. 1992. *Policymaking, Politics, and Urban Governance in Chihuahua*. U.S.–Mexican Policy Report No. 3. Austin, Tx.: Lyndon B. Johnson School of Public Affairs, University of Texas at Austin.

Schulz, Ann. 1979. *Local Politics and Nation-States*. Santa Barbara, Calif.: Clio.

Ureña, José. 1991. "Clase política," *La Jornada*, August 16.

Ward, Peter. 1995. "Policy Making and Policy Implementation among Non–PRI Governments: The PAN in Ciudad Juarez and in Chihuahua." In *Opposition Government in Mexico*, edited by Victoria Rodríguez and Peter Ward. Albuquerque: University of New Mexico Press.

Wilkie, James, ed. 1995. *Statistical Abstract of Latin America*. Vol. 31, Part 1. Los Angeles: Latin American Center, University of California, Los Angeles.

3

Democratization and Local Party Building: The PAN in León, Guanajuato

David Shirk

Democratization exposes political actors at all levels to a fresh set of opportunities and dilemmas. Political success, as well as the long-term viability of the democratic process, requires that these actors rise to meet the new circumstances. Among the most important of these are the challenges that political parties face in developing effective organizations capable of winning elections and governing effectively. By looking at the experience of Mexico's National Action Party (PAN), this chapter explores how local and regional political factors have affected the process of democratization in León, Guanajuato.

There is nothing new in the claim that major shifts in a political party's external institutional environment have an impact on the party itself. The earliest analyses of political parties—heavily focused on their organizational features—were explicitly concerned with this problem.[1] However, scholarly interest in political parties as organiza-

The field research for this project was funded in part by an NSF Fellowship for Minorities and a grant from UC MEXUS. The wisdom, encouragement, and patience of Ann Craig were invaluable in the project's development and write-up. The author also thanks Amy Bridges, Wayne Cornelius, Karla de la Peña, Alain de Remes, Emily Edmonds, Todd Eisenstadt, Stephen Erie, Steph Haggard, Jane Hindley, Kevin Middlebrook, Luis Miguel Rionda, María and Guadalupe Valencia, and Chris Woodruff for their assistance. Most importantly, he thanks the many PANistas, officials, and citizens of León who contributed their narratives.

[1] In 1902 and 1915, respectively, Ostrogorski, Weber, and Michels paid considerable attention to the rise and transformation of party organizations during the industrial

tions was gradually eclipsed by a general interest in the relation of political parties within a given system (Panebianco 1988; Lawson 1994). Such analyses have generated valuable insight into the nature of "party systems," but most have done so to the neglect of processes internal to the party organizations themselves. Yet the internal processes of party organizations are essential to understanding how parties ultimately react to the external factors that supposedly determine party behavior within a party system.

How environmental constraints and opportunities interact with the organizational characteristics of a party to shape its behavior must be considered in order to evaluate the prospects for political parties in a context of democratization. In the Mexican case especially, where parties were allowed to "compete" but were effectively excluded from political power for several decades, the prospect of political liberalization would seem to be a great boon for the parties. Yet a closer analysis illustrates the complexities of their internal adjustments to this transition.

The National Action Party is one of Mexico's most successful and experienced opposition parties and has a strong local presence in León. Both criticized and commended for its ability to negotiate the treacherous waters of the Mexican system on its precarious course toward political liberalization, the PAN has done better than any other opposition party in placing its candidates in office. By 1998 the PAN had won nine governorships in six states, hundreds of state and local deputyships, and over two hundred municipal governments, including Mexico's most important cities.[2] Given its electoral accomplishments, the PAN provides an excellent case in which to evaluate the opportunities and constraints that come with survival and success under conditions of political opening.

Several scholars have noted the organizational concomitants of the PAN's successes in recent years. Mizrahi, for example, observes that "the PAN has emerged from its old-time condition akin to a sect (small, ideologically strong and closed, yet politically irrelevant) and has transformed itself into a more open and loosely defined, but

---

revolution (Michels 1966; Ostrogorski 1964). Weber (1946) traced shifts in the composition and structure of party organizations in response to external pressures, such as the expansion of suffrage and the industrial revolution in the nineteenth century.

[2] In 1997 the PAN controlled four state governments (Baja California, Guanajuato, Chihuahua, and Jalisco) and won three new ones (Querétaro, Nuevo León, and Aguascalientes), but it lost Chihuahua. With the notable exception of Mexico City, by the end of 1997 the PAN controlled most of Mexico's important cities: Guadalajara, Monterrey, Mexicali, Zapopan, Tijuana, León, Ciudad Juárez, Puebla, Veracruz, Tampico, and Ciudad Madero. By 1997 the PAN also governed several more state capitals, including Mérida, Oaxaca, San Luis Potosí (recaptured in 1997), Culiacán, Morelia, and Aguascalientes.

electorally more effective and competitive party" (1996: 2).[3] In other words, democratization has brought the PAN both electoral benefits and organizational changes.

This chapter analyzes how the PAN has adjusted to these new circumstances in León, the most important of Guanajuato's forty-six municipalities in both demographic and economic terms. With an estimated one million inhabitants, it holds over 20 percent of the state's population. It is also the strongest and northern-most link in Guanajuato's industrial corridor and the center of the state's economic wealth. León's footwear industry dominates the domestic market and caters to a growing international market. Furthermore, León lies in the heart of Mexico's "bible belt,"[4] making it fertile ground for the PAN, which is commonly described as a conservative and religious party.[5]

León is also of political interest. It is fairly typical of the large, urban municipalities of northern and central Mexico where the PAN has been most successful. León has long been the bastion of the PAN in Guanajuato and has produced many of the party's prominent state figures, including Guanajuato's first PAN governors, Carlos Medina Plascencia (1991–1995) and Vicente Fox Quesada (1995–2001). In addition, León is the first major municipality to host four consecutive PAN administrations.[6]

As a case study, León helps to demonstrate the impact of political success on the PAN's party organization. At the same time, it affords an opportunity to evaluate electoral success and organizational change in the context of the local-national dynamics of democratization. In particular, the PAN's experience in León highlights local

---

[3] Reveles has provided comprehensive analyses of the PAN's national-level organizational development and the problems the party has confronted (1993, 1996). Rodríguez and Ward (1994) also note the organizational challenges facing the PAN in an increasingly democratic context.

[4] Roughly equivalent but not limited to El Bajío, the agricultural corridor between Mexico's Federal District and Guadalajara. It was in this region, which spans the states of Guanajuato, Jalisco, and Querétaro, that Mexico's most important antigovernment religious movements were strong in the 1930s and 1940s. The Catholic Church continues to play a central role in the region's society and politics (Ruiz 1992: 75).

[5] Although the PAN's ideological roots are heavily based in Catholicism, there is substantial variation in the "religiosity" of the party and its militants. Camp's findings on the similarity of PAN and PRI militants' religious affiliations seem to support this view (1996).

[6] Multiple consecutive PAN governments have occurred in smaller municipalities. According to data from the PAN's National Executive Council (CEN), the 1980–1983 administration of Darío Torres Vázquez was the fourth consecutive PAN municipal government in Asunción Cuyotepeji, Oaxaca, and the 1995 victory of Fabián Artemio González Rosas in San Juan Ihualtepec, Oaxaca, ushered in that municipality's fourth consecutive PAN administration.

manifestations of Mexico's unique brand of PRI authoritarianism and the resulting constraints on the organizational prospects of opposition parties. Most importantly, reflection on the PAN's experience in León helps to underscore the notion that political liberalization holds significant organizational consequences for political parties, which in turn complicates the nexus of "the local" and "the national" in the process of democratization.

PAN Origins and PRI Hegemony in León

The León chapter of the PAN was founded in 1943 as Acción Nacional–León. In 1946 it joined with the National Sinarquist Union (UNS) and the Civic Union of León (UCL) to support a common independent candidate, Carlos A. Obregón, for municipal president, against the "official" candidate of the Party of the Mexican Revolution (the PRM, an earlier incarnation of today's ruling Institutional Revolutionary Party, or PRI).[7] Obregón advocated clean elections, standards of good government, citizen involvement in decision making, open and transparent planning of public works, education, and respect for human rights.

On the evening of election day, December 16, 1946, Obregón was believed to have triumphed. According to the coalition's unofficial tally, the PRM's candidate, Ignacio Quiroz, had logged only 58 votes against an overwhelming 22,173 cast for Obregón. Yet almost two weeks later, government officials declared Quiroz the winner. On New Year's Day 1947, Governor Hidalgo ordered Quiroz to take office.

The next day demonstrators gathered in the plaza to await Obregón, who planned to stage his own public—but unofficial—inauguration that evening. By nightfall, a crowd of approximately five thousand Obregón supporters raged out of control. When demonstrators began to hurl stones at the municipal palace, military forces opened fire. At least fifty people were killed, and dozens more were wounded (Alemán 1993: 22–26).

The massacre was an embarrassment for the PRI regime. Physical evidence seems to contradict official claims that the troops had acted in self-defense; many unarmed civilians were shot from behind, and several met their fate blocks from the plaza.[8] Eventually the national

---

[7] Obregón's candidacy was fueled in part by dissatisfaction among businessmen, merchants, and agriculturalists over rent freezes, increased taxes for public services, and additional levies for public works. He may also have benefited from national cleavages in the local PRI (Alemán 1993: 19–20).

[8] This site is now known as the Plaza de los Mártires del 2 de Enero (author interview with Professor José Lozano Padilla, May 1997). See also Alemán 1993: 22–26.

Senate was forced to intervene, instructing Governor Hidalgo to appoint a nonpartisan "citizens' council" with Obregón at the head.

Despite this small victory, the massacre was followed by a period of political inactivity for the PAN. Opposition forces were exhausted, and the people feared that even minor political activity could cost them their lives (author interview with Professor José Lozano Padilla, May 1997). The consequences for the local and state organizations of the PAN were predictable. Those few who remained politically active in organizations like the PAN found it difficult to attract much interest to their cause.

Other factors contributed to hinder the PAN's organizational development over the next several decades. For example, when the regime began to implement reforms to encourage "loyal" opposition parties in the 1970s, the PAN's national leadership firmly refused to accept the public funding that electoral reforms had made available. Instead, they held fast to the party's long-standing opposition to any hint of complicity with the PRI regime (Reveles Vázquez 1996: 65).[9] As a result, PAN candidates often had to shoulder a considerable share of their own campaign costs and could rely little on the their party's loose organization. Party members cooperated to give whatever time they could spare, but a permanent, professional staff was an unaffordable luxury.

Despite these obstacles, the PAN did score some electoral victories in León. For example, local party founder José Ayala Frausto won the PAN's first federal deputyship in León in 1964, despite massive fraud (Ling Altamirano 1992: 12). Yet such victories were small compensation for repeated electoral abuses. Ayala's was one of only two PAN victories out of Mexico's 178 electoral districts—and was clearly part of the PRI's broader strategy of regime legitimization in the guise of democracy.[10]

Impacts of Political Liberalization

In the late 1970s and early 1980s, serious divisions surfaced within the PRI, and by the late 1980s several prominent PRI public officials were

---

[9] Anecdotal evidence suggests that this reluctance is not universal within the party. There are reports of PAN militants elsewhere accepting bribes and kickbacks from the ruling party.

[10] Parties that win more than 2.5 percent of the vote, but fewer than twenty plural majority seats, in a national election are guaranteed between five and twenty seats in the Chamber of Deputies (seats which are not subtracted from the total number controlled by the PRI). These "party deputy" seats in the legislature actually serve as a disincentive for opposition parties to increase their share of the national vote for fear of losing this guaranteed access to Congress.

discredited and eventually ousted in a wave of corruption scandals throughout Guanajuato. The PRI's difficulties clearly created new opportunities for the PAN. At the same time, changes in the institutional structure of local government in the early 1980s helped give Mexico's opposition parties a vantage point from which to attack the PRI and gain recognition and support from civil society. It was in this context that the PAN racked up new successes in advancing its candidates to public office, particularly in León.

The divisions that helped disable the PRI locally were significantly related to national-level politics. President José López Portillo's (1976–1982) appointment of Governor Velasco Ibarra in 1979 brought major changes to Guanajuato. Velasco sought to return the PRI to its revolutionary bases by promoting the interests of industrial and agrarian labor. His efforts were accompanied by an unprecedented tolerance of the Left, including leftist parties and campesino and worker organizations. Velasco also promoted decentralization through legislative initiatives that helped generate more local revenue and regularize the distribution of resources (Valencia García 1996: 93–94).

Velasco's political and administrative reforms were particularly noteworthy because they preceded national-level reforms by President Miguel de la Madrid (1982–1988) to democratize and decentralize local government. However, Velasco's efforts sparked resentment among the state's business community and members of his own party, and they threatened the center-periphery connections that traditionally undergirded gubernatorial power and local PRI unity. When de la Madrid, the bearer of a markedly different economic agenda, succeeded López Portillo, Velasco was forced to resign and was replaced by interim governor Salvador Rocha Díaz. Rocha Díaz proceeded to undo much of Velasco's work by confiscating lands granted to campesinos and mending relations with the business community.

PRI hegemony in Guanajuato also suffered as a result of Mexico's economic crisis of the 1980s.[11] In 1985, the PRI gubernatorial candidate, Rafael Corrales Ayala, was elected with just over 400,000 votes, while conservative parties (the PAN and the Mexican Democratic Party, or PDM) obtained nearly 200,000 votes and the Left scored its first significant showing, with 30,000 votes (*La Jornada* 1990a: 11).

At the same time, reforms to Article 115 of the Mexican Constitution in 1983 created new opportunities for opposition parties by introducing proportional representation to local government. Under the reformed rules, the winning party was always guaranteed a majority,

---

[11] The discovery of large petroleum deposits in the late 1970s helped generate credit to drive massive government spending. In 1982 the Mexican economy collapsed when petroleum prices plummeted and interest rates soared.

but opposition parties could win positions on the municipal council, from which they could monitor local government and denounce corruption and abuses to the state legislature.

In fact, during Corrales's term as governor of Guanajuato, five municipal presidents were forced to resign amid accusations of "diverting funds." The most significant of these was the forced resignation of León's municipal president, Antonio Hernández Ornelas, because of corruption within his staff.[12]

Federal and state-level elections were held on July 6, 1988, in the wake of this scandal and midway into Governor Corrales's term. Carlos Salinas de Gortari won the race for the presidency despite intense competition from the opposition and allegations that he had triumphed only through massive fraud. Indeed, fraud was blatant and ubiquitous in León. Although the president of the PRI in León, Félix Vilches Ríos, had predicted peaceful elections, citizens of León who arrived early at polling stations found ballot boxes already filled with ballots pre-marked for the ruling party. The indignant voters emptied the ballot boxes and burned ballots or took them to the newspapers as evidence of the PRI's attempt to steal the election. The voters then cast their ballots and observed the remainder of the electoral process to assure that the elections were clean and fair (*A.M.* 1988a).[13]

At the end of the day, the election results were not very favorable for the PRI. In fact, early results strongly favored the PAN across the board. When predictions of a PAN sweep became known, local members of the leftist Cardenista Front (Frente Cardenista) readily expressed their support for the PAN victory, but PRI officials withheld their recognition of the PAN's triumph, awaiting a signal from their national leaders.[14] The next day, the state's electoral commissions determined that PAN candidates Elías Villegas, Vicente Fox Quesada, and José Pedro Gama Medina had indeed carried León's three federal

---

[12] In March 1987 the five PAN city council members helped publicize the fact that Hernández's director of housing had defrauded three hundred people. Hernández's reputation was badly damaged by the scandal; many people believed that he had known about, was involved in, or somehow benefited from the incident (*A.M.* 1987a). Hernández attempted damage control by imposing a "muzzle law" on media reports deemed too sensitive by the administration. These efforts were unsuccessful, and within twenty-four hours the restrictions were retracted (*A.M.* 1987b, 1987c).

[13] Even so, other types of irregularities abounded: voters with legal voting credentials found they were not listed on official rolls; local heads of polling booths hid election materials in their homes; and polling stations were moved without warning.

[14] Later, after gaining permission from the national leadership to concede the election to the PAN, some local PRIistas actually blamed the national leadership for their defeat (*A.M.* 1988b, 1988c, 1988d).

districts to win seats in the federal Chamber of Deputies, the lower house of the Mexican Congress.[15]

The July elections paved the way for Carlos Medina's victory in municipal elections later that year. An experienced municipal councilman who had helped oust Municipal President Antonio Hernández Ornelas, Medina captured the PAN nomination for municipal president without a fight and went on to defeat the PRI's Joaquín Yamín Saade in December. Medina's victory was recognized by the Electoral College on December 21, 1988, beginning a dynasty of PAN administrations in León (*A.M.* 1988f, 1988g, 1988h).

The PAN's victories after 1988 served to consolidate the party's place in Guanajuato. The PAN has not lost a municipal contest in León since Carlos Medina took office. The election of the PAN's Jorge Carlos Obregón to the municipal presidency in 1997 reaffirmed the electorate's support for the party. That victory also made León one of the few municipalities that have been governed by the PAN consecutively for four terms.

Since 1988, León has been something of a PAN island in a widely fluctuating tide of PRI dominance in Guanajuato's other municipalities. Medina's was the PAN's only municipal victory in Guanajuato in 1988. It was followed by victories in twelve of the state's forty-six municipalities three years later, due in part to votes drawn by the PAN's charismatic gubernatorial candidate, Vicente Fox Quesada.[16] In the 1994 elections, the PAN lost ten of the twelve municipalities won in 1991, though it won three new ones.[17]

Then in 1997 the PAN surged once again to gain control of a plurality of the state's municipalities. The party also fared well in local and federal deputy elections in León and gained some ground in other parts of the state. For many years, the PAN had performed poorly in local congressional districts in the predominantly rural ar-

---

[15] The PAN triumphed across the board in León, even in the presidential race. In all other parts of the state, Salinas was declared the official winner (*A.M.* 1988e).

[16] The 1991 gubernatorial race is an important part of PAN history in Guanajuato, though the story is too long and complicated to be told here. Many believe that Fox won the election, but "irregularities" were widespread and PRI candidate Ramón Aguirre was declared the winner. Aguirre "resigned" before taking office, and President Salinas named PANista Carlos Medina as interim governor until new elections could be called under reformed electoral rules. The fact that new elections were not held until August 1995 led some to suggest that Salinas wanted to keep Fox out of the governorship until his presidential term was over. Some observers, notably Alemán (1993), suggest that Medina's appointment was part of a tacit pact between the government and the PAN leadership, and that by opting for conciliation rather than defending the vote, the PAN dealt a blow to democracy in Guanajuato.

[17] Nationally, the PRI rebounded dramatically, thanks, no doubt, to the tremendous increase in public support for Salinas and his new brand of rational populism via the National Solidarity Program (PRONASOL).

eas outside León, largely because of a political structure that empowered local PRI bosses. However, the PAN worked hard to build support in these areas, making enormous efforts to complete long-neglected public work projects. The payoff came when it captured a majority in the local congress in 1997.

Explaining the PAN's Electoral Success

The preceding discussion alluded to two of the factors that contributed to the PAN's triumph in León: (1) strife within the PRI and the corruption of PRI officials, and (2) a national economic crisis that was attributed to PRI mismanagement of the federal government. But other factors also contributed to the PAN's electoral success. For example, León's citizens and the party itself played an important part in forging new political spaces. Furthermore, several factors benefited the PAN in particular, both locally and nationally.

As noted above, the 1983 reforms to the Mexican Constitution altered the institutional structure of municipal councils,[18] and this effect was enhanced during Governor Velasco's administration as spaces opened for "loyal" opposition parties. The new spaces seem particularly relevant for efforts to explain the ability of the local PAN to draw attention to and benefit from PRI administrative failures.

At the same time, the PAN was taking an active part in determining its own opportunity structure by making strategic decisions to adjust to its political environment. One major strategic initiative was the decision to recruit more marketable candidates, both locally and nationally. For example, Manuel Clouthier, a charismatic businessman and the PAN's presidential candidate in 1988, rallied tremendous support in León during the campaign, carrying León's three electoral districts by a margin of two to one.

Carlos Medina came from the same mold, a businessman with wide appeal. He was a new recruit to the PAN in 1986, when he ran as the party's candidate for a seat on the municipal council. Although the PAN's candidate for municipal president lost that year to the PRI's Antonio Hernández, Medina won his seat through proportional representation. Then in 1988 he ran successfully to become León's first PAN municipal president, holding that office from 1989 to 1991.[19]

---

[18] This political opening might easily be mistaken for the act of a benevolent democrat, were it not for the fact that de la Madrid's reforms were a response to widespread political discontent following the currency devaluations and bank nationalizations of the last days of the López Portillo administration.

[19] Medina would take his place in a long line of businessmen municipal presidents in León. As of 1998, eight of the city's last eleven municipal presidents had been important members of the local business community.

With Clouthier energizing the party at the national level and the equally popular Medina in local government, the party was able to garner substantial support among the business community (*La Jornada* 1990b: 13).

Another factor that may have contributed to the initial success of the PAN in León was the Salinas administration's acceptance of PAN victories as an unpalatable but necessary concession. At the beginning of his term, Salinas faced a severe legitimacy crisis and needed the PAN's political and legislative support.[20] Especially important was the PAN's recognition of Salinas's victory in the highly challenged presidential elections, the party's support for the president's neoliberal package, and its role in passing constitutional amendments. In exchange for supporting the PRI, the PAN apparently obtained government recognition of several significant electoral victories, as well as longer-term political concessions in the form of three major sets of electoral reforms during Salinas's term (1988–1994) (Klesner 1993; Stansfield 1996).

Despite this apparent cooperation between the PRI and the PAN, one must not overlook the PAN's tremendous efforts to protest local and state fraud through legal complaints, demonstrations, marches, takeovers of government buildings, and hunger strikes. While the recognition of PAN victories may have been facilitated by a thinly veiled alliance between the PAN's national leadership and the Salinas administration, these concessions were also earned through persistent, courageous, and skillful political maneuvering at both the national and subnational levels.

The national leadership's dialogues with the regime also seem to indicate that the PAN had adopted a more pragmatic position than in the past. In part, this was due to changes in the national leadership that allowed the party to shift away from its long practice of rejecting any collusion with the PRI regime. Thus the transformation of the PAN into a more pragmatic party that could actually win—or be allowed to win—elections involved a complex and controversial struggle of self-definition. Moving from the ideological extreme of noncooperation required an internal restructuring of the party's preferences via membership and leadership changes.

A final factor contributing to the PAN's success has already been mentioned: massive citizen participation in the electoral process. The activism of León's citizens in the 1988 electoral process certainly played an important part in creating new opportunities for the party, confirming the notion that citizen participation is an important contributing factor to democracy.

---

[20] For the most comprehensive analyses of the political circumstances following Salinas's election, see Cornelius, Gentleman, and Smith 1989.

Organizational Developments within the PAN

The preceding section considered some of the dramatic organizational changes that coincided with the PAN's electoral success in León, particularly those that led to further organizational development. Consideration is given below to three types of organizational development that had an important impact on party behavior: a surge in the number of party militants, the professionalization of the PAN's internal structure and processes, and increasing factional conflict within the party.

Party Membership

During the years when political opposition was effectively repressed in Mexico, the number of PAN sympathizers who registered as party members was extremely low. In the absence of tangible political benefits and in the presence of observable political costs—including risks to themselves, their families, and their businesses—people had few rational incentives to participate openly in the PAN. However, as new opportunities opened for the party, the PAN's ability to attract candidates and rank and file rose dramatically.[21]

As mentioned above, Manuel Clouthier was instrumental in drawing new blood into the organization in the 1980s, nearly tripling the party's base of active members in León from just over one hundred in 1986 to nearly three hundred in 1988, the year of Clouthier's presidential campaign. The PAN's electoral performance in León in 1988 for both federal and local offices also attests to Clouthier's impact on the party's ability to draw support from outside the PAN.

The PAN has long been perceived as the party of "the landed rich" and "wealthy entrepreneurs." Yet this identification ignores the fact that for decades Mexico's business community has maintained very strong links with the PRI–government. In Guanajuato, for example, the business community is a complicated web of families and groups connected to the PRI, and politically active businessmen in León typically place their bets on this longtime favorite. Clouthier was able to break this PRI–business link, drawing businessmen from all over

---

[21] Reliable figures on the history of PAN local membership are practically nonexistent. However, in 1994 all PANistas were required to reaffiliate to the party and complete a small survey regarding their militancy and demographic characteristics. While there are problems with measurement through these reaffiliation data (which naturally tend to underestimate membership increasingly backwards over time due to death and other failures to reaffiliate), these are the only hard data available and they are generally confirmed by personal accounts. Current membership figures were compiled by the PAN's national membership registry staffer, Karla María de la Peña Jiménez.

Mexico into the PAN. In León, for example, he recruited Vicente Fox Quesada to the party by appealing to his sense of civic duty. Fox recalled the phone call from Clouthier that forced him to set aside his fear of entering politics:

> It was a tough decision. I had always participated in civic social activities, but that phone call implied a different responsibility, mainly because we in Mexico were acculturated to fear political participation. All the decent people of this country have considered political activity to be dirty and corrupt, and that participating in the opposition placed one's livelihood, the safety of one's family, and oneself at risk.[22]

Clouthier's example no doubt helped convince others like Fox to put both feet squarely in the PAN camp. He also drew large numbers of women into the ranks of the PAN (author interviews with council member Leticia Villegas and others, April–May 1997) (figure 3.1).

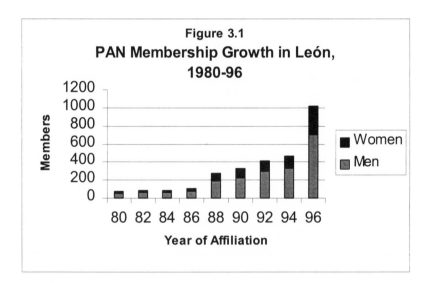

Figure 3.1
PAN Membership Growth in León, 1980-96

After Carlos Medina's 1988 victory in the race for municipal president of León, crises in several basic industries and the initial shock of Mexico's entry into the General Agreement on Tariffs and Trade

---

[22] Fox himself seemed to draw a fair number of individuals to the party in both 1991 and 1994, including future municipal presidents Eliseo Martínez Pérez and Luis Quirós Echegaray (*El Proceso* 1990).

(GATT) began to swing business support toward the PAN. The hit to the footwear industry—León's industrial base—promoted the business sector to seek good terms with local power holders as a key to corporate survival (*La Jornada* 1990b: 13).

What was obviously even more important to the party's development was the number of small and midsized businessmen who joined the PAN in León.[23] The party's rapid growth in the late 1980s and early 1990s came about as a result of the increased participation of these individuals, much more than by drawing León's wealthiest citizens into its ranks, again belying the portrait of the PAN as the party of the rich.

Another potentially important factor in explaining the party's growth was its ability to draw supporters away from other opposition parties. In the July 1988 elections, Felipe Pérez Gutiérrez, one of the founding fathers of the Mexican Democratic Party (PDM), publicly admitted that his party had lost nearly half of its supporters to the PAN and that nationally the PDM would have difficulty meeting the 1.5 percent threshold necessary to maintain registration as a political party (*A.M.* 1988i).[24]

Electoral Success and Organizational Professionalization

As the PAN's political opportunities in León and the rest of Guanajuato increased, the party changed its organizational structure to take best advantage of the challenges presented by political liberalization. Many of these changes proved very successful, though some generated considerable tension within the party.

Changes in the PAN's organizational schema enabled the party to perform an increasing number of functions more fully and efficiently than in the past. Many of these changes were part of the national leadership's effort to energize and professionalize the party in order to cope with the new electoral situation. The national party organization also pressed for reforms to increase the freeness and fairness of political competition. Of particular importance was the party's decision to accept public funding.[25]

---

[23] Author interviews with several longtime PANistas—including Professor Lozano Padilla, Refugio Camarillo, Miguel Segura Dorantes, and others—suggest this to be the case.

[24] The PDM's stint in power in the state capital of Guanajuato (it controlled the municipal government from 1983 to 1986) had actually raised new problems for that party; a sudden influx of members was soon followed by factional divisions that complicated the task of governing and maintaining the organization. Thus the PDM's experience seems to have foreshadowed the difficulties later encountered by the PAN.

[25] Following electoral reforms in 1977, the PAN's national leadership had agreed to accept publicly funded materials, over the protests of several high-ranking party

In 1987, with the enactment of the Federal Electoral Code (CFE), the system for distributing funding to parties changed. Whereas these public funds previously had been distributed to opposition parties by the executive branch (through the Ministry of the Interior), under the CFE they would be allocated according to a formula based on campaign costs, the number of candidates in a race, and the number of votes obtained by each party. In light of this change, the PAN leadership decided to revisit the question of public funding and, after twice putting the issue to a vote, decided in 1988 to accept it. The "yes" vote primarily reflected the PAN's need to increase its organizational capacity on par with its growing membership (Reveles Vázquez 1996: 66).

The resulting influx of monies to the PAN's financial base generated opportunities for professionalizing the León organization. The party was at last able to acquire the material resources that had been sorely lacking in the past. And even more important, its ability to purchase office space to house a full-time party organization kept the party from disappearing between elections, as it had in the past.

Another important part of the transition from intermittently active to full-time organization was the opportunity to hire a full-time staff and offer compensation to party leaders. With a professional staff in place to manage the party's daily affairs, the PAN could refocus volunteer activity away from mundane clerical activities and toward more politically productive pursuits, such as recruiting and mobilizing militants and launching counterattacks against the PRI and the state government. And compensation for party leaders made it possible for these individuals to devote their full attention to the problems of the party. New human, material, and financial resources also facilitated (and necessitated) organizational specialization. New administrative capacities were developed within the organization to oversee electoral activities, the training of public officials, and information management.

As party leadership or "management" functions were professionalized, the organization of the party's rank-and-file or "labor" functions were decentralized through the establishment of committees and subcommittees distributed throughout León's electoral districts. These ward-like units helped encourage greater neighborhood participation, which in turn helped simplify the assignment of elec-

---

members who resigned in protest. The party had already accepted the limited free television and radio access, tax exempt status, and franking privileges for postage and telephone expenses that were contained in electoral reforms implemented in 1973. However, the national leadership had always refused to accept direct subsidies. The general sentiment within the organization was that accepting direct subsidies would put the party at the mercy of the PRI regime and therefore jeopardize the PAN's integrity (Reveles Vázquez 1996: 66).

toral activities and other tasks. The subcommittee structure also helped establish new links to civil society. Statewide, this restructuring was an important part of the PAN's strategy to take the Guanajuato governorship in 1991, helping to fortify the thirty-five existing local party organizations in the state while inaugurating new ones in the nine municipalities where the PAN had yet to establish itself.

Yet despite the very real progress made at the local level, deficiencies still remained. First, given the very low level of development that the local organization had achieved in the past, the advancements, although tremendous, were insufficient. The party still lacked adequate archives, record-keeping facilities, and modern office conveniences.[26] Second, the degree of professionalization and organizational development achieved at the national level far outstripped corresponding efforts at the state and local levels, suggesting a skewed or centralized pattern of organizational development that contradicts notions about the PAN's internal federalism.

Electoral Success and Intra-Party Relations

Not all PANistas saw professionalization in a positive light. Some, especially those who were opposed to accepting public funds, now objected to using these monies to pay people for doing tasks that had long been undertaken as a labor of love. Proponents of organizational change responded that personal commitment was no longer enough; if party leaders were forced to earn a living outside the organization, they would be unable to direct their complete attention to activities of the party.

The organization also had to deal with the frictions that arose from the party's rapid increase in membership. At the national level, the PAN leadership took measures to prevent a wholesale transformation of the base as the party grew. One strategy was to tighten restrictions on the admission of new party members; under the tightened regulations, only an individual who was endorsed by a current party member and who embraced the party's political philosophy in full would be given party membership. These regulations clearly limited the party's growth; with a 1997 membership of just over one thousand in a city of over a million, Leon's PAN could hardly be described as a "mass" organization.

---

[26] Comparisons with other local PAN organizations suggest variation in the availability of (or focus on) such resources. For example, the offices of León's local PAN are in a dank (though historic) building and have little office equipment; local party offices in Tijuana are in a more modern facility and are equipped with much more sophisticated support technologies.

Nevertheless, the tenfold expansion of the party's membership base in less than a decade also meant that new ideas and interests were penetrating the organization, including alternative ideas about the party's basic objectives and different strategies about how to achieve existing goals. Some party members have observed cynically that the PAN has also attracted some opportunists for whom power, not principle, is the primary focus.

Other observers have noted the tensions between old and new party members (Mizrahi 1995), especially in the early 1990s when the "Foristas," a group of longtime party militants, defected from the PAN, claiming that the leadership was leading the party away from its basic principles.[27] Despite major media coverage of the schism, the Foristas actually represented a very small portion of the PAN's membership and were not a real threat to party unity (author interview with Luis H. Álvarez, June 1997), and relatively few members withdrew from the party at either the local or national level.

Although such conflicts were not insignificant, to say that the major schisms within the party lay between old-timers and newcomers would be an oversimplification. In reality, on issues of major dispute within the party, the opposing factions do not seem to be differentiated strictly by years of party membership. Newcomers and old-timers are often to be found on both sides of a debate, with younger members sometimes defending traditional ideological principles and lifetime militants arguing on the side of a more pragmatic approach. For example, both Fox and Medina qualify as "neo-PANistas"; Medina entered the organization in 1986, Fox in 1987. Yet, although both are new to the party, Fox is renowned for his pragmatism and Medina for his adherence to ideology.[28]

The most significant showdown between party factions came in 1996–1997, during the PAN's pre-campaign for its fourth municipal administration; this incident is highly representative of the most important lines of division in León. Despite the party's claims of internal democracy and equality, the nominating process for the PAN's 1997 candidate to the municipal presidency began behind closed doors one early October evening in 1996, when seven of León's prominent PANistas[29] met to consider possible candidates.

---

[27] The Foristas were primarily concerned over the party's undue and antidemocratic cooperation with the government, the business sector's growing influence in party life, and intolerance of different groups and opinions within the party (Reynoso 1994: 194).

[28] Paradoxically, in the controversial 1997 nomination of PAN candidates, Fox was linked to the local party leadership and Medina was among the "undisciplined" government officials who fought against them.

[29] The impressive list of attendees included PAN state secretary Elías Villegas; then–municipal president Luis Quirós Echegaray; former municipal president Eliseo

This was not the first time that an exclusive group had selected the PAN candidate for municipal president. Similar meetings were held in 1991 and 1994. The 1991 meeting was the first informal gathering of PANista notables (the so-called Consejo Político), convened to select a successor for Carlos Medina. They ultimately chose Eliseo Martínez Pérez.[30] In 1994 the Consejo met to evaluate Luis Quirós Echegaray and Gabriel Hernández Jaime, ultimately choosing the former as the PAN candidate.[31]

Events unfolded differently in the selection of the PAN candidate to run in 1997. The Consejo considered three individuals for possible nomination: Luis Ernesto Ayala, head of the local association of footwear manufacturers; Jorge Carlos Obregón, president of the organizing committee for León's municipal fair; and Ricardo Torres Origel, municipal director of social development. Each had a strong base of support within the party, although none had voiced his intention to seek the nomination. The assembled PANistas had come together to evaluate the three in terms of leadership skills, personality, public image, work for the party, intelligence, administrative skills, honesty, and moral values.[32] At the end of the meeting, their handpicked choice was Luis Ernesto Ayala.

When Jorge Carlos Obregón learned of the October 1996 meeting and the Consejo's decision to back Ayala, he was not pleased. Rather than cede the nomination gracefully, Obregón continued to jockey for the candidacy, ultimately gaining the backing of all three PANistas who had served previously as municipal president of León (Medina, Martínez, and Quirós).[33] His slate was packed with notables, including

---

Martínez Pérez; PAN state president Juan Manuel Oliva; León's current municipal president, Gabriel Hernández Jaime; Governor Vicente Fox Quesada; and Refugio Camarillo, secretary general of the Municipal Management Committee. Former municipal president and interim governor Carlos Medina was also invited but was unable to attend.

[30] In that meeting, the Consejo chose Martínez over Gabriel Hernández Jaime. A bitter Hernández went on to launch a disastrous pre-campaign against Martínez. Hernández finally conceded after two rounds of voting at the party convention (*A.M.* 1994a).

[31] In exchange, Hernández was rewarded with one of two municipal prosecutor positions on Quirós's slate. At that time, the PAN had just lost all three of León's federal deputyships, and Hernández, unwilling to provoke a division within the party that might cause the PAN to lose the election for municipal president, readily accepted the Consejo's decision. Thus, despite Quirós's public statements that internal competition was welcome, the PAN launched a "unity" candidate, who later defeated the PRI's Arturo Villegas by the slimmest of margins (*A.M.* 1994b).

[32] Incumbent municipal president Luis Quirós backed Obregón; the others leaned toward Ayala.

[33] Medina also brought former interim municipal president Facundo Castro into his camp, technically giving Obregón the support of four PANistas who had served as municipal president.

two former municipal presidents as his candidates for municipal council seats. Obregón also had strong popular support, though not among longtime members of the party despite his family's long identification with the PAN in León.[34]

Ayala soon responded by launching his own pre-campaign with a slate of party leaders drawn from the local and the state level. Ayala's popularity with state party leaders like José Lozano Padilla, a prominent member of the PAN since the 1940s, drew criticism from Obregón's supporters, who presented themselves as defenders against any party politics that involved candidate imposition from above. Eliseo Martínez Pérez was a vocal opponent of the leadership's behavior: "This contest is not between two candidates; it is between one candidate and the municipal leadership" (*A.M.* 1997). Martínez was also swift to rebuke the state leadership, including Governor Vicente Fox Quesada, for their open and unwarranted public support for Ayala. Ironically, the support Ayala received from the governor and other party leaders may have strengthened support for Obregón because it was viewed as further evidence of imposition politics.

When the votes to select the PAN candidate to the municipal presidency were counted at the local party convention, Obregón had 523 against Ayala's 346. Although the party leadership put on a face of unity and claimed that the pre-campaign had left no scars, Ayala's supporters clearly had difficulty accepting defeat (author interview with Leticia Villegas, May 1997). This conflict—an open effort by the local and state party leadership to capture control of the municipal government, which pitted the party leadership against both current and former municipal officials—illustrates the kinds of tensions that can accompany rapid party growth.

Internal conflicts such as this seem to have become both more common and more intense as Mexico's political context has turned increasingly in favor of the PAN. Potential nominees and their supporters now see elective office as an attainable goal and are more likely to challenge one another for candidate nominations. This party, which once had to beg people to run on its ticket, now has to keep competing pre-candidates from tearing the organization apart.

What was ironic in this rivalry is that self-declared pragmatists like Governor Fox attempted to impose their candidate by exploiting their control over the party leadership. The power struggles that surrounded the selection of Jorge Carlos Obregón were not unique; similar incidents occurred in the nomination of candidates for local deputyships, federal deputyships, and Senate seats.

---

[34] Jorge Carlos Obregón is two generations removed from Carlos A. Obregón, the 1946 UNS–UCL–PAN coalition candidate.

Even as the party in León was dividing along the lines described above, PANistas across the state were unified in terms of their position on national-level politics. In this arena, local-level differences were downplayed for the sake of more regionally defined interests. This became quite evident, for example, in the Guanajuato PAN's strong support for Ernesto Ruffo's candidacy for the national party leadership in 1996. Joining with PANistas from the northern states, Guanajuato backed Ruffo against Felipe Calderón Hinojosa, the protégé of then–national president Carlos Castillo Peraza.

Such schisms between local PAN organizations and party leadership at the state or even the national level simply had no place in the party's earlier development. During the decades in which the PAN was largely excluded from power, local party organizations had little capacity to influence the national leadership. Although the national leadership still enjoys enormous advantages in terms of resources and its level of professionalization when compared to subnational party organizations, as the party's local and regional organizations have developed their own leadership structures, membership, and support base, they have become increasingly able to challenge and pressure the national leadership.

The dangers that result from cleavages such as those described above are considered in the concluding section. Meanwhile, it is important to note that, although the PAN's electoral successes have brought about a very positive organizational transformation, they have generated potential liabilities for the party as well. One important negative outcome has been the emergence of factions that contest against one another from within the party structures, as in the struggle between local and state party leadership in León.

Lessons for National-Local Intra-Party Relations

While the experience of the PAN in León is interesting in itself, this case holds important lessons about some of the general problems the party faces in today's liberalized political setting. First, the PAN has established strong regional bases of support. This pattern can become a source of conflict as local and regional cliques develop within the party and vie for influence within the national organization.

Second, as electoral victories stack up at the local level, the national leadership needs to foster the party's organizational development and prepare it to take on new functions. The national leadership has gone some way toward this goal. However, the current national leadership has been slow and/or reluctant to develop the organization to its maximum potential. For example, federal monies allocated prior to the 1997 midterm elections included funds that would nor-

References

Alemán, Ricardo. 1993. *Guanajuato: espejismo electoral.* Mexico City: La Jornada Ediciones.

A.M. [León, Guanajuato]. 1987a. "Hablan los leoneses sobre el fraude en Promoción de Vivienda," April 7.

———. 1987b. "No renunciaré; sería una cobardía: A. Hernández O," April 1.

———. 1987c. "Solamente un día duró 'la Ley Mordaza' en la presidencia local," April 4.

———. 1988a. "En la casilla 65-A los votantes se apoderaron de urnas 'rellenas'," July 7.

———. 1988b. "Arrasa el PAN en León: Cardenistas," July 9.

———. 1988c. "Reconoce el PRI el triunfo de Acción Nacional pero impugnará 60 casillas," July 10.

———. 1988d. "Por falta de dirigencia perdió en León el PRI: Alfonso Sánchez," July 12.

———. 1988e. "León votó por Clouthier; en Guanajuato Salinas sigue adelante," July 13.

———. 1988f. "Reconoce T. Landa la ventaja panista," December 5.

———. 1988g. "Inconforme PRI con el proceso," December 6.

———. 1988h. "PAN 65,958; PRI 39,889," December 12.

———. 1988i. "La mitad de nuestra gente votó por el PAN, reconoce PDM," July 15.

———. 1994a. "Elecciones municipales de 1991," September 9.

———. 1994b. "Con más gallos es mejor el mole," September 8.

———. 1997. "'Apoyé a Jorge Carlos porque vi que la competencia no era pareja', Eliseo," February 15.

Camp, Roderic A. 1996. *Politics in Mexico.* 2d ed. New York: Oxford University Press.

Cornelius, Wayne A., Judith Gentleman, and Peter H. Smith, eds. 1989. *Mexico's Alternative Political Futures.* Monograph Series, 30. La Jolla: Center for U.S.–Mexican Studies, University of California, San Diego.

El Proceso. 1990. "Reclutado por Clouthier, el neopanista Vicente Fox, seguro de convertirse en el segundo gobernador de oposición," October 29.

Klesner, Joseph L. 1993. "Modernization, Economic Crisis, and Electoral Alignment in Mexico," *Mexican Studies/Estudios Mexicanos* 9 (2): 187–223.

La Jornada. 1990a. "En 10 años el PRI perdió 60 por ciento de las preferencias electorales en Guanajuato," August 27.

———. 1990b. "Los empresarios de León, con el PRI y con el PAN," August 31.

Lawson, Kay, ed. 1994. *How Political Parties Work: Perspectives from Within.* Westport, Conn.: Praeger.

Ling Altamirano, Ricardo Alfredo. 1992. *Vamos por Guanajuato.* Mexico: EPESSA.

Michels, Robert. 1966. *Political Parties: A Sociological Study of the Oligarchical Tendencies of Modern Democracy.* New York: Free Press.

Mizrahi, Yemile. 1995. "Entrepreneurs in the Opposition: Modes of Political Participation in Chihuahua." In *Opposition Government in Mexico,* edited by Victoria E. Rodríguez and Peter M. Ward. Albuquerque: University of New Mexico Press.

———. 1996. "The Costs of Electoral Success: The Partido Acción Nacional in Mexico." Paper prepared for the Institute of Latin American Studies, University of London, November.

Ostrogorski, M. 1964. *Democracy and the Organization of Political Parties*, edited and abridged by Seymour Martin Lipset. Chicago: Quadrangle Books.

Panebianco, Angelo. 1988. *Political Parties: Organization and Power*, translated by Marc Silver. Cambridge: Cambridge University Press.

Reveles Vázquez, Francisco. 1993. "Sistema organizativo y fracciones internas del Partido Acción Nacional, 1939–1990." Master's thesis, Universidad Nacional Autónoma de México.

———. 1996. "El proceso de institucionalización organizativa del Partido Acción Nacional (1984–1995)." Ph.D. dissertation, Universidad Nacional Autónoma de México.

Reynoso, Víctor Manuel. 1994. "El PAN en 1993: Los Foristas se van, Castillo llega a la presidencia del partido y Diego es elegido candidato a la presidencia de la República." In *Elecciones y partidos políticos en México, 1993*, edited by Leonardo Valdés. Iztapalapa: Universidad Autónoma Metropolitana.

Rodríguez, Victoria E., and Peter M. Ward. 1994. *Political Change in Baja California*. Monograph Series, no. 40. La Jolla: Center for U.S.–Mexican Studies, University of California, San Diego.

Ruiz, Ramón Eduardo. 1992. *Triumphs and Tragedy: A History of the Mexican People*. New York: W.W. Norton.

Stansfield, David E. 1996. "The PAN: The Search for Ideological and Electoral Space." In *Dismantling the Mexican State?* edited by Rob Aitken et al. New York: St. Martin's.

Valencia García, Guadalupe. 1996. "La administración Panista del municipio de León, Guanajuato (1989–91)." In *La tarea de gobernar: gobiernos locales y demandas ciudadanas*, edited by Alicia Ziccardi. Mexico City: Miguel Angel Porrúa.

Weber, Max. 1946. *From Max Weber: Essays in Sociology*, edited and translated by H.H. Gerth and C. Wright Mills. Oxford: Oxford University Press.

4

Alternation and Political Liberalization: The PAN in Baja California

Víctor Alejandro Espinoza Valle

In 1994 and 1995, the Mexican political system underwent a dramatic crisis that for many observers signaled the end of the regime. Like all political crises, this one was characterized by the regime's inability to satisfy social demands using existing strategies. What differentiated it from past crises was that the administration's efforts to employ new strategies of "political opening" served only to undermine the corporatist pillars on which the governing structure was based. The outcome was increasing uncertainty about the future configuration of state-society relations and the means for arriving at new political agreements.

Uncertainty is a defining characteristic of all political liberalization processes. Political liberalization in Mexico dates from the political opening that occurred during the administration of President Luis Echeverría (1970–1976) in response to the democratic student movement of 1968.[1] In the late 1980s and 1990s, political opening expanded to include recognition by Mexico's ruling Institutional Revolutionary Party (PRI) of opposition-party electoral victories in races for municipal government posts and state governorships. But these advances in formal democracy have proved insufficient. Liberalization has not brought about the dismantling of Mexican authoritarianism. In fact, it

---

Translation by Sandra del Castillo.

[1] Editors' note: On October 2, 1968, students assembled in downtown Mexico City to demand democracy. Hundreds were slain by members of the Mexican army. Luis Echeverría, then minister of the interior, was blamed for ordering the use of the military force against the demonstrators.

"normalization") or democratization.... Successful liberalization does not necessarily produce democratization.... It can also produce an outcome that responds to its own logic.... Mexico's successive liberalizations have sometimes been aimed at preserving the status quo rather than responding to a supposed democratizing imperative" (Loaeza 1993: 48–49, 51–52). Given that liberalization is an open process with little institutionalization, it creates a high level of uncertainty in regard to its outcome and the future.

The Presidency and Presidentialism

Mexico's presidentialist form of government is mirrored in the political structure that exists within the individual states. At the state level, as at the federal level, legislative and judicial authorities are subordinate to the executive and to the clientelistic practices of the corporatist sociopolitical structure (Espinoza 1994a). This pattern holds true at the level of local government as well (see Ziccardi 1995; Espinoza 1992a: 119–22). The experience of Ernesto Ruffo Appel is illustrative. Before being elected governor of Baja California in 1989, Ruffo was elected municipal president of Ensenada, in 1986. One of Municipal President Ruffo's primary objectives was to increase the share of revenues that the state government returned to the municipality. He succeeded in his efforts, and Ensenada's share of state funds was increased substantially as of January 1, 1990. By this time, however, Ruffo had already been elected governor, and during his tenure in this latter post, with a PAN majority in the state legislature, Ruffo was able to reduce Ensenada's municipal budget to its previous level. He justified his action as follows: "If we increase the revenues that are returned to the municipalities, we will be unable to grant salary increases to teachers and government workers." His actions make it undeniably clear that, party affiliations aside, local governments' requests for resources to meet social demands are not a priority in Mexico's centralized political structure. Ruffo's response also demonstrates how quick the transition can be from opposition party to party in power (Espinoza 1993: 302–305).

The reform initiatives that the Mexican government proposed from the 1980s forward included programs whose purported objective was to promote political and administrative decentralization. Paradoxically, many decentralizing efforts served to reinforce the centralized political system. For example, a study of the spatial distribution of public employment conducted by the author found that the number of federal bureaucrats in Mexico City declined from 885,608 to 813,556 between 1982 and 1989. Concurrently, the number of federal employees distributed throughout the rest of the country increased from 1,147,306 to 1,596,204. Measured another way, in 1982 there were 0.44 local employees for every federal employee; in 1989, the ration was 0.39 local workers per federal employee.[4] What had happened was that federal *employees*, not political power, had been decentralized, effectively increasing the reach of the federal government into the states and hence strengthening even more the power of the centralized government (Espinoza 1993: 88–94).

This example suggests that structural constraints can limit the chances for substantive democratization at the level of state government. And this, in turn, implies that we must include "national factors" if we are fully to understand local politics.[5] The importance of national factors at the local level is reiterated by Lorenzo Meyer in his review of the PRI's recognition of Francisco Barrio in 1991 as the second PANista to be elected governor of a Mexican state. According to Meyer, this outcome was possible only in light of agreements signed by the PRI and the PAN prior to the 1988 presidential election, agreements intended to marginalize the leftist Party of the Democratic Revolution (PRD) during that campaign. From that time forward, the federal government viewed the PAN as its "loyal opposition," not as a threat to national sovereignty. Hence, there was no need to resort to electoral fraud to keep it out of office.[6]

Losing local offices to the loyal opposition is no longer seen as a threat to the stability of the Mexican political system. To the contrary, since 1989 the PRI government has viewed the PAN's electoral victories as an investment in its own legitimacy. Nevertheless, the system is certainly not fully open; opposition victories become less likely the higher the elective office in question. That is, a loyal opposition has a better chance of winning—and gaining recognition for its victory—in local races than in state-level races, and virtually no chance at claiming the presidency. In this regard, Mizrahi notes that "at the state and municipal levels, electoral contests tend to be two-party races, either between the PRI and the PAN or between the PRI and the PRD, which

---

[4] The federal bureaucracy has long been "big business" in Mexico and a major source of the government's legitimacy. See Aguilar Villanueva 1991.

[5] According to Alberto Aziz Nassif, since 1988 regional events have become interlinked with events at the national level, and together the two mark the pace of democratization. Thus, gains at either the regional or municipal level are not necessarily the forerunners of change. For that we must look to the interaction of regional advances with extraordinary happenings on the national stage (Aziz Nassif 1994a: 209–10). Also see Aziz Nassif 1994b: 8–9, for the interaction of national and local factors in the state of Chihuahua.

[6] The change in campaign rhetoric is almost certainly due more to external factors than to the situation in Chihuahua itself. In 1992, the major threat to the government and the PRI was not the PAN but the PRD under the leadership of Cuauhtémoc Cárdenas. The government's objective was to block any possible alliance between the PRD and the PAN. See Meyer 1994: 13.

increases the opposition's chances of winning." By recognizing the opposition's victories at these levels, "the PRI can share power with the opposition within a circumscribed territory without losing control of the presidency and the highest levels of power. And giving the opposition parties the opportunity to govern states and municipalities spurs these parties to moderate their positions and work toward achieving consensus between the opposition and the government" (Mizrahi 1995: 187–99).[7]

Baja California, 1989–1995: Contained Alternation

The PAN's rising political fortunes in Baja California reflect the state's highly politicized and independent-minded society. Recent political history in the state traces an unbroken struggle to win recognition of PAN victories in state and municipal elections. Yet the deciding factor in winning PRI–government recognition for Ruffo's gubernatorial win in 1989 was not the efforts of civil society to assure a free and fair election but, rather, a deliberate decision on the part of President Carlos Salinas de Gortari (1988–1994).[8] It proved to be a wise decision and one that gave an excellent rate of return in legitimacy for the Salinas administration—although it did damage the relationship between the PRI's local contingent and the party's National Executive Committee (see Espinoza 1992b).[9] There can be little doubt that this "selective democracy" is the result of the ruling party's calculated generosity toward the PAN, a strategy designed to undermine the threat from the Left.[10]

---

[7] Meyer (1994: 15) notes that "bipartisanship ... in a macropolitical scenario in which there are three, not two, major factions—and where an alliance between oppositions could dismantle an authoritarian system—would appear, for the time being at least, impossible."

[8] "In the state and municipal elections that followed the installation of the Salinas administration, some PAN victories were allowed to stand, others were not; and winning recognition of opposition election victories sometimes required demonstrations, threats of violence, and appeals to the international community. Thus, in 1989, *by presidential decision*, election authorities and the PRI accepted the election of Ernesto Ruffo as governor of Baja California" (Meyer 1993, emphasis added).

[9] The political costs had it *not* acknowledged the PAN victory inclined the Salinas administration to set aside the concerns of the local PRI contingent.

[10] The PRD (in 1988 still called the National Democratic Front, or FDN) showed substantial strength in the 1988 presidential elections, coming very close to winning Mexico's highest office. According to Mauricio Merino Huerta: "The PRI has adopted a posture of 'calculated generosity' toward PAN candidates in local elections ... in a strategy that serves, with increasing effectiveness, to challenge the PRD in areas that it has claimed for itself" (1993: 65).

There are two points of particular interest regarding the election and time in office of Governor Ruffo. First, although the 1989 gubernatorial campaign was run amid widespread calls for alternation of parties in power and intense efforts on the part of local citizens to protect the vote on election day, in fact, Ruffo won the governorship with a smaller percentage of the electorate participating than in the five preceding gubernatorial elections. Abstentionism in 1989 measured 52.3 percent. Moreover, a significant proportion of the votes cast for the National Action Party candidate came from disaffected PRI partisans.

Second, after the 1992 elections no party held a majority in the Baja California state legislature, which was composed of eight delegates from the PAN, seven from the PRI, and four from the PRD. While an alliance between the PRI and PRD delegates could have placed the PAN in a minority position—and made the task of governing extremely difficult—such an alliance never materialized. Instead, two PRI delegates regularly allied themselves with the PAN legislators to ensure the passage of practically all initiatives presented by the governor to the legislature,[11] giving further support to allegations that it was President Salinas himself who was easing the way for the Ruffo administration.[12]

For its part, the PAN made good use of its first governorship and its special relationship with the Mexican president. Its strategy was to close in on the political center, taking ground bit by bit until it reached the heart of the system. The date for reaching this happy goal was set for the year 2000. Regarding his party's strategy, Ruffo observed: "The official party is like a retreating army; in order to avoid total defeat it must yield ground [governorships], although soon it will have to hand over the general headquarters [the presidency]" (Chávez 1994: 6; see also Merino Huerta 1993: 79).

One of the central paradoxes of the Mexican government's modernization process begun in 1982 is that the project is being implemented at the local level by opposition governments. This is certainly the case in Baja California. For example, reducing the state's budget by cutting the state-level bureaucracy began in Baja California in 1989, under Ruffo.[13] Ruffo's argument in support of this action was the same as the president's justification six years earlier at the national level: it was high time to make the private sector serve as the engine of growth to achieve social and economic development.

---

[11] Efforts by the local PRI to expel these two legislators from the party were unsuccessful.

[12] This opinion was expressed frequently in Zeta. See, for example, Barroso 1995.

[13] Budget reductions were achieved by slowing the rate at which new personnel were hired, restructuring some municipal offices, and modernizing work processes.

Yet the consequences of enlarging the private sector's role were different at these two levels of government. Salinas enjoyed the support of the traditional union bureaucracy, including the unconditional backing of corporatist organizations such as the CROM, the CROC, and the FSTSE—even though the reform reduced the economic benefits that these organizations received in exchange for their support of the system. In contrast, Ruffo not only lacked such support, he had to implement his program over the objections of the local labor leadership. (The most visible case involved the union of state employees; see Espinoza 1992b.) And yet his credentials as someone who came up through the opposition gave him the maneuvering room necessary to transform the local corporatist system by naming traditional labor leaders to positions in teacher organizations, taxi drivers' unions, and popular movements (Espinoza 1994b; Hernández Vicencio 1995).

Thus, alternation in government allowed for the opening up of the corporatist system, the first salvo in the process of political liberalization. Formal democratization of Baja California's political system built up momentum during the Ruffo governorship. For example, it was Ruffo's administration that developed a voter identity card that included the individual's photograph. Six years later, this type of voter card was adopted at the federal level, passed over strong PRI opposition in the Mexican Congress.[14] Another important advance was the state's "New Law of Institutions and Electoral Processes," passed unanimously in December 1994. This law eliminated the self-certification of elections, and the leadership of state-level electoral institutions was broadened beyond parties and public officials to include nonpartisan citizen ombudsmen as voting members. The only direct role in elections that was left to the president was his right, vigorously criticized by the opposition, to name the presidential adviser to the State Electoral Council.

As significant as these advances in procedural democracy may be, there is still a possibility that they could be reversed. This susceptibility to reversal extends to include the alternation of political parties in power. Regarding changes to Mexico's corporatist structure, there is a danger of regression here as well because the PAN has failed both to propose an alternative structure and to fill the vacuum left by the displacement of the traditional corporatist leadership. Mizrahi notes: "The PAN ... has presented no alternative model for state-society relations" nor an economic project that differs from the one implemented by the federal government since 1982" (1995: 200–201). The

---

[14] Ruffo cited as the most important achievement of his administration the opportunity he had to present his own voter identification card to President Salinas and say, "Yes, Mr. President, it can be done" (reiterating the slogan he had used throughout his campaign and time in the governor's office).

PAN's sole differentiating characteristic, according to Lorenzo Meyer, is that, beginning with Manuel Clouthier's leadership of the PAN in 1988, the party had not "addressed the direction of structural change so much as the authoritarian manner in which it is being implemented" (Meyer 1993: 70).

Although the relationship between the governor's office and the national executive has remained positive, on the whole, throughout Baja California's opposition governments, two factors did undercut state-federal relations during the second half of Ruffo's term in office. The first topic of contention involved the state's share of public revenues, discussed above (Espinoza 1995). Ruffo was highly critical of Mexico's fiscal centralism, which allocated 81 percent of each peso collected to the central government, 16 percent to the states, and 3 percent to the municipalities, asserting that the state failed to recover an amount equivalent to its contribution to the federal budget. He eventually carried his complaint directly to the federal Ministry of Finance (SHCP). The state's share of federal funding was reduced even further in December 1992 when additional resources were directed away from the states to support a new program to improve the nation's schools (Espinoza 1996). Ultimately the minister of government stepped in to resolve the conflict between Ruffo and Ministry of Finance officials by authorizing a study to ascertain whether Baja California's contributions in fact outweighed federal returns to the state. The study found that the Baja California state government was receiving 13.5 percent *more* in funding from the federal government than it contributed to the federal tax base (Espinoza 1995: 274).

Narco-trafficking was the second source of conflict between Baja California and the federal government during the Ruffo administration. In 1994 and 1995, Baja California was in the eye of the drug-trafficking hurricane. The drug trade and the violence associated with it were among the foremost issues of public concern, and the state's citizens were quick to point out the PAN government's inability to mount an effective policing effort. In his own defense, Ruffo noted that drug trafficking falls under federal, not state, jurisdiction, and that enforcement is the responsibility of the federal attorney general.

Baja California's gubernatorial elections scheduled for August 1995 were thought likely to mark the next step in party alternation by returning control of the state government to the old guard—the so-called dinosaurs—of the PRI. The reappearance of traditional campaign strategies came accompanied by expectations that the former corporatist relationship between the state and society would be reestablished as well, for, although the old leadership had been displaced, the corporatist organizational structure, and especially the corporatist political structure, remained in place.[15] In the end, the PAN candidate, Héctor Terán Terán, won the governorship, postponing for the moment the scenario of a full return to the old model.

Clearly, the frictions that had emerged during Ruffo's term as governor had not decreased the popularity of the National Action Party in Baja California. The state's citizens had elected their second PAN governor with a decisive margin (Terán Terán defeated his PRI opponent, Francisco Pérez Tejada, by 8.4 percent of the vote). The PAN also won the municipal presidencies in Tijuana and Mexicali, while the PRI carried Tecate and Ensenada. The newly elected state legislature included thirteen deputies from the PAN, eleven from the PRI, and one from the PRD. This marked numerical equilibrium between parties in the legislature presents an optimal opportunity for reestablishing more harmonious relations between the state and federal levels of government, something that would benefit both sides. Conflict between the PAN and the PRI in Baja California would only deepen Mexico's political crisis, something the administration of Ernesto Zedillo Ponce de León (1994–2000) clearly hopes to avoid. And state authorities are eager to build consensus, having found that a friendly relationship with the central government is indeed more profitable than an inflexible strategy such as the one pursued by Ruffo during the second half of his term (see Rodríguez and Ward 1994: 110). Zedillo spoke to this "new era" in the relationship between the two levels of government during his visit to Baja California only days after Terán Terán's inauguration on November 1, 1995: "We look forward," Zedillo affirmed, "to a relationship built on mutual trust, a relationship free of discord.... We have left the phase of political conflict behind us." He appealed to local legislators to close ranks with the governor and to join in efforts to develop workable solutions (*Cambio* 1995; Heras and Garduño 1995: 10).

Conclusion

The importance of political opening in Baja California since 1989 in advancing democratization is undeniable. Alternation catalyzed a process of liberalization which, although it has not yet brought about radical change, has transformed local political life. And yet its future remains tenuous. Advances still seem fragile and are potentially re-

---

[15] The belief that corporatist and clientelistic relations could be revived relied on the fact that Ruffo had not been able to modify the PRI–government's corporatist organizations at their core. Such a transformation requires more than the six years of a governor's term for full consolidation. The future of Mexican corporatism, at both the national and local levels, depends on democratization of the Mexican political regime.

versible as long as there is no institutional framework for transitioning to a new political regime. Moreover, the likelihood that the National Action Party will continue to be a viable challenger to the PRI in a system of alternating political parties is twice constrained: first by the PAN's lack of a unique economic and social project, and second by the predominance of a presidentialist, authoritarian government that continues to recreate itself at all levels of Mexico's political geography. Thus it seems highly unlikely that the PAN's electoral successes in Baja California are the vanguard of a new democratic regime and a long-awaited transition in the national political system. Many Mexicans still doubt that Baja California's successful foray into alternation of the executive at the state level can be successfully replicated at the federal level.

References

Aguilar Villanueva, Luis F. 1991. "Cambios en la gestión gubernamental y reforma del Estado." Cuadernos de Discusión, no. 1. Tijuana, B.C.: El Colegio de la Frontera Norte.

Aziz Nassif, Alberto. 1994a. "Municipio y transición política: una pareja en formación." In *En busca de la democracia municipal. La participación ciudadana en el gobierno local mexicano*, edited by Mauricio Merino. Mexico City: El Colegio de México.

———. 1994b. *Chihuahua. Historia de una alternativa*. Mexico City: La Jornada Ediciones/CIESAS.

Barroso, Santiago. 1995. "Por nocaut técnico, Ruffo le ganó a Fierro Márquez," *Zeta* [Tijuana], September 22–28.

Cambio. 1995. "Nueva relación con BC: Zedillo," December 22.

Chávez, Elías. 1994. "Ejército en retirada, el PRI 'cede' espacios, pero tendrá que entregar el cuartel general; para el 2000, 'soy materia dispuesta': Ernesto Ruffo," *Proceso* 980 (August 14).

Espinoza, Víctor Alejandro. 1992a. *Don Crispín. Una crónica fronteriza. Memoria y diálogos de don Crispín Valle Castañeda*. 2d ed. Tijuana, B.C.: El Colegio de la Frontera Norte.

———. 1992b. "Las transformaciones del corporativismo regional. Relaciones Estado-sindicato en el sector público de Baja California," *Frontera Norte* [El Colegio de la Frontera Norte] 4 (8): 79–110.

———. 1993. *Reforma del Estado y empleo público. El conflicto laboral en el sector público de Baja California*. Mexico City: Instituto Nacional de Administración Pública.

———. 1994a. "Interrogantes de la transición," *Cuadernos de Nexos* 71 (197).

———. 1994b. "El SNTE ante la modernización educativa y la alternancia política en Baja California." Tijuana, B.C.: El Colegio de la Frontera Norte. Mimeo.

———. 1995. "Gestión pública y alternancia política. Baja California, 1989–1994," *Revista de Administración Pública* 89: 265–80.

————. 1996. "Modernización educativa y cambio político en Baja California," *El Cotidiano* [UAM–Azcapotzalco] 12 (74): 44–48.

Gilly, Adolfo. 1988. *Nuestra caída en la modernidad*. Mexico: Joan Boldó i Clement.

Heras, Antonio, and Roberto Garduño. 1995. "Pide Zedillo a legisladores de BC cerrar filas con Terán," *La Jornada*, December 23.

Hernández Vicencio, Tania. 1995. *Los gremios de taxistas en Tijuana. Alternancia política y corporativismo cetemista*. Colección Cuadernos, no. 7. Tijuana, B.C.: El Colegio de la Frontera Norte.

Loaeza, Soledad. 1993. "La incertidumbre política mexicana," *Nexos* 186 (June): 47–59.

Marcos. 1996. "De árboles, transgresores y odontología, *La Jornada Semanal* 45 (February 14).

Merino Huerta, Mauricio. 1993. *La democracia pendiente. Ensayos sobre la deuda política de México*. Mexico City: Fondo de Cultura Económica.

Meyer, Lorenzo. 1993. "El presidencialismo. Del populismo al neoliberalismo," *Revista Mexicana de Sociología* 55 (2).

————. 1994. "Prólogo." In *Chihuahua. Historia de una alternativa*, by Alberto Aziz Nassif. Mexico City: La Jornada Ediciones/CIESAS.

Mizrahi, Yemile. 1995. "Democracia, eficiencia y participación: los dilemas de los gobiernos de oposición en México," *Política y Gobierno* [Centro de Investigación y Docencia Económicas] 2 (2).

Ramírez, Carlos. 1995. "Archivo político," *La Crónica* [Mexicali], November 19.

Rodríguez, Victoria E., and Peter M. Ward. 1994. *Political Change in Baja California: Democracy in the Making?* Monograph Series, no. 40. La Jolla: Center for U.S.–Mexican Studies, University of California, San Diego.

Ziccardi, Alicia. 1995. "La tarea de gobernar: las ciudades y la gobernabilidad." In *La tarea de gobernar: gobiernos locales y demandas ciudadanas*, edited by Alicia Ziccardi. Mexico: Miguel Angel Porrúa/Instituto de Investigaciones Sociales, Universidad Nacional Autónoma de México.

5

A Case of Opposition Unity: The San Luis Potosí Democratic Coalition of 1991

Tomás Calvillo Unna

"We began this undertaking thirty-five years ago. We have never veered off course, nor turned back. We are getting nearer; the distance is closing. . . . I want to see democracy with my own eyes. That is my desire."—*Dr. Salvador Nava, 1992*

Mexico's 1991 midterm federal congressional elections marked a crucial point in the presidency of Carlos Salinas de Gortari (1988–1994). They were an opportunity to assert the legitimacy of his policies, the continuing popularity of the ruling Institutional Revolutionary Party (PRI), and the weakness of the emergent opposition parties—and thus resolve the legitimization crisis provoked by the events of the 1988 presidential election. In other words, the midterm elections were a means to legitimize retroactively the first three years of Salinas's administration. But they were also a means to demonstrate support for the president's political and economic policies, thereby providing a popular mandate for continuity as well as approval for controversial initiatives—like the North American Free Trade Agreement (NAFTA)—in the second half of his six-year term. In preparation for these elections, considerable efforts had been made to rebuild the

The author is grateful for the support and comments of Wayne A. Cornelius, Jane Hindley, and Todd Eisenstadt. He also wishes to thank Lydia Torre and Isabel Monrroy for their help in San Luis Potosí, along with Martha Rivera and Eduardo Baños. Translation by Jennifer Collins.

bases of PRI support (most notably through the National Solidarity Program, known as PRONASOL; see Cornelius, Craig, and Fox 1994) and to ensure that the most crude and blatant forms of electoral fraud could not undermine the official outcome. Such efforts were largely successful: the official returns gave the PRI 60 percent of the total vote and two-thirds majority control of the federal Chamber of Deputies. Moreover, accusations of fraud notwithstanding, the 1991 elections were widely recognized as the cleanest midterm federal elections in the postrevolutionary period.

If the federal election results were presented as a partial vindication of Salinas's project, including his claims to have modernized the PRI, concurrent state elections in Guanajuato and San Luis Potosí raised important questions about his program of political reform and democratizing credentials. Following high-profile campaigns, both Vicente Fox Quesada, the National Action Party's (PAN) gubernatorial candidate in Guanajuato, and Dr. Salvador Nava, candidate of the Potosí Democratic Coalition (CDP) for the governor's seat in San Luis Potosí, refused to recognize the official returns, which, as anticipated, gave victory to their PRI opponents. Instead, both Fox and Nava spearheaded a series of political protest actions denouncing electoral fraud. For a brief period their actions captivated the political imagination of the nation, exposing the weakness of the supposedly reformed electoral institutions and the discretionary control of the president, and giving new momentum to the halting process of political reform.

The post-electoral conflict in Guanajuato was resolved quickly. Mass mobilizations of PAN supporters in the state, concomitant with negotiations between the PAN national leadership and President Salinas, resulted in the resignation of the PRI candidate, Ramón Aguirre. Victory was not conceded to Fox, however; Salinas announced an interim replacement for Aguirre, a well-known member of the PAN, Carlos Medina Placencia.

In contrast to the expeditious resolution of the conflict in Guanajuato, events in San Luis Potosí took a different course, one that ultimately exposed the vulnerability and inconsistency of the Salinas administration's political reform program. Building on a long tradition of local political struggle, the Potosí Democratic Coalition unified Mexico's two most important opposition parties, the PAN and the Party of the Democratic Revolution (PRD), along with the regionally significant Mexican Democratic Party (PDM) behind Nava's 1991 gubernatorial bid. The coalition was an entity without precedent in the country's political history (Caballero 1992: 43; see also *Proceso* 1991). It presented a challenge not only to the Salinas administration, which sought to prevent any form of opposition unity, but also to the national opposition forces themselves. The project of uniting the opposition around a single candidate in order to defeat the official PRI candidate and establish a government of democratic transition demonstrated one possible way to accelerate and deepen the process of political change occurring in the country.

This chapter describes Nava's project in detail, analyzing the coalition that unified the PAN, PRD, and PDM behind Nava's 1991 gubernatorial campaign. A discussion of the coalition, its origins, internal characteristics, and trajectory is relevant to the political history of San Luis Potosí; it can also shed light on important aspects of the political process nationwide during this period of regime transition.[1] In particular, this case demonstrates the significant role that local actors played in Mexico's complex transition, as well as the articulations between local and national forces and domains.

The basic elements that will be employed to describe and explain the origin and dynamics of the Potosí Democratic Coalition include the Navista movement itself, state-level organizations of national-level political parties, and national party structures and leaderships. The relationships between these three sectors and each one's actions in the course of events will be examined in three distinct periods, covering the coalition's formation, the electoral campaign, and the period of civil resistance that followed the election. Other factors also had direct or indirect impacts on the 1991 experiment in political unity; these include the local and national media, the president of Mexico, and the PRI and its own local candidate. These will be considered as well.

Origins of the Navista Movement

It is not the intention here to provide a historical account of the Navista movement. However, in order to explain the events of 1991 and understand why by this date Salvador Nava had become a powerful symbol of good government—and thus a desirable and trustworthy

---

[1] Regime transition here refers to political changes that began in the early 1980s, such as the alternation of political parties in power and opposition access to state governments, town councils, and local legislatures. In a highly centralized political system like Mexico, the culmination of this regime transition would be signaled by full opposition access to the central government in Mexico City, the end of the governing party's majority control of the federal Congress, and the ability of a candidate proposed and supported by the opposition to run in an open and fair race for the presidency. Regime transition consists of two parallel processes: democratization and decentralization. Its main goal is to avoid either national disintegration or a return to an authoritarian regime.

Editors' note: some but not all of these conditions were met by the surprise showing of opposition parties in Mexico's 1997 midterm congressional races.

candidate for the principal opposition forces—a brief overview of the history and characteristics of Navismo is advisable.

In 1958 Dr. Nava had competed successfully for the municipal presidency of San Luis Potosí as a coalition candidate, representing a broad array of opposition political forces. Although he was a member of the PRI at the time, the PRI's electoral apparatus in San Luis was controlled by a notorious regional cacique, Gonzalo Santos,[2] a situation that forced Nava to stand as an independent. As municipal president, Nava brought together wide sectors of the population in a process that succeeded in partially dismantling Santos's political machine.

In 1961, supported by the local PRI establishment and social groups that had emerged under the protective wing of the movement, Nava sought to run as the PRI's gubernatorial candidate. However, despite his local popularity, Nava's bid was blocked by the PRI's national elite.[3] In response, Nava and his political group publicly renounced their PRI membership, and Nava ran as an independent. The elections were marred by fraud and violence; towns were occupied by the army, and leaders of the Navista opposition were arrested. On their release from prison, this core group of Navista leaders and activists tried to a form a regional political party, the Potosí Democratic Party, but local PRI forces soon forced them to abandon the project. They then halted their political activities, biding their time for more propitious political conditions.

It was not until 1982 that the Navistas regrouped around Salvador Nava and formed the Potosí Civic Front (Frente Cívico Potosino). The resurgence of Navismo can be attributed to two main factors. The first was the increasing subordination of the local PRI to the political will and dictates of a new governor, Carlos Jonguitud Barrios (1979–1985), whose regional power base was reinforced by his position as leader of the National Education Workers' Union (SNTE). The second factor was the development of a new national political climate, as democratic movements emerged in Chihuahua, Sinaloa, Durango, Baja California, and Oaxaca.

The trajectory of the Navista movement between 1982 and 1990 bears many similarities to the earlier cycle: popular mobilization, electoral victory, control of municipal government, expanded social participation, and repression. Indeed, the main characteristics of Navismo changed little from the earlier to the later period. From its inception, this political movement has emphasized electoral participa-

---

[2] Santos was governor of San Luis Potosí from 1943 to 1949, but he retained de facto control of political power through the 1950s, imposing governors and municipal presidents.

[3] He was summoned to Mexico City and warned that he would not be chosen as the party's gubernatorial candidate in San Luis Potosí.

tion as an important tool for citizens in their attempts to challenge local bosses, regain control over public institutions monopolized by the official party, and contest authoritarian excesses. It has always combined a resolute espousal of nonviolence with a discourse of civic responsibility that stresses ethical values rather than ideology. Navismo has mainly been an urban movement, with its stronghold in the state capital of San Luis Potosí and its core support drawn mostly from the middle classes. Furthermore, Navismo has always been a plural movement, seeking to promote and build coalitions among both local and national opposition forces and parties. Even though on two occasions attempts were made to organize a regional political party—the Potosí Democratic Party (1961–1963) and the Navista Political Party (1993)—during the most important periods of political activity Navismo has been a nonpartisan movement (Gómez Tagle 1993).

Beginning in 1990, members of the Navista movement founded the Open Opposition Movement (Movimiento de Oposición Abierta). Local leaders of the state PAN, PRD, and PDM soon joined this organization which sought to prepare a joint platform and promote a single candidate in the 1991 gubernatorial elections.[4] There were three main reasons why the Navistas decided to form a coalition with opposition political parties. First, they believed that only a unified opposition would be capable of defeating the ruling party, a conviction based on past experience. Even if they could count on a majority of votes in and around the state capital, for about 33 percent of the voting population, they would still need to strengthen their presence in the rest of the state. Such a presence was important for the campaign itself, but also to ensure effective monitoring of the electoral process and, if necessary, to file complaints or charges regarding electoral irregularities. Second was the legal requirement that Nava's candidacy be entered under a registered political party. And third, the Navistas viewed the ideological differences and separate platforms of the various parties in the proposed coalition as secondary to the overriding priority of ending the one-party system and its local manifestations.

Navismo's Alliances with Opposition Parties

The resurgence of the Navista movement as the Potosí Civic Front in 1982 coincided with, and was reinforced by, the concurrent emergence of the PAN as a significant electoral player in San Luis Potosí and other parts of northern Mexico. The convergence of forces for

---

[4] It was even suggested that joint lists of candidates for federal Chamber of Deputies and Senate seats be drawn up. See the interview in *Expresiones de San Luis*, March 1991.

democratic electoral participation in San Luis was strengthened by the PAN's electoral struggles in Chihuahua, Sonora, Durango, Sinaloa, and Guanajuato. Navistas, in alliance with the PAN, had won three consecutive municipal elections in the state capital of San Luis Potosí—although in one case electoral fraud prevented their candidate from assuming office.

There was also a convergence in the conformation of the leaderships of these two organizations. Prominent among the Navista leaders were young, dynamic entrepreneurs—like Guillermo Pizzuto, winner of the 1988 election for municipal president in the city of San Luis Potosí—with political profiles similar to a new generation of PAN leaders in other states. In fact, the Navistas' local organization, the Potosí Civic Front, became a training ground for future PAN leaders. The PAN was clearly a natural ally for the Navista movement in 1991 and a logical partner to be included in the Potosí Democratic Coalition.

Although the Left has never been strong in the state of San Luis Potosí, the Navistas' links with local branches of left-wing parties date back to the movement's early years. In 1958, the San Luis Potosí Communist Party participated in the Navista alliance against Gonzalo Santos, and when Nava successfully took office as municipal president, local Communist Party leader Prisciliano Pérez became a member of the town council. Likewise in 1986, the Mexican Unified Socialist Party (PSUM) actively participated in the creation of the Committee for the Defense of the Rights of the People of Potosí (Comité de Defensa de los Derechos del Pueblo Potosino) which, under the leadership of Nava and Pizzuto, organized opposition forces to denounce electoral fraud and repression.

For the Navistas, an alliance with the leftist PRD made sense for four reasons. First, the PRD served as a counterweight to the PAN's presence in the coalition, enabling the Navista leadership to distance itself from certain policies that the PAN's national directorate pursued, such as the PAN's decision not to challenge Salinas's policy of "selective democracy" (discussed below) more decisively and its apparent willingness to postpone deep political reform in favor of a policy of "gradualism." Second, one Navista strategy was to ensure that the electoral campaign in San Luis attracted national attention; an alliance with the PRD guaranteed national press coverage and support from prominent intellectuals identified with that party. Third, the PRD shared with the Navistas a strong stand in favor of deep political reform and a demonstrated willingness to form broad alliances in order to achieve this goal. And fourth, cooperation with the PRD was an important means to broaden bases of support for Nava's campaign in the remote rural and indigenous regions of the state; the PRD could claim some degree of presence and organizational capacity in the Huasteca, traditionally a PRI stronghold.

The Navistas' alliance with the right-wing PDM also had deep historical roots. The local PDM leadership, which had its origins in the Sinarquista movement of the 1940s and 1950s, had participated in the Navista-led struggles against Gonzalo Santos.[5] In 1982, the PDM, along with the PAN, backed Nava's bid for the municipal presidency of San Luis Potosí. Like the PRD, the PDM had a following in certain rural areas of the state where Navismo was historically weak. The PDM's participation in the Potosí Democratic Coalition was more than symbolic. It helped Nava position himself in the ideological center of the local political spectrum, a position he sought to wrest from the PRI; and it gave him maneuvering room to counter PAN attempts to dominate his gubernatorial campaign.

Navismo and National Parties

At the national level the most important opposition parties were the PAN and the PRD. The national leadership of each had its own opinions about the strategies to be pursued in San Luis Potosí, which at times differed from those of their state branches.

Initially, the PAN's national directorate was reluctant to join the proposed coalition, and on February 1991 PAN General Secretary Abel Vicencio Tovar announced that the PAN's National Committee had decided not to join the Potosí Coalition. The party's national directorate felt that the project of constructing an opposition coalition in San Luis would directly violate their recent tacit alliance with President Salinas, an agreement which they hoped would guarantee recognition of their party's electoral victories. The PAN national leadership proposed instead that Nava run on the PAN ticket. Nava responded by reaffirming his determination to run as a coalition candidate (Caballero 1992: 43–44). Other factors that help explain the national directorate's refusal to join the Potosí Coalition include a distrust of the PRD and the view that the latter had little political presence in San Luis and therefore had no legitimate claim to share the political capital of Navismo.

This first source of tension in the efforts to build a coalition stemmed from differences between the political interests of the PAN's national directorate and those of the local Navista movement. But it was also a product of more fundamental differences over political principles and strategy. Nava had implicitly denounced Salinas's

---

[5] The Sinarquistas were a group of Catholic activists that formed in the 1950s to oppose Santos's political machine; it was the best organized and strongest wing of the political opposition in the region at that time.

"selective democracy policy," in which the federal executive refused to recognize PRD electoral victories but did accept those of the PAN. Opposed to informal, exclusionary elite agreements of this sort, Nava publicly announced his faith in the president's pledge that the popular will would be respected in the upcoming elections—emphasizing his own commitment to the formal democratic rules while at the same time placing responsibility for clean elections in the hands of the president.

What, then, prompted the PAN's national leadership to change position and decide to support the Potosí Coalition and join forces in Nava's campaign? The simplest answer is that it found no viable alternative. Attempts were made to identify a suitable person to run against Nava, including efforts to recruit Municipal President Guillermo Pizzuto. But Pizzuto refused to oppose his longtime ally. Leaders of the state PAN, meanwhile, remained more flexible toward the proposed coalition, supporting Nava's attempts to establish a "government of democratic transition" and acknowledging that grassroots PAN supporters would vote for Nava in the elections. If the only way to back Nava's candidacy was as a member of the coalition, this proposal would be adopted at the state party's nomination convention—whatever the national directorate's position.

After carefully considering the repercussions of refusing to participate in Nava's proposed coalition, the national PAN joined up. Not joining would probably have been tantamount to renouncing any possibility of contesting the gubernatorial elections, because running a candidate against Nava would almost certainly result in defeat. Furthermore, such an action would mean abandoning the party's long-standing strategic alliance with Navismo, and risk jeopardizing local party unity and opening a political void to be filled by the PRD. Additionally, Nava was seventy-seven years old and in failing health; if local conditions changed, perhaps the PAN could capitalize on his political legacy. Finally, a PAN victory was likely in the gubernatorial race in Guanajuato, where the candidate was fully identified with the party. Participating in the San Luis race could provide a low-cost bargaining chip for future negotiations in the event of an electoral conflict in either state. In any event, by mid–February Abel Vicencio had made it clear that the PAN's national directorate no longer insisted that Nava run on their ticket; they would, however, require the coalition to adopt the PAN platform in its entirety. On February 23, 1991, the state-level convention of the PAN elected Nava as their gubernatorial candidate.

Regarding the PRD, efforts to build personal contacts between Dr. Nava and members of the party's national leadership, mainly Cuauhtémoc Cárdenas, began in 1989, initially through channels outside the structural confines of the two organizations. Key in this process were a handful of political figures who served as intermediaries, facilitating communication between the two parties and breaking down barriers of distrust and ideological differences.[6] For the PRD, an alliance with the centrist Navista movement offered an ideal way to broaden the party's political base. Furthermore, although Navismo had not emerged out of traditional struggles of the Mexican Left, its local political demands coincided with the thrust of the PRD's national platform. Thus the PRD was able not only to extend its reach geographically beyond its existing strongholds in Michoacán, Guerrero, and other southern states, but also to move toward the political center. This was the first time the PRD had made an alliance with a political leader and a movement commonly associated with the rightist PAN. However, the party had a clear policy of seeking out electoral alliances with independent, locally based, social and political movements and had done so to good effect with the Coalition of Workers, Peasants, and Students of the Isthmus (COCEI) in Oaxaca and with urban movements in Mexico City, to mention just two examples. Indeed, the party itself had emerged from the broad-based coalition of leftist parties and grassroots movements that had fought the 1988 elections under the rubric of the National Democratic Front (FDN). Moreover, it is possible that the party was seeking to organize broader opposition coalitions in order to contest the 1994 federal and presidential elections.

In sum, the PRD had little to lose and much to gain by joining Nava's proposed coalition. On the afternoon of February 23, 1991, in Ciudad Valles, the PRD designated Nava as its official candidate. Referring to Nava as "the candidate of the democratic forces of San Luis Potosí," Cuauhtémoc Cárdenas indicated that democratic change in Mexico "will be less difficult if forces are united and agreements to support specific joint candidates can be concretized" (Caballero 1992: 49).

The Campaign

Differences between the coalition's main political players surfaced again during the final stages of formalizing the political alliance when the State Electoral Commission (CEE) rejected a proposal to put Nava's name in the center of the Potosí Coalition's campaign logo, thereby unwittingly sparking an acrimonious debate among the coalition partners. The three parties finally accepted a PAN proposal (which Nava supported) to use the general format of the PAN logo and include within it the symbols of the three participating political

---

[6] One of the most important mediators in this process was Dr. Samuel I. del Villar.

parties.[7] In contrast, no conflict arose over the coalition's manifesto. Drafted by the Navista leadership (the Potosí Civic Front), it was restricted to general pronouncements about democratic principles: to fight for a democratic electoral law and independent electoral institutions; to end government corruption at all levels; and to strengthen freedom of the press and association.

By the end of February 1991, the Navistas' first strategic goal had been accomplished: the Potosí Democratic Coalition had become a viable electoral vehicle. From the moment of its formalization, if not before, the coalition had an impact beyond the Potosí region. Even though President Salinas's policies were aimed at dividing the opposition parties at the national level, he nonetheless paid close attention to local races. In the case of San Luis Potosí, he had sought to negotiate directly with Nava. A month before Nava decided to make public his candidacy, he had presented his project of unifying the opposition in San Luis Potosí to Salinas at the presidential residence in Mexico City. Salinas's reply was simple: "Watch out for those who want to take advantage of your prestige"—a clear reference to the PRD. But Nava was not deterred either by the president's warning or by changes in electoral laws that made it more difficult to unite opposition groups behind a single candidate.

The coalition soon moved forward with two main strategies. The first was to extend its support base. The Navistas continued to build on their experience in community organizing, using door-to-door canvassing and community meetings to build a broad social network.[8] The coalition's main efforts were directed toward consolidating support outside the state capital, especially in the Huasteca, the most rural and underdeveloped portion of the state.

The coalition's second strategy in the early months of the campaign was to generate national publicity. In particular, strategists sought to publicize the rationale underpinning the Potosí Democratic Coalition: "to join forces in order to defeat the common enemy—the PRI government—and thereby establish a regime of democratic transition." To this end, the Navistas organized various high-profile events during the six-month campaign. At key moments Nava staged press conferences in Mexico City. The PAN, meanwhile, was working to win the support of the business sector and groups associated with the Catholic Church. The PRD sought out support from journalists

---

[7] To some extent the agreed-upon design was a concession to the PAN's demand that its importance in the coalition be explicitly recognized.

[8] Although this approach proved generally successful, relations with the business sector had deteriorated somewhat. Business leaders had decided not to support Nava, in part because of the PRD's presence in the coalition, but mainly because they supported Salinas's economic policies and felt that the PRI candidate, Fausto Zapata, would better represent their interests.

prominent in the national press, well-known intellectuals from the Mexico City academic community, and indigenous communities in the Huasteca. The PDM got the Sinarquistas involved.

Although the political parties all collaborated in mobilizing social forces behind Nava's candidacy, it had been agreed that each party would pursue its own campaigns for Chamber of Deputies and Senate seats independently and that primary responsibility for the gubernatorial campaign strategy should rest with the Navistas. In fact, the coalition's campaign headquarters were housed in the offices of the Potosí Civic Front.

Some members of Nava's campaign team had close links with the PAN, others with the PRD, but the majority had been involved with Nava's movement since the early 1980s and a few since the late 1950s. Most were professionals, merchants, and industrialists in their forties. Two owned local printing shops, a circumstance that reduced the costs and facilitated the production of campaign materials.

Needless to say, the coalition's strategies and tactics were shaped in part in response to those of Fausto Zapata, who had been chosen as the "candidate of PRI unity" in February 1991. Zapata had returned to San Luis Potosí after a thirty-year absence, during which time he had served as Mexico's ambassador to China and held other government posts. He moved quickly to rehabilitate the local PRI, which had been seriously weakened by internal divisions. Alongside his efforts to build party cohesion, Zapata also sought to unify the Potosí economic elite. In order to win over business leaders, he promised to use his strong economic and political connections to attract investment and federal funding for state development; he also invited local businessmen to dine with prominent national bankers and industrialists such as Carlos Abedropp and Emilio Azcárraga.

The PRI's campaign relied heavily on presenting Zapata as the candidate of modernity and harmony. Television spots showed him greeting the queen of England and Yasser Arafat, and ended with his campaign slogan, "Proud To Be Potosino." He marketed himself as a son of San Luis who had been highly successful in the diplomatic world and who had come home to share his experiences. Catchy billboards and print ads all conveyed a political message of civility—of a candidate gracious enough to acknowledge the merits of his opponent.

The other facet of Zapata's campaign, which relied on the PRI's control of the local media, was to undermine the coalition by portraying Nava as outdated and out of touch. According to this portrayal, whatever Nava's good intentions, he could only lead San Luis down the road to violence. Both his political trajectory and the presence of the PRD in the coalition confirmed this.

Zapata's strategy, then, was to present contrasting images of the two candidates: the present versus the past; the internationally experienced politician versus the community doctor; a program offering progress, security, and peace versus one that would lead to confusion, violence, and chaos. This strategy had some success during the first few months of the campaign, thanks to the unabashed collaboration of the local media (Calvillo 1992: 45–46).

During the campaign, Zapata challenged Nava to a public debate.[9] Nava responded by convening a special press conference in Mexico City at which he publicly denounced the PRI candidate's control of the San Luis media. Nava went on to propose that the candidates hold not one but two debates—the first covering the political conduct of each candidate in the context of the wider themes of freedom of speech, democracy, and family values; and the second addressing the problems facing the state of San Luis Potosí and outlining each candidate's proposals to address these problems during his term as governor.

With this counterchallenge Nava succeeded in shifting the locus of debate from the local to the national stage—and to the national press.[10] Coverage of the gubernatorial race in the national press discredited Zapata's image as the candidate of civility and political modernity, and it also brought alternative views of the race to the state's voters.

In May 1991 a public rally in Nava's home neighborhood in San Luis clearly demonstrated the high level of outside support the coalition's experiment in political unity enjoyed. Speaking at the rally were Rogelio Sada and Lucas de la Garza, the PAN and PRD gubernatorial candidates in Nuevo León, and Vicente Fox Quesada, the PAN candidate for governor of Guanajuato. All expressed their commitment to achieving unity among the political opposition.

Building on its swelling support, the Potosí Coalition organized a dinner for the local business community to honor four opposition gubernatorial candidates, as well as Jorge Ocejo, former president of COPARMEX (the Mexican Employers' Confederation). Addressing the assembled businessmen, Nava had an opportunity to reiterate the rationale behind the coalition: "To make the vote count and to guarantee a clean and efficient electoral system, so that each party can defend its ideology and principles and the people can truly determine electoral outcomes."

---

[9] It should be emphasized that public debates between opposing candidates were almost without precedent in Mexico at this time.

[10] Zapata was at a disadvantage vis-à-vis journalists from the national press because of his role in clamping down on press freedom in the late 1970s. His involvement was not forgotten by the reporters who covered his 1991 gubernatorial bid.

Throughout the campaign, Zapata was clearly able to dominate within the state as a whole. On election day, his dominance over the local mechanisms of political control gave him the needed margin of victory. According to the official count, Zapata garnered 329,292 votes, compared to 170,646 for Nava. However, the Potosí Coalition was able to maintain its preeminence in the state capital, where it soundly defeated Zapata. And in the national arena, the coalition succeeded in projecting an image of trustworthiness and credibility. This network and image were crucial in generating public pressure after the election.

Toward the end of the campaign, Zapata admitted: "I need a clear win and clean elections; I need a strong showing in the capital. Without these I will face a problem of ingovernability" (Caballero 1992: 62). As Silvia Gómez Tagle later summarized: "The 1991 local elections in San Luis Potosí, Guanajuato, Sonora, and Tabasco all highlight the difficulties and uncertainty that can result from opposition electoral struggles. For this reason, the political value of votes for the opposition cannot be directly equated with those for the PRI; while the latter may be more numerous, a vote for the opposition is usually an active vote" (Gómez Tagle 1993: 33–34).

The Navistas began preparing the ground for post-electoral actions in July with a public forum entitled "Challenges in the Transition to Democracy," attended by a number of renowned Mexican intellectuals and independent political activists.[11] Virtually every wing of the political opposition and civic reform movements was represented—an implicit acknowledgment of the significance of Nava's and the coalition's political project. Participants discussed how to create and develop a common political discourse that could unify opposition forces in a national project of political transition. They examined the role of intellectuals as shapers of public opinion and as advisers to political elites. They noted the federal government's interest in the process under way in San Luis Potosí and how this opposition coalition had become a crucial part of national political debate. They also acknowledged the important role that the Navista struggle and its leader had played in opening up political space within the country. Finally, they debated the possibility of replicating the Potosí experiment in political unity at the national level for the 1994 presidential elections. Additionally, as preparation for anticipated electoral irregularities, the Mexican Human Rights Academy (AMDH), together with the Potosí Human Rights Center, organized a 300–person team to monitor the electoral process.

---

[11] Attendees included José Agustín Ortiz Pinchetti, Adolfo Aguilar Zinser, Rolando Cordera, Francisco José Paoli, Diego Fernández de Cevallos, Jorge Alcocer, Carlos Monsiváis, Lorenzo Meyer, Miguel Granados Chapa, Jorge Castañeda, and Luis Javier Garrido.

The candidates' closing campaign rallies signaled that a post-electoral conflict was inevitable. The Potosí Coalition's rally was the largest in the state's history. Zapata's closing rally also filled the main square, but in Zapata's case, the obvious disinterest of the assembled crowd spoke eloquently to the PRI candidate's weak political appeal.

Contesting the Electoral Outcome

The elections, held on August 18, 1991, took place without violence, but there were multiple irregularities. Indeed, the PRI's manipulation of the process was documented even before voting commenced. Days before the election, the Potosí Coalition released a study by scholars at Mexico's National Autonomous University, which claimed that approximately 280,000 voting-age citizens had been "shaved" from the new electoral roll (Rivera Godines 1991). On election day itself, reports of irregularities flooded the Potosí Civic Front's headquarters; the most significant concerned incidents barring coalition representatives from the polling stations. The Mexican Human Rights Academy's subsequent report on the elections listed fifty observed irregularities, including violations of ballot secrecy, overt inducement to vote for the PRI, voter intimidation, stuffing of ballot boxes, and forceful removal of opposition representatives. Overall, the report concluded, the serious irregularities observed by the Academy's monitoring team put the legality (and morality) of the whole process into question (*Proceso*, September 9, 1991).

Following the election, Nava refused to submit complaints of irregularities to electoral authorities, stating that "the electoral authorities in San Luis Potosí have betrayed President Carlos Salinas de Gortari's promise that these elections would be transparent and that the will of the people would be respected. A Zapata triumph in these elections would be illegitimate" (Caballero 1992: 76). By appealing directly to the voters' sense of ethics and morality, Nava raised serious doubts in their minds about the very foundations of prevailing political practices. And by refusing to recognize the legitimacy of the local authorities' decisions, he radicalized the struggle and underlined the importance of establishing independent electoral agencies.

Instead of turning to the electoral authorities, Nava relied on the willingness of his followers and national allies to mobilize. He held a press conference in Mexico City to assess how strongly the PAN and PRD national leaderships might support demonstrations to protest the outcome of the San Luis Potosí gubernatorial election. In Guanajuato, Vicente Fox had already organized several demonstrations to protest against fraud in his gubernatorial contest with Aguirre.

On August 21, 1991, Nava denounced the San Luis Potosí electoral fraud to journalists from the national and international press; he was accompanied on this occasion by Luis Álvarez, Cuauhtémoc Cárdenas, and Víctor Atilano. In the course of this public show of unity, these national presidents of the PAN, PRD, and PDM, respectively, all confirmed their parties' continued support for the Potosí Coalition and agreed that decisions about how to proceed should rest with the people of San Luis Potosí.

Civil Resistance

Nava had defined the Potosí Coalition's struggle as an ethical battle about core values, shifting the terms of public debate surrounding the electoral process from questions of vote counts to questions of principle. In line with their repudiation of the legal and moral authority of Mexico's electoral institutions, the Navistas asserted that their claims of fraud should be judged by actors from civil society. Therefore, they presented their evidence of electoral irregularities to businessmen, professionals, students, and the press. This act signified a challenge not only to the legitimacy of the electoral bodies but also to President Salinas, given that the entire process had taken place under his tutelage.

In the week following the election, the Navistas sought, but failed, to link the struggle in San Luis with Fox's post-electoral protest campaign in Guanajuato.[12] When Fausto Zapata received approval of his winning majority from the state legislature and called for the opposition to support his government (*Pulso* [San Luis Potosí], August 26, 1991), the Potosí Coalition responded with a rally, filling the main square in San Luis with Nava supporters. Addressing a crowd of 30,000 and accompanied by national leaders from the coalition's member parties, Nava asked the people to forgive him for having trusted the authorities to respect the transition to democracy. He then directed his words to the president in Mexico City: "In the face of injustice, hear the painful silence of my people" (*La Jornada*, August 27, 1991). With this he ended the rally. As journalist Miguel Granados Chapa later described the event: "[a] wave of disillusionment spread

---

[12] The PAN's national leadership was clearly pursuing a distinct strategy. On August 25, President Salinas, via the minister of the interior, informed PAN leader Diego Fernández de Cevallos that the federal government had decided to resolve the Guanajuato conflict. The PRI candidate, Ramón Aguirre, would not take office as governor, nor would victory be conceded to Vicente Fox. Instead, a well-known PAN member, Carlos Medina Placencia, would be appointed as interim governor, with key members of his cabinet nominated by the federal government. The PAN accepted. The party's critics accused the deal as a sell-out.

throughout the crowd when Dr. Nava, with a political gesture so simple as to be difficult to comprehend, sent his supporters home to await new actions, ones which, though less dramatic, would have deeper and more enduring effects in the long run" (Granados Chapa 1992: 153–54). In effect, what Nava had done was to put the president squarely in the center of this local battle, leaving no room for doubt about where final responsibility rested.

Days later, the Potosí Coalition held a rally at which Nava was declared governor. Municipal President Guillermo Pizzuto welcomed him with these words: "Two and a half years ago I pledged to defend the people of San Luis Potosí through legal means, and today I have come here to do just that, to give a warm welcome to our new governor, Dr. Salvador Nava Martínez" (Caballero 1992; Granados Chapa 1992).

In an effort to resolve the Potosí conflict, the Salinas administration then proposed a deal very similar to that accepted by the PAN in Guanajuato. Fausto Zapata would resign, and Nava would be given the post of interim governor; in turn, the federal government would appoint the state's government secretary, finance minister, and attorney general. Nava rejected the proposal and demanded new elections.

Unable to negotiate a settlement, on September 3, Salinas publicly recognized Zapata's electoral victory. This act marked a new phase in the coalition's post-electoral struggle, which began with a public forum on September 5–6. Among those attending were writer Enrique Krauze and PAN leader Luis Álvarez. The presence of these two men strengthened Nava's leadership position and his claim to represent a broad political spectrum at a time when the PAN was under pressure to withdraw from the Potosí Coalition (Frente Cívico Potosino 1991). In the state capital, acts of civil resistance—rallies, marches, and roadblocks—continued to multiply, many of them spearheaded by women, who as a group would come to play a key role during this period of civil resistance.

On September 26, 1991, as Zapata was inaugurated as governor of San Luis Potosí in a ceremony presided over by President Salinas, the Potosí Coalition held another rally. At this rally, Nava announced that on September 28 he would begin a protest march to Mexico City, planning to arrive there on November 1, the day of President Salinas's State of the Nation address. Finally, Nava also invited the women who supported him to form a human chain around the government palace in San Luis. These two actions would be decisive in bringing about the fall of Fausto Zapata.

"The Dignity March" was the name given to the 463–kilometer trek that 77–year–old Nava proposed to walk from San Luis Potosí to Mexico City to protest the election. Resonating with the popular practice of religious pilgrimage, Nava's gesture was a dramatic demonstration of his great moral courage and unwavering commitment to the struggle for democracy. Each day, Nava was joined in his march by some important public figure—such as Vicente Fox, who accompanied Nava on October 4 as he crossed into the state of Guanajuato.[13] As one political analyst phrased it: "The nation hears his every step."[14]

While Nava marched toward Mexico City, Zapata was facing further political embarrassment in the heart of San Luis Potosí. On the fourth day of the women's blockade, the new governor decided to take possession of his offices in the government palace; his entry was accomplished by force, and several women were assaulted in the process.

On October 9, while Carlos Biebrich, the PRI's new regional coordinator in San Luis, was denying the possibility that the newly installed Zapata might be asked to resign the governorship, federal government representatives were delivering a proposal to Nava for resolving the conflict. It included the following observations:

- If more time were allowed to elapse, the level of confrontation would increase. This could lead to a situation where national interests would militate against a political solution.
- The time for a political solution had arrived. Yet the governorship could not be conceded at the expense of President Salinas's political prestige, which had to be respected for the sake of national interests, both within Mexico and abroad.
- A possible solution would be that a full agreement be reached, within a matter of hours, that would include a public explanation that harmed neither the government nor the Navista movement and that contributed, moreover, to the democratic education of the country.

This agreement would contain the following points:

- Fausto Zapata would resign the San Luis governorship.
- A new government would be inaugurated that would maintain a close association with President Salinas while also reaching out to the Navistas.
- The conflict would end, and efforts would be redirected toward electoral reform and other administrative reforms to ensure that future municipal elections would be both clean and peaceful.

---

[13] When Nava crossed the state line into Guanajuato, he said, "I knew there was a place where San Luis Potosí ended and Guanajuato began;... I left dignity and I found dignity" (*Proceso*, October 14, 1991).

[14] René Delgado, on the radio news program *Para Empezar*, October 3, 1991.

- Electoral results would be respected. In cases of opposition victories, municipal governments would work in conjunction with the
  state and federal governments.
- Nava would make a joint political declaration with government
  representatives and return to San Luis Potosí.
- Henceforth, the Navistas would participate with state authorities
  in matters concerning the state.[15]

Conclusions

A fortnight after assuming the governorship of San Luis Potosí,
Fausto Zapata was asked by President Salinas to resign; he never returned to his home state. The Potosí opposition had effectively mobilized support from national forces in order to pressure Salinas to
withdraw his support from the governor. Ironically, this authoritarian
decision at the center served to open up democratic space at the local
level. The Potosí Coalition's struggle took place at a time when the
federal government was seeking to consolidate new bases of support
for Salinas's political project, and in this regard it constituted a significant challenge to the administration's claim to have reconstituted
its legitimacy through the 1991 federal elections.

The coalition's political struggle succeeded in modifying the rules
of the political game in San Luis Potosí. It brought about reforms of
the local electoral process which, although producing no direct
benefits in terms of electoral results for the opposition in the short
term, were fundamental to democratizing the regional political process in the medium term. Products of this struggle included: (1) the
incorporation of representatives from civic organizations and opposition parties into electoral institutions; (2) the consolidation of a network of civic groups serving as observers of the political process and
as obstacles to authoritarian behavior; (3) changes within the local
PRI, obliging the party to uphold basic rules of democratic conduct
and to recognize opposition victories; and (4) some preliminary reforms of the local media, which had been widely condemned for its
biased coverage of the 1991 electoral process.

As previously mentioned, at the national level the Potosí case and
the experience of the Potosí Democratic Coalition contributed to the
restructuring of the nation's electoral agencies, ensuring that they
would no longer be controlled exclusively by the PRI. It also provided
a practical example of one political strategy that could contribute to
dismantling the authoritarian system of dominant party rule: the uni-

---

[15] Document held in the Potosí Democratic Coalition archives (Frente 1991). Although
the first point was carried out in full, the other points were at best only partially respected.

fication of all wings of the opposition in order to compete effectively for key political positions—municipal presidencies, governorships, and even the federal presidency.[16] Nava's strategy was simple but decisive: to unite the opposition in order to establish a regime of democratic transition, thereby avoiding violent conflicts in the country. One of the keys to the success of the 1991 Potosí Democratic Coalition was Nava's historic commitment to the political and ideological center; as he showed in practice, occupying the center can be a radical position, capable of mobilizing popular support and of effectively challenging authoritarian decision making.

While Nava's campaign succeeded in bringing national political forces into dialogue, albeit briefly, his death in 1992 prevented the consolidation of his broader project to unify the major opposition political forces in the country behind a single presidential candidate in 1994. The example of the Potosí Democratic Coalition and Nava's position at the center of the political spectrum, together with his reputation as an honest broker, meant that this option began to emerge as a serious possibility in 1992. In March of that year, a new civic organization—the Citizens' Movement for Democracy (MCD)—came into being and was presided over by Nava. Its first meeting in San Cristóbal de las Casas, Chiapas, brought together leaders from across the political spectrum. Thus Nava sought not only to bridge the ideological gap between the two main opposition parties but also to create links between the business-led PAN regions of northern Mexico and the PRD rural and indigenous regions of the south. However, after Nava's death, the institutionally weak nature of the political project that he had begun to lead and the divergent interests of the PAN and the PRD impeded further advancement. The window of opportunity for a PRD–PAN alliance seems to have closed in early 1994 when the Zapatista uprising led to a further polarization between the two parties.

References

Caballero, Alejandro. 1992. "Salvador Nava: las últimas batallas," *La Jornada*.
Calvillo, Tomás. 1992. "Parcialidad del periodismo potosino," *Este País*, April.
Cornelius, Wayne A., Ann L. Craig, and Jonathan Fox. 1994. *Transforming State-Society Relations: The National Solidarity Strategy*. U.S.–Mexico Contemporary Perspectives Series, no. 6. La Jolla: Center for U.S.–Mexican Studies, University of California San Diego.

---

[16] Such a PAN–PRD alliance was sustained in a close but ultimately unsuccessful electoral battle for the governorship of Durango in 1992. However, efforts to forge such opposition party alliances for electoral contestation have failed at the national level and in almost all subsequent local races.

Frente Cívico Potosino. 1991. "Análisis y balance de elecciones." Colección Transición a la Democracia. San Luis Potosí: Frente Cívico Potosino.

Gómez Tagle, Silvia. 1993. "Las elecciones de 1991, la recuperación oficial," *La Jornada.*

Granados Chapa, Miguel. 1992. *Nava Sí, Zapata No! La hora de San Luis Potosí: crónica de una lucha que triunfó.* Mexico City: Grijalbo.

Proceso. 1991. "Los partidos políticos así decidieron llegar a una coalición nunca antes conseguida en el país," October 14.

Rivera Godines, Cuauhtémoc. 1991. "Siete puntos sobre el padrón electoral de San Luis Potosí, 1991." Cuadernos de Comunicación y Sociología Alternativas. Mexico City: Nueva Sociología Práxis.

PART III

Popular Movements and Democratization

6

The Movimiento de Damnificados: Democratic Transformation of Citizenry and Government in Mexico City

Ligia Tavera-Fenollosa

In July 1997, after almost seventy years of nondemocratic rule and severe curtailment of their political rights, the residents of Mexico City were at last able to elect their head of local government. The direct election of the mayor of Mexico City was the culmination of a long process of reforms that began just two months after severe earthquakes hit Mexico City in September 1985,[1] sparking the most intense social mobilization in the city's history.

Mexico City residents are not unacquainted with earthquakes. However, the 1985 quakes were of exceptional magnitude and destructiveness. No one could recall earthquakes of such violence; nor could anyone recollect anything like the mobilization and solidarity with which the population responded. Almost every sector of Mexican society contributed to the relief effort. Some helped directly in rescue activities, others gathered and distributed food and other

---

[1] At 7:19 AM on September 19, 1985, the most severe earthquakes in Mexico's modern history shook the capital, Mexico City. The first quake measured 8.1 on the Richter scale and was followed the next evening by an aftershock of magnitude 7. Although the earthquakes were felt over much of the country, their destructive power was concentrated in downtown Mexico City. Due to a combination of geological factors (long wave motion interacting with water-laden soils) and political factors (corruption and negligence), the devastation was without precedent. Of Mexico City's population of 18 million people, an estimated 10,000 were killed and 50,000 injured. Property damage totaled U.S.$5 billion (U.S. Department of Commerce 1990).

supplies, and still others contributed to the rebuilding fund. For some, their involvement lasted only a few days; others continued to provide aid to the earthquake victims well beyond the "emergency period."

Supported by churches and left-wing organizations and parties, earthquake victims came together in one of the most—if not *the* most—successful urban popular movements of recent decades: the Movimiento de Damnificados, or Earthquake Victims' Movement. The movement demanded, and got, expropriated land on which to construct low-cost housing for the earthquake victims and then set about the rebuilding process. But beyond such tangible achievements, the Earthquake Victims' Movement had important political consequences. Framed as an icon of civic competence and democracy, the movement undermined the "repressive discourse" with which the government justified its exclusion of citizens from local government, challenged the legitimacy of the political status quo in the Federal District (DF), and opened the door to the democratization of government and citizenry in Mexico City.

This chapter examines the process of democratizing the Federal District—from the first public hearings to the creation of the Assembly of Representatives seventeen months later—and the contribution that the Earthquake Victims' Movement made to it. In order to evaluate the political consequences of this and other social movements, one must heed the cognitive and interpretative dimensions of social movement activity, as well as the role of the media and other actors in such processes. Because, as Gamson (1988) noted, movements are vehicles for creating contesting discourses, public opinion is a key factor in shaping their contribution to democratic change. If social movement activity is framed in such a way that it delegitimizes the cultural assumptions that preclude political participation, then social movements can contribute to processes of democratization.

The chapter is divided into four sections. The first describes government in Mexico City and examines the bases on which authorities offered to expand citizen participation in local affairs. The second analyses the Earthquake Victims' Movement as a framing opportunity. How the movement challenged the symbolic codes of civil society is addressed in section three. The concluding section covers the democratizing impact of social movements in nondemocratic contexts.

Democratizing Mexico City's Government

Like other capital cities in federal states, Mexico City does not fall within any state. Instead, it is formally designated as a federal district. Until the 1980s, it had no locally elected legislative body to represent its millions of residents and no directly elected local authorities. The Federal District was governed by a "regent" appointed directly by the president. The regent served as head of the Department of the Federal District (DDF), an administrative body in charge of the city's management. In addition to appointing the regent, the president named or confirmed the second tier of DDF officials. Since 1928, political arrangements in Mexico City had offered no opportunity for local participation (Meyer 1987), leading many city residents to decry their "second-class citizenship."

Until 1988, citizen representation was channeled through a pyramid of neighborhood organizations comprising (from the bottom up) block committees and residents associations, both created in 1978; neighborhood councils, in place since 1970 but activated in 1978; and the Consultative Council of the Federal District, established in 1929. Although formally a participatory structure, this pyramid of organizations was really administrative in nature and did not give Mexico City citizens true political representation.

Even though local government tends to be limited in federal districts everywhere, the degree of citizens' exclusion from local government does vary, as do its implications for democratic life at the national level.[2] In 1985, Mexico City was an extreme example of exclusionary political practices in a federal district; its residents did not vote for any of their local authorities. This is particularly important when one considers that the Federal District is not only the political center of Mexico; it is also the country's economic and demographic hub.[3]

If the elimination of authoritarian enclaves is required for the consolidation of democracy in general (Fox 1994), then the democratization of Mexico City was a necessary (though not sufficient) condition for Mexico's full transition to democracy. This is the case of an enclave—not in a rural, underdeveloped area or in a region where democratic political parties are weak or absent—but in the capital city, the huge, developed urban center where all parties—the ruling Institutional Revolutionary Party (PRI) and opposition parties—have a presence. Mexico could hardly undertake its transition to democ-

---

[2] Residents of the Federal District of Columbia (on which the Federal District of Mexico was modeled) do not vote for president, do vote for mayor, have a voice but no vote in the House of Representatives, and have neither voice nor vote in the Senate. While citizen participation in Mexico City's government has been increasing steadily since 1985, residents of the District of Columbia have seen their local rights reduced, especially since 1997, when the mayor was replaced by a governing committee.

[3] By 1985, the Federal District accounted for 13 percent of the nation's population, 37 percent of service-sector GNP, 41 percent of commerce, and 37 percent of Mexicans enrolled in higher education (INEGI 1984).

racy without opening the DF to electoral competition and extending full political rights to its residents.

Prior to 1985, Mexico's presidents had been very successful in keeping the potentially disruptive issue of full citizenship and electoral competition in the Federal District off the political agenda. The present analysis suggests that, were it not for the Earthquake Victims' Movement, the administration of President Miguel de la Madrid (1982–1988) would probably have succeeded here as well.

The issue of introducing more democratic structures into Mexico City's government had reemerged during de la Madrid's presidential campaign. Responding to generalized pressures to reform existing political arrangements (Cámara 1983: 40), de la Madrid spoke to the problem of citizen participation in local government, noting the need to:

> achieve coordination and collaboration between citizens and government on goals and tasks in order to build true instances of democratic action at all levels, from the National Congress to the *block committees* (de la Madrid 1982a: 158; emphasis added).

Months later, in his inaugural speech, the newly elected president committed himself to convening

> a public debate to examine the state of the political reform process, the function and composition of the Mexican Senate, citizen participation in the government of the Federal District, and reform of the judiciary (de la Madrid 1982b: M7).

Nevertheless, in its first three years, the de la Madrid administration took no public action toward democratic reform. Indeed, when reforms to the Organic Law for the Federal District were being considered in the Chamber of Deputies in December 1983, the administration actually favored limiting these reforms to administrative changes and further increasing presidential power in the DF, to include the appointment of the regent's closest aids in the DDF (Cámara 1983). Despite the fact that all opposition parties supported full political rights for Mexico City residents and democratization of the DF government, the de la Madrid administration blocked any discussion on the issue.[4] As Iván García Solís, a member of the federal Chamber of Deputies from the Mexican Unified Socialist Party (PSUM), put it:

---

[4] Although the Mexican Democratic Party (PDM) voted in favor of the new law, it noted the undemocratic character of Mexico City's government. The PDM representative demanded the direct election of the mayor, the creation of a local congress,

> Instead of actions that accord with the words spoken pub-
> licly, we find ourselves with the opposite, a set of reforms
> that will not modify the structure of government in this
> city but, to the contrary, will validate it, consolidate it, and
> perpetuate it (Cámara 1983: 41).

Two years later, the PRI's poor performance in the 1985 midterm
elections made discussion of this contentious issue even less likely.
The official party received its lowest level of electoral support in
Mexico City. In rural districts, the PRI managed to win 79.5 percent of
the vote; in the DF, the official party won only 42.6 percent, down
nearly 6 percent from its performance in 1982 (Molinar Horcasitas
1991: 144).

In sum, despite opposition pressure, and despite de la Madrid's
pledge to open a public debate on citizen participation in the Federal
District government, the democratization of Mexico City was kept off
the political agenda until late 1985.

Then on November 1, 1985, just two months after the September
earthquakes, Ramón Aguirre, regent of Mexico City, suddenly announced to the Chamber of Deputies that President de la Madrid was
ready to hold public hearings on citizen participation in the Federal
District government. These were not isolated events. De la Madrid's
recognition of the need to democratize Mexico City and to expand the
political rights of its residents was clearly linked to the Movimiento
de Damnificados. In explaining why the administration was finally
willing to reconsider the status of these "second-class citizens,"
Aguirre noted:

> The way in which Mexico City's society has responded to
> very critical circumstances [the earthquakes] indicates that
> the foundations of an extraordinary civic maturity have
> been laid down. The conditions are ripe for the analysis,
> discussion, and presentation of alternatives regarding the
> transcendental issue of citizen participation in the govern-
> ment of the capital (Cámara 1985: 22).

Besides finally putting democracy in the DF on the agenda,
Aguirre's announcement also signaled the emergence of a new frame
within which possible alternatives for citizen participation in local
government would henceforth be evaluated and acted upon. Prior to

---

and the establishment of a local judicial authority (Cámara 1983: 33, 51–52). Only
two months before the Organic Law was discussed in the Chamber of Deputies, the
Socialist Workers' Party (PST), which supported the president's initiative, had presented a reform bill to Congress that contemplated direct election of the Mexico City
mayor. In December 1980 the Socialist Popular Party (PPS) had proposed a reform
project that envisioned creating a local congress for Mexico City (Monterrosas n.d.).

1985, the situation of Federal District inhabitants was framed as being unalterable. As the site of federal power, the DF was a special political entity needing special political arrangements which implied the people's exclusion from local government. Nonetheless, it was argued, Mexico City residents were not second-class citizens. By voting for the president, they were, in effect, electing their mayor. And since they voted for the national Congress, which legislated for the DF, they were also electing their local representatives (Ward 1989). However, Aguirre's quote suggests that, in the aftermath of the earthquakes, the frame within which political arrangements for the DF had been justified crumbled, and the government publicly recognized that the nonexistence of local democratic structures was unfair. The justifications that had been advanced in the past to keep the issue off the political agenda became, suddenly, less legitimate.

The Movimiento: A Framing Opportunity

Although the government's readiness to reconsider citizen participation in local government did stem from the residents' initial response to the earthquakes and to the autonomous organization of earthquake victims and their neighbors that followed, this was not something demanded by the individuals involved in the movement. As with other popular movements, the goals of the Earthquake Victims' Movement did not include bringing about political change. Although its leaders sometimes criticized the lack of a democratically elected, and therefore more accountable, government in the Federal District, they were not actively seeking the extension of full political rights for the residents of Mexico City or the introduction of a more democratic political structure for the city.

The government's position vis-à-vis the Movimiento de Damnificados was not only highly responsive but also qualitatively different from its posture with regard to previous movements. At a time when repression of urban popular organizations was at its peak (Hernández 1987), the de la Madrid administration was negotiating with movement representatives from the very outset and meeting their most important demands (see Tavera-Fenollosa 1998).

Even before the earthquake victims had formally constituted their social movement organization, the Earthquake Victims' Coordinating Committee (CUD), but after they had organized a massive silent march to the president's residence, the government had recognized the movement as an "valid interlocutor." Less than two weeks after the quakes, on October 2, President de la Madrid met with spokespersons for the earthquake victims.[5] This audience with the president, something rarely accorded social movement leaders in Mexico, was very important for the development of the movement. In a regime as strongly presidentialist as Mexico's, this meeting constituted official recognition of the movement as a legitimate actor, something previous movements attained, if at all, only after years of protests and mobilizations. It was particularly significant because, as Foweraker notes, the survival and success of popular movements in authoritarian contexts largely depend on the effective representation they can achieve (1990: 44). In this meeting, the victims' representatives demanded the expropriation of buildings and plots affected by the quakes (to be used for the benefit of the victims), the resumption of urban services, and government assistance in rebuilding.

The petition for expropriation was a radical one, especially in the context of the de la Madrid administration's withdrawal from the public sphere and its protection of capital and private property. On October 11, 1985, de la Madrid took the surprising step of expropriating 5,563 buildings to benefit the earthquake victims. Although the list of expropriated buildings was later amended, it met the earthquake victims' primary demand: it allowed most of them to remain in their neighborhoods.

The expropriation also defined the institutional-legal terrain in which the movement developed. Because of its strong and early links to the administration, the Earthquake Victims' Movement never contemplated pressing for political reform, and the CUD chose not to echo other social actors' demand for democratizing the Federal District.[6] Clearly, the challenge that the movement posed to the legitimacy of political arrangements in the DF was not direct.

Why, then, did de la Madrid decide to open the debate on the democratization of Mexico City only two months after the 1985 earthquakes? Why did his government link the need to reconsider alternatives for citizen participation in governing the Federal District with the post-disaster social movement activity? What does this case teach about the political consequences of social movements in contemporary Mexico?

The Movement Is the Message

Mediating between the post-disaster situation and the government's sudden willingness to publicly discuss democracy in the Federal Dis-

---

[5] This was seventeen years to the day after the government had brutally repressed the student-popular movement at Tlatelolco in 1968.

[6] For an excellent discussion of the relationship between social movements and the political system, see Foweraker 1990.

trict is what Snow and his colleagues call "framing processes," or the "collective processes of interpretation, attribution, and social construction that mediate between opportunity and action" (Snow 1996: 2).

Just as changes in the "political opportunity structure" do not automatically lead to collective action and the emergence of social movements, the impact of social movement activity on democratic processes is not immediate. Like any event or situation, social movement activity is interpreted differently by different actors. Competing actors, particularly, assign different meanings and sponsor diverse interpretations of what is going on (Klandermans 1988: 175). These interpretations are of critical importance for determining how society and government will react to social movements. As Donatella Della Porta aptly put it, "whether a protest action is defined as a citizen right or as a 'disturbance of the public order' has a vital effect on the legitimation of the different actors" (1996: 65). This is especially true in nondemocratic contexts where the political impacts derive not from a movement's goals but from the meaning assigned to the movement itself.

A wide number of scholars from various theoretical backgrounds have analyzed the sources and functions of subjectivity within social movements. For example, issues of identity formation and meaning have been crucial concerns for European scholars working within the new social movements perspective (Touraine 1981; Melucci 1985, 1980). U.S. scholars writing from the political process approach— especially McAdam (1982), Klandermans (1988), and Gamson (1992)— have also emphasized the importance of ideas for the emergence of social movements. Nonetheless, it is perhaps the small but influential group of U.S. social and political scientists led by David Snow that has specifically addressed issues surrounding the social construction and interpretative dynamics of social movement activity (Snow et al. 1986; Snow and Benford 1988, 1992).

Building on sociologist Erving Goffman's notion of frame, Snow and his colleagues have developed a framing perspective that views movements not merely as carriers of existing ideas and meanings, but as signifying agents actively engaged in fabricating and maintaining meaning for society at large. According to Snow and Benford, one of the tasks of social movements is the production of meaning for participants, antagonists, and observers alike. In their words:

> Movements frame or assign meaning and interpret rele-
> vant events and conditions in ways that are intended to
> mobilize potential adherents and constituents, to garner
> bystander support, and to demobilize antagonists (Snow
> and Benford 1988: 198).

More recent work has extended the framing notion to suggest not only that the production of meaning is instrumental to a movement's interests, but also that it does not exclusively take a discursive form, as the work of Snow and his colleagues assumed.[7] As McAdam noted, the ideational bias in the work of Snow and his collaborators has prevented scholars from looking at the messages encoded in group actions and tactics. In his opinion, "the old adage is true: actions do speak louder than words" (McAdam 1996: 341). That is, movements indeed produce meaning, but they also become messages themselves or, as Melucci (1985: 801) puts it, "the movement itself as a new medium is the message."

Moreover, Szasz has suggested that the process through which society comes to believe consensually that a problem exists increasingly takes the form of iconography. Iconic communication is a particular type of political communication in which "political messages are carried by images rather than words, so that the meaning or signification takes place more through nonverbal spectacles than through narrative" (Szasz 1994: 57, 62). Iconic communication is of particular relevance in authoritarian contexts where social movement activity is often assigned a political meaning that goes beyond social movements' stated goals, actions, and tactics. To wit, José Woldenberg's remark on the social mobilization and organization that followed the earthquakes:

> In a routinary and bureaucratic environment, impermeable to citizens and their organizations, pyramidal and authoritarian, any citizen expression is transformed into a paradigm (*La Jornada*, October 12, 1985).

Or note the observation by the late PRI president José Francisco Ruiz Massieu on the Movimiento de Damnificados:

> When society mobilizes, and the mobilization is not promoted by the state, political parties, or unions, a political phenomenon occurs that requires a political solution (*La Jornada*, October 8, 1985, p. 5).

However, in order to become an icon that can contribute to political change, a social movement emerging from "suddenly imposed major grievances" (Walsh 1981) must be framed in a particular way.

---

[7] For an excellent and updated discussion on framing processes, see McAdam, McCarthy, and Zald 1996: 1–20.

Changing Symbolic Codes of Mexican Civil Society

The relationship between ideological factors (values, beliefs, meanings) and social movements—whether in terms of participation, success, or political outcome—exists in a wider social context. As Snow and his colleagues noted, framing processes are embedded in the symbolic and institutionalized cultural assumptions of a society. In their view, processes of interpretation and attribution of social movement activity draw on "cultural narrations" or "the stories, myths, and folk tales that are part and parcel of one's cultural heritage and that thus function to inform events and experiences in the immediate present" (Snow and Benford 1988: 210). As will be demonstrated below, in nondemocratic contexts, cultural assumptions concerning citizens' civic competence are particularly relevant for framing collective action.

Social Movements, Civic Competence, and Democratic Discourse

What sociologist Jeffrey Alexander calls the "symbolic code of civil society" is particularly relevant for understanding the process by which the Earthquake Victims' Movement, and social movements more generally, can become vehicles for creating contesting discourses conducive to democratic reform. According to Alexander, civil society is a moral community, a "network of understandings that operates beneath and above explicit institutions and the self-conscious interests of elites"—that is, the symbolic codes of civil society (1992: 290).

Although the formation of the symbolic code draws upon many movements and intellectual traditions—from Greek philosophy to Protestantism, the Enlightenment, and liberal thought—Alexander argues that its has a universal structure:

> It seems clear that many different historical movements contributed to the emergence of democratic discourse and practice and that, indeed, each is responsible for the particular emphasis, constructions, and metaphors that make every national and even regional configuration of democracy unique. At the same time, it is also clear that there is an overarching "structure" of democratic discourse that is more general and inclusive than any of these particular parts (1992: n. 4).

This overarching structure is formed by a set of binary oppositions, a code and counter code. The positive side constitutes the discourse of inclusion, whereas its negative side forms what Alexander calls the "discourse of repression." Thus, through civil society's symbolic codes, groups and individuals are divided into pure/impure, worthy/unworthy, friend/enemy.

> The codes supply the structured categories of pure and impure into which every member, or potential member, of civil society is made to fit. It is in terms of symbolic purity and impurity that centrality is defined, that marginal demographic status is made meaningful and high position understood as deserved or illegitimate (Alexander 1992: 290).

In general, the binary codes that constitute the symbolic order do not vary across social groups. There is consensus on what is civic virtue and what is civic vice. What is contested is how the code and counter code are applied. Who is going to be placed on which side of the discourse? In Alexander's view, people exhibiting the positive side of the binary set are held to be deserving of inclusion, whereas those exhibiting the negative side are deemed not worthy and are excluded.

Liberal political scientists have generally defined worthy democratic citizens on the basis of certain qualities considered to be axiomatic of democracy. To be members of the democratic polity, liberal democrats argue, actors must be active rather than passive, autonomous rather than dependent, rational instead of irrational, reasonable and not hysterical, and so on. The relationships they establish should be open, trusting, critical, and honorable, as opposed to secretive, suspicious, deferential, and self-interested. Finally, democratic institutions should be regulated by law rather than arbitrarily administered, egalitarian rather than hierarchical, impersonal rather than based on personal loyalty, and inclusive rather than exclusive (Alexander 1992: 292–95). Thus,

> civil society becomes organized around a bifurcating discourse of citizen and enemy, defining the characteristics of worthy, democratic citizens and also of unworthy, counter-democratic enemies (Alexander and Jacobs n.d.: 18).

Those who are unfortunate enough to be constructed under the counter-democratic code, Alexander argues, must ultimately be repressed, because their supposedly anti-civil qualities make it necessary to deny them access to rights and the protection of law (1992: 296). In other words, if people are portrayed as passive, dependent, and unable to behave reasonably—that is, as exhibiting the qualities associated with the negative side of the democratic discourse—their exclusion from full participation in the community is presented as a justified, legitimate act.

The symbolic basis of citizen inclusion and exclusion implies that segregated individuals and groups must be construed under the positive side of the democratic discourse in order to be incorporated into the civic sphere:

> The incorporation of previously excluded groups cannot take place simply through a restructuring of power relationships or an extension of legal rights. These steps will be ineffective unless the previously excluded group is redefined in terms of the "timeless qualities" which citizens in good standing putatively possess (Alexander and Jacobs n.d.: 3).

In other words, the process of inclusion of marginalized groups must be preceded by the redefinition of such groups in more favorable terms. That is, in order to become full members of society, formerly excluded groups must first be construed as worthy of inclusion.

From Victim to Citizen

A depiction of Mexicans as being politically incompetent has long been used to justify their exclusion from political life. The most famous declaration of this logic dates from an interview that President Porfirio Díaz gave U.S. journalist James Creelman in 1908. By that time, Díaz had been in power for twenty-seven years, and national and international observers feared he would run for reelection to a sixth term. Díaz's justification for his longevity in office speaks directly to Alexander's symbolic codes of civil society:

> Indians, who constitute more than 50 percent of the total population, do not care about politics. They are used to letting themselves be guided by those who hold the reins of power. They inherited this tendency from the Spaniards, who taught them not to participate in public affairs but to trust the government to guide them (in López Portillo 1975: 366).

As for the impoverished, Díaz noted:

> Poor people are, in general, too ignorant to be trusted. Democracy needs an active and participatory middle class that strives to improve its condition and cares about politics and the nation's progress (in López Portillo 1975: 365–66).

Construed as ignorant, passive, servile, and untrustworthy, the majority of Mexicans were, according to President Díaz, incapable of participating in public affairs and, consequently, had to be excluded from political life.

In the context of today's myth of the indifferent, apathetic Mexican, the social mobilization and organization of earthquake victims, neighbors, institutions, and organizations in 1985 acquired a special meaning, one that severely undermined the legitimacy of citizen exclusion from local government. The political message of the Movimiento de Damnificados was clear: Mexico City now had a more competent citizenry and, therefore, its government had to be democratized. This newly voiced capacity for self-government was acknowledged by Regent Ramón Aguirre. In his announcement of public hearings on possible changes to the governmental structure of the Federal District, Aguirre noted:

> Once more, the residents of Mexico City have shown why the Federal District is the pulse of the nation. Their ability to react immediately to the emergency situation, to spontaneously organize voluntary participation, and their promptness in helping their fellow citizens in need reflect the high moral value of all Mexicans. The dark myth of the *capitalino* as indifferent and apathetic has been expunged (Cámara 1985: 22).

Opposition parties also took note of the changing status of Mexico City residents. Efraín Calvo, a member of the Chamber of Deputies from the Revolutionary Workers' Party (PRT), addressed the subject as follows:

> During these ill-fated days [following the earthquakes], the false myth of the apathetic Federal District resident has crumbled, initially undermined by the explosion of citizen participation, and then later, when that first spontaneous reaction subsided, by the emergence, virtually out of nowhere, of multiple, massive, autonomous organizations of earthquake victims. These phenomena put a definitive end to paternalistic theories about the citizen of Mexico City. The *capitalino* is not a child incapable of self-government, but an adult who requires, who demands, self-government. Nothing, absolutely nothing, can substitute for the right of the citizens of the Federal District to elect their own government (Cámara 1985: 82).

As these statements indicate, the political rationale for considering awarding residents of Mexico City full political rights was framed within what Alexander calls the symbolic codes of civil society. Implicit in Aguirre's and Calvo's arguments was the idea that, until 1985, citizens of the Federal District had not deserved full membership in Mexican society, presumably because they had not exhibited the qualities deemed necessary for inclusion. Classified under the counter-democratic code—which defined them as dependent, irrational, excitable, and untrustworthy—people living in Mexico City were not worthy of enjoying full political rights. Discussions regarding their possible participation in local government could only take place once they exhibited the qualities associated with the positive side of the democratic discourse. Congruous with Alexander's observation that excluded groups must first be construed under the democratic code in order to be worthy of inclusion, Aguirre noted that the social response to the emergency signaled the "coming of age" of Mexico City's residents. Consequently, conditions suddenly were "ripe" for publicly discussing their incorporation into local government.

It is obvious that the Earthquake Victims' Movement significantly altered political discourse on democracy in the Federal District. By undermining the cultural beliefs that supported the absence of democratic structures, the Movimiento de Damnificados exposed the hollowness of official discourse. To fill the vacuum, a new discourse had to be generated, one that was supportive of democratic change, given that at its core lay the democratic qualities demonstrated by the earthquake victims and their neighbors.

The Role of the Media

Public opinion played a crucial role in redefining Mexico City's residents in ways that made their exclusion from full citizenship appear illegitimate and arbitrary. In fact, it was through the media that the movement was first construed as an icon of civic competence and the demand for democratization of the DF first emerged.

Frames can be generated by a diverse set of actors, but some actors possess more framing power than others. According to Gamson and Meyer, because the media spotlight "validates the movement as an important player," media leaders "play a crucial role in defining for movement actors whether they are taken seriously as agents of possible change" (1996: 285). Therefore, the opening and closing of media access and attention are crucial for shaping a government response to social movement activity. Gamson and Meyer's analysis is consistent with Alexander's understanding of the media's role in the construction and reconstruction of the civil realm. In the case of the Earthquake Victims' Movement, the media were centrally involved in redefining the residents of Mexico City under the democratic code. The press emphasized the deplorable distance between the symbolic and institutional levels of civil society and thus created a cultural climate conducive to change.

As in any major disaster, the 1985 earthquakes attracted national and international media coverage, all highly sympathetic toward the earthquake victims. It was also critical of the political system. In the weeks that followed the disaster, many articles focused on the human aspect of the tragedy, emphasizing the courage and solidarity of the Mexican people (for example, *El Día* 1985a, 1985b; Bolaños 1985; *El Heraldo* 1985; *La Jornada* 1985; Canale 1985; Aguilera Gómez 1985). Others focused on the negative consequences of economic centralization and unplanned urban growth that were laid bare by the earthquakes (Carrión 1985; Haas 1985; de la Borbolla 1985; Gutiérrez Espíndola 1985, among others). Still others underscored the changing civic and political character of Mexico City residents and the need to introduce more democratic structures into the city's government.

Informed by a set of shared cultural assumptions concerning the lack of civic culture among the city's residents, journalists, columnists, experts, and politicians alike attributed a very similar political meaning to the social mobilization and organization of the earthquake victims and their fellow citizens. As a journalist for the daily *El Universal* put it:

> Because we usually pay little attention to the signals coming from society, some of us have been caught off guard by the response of our fellow citizens. We forged a myth about Mexicans' unwillingness to engage in collective action. We believed that apathy and individualism dominated our fellow citizens' attitudes. Now we see that this is not the case (*El Universal*, September 23, 1985, p. 4).

The breakdown of cultural assumptions regarding Mexico City residents' civic proficiency had clear political connotations:

> The wide popular mobilization that arose on September 19 shows us a city that is radically different from the image that the regent presents. Here is a city, a *people*, that is infinitely superior to the bureaucratic government that has been imposed on it (Pablo Gómez, opposition member of the Chamber of Deputies, *La Jornada*, October 1, 1985, p. 5).

In the same vein, the editors of the influential magazine *Nexos* analyzed the political impact of the movement in the following terms:

> It was an eruption of unknown forces that will forever modify our understanding of urban life and of its institu-

tional reality, of the political system and the exercise of citizenship, of the social and administrative organization of the Federal District. What we knew by fractions revealed itself in its totality: the Federal District can no longer be governed through antidemocratic and archaic methods (in *La Jornada*, October 8, 1985, pp. 1, 12).

By redefining the civic character of Mexico City residents in terms of the democratic discourse, the Earthquake Victims' Movement contributed to the construction of a new interpretative framework within which political arrangements in the DF would now be understood and evaluated. The mobilization of city residents in the aftermath of the earthquakes created a rift between the symbolic code of civil society and its institutional dimension.

Loss of Legitimacy and Framing Processes

The discrepancy between Mexico City residents' civic competence and existing channels for political participation was further magnified by the government's responses following the earthquakes. Even though any government would have had difficulty responding to a disaster of this scale, the Mexican government's disorganization, its initial reluctance to coordinate its efforts with civil society or to accept aid from other nations, and its insensitivity to the victims were remarkable. Moreover, government responses were in sharp contrast to society's response, characterized by promptness, efficient self-organization and coordination, and, above all, solidarity.

The government's failure to provide rapid and appropriate assistance to the earthquake victims brought into question its capacity to manage the city. Moreover, the earthquakes—in addition to killing thousands of people and leveling thousands of buildings—unveiled the extensive corruption pervading the Mexican system. The "high moral standards" that Aguirre lauded in his speech before the Chamber of Deputies contrasted acutely with the corruption that the earthquakes exposed in the construction sector, in the administration of justice, and in the labor sector.[8]

---

[8] Among the most dramatic illustrations of government corruption unveiled by the earthquakes was the collapsed Nuevo León building in Tlatelolco, whose residents had long been petitioning the government (builder and owner of the building) to provide adequate maintenance. Another horrible example was the discovery of corpses of torture victims in the rubble of the collapsed offices of the Attorney General of the Federal District (PGJDF), revealing the Mexican police's violations of human rights and the judicial system's repressive character. A third instance was the exploitation uncovered in the garment industry, when the earthquakes leveled

So pervasive was the unveiled corruption that international organizations and NGOs refused to funnel their aid through official channels. Instead, they sent it directly to earthquake victims' organizations, universities, local NGOs, and church parishes. In the aftermath of the natural disaster, only a portion of the destruction was attributable to the earthquakes themselves. The remainder was credited to the "fraud, inefficiency, and incapacity of a corrupt government."[9] The tragic effects of having no democratic, accountable government in the Federal District intensified the public's framing of the Earthquake Victims' Movement as an icon of civic competence and democracy. And the government's failure to respond rapidly and appropriately prevented it from offering an alternative frame for interpreting society's mobilization and organization.

The Democratizing Power of Social Movements
Undermining the Legitimacy of Authoritarian Rule

Scholars have argued that social movements in Latin America have a democratizing impact because they undermine the legitimacy of authoritarian rule (Mainwaring and Viola 1984; Mainwaring 1987, 1989). But in order to achieve a thorough understanding of the democratizing potential of social movements and, in this case, to understand the process by which the Earthquake Victims' Movement undermined the legitimacy of political arrangements in Mexico City, one needs a more highly refined conceptualization of legitimacy, a virtual tool that reveals the processes by which legitimacy is built up and torn down. David Beetham's definition of legitimacy is particularly well suited for this task.

Elaborating on Max Weber's legacy, Beetham develops a multilayered definition of legitimacy. In his view, just as the concept of power is better understood from a multidimensional perspective (cf. Lukes 1974), the "key to understanding the concept of legitimacy lies in the recognition that it is multidimensional in character" (Beetham 1991: 15). More precisely,

> Legitimacy is not a single quality that systems of power possess or not, but a set of distinct criteria, or multiple dimensions, operating at different levels, each of which provides moral grounds for compliance or cooperation on the

---

sweatshops in downtown Mexico City that employed hundreds of women without benefit of any labor protections.

[9] Author's fieldwork. See also Poniatowska 1988 and Cazés 1995, among others.

part of those subordinate to a given power relation (1991:
20).

According to Beetham, the legitimation of power occurs at three
different levels. All three levels contribute to legitimacy but are
qualitatively different, and they lead to different nonlegitimate power
situations. The first and most basic level of legitimacy is that of rules.
Legal validity, however, is insufficient to secure legitimacy because
the rules of power stand in need of justification. The second level of
legitimacy is that of the shared beliefs on which the justification of
power is based. The third level of legitimacy involves actions expres-
sive of consent. These actions create a normative commitment on the
part of those engaging in them, and they have a symbolic or declama-
tory force. Thus, legitimate power has to be acquired according to the
rules, the rules have to be justified in reference to shared beliefs, and
subordinates need to consent to prevailing power relations.[10]

Following Beetham, then, social movement challenges to the legitimacy of authoritarian rule can occur at various levels. They can
take the form of a direct contestation of power relationships, as would
be the case in level three. Alternatively, they can be indirect challenges that break or undermine the rules of power:

> Rules of power will lack legitimacy to the extent that they
> cannot be justified in terms of shared beliefs: either because
> no basis of shared belief exists in the first place; or *because
> changes in belief have deprived the rules of their supporting ba-
> sis; or because circumstances have made existing justifications
> for the rules implausible, despite beliefs remaining constant*
> (1991: 17; emphasis added).

The challenge that the Movimiento de Damnificados posed to the
legitimacy of authoritarian rule in the Federal District occurred at
level two. Framed as an unquestionable demonstration of political
proficiency, the Earthquake Victims' Movement changed existing
shared beliefs about the civic competence of Mexico City residents
and thereby pointed to a discrepancy between the structure of the DF
government and its supporting basis. This explains why, although not
explicitly oriented toward political change, the Earthquake Victims'

---

[10] These three levels of legitimacy correspond to Weber's typology of legitimate
authority. The first level becomes a "rational-legal" type. One example of the second-
level basis for legitimacy is Weber's traditional type, whereas charismatic legitimacy
exemplifies legitimacy deriving solely from consent. In contrast to Weber's typology,
which Beetham feels "represents the elevation of a different level of legitimacy into a
self-sufficient type," Beetham distinguishes the three levels but accords each one the
status of one element in the totality and focuses on their interrelations (Beetham
1991: 25).

Movement was a vehicle for creating a civil discourse that questioned the legitimacy of political arrangements in the Federal District and opened the door to the democratic reassessment of its citizens and government.

Creating a More Democratic Political Culture

Perhaps one of the most accepted political effects of social movements is their contribution to the creation or redefinition of a more democratic political culture. Movements work as "schools for democracy" and encourage the expansion of democratic values. They "foster a political culture that is supportive of democracy" (Sonia Álvarez, quoted in Hellman 1992: 58) and open the way to the development of effective nonclientelistic links (Hellman 1992: 58). "At the most basic level, social movements must be seen as crucial forces in the democratization of authoritarian social relations" (Escobar and Álvarez 1992: 326). However, as Foweraker noted, the creation of a more democratic political culture does not necessarily lead to the democratization of the state:

> There are no guarantees, either in history or in theory, that the democratization of civil society will necessarily be reflected in the democratization of the state. On the contrary, the state may become more repressive and authoritarian (1989: 95).

The case of the Movimiento de Damnificados suggests that, more than through the creation of a more democratic political culture, it is through "cultural contradictions" that social movements can contribute to processes of democratic change. "Cultural contradictions" occur

> when two or more cultural themes that are potentially contradictory are brought into active contradiction by the force of events, or when the realities of behavior are substantially different from the ideological justifications (Zald 1996: 268).

Mexico City residents' mobilization in the aftermath of the earthquakes brought political arrangements in the Federal District into active contradiction with these citizens' clear ability to participate actively in the public sphere. By pointing to a discrepancy between existing channels of citizen participation in local government and the civic competence of Mexico City residents, the Movimiento de Damnificados called attention to a cultural contradiction that challenged the legitimacy of authoritarian rule in Mexico City. This political contradiction was perceived by journalists and intellectuals, politicians and specialists, who helped create a contested discourse on democracy. This discourse weakened the "official package" and forced the government to examine alternatives for citizen participation in local government.

Placing Issues on the Agenda: Parties vs. Movements

In assessing social movements' contributions to processes of democratization, scholars have stressed that:

> Even when they appear to be inefficient political actors, social movements can play an important role by sensitizing other forces, especially political parties and the State, to the need to redefine the political arena. The movements themselves may die out, but they can promote lasting change by placing new questions on the agenda—questions which are ultimately adopted by political parties and acted upon by the State (Mainwaring 1989: 197).

The case of the Movimiento de Damnificados and the democratization of Mexico City's government indicates that social movements can contribute to political change, not only by creating and placing new issues on the agenda but also by recasting old ones, especially politically sensitive issues that governments have successfully kept off the agenda and which other actors, especially political parties, have failed to bring into the legislative arena. By recasting prevailing definitions of a situation—and thus changing perceptions of the costs and benefits (and the injustice) of the status quo—social movements can force public and legislative debate on issues that would otherwise remain undiscussed and probably unaddressed.

Because they are the primary instruments for gaining access to power in a democratic system, political parties are generally presumed to be more effective than social movements in promoting political change. Yet the evidence suggests that, had it not been for the Movimiento de Damnificados, it is very unlikely that there would have been any discussion on citizen participation in the DF government. Although opposition parties in Mexico had been eager to assert the principles of local participation before 1985, their efforts—public statements, legislative initiatives, and opposition to administrative reforms—had not borne fruit.

Parties were also not particularly successful in advancing the issue once it got on the agenda. Public hearings on the democratization of Mexico City's government began in summer 1986. During six sessions, representatives of all political parties, as well as jurists and intellectuals, discussed various alternatives for citizen participation in local government. Debate centered on the feasibility of making the Federal District Mexico's thirty-second state, creating a local congress for the city, and direct election of the regent. But no consensus was reached. Some opposition parties favored the state option; others backed the direct election proposal. The Federal District PRI backed the establishment of a local congress; speaking in support of this option were high-ranking PRIistas like Jesús Salazar Toledano, president of the PRI in the Federal District, and Guillermo Cosío Vidaurri, secretary of government in the DDF.

On December 28, 1986, President de la Madrid sent his reform project to the Mexican Congress. It did not include the proposals advanced by the opposition or by members of his own party. Instead of recommending the direct election of the regent and/or the creation of a local congress, de la Madrid devised an Assembly of Representatives of the Federal District (ARDF) with no legislative powers. The new political institution was to comprise sixty-six members, forty elected through direct vote and twenty-six through proportional representation. The first election of these representatives was to take place in the 1988 federal elections, and elected members would serve for a three-year period. Under de la Madrid's proposal, the regent would still be appointed by the president. Four months later, on April 23, 1987, de la Madrid's initiative was discussed in the Chamber of Deputies and then approved by the PRI bloc; opposition party members had already walked out in protest (*La Jornada*, April 24, 1987; Unidad 1988).

Nearly all political actors saw the Assembly of Representatives as an inadequate solution, because it basically kept intact the organization and functioning of the Federal District government. Yet the Assembly was not just one more effort designed to curtail demands for full democratization in the Federal District. To view it as such would be to ignore the fact that, despite its limited impact, the initiative represented a major qualitative change from previous reforms: the Assembly finally opened the Federal District to electoral competition. Moreover, from the very beginning, its members sought to expand their mandate. "In a short time, the ARDF exceeded its administrative functions and transformed itself into a political interlocutor for the regent" (Ballinas and Urrutia 1992).

Even if the outcome of the hearings was not wholly satisfactory,[11] the fact that, for the first time, the issue of democratizing the Federal District was discussed publicly by all political parties is an indication

---

[11] The reform does not provide for the election of delegates, nor does it give the Assembly full autonomy vis-à-vis the federal government.

of how and how much social movements can impact democratic reform. As Gamson and Meyer noted, the stable elements of the political opportunity structure—that is, those "deeply embedded in political institutions and culture"—are from the standpoint of social movements "essentially fixed and given, barring dramatic and unforeseen changes beyond their control" (1996: 277). Within these constraints, however, movements can affect other aspects of the political opportunity structure and thus contribute to political democratization.

No matter how short the actual reform fell from the democratic ideal, the democratization of the Federal District became a central part of the political agenda from 1985 forward. Although limited, it clearly established the framework for subsequent amendments, which have further increased democratization. In 1993, for example, the Assembly of Representatives gained some legislative functions, including the authority to approve the electoral law for the Federal District. The reform also stipulated indirect election of the mayor and the creation of citizen councils.

Another reform, passed in 1996, further advanced democratization of the Mexico City government. As a result of this reform, in 1997 the residents of the Federal District elected Cuauhtémoc Cárdenas as their first mayor.

References

Aguilera Gómez, Manuel. 1985. "Ante la tragedia, refrendo de entereza," *Excélsior*, September 25.

Alexander, Jeffrey. 1992. "Citizen and Enemy as Symbolic Classification: On the Polarizing Discourse of Civil Society." In *Cultivating Differences. Symbolic Boundaries and the Making of Inequality*, edited by Michèle Lamont and Marcel Fournier. Chicago: University of Chicago Press.

Alexander, Jeffrey, and Ronald N. Jacobs. n.d. "Toward a Voluntaristic and Cultural Approach to Mass Communications: Elihu Katz and the Communicative Understanding of Civil Society." In *Essays in Honour of Elihu Katz*, edited by Tamar Liebes and James Curran. London: Routledge. Forthcoming.

Ballinas, Víctor, and Alonso Urrutia. 1992. "Hacia la democratización del Distrito Federal," "Perfil de la Jornada," *La Jornada*, March 3.

Beetham, David. 1991. *The Legitimation of Power*. Atlantic Highlands, N.J.: Humanities Press International.

Bolaños, Laura. 1985. "La hermosa gente del D.F.," *El Universal*, September 21.

Cámara de Diputados. 1983. *Debate y legislación sobre el Distrito Federal*. Mexico City: Cámara de Diputados, Período Ordinario de Sesiones, LII Legislatura.

————. 1985. *Comparecencia del Jefe del Departamento del Distrito Federal Ramón Aguirre Velázquez ante la LII Legislatura.* Mexico City: Cámara de Diputados, LII Legislatura.

Canale, Sergio Antonio. 1985. "Adelante a pesar de la tragedia," *El Nacional*, September 23.

Carrión, Jorge. 1985. "Los recursos del porvenir. Desigualdades al descubierto," *Excélsior*, September 30.

Cazés, Daniel. 1995. *Volver a nacer. Memorial del 85.* Mexico City: Ed. La Jornada.

de la Borbolla, Juan. 1985. "No todas las causas del desastre son fortuitas," *El Universal*, October 8.

de la Madrid, Miguel. 1982a. *Nacionalismo revolucionario. Siete tesis fundamentales de campaña.* Mexico City: Secretaría de Información y Propaganda, Partido Revolucionario Institucional.

————. 1982b. "Inaugural Speech." Mexico City: Domestic Service in Spanish 1701 GMT, December 1.

Della Porta, Donatella. 1996. "Social Movements and the State: Thoughts on the Policing of Protest." In *Comparative Perspectives on Social Movements*, edited by Doug McAdam, John D. McCarthy, and Mayer N. Zald. Cambridge: Cambridge University Press.

El Día. 1985a. "Ante nuestro luto y voluntad de vivir," September 20.

————. 1985b. "Solidaridad con mayúsculas," September 30.

El Heraldo de México. 1985. "Se humanizó la capital," September 20.

Escobar, Arturo, and Sonia E. Álvarez, 1992. "Theoretical and Political Horizons of Change in Contemporary Latin American Social Movements." In *The Making of Social Movements in Latin America: Identity, Strategy, and Democracy*, edited by Arturo Escobar and Sonia E. Álvarez. Boulder, Colo.: Westview.

Fox, Jonathan. 1994. "Latin America's Emerging Local Politics," *Journal of Democracy* 5 (2): 105–16.

Foweraker, Joe. 1989. "Los movimientos populares y la transformación del sistema político mexicano," *Revista Mexicana de Sociología* 51 (4).

————. 1990. "Popular Organization and Institutional Change." In *Popular Movements and Political Change in Mexico*, edited by Joe Foweraker and Ann L. Craig. Boulder, Colo.: Lynne Rienner, in association with the Center for U.S.–Mexican Studies, University of California, San Diego.

Gamson, William A. 1988. "Political Discourse and Collective Action." In *From Structure to Action: Comparing Social Movement Research across Cultures*, edited by Bert Klandermans, H. Kriesi, and Sidney Tarrow. Greenwich, Conn.: JAI Press.

————. 1992. *Talking Politics.* Cambridge: Cambridge University Press.

Gamson, William A., and David S. Meyer. 1996. "Framing Political Opportunity." In *Comparative Perspectives on Social Movements*, edited by Doug McAdam, John D. McCarthy, and Mayer N. Zald. Cambridge: Cambridge University Press.

Gutiérrez Espíndola, José. 1985. "Reconstruir la ciudad," *El Universal*, October 2.

Haas, Antonio. 1985. "El sistema al desnudo," *Excélsior*, October 9.

Hellman, Judith Adler. 1992. "The Study of Social Movements in Latin America and the Question of Autonomy." In *The Making of Social Movements in Latin America: Identity, Strategy, and Democracy*, edited by Arturo Escobar and Sonia E. Álvarez. Boulder, Colo.: Westview.

Hernández S., Ricardo. 1987. *La Coordinadora Nacional del Movimiento Urbano Popular, CONAMUP: su historia 1980–86.* Mexico City: Equipo Pueblo.

INEGI (Instituto Nacional de Estadística, Geografía e Informática). 1984. *Anuario Estadística del Distrito Federal.* Mexico City: INEGI.

Klandermans, Bert. 1988. ""The Formation and Mobilization of Consensus." In *From Structure to Action: Comparing Social Movement Research across Cultures*, edited by Bert Klandermans, H. Kriesi, and Sidney Tarrow. Greenwich, Conn.: JAI Press.

La Jornada. 1985. "Solidaridad y organización," September 23.

López Portillo, José. 1975. *Elevación y caída de Porfirio Díaz.* Mexico City: Porrúa.

Lukes, Steven. 1974. *Power: A Radical View.* London: Macmillan.

Mainwaring, Scott. 1987. "Urban Popular Movements, Identity and Democratization in Brazil," *Comparative Politics* 21 (2): 131–59.

———. 1989. "Grassroots Popular Movements and the Struggle for Democracy: Nova Iguacu." In *Democratizing Brazil*, edited by Alfred Stepan. Oxford: Oxford University Press.

Mainwaring, Scott, and Eduardo Viola. 1984. "New Social Movements, Political Culture, and Democracy: Brazil and Argentina in the 1980's," *Telos* 61: 17–52.

McAdam, Doug. 1982. *Political Process and the Development of Black Insurgency, 1930–1970.* Chicago: University of Chicago Press.

———. 1996. "The Framing Function of Movement Tactics: Strategic Dramaturgy in the American Civil Rights Movement." In *Comparative Perspectives on Social Movements*, edited by Doug McAdam, John D. McCarthy, and Mayer N. Zald. Cambridge: Cambridge University Press.

McAdam, Doug, John D. McCarthy, and Mayer N. Zald, eds. 1996. *Comparative Perspectives on Social Movements.* Cambridge: Cambridge University Press.

Melucci, Alberto. 1980. "The New Social Movements: A Theoretical Approach," *Social Science Information* 19: 199–226.

———. 1985. "The Symbolic Challenge of Contemporary Movements," *Social Research* 52 (4): 789–816.

Meyer, Lorenzo. 1987. "Sistema de gobierno y evolución política hasta 1940." In *El Atlas de la Ciudad de México*. Mexico City: Departamento del Distrito Federal/El Colegio de México.

Molinar Horcasitas, Juan. 1991. *El tiempo de la legitimidad: elecciones, autoritarismo y democracia en México.* Mexico City: Cal y Arena.

Monterrosas, Daniel. n.d. *Reforma política del D.F. Reformas legales, plataforma electoral, opinión pública.* Mexico City: Fundación Distrito Federal Cambio XXI.

Poniatowska, Elena. 1988. *Nada, Nadie, las voces del temblor.* Mexico City: Era.

Snow, David A. 1996. "Introduction: Opportunities, Mobilizing Structures, and Framing Processes—Toward a Synthetic, Comparative Perspective on Social Movements." In *Comparative Perspectives on Social Movements*, edited by Doug McAdam, John D. McCarthy, and Mayer N. Zald. Cambridge: Cambridge University Press.

Snow, David A., and Robert D. Benford. 1988. "Ideology, Frame Resonance, and Participant Mobilization." In *From Structure to Action: Comparing Social Movement Research across Cultures*, edited by Bert Klandermans, H. Kriesi, and Sidney Tarrow. Greenwich, Conn.: JAI Press.

———. 1992. "Master Frames and Cycles of Protest." In *Frontiers in Social Movement Theory*, edited by Aldon Morris and Carol M. Mueller. New Haven, Conn.: Yale University Press.

Snow, David A., et al. 1986. "Frame Alignment Processes, Micromobilization, and Movement Participation," *American Sociological Review* 51: 464–81.

Szasz, Andrew. 1994. *Ecopopulism. Toxic Waste and the Movement for Environmental Justice*. Minneapolis: University of Minnesota Press.

Tavera-Fenollosa, Ligia. 1998. "Social Movements and Civil Society: The Mexico City 1985 Earthquake Victims' Movement in Mexico City." Ph.D. dissertation, Yale University.

Touraine, Alain. 1981. *The Voice and the Eye: An Analysis of Social Movements*. Cambridge: Cambridge University Press.

Unidad de la Crónica Presidencial. 1988. *Las elecciones de 1988. Serie Las Razones y las obras. Crónica del Sexenio de 1982 a 1988*. Mexico City: Fondo de Cultura Económica.

U.S. Department of Commerce. 1990. *The Earthquake in Mexico City, Mexico September 19, 1985*. Boulder, Colo.: National Oceanic and Atmospheric Administration, National Geophysical Data Center.

Walsh, Edward. 1981. "Resource Mobilization and Citizen Protest in Communities around Three Mile Island," *Social Problems* 29 (1): 1–21.

Ward, Peter M. 1989. "Government without Democracy in Mexico: Defending the High Ground." In *Mexico's Alternative Political Futures*, edited by Wayne A. Cornelius, Judith Gentleman, and Peter H. Smith. La Jolla: Center for U.S.–Mexican Studies, University of California, San Diego.

Zald, Mayer. 1996. "Culture, Ideology, and Strategic Framing." In *Comparative Perspectives on Social Movements*, edited by Doug McAdam, John D. McCarthy, and Mayer N. Zald. New York: Cambridge University Press.

7

The El Barzón Debtors' Movement: From the Local to the National in Protest Politics

Gabriel Torres

Mexico's difficult circumstances in 1994 and 1995 (the guerrilla rebellion in Chiapas, political assassinations, the unheralded electoral triumph of the Institutional Revolutionary Party, or PRI) reflected the dark side of the dramatic transformations that had taken place in the economic realm under Presidents Carlos Salinas de Gortari (1988–1994) and Ernesto Zedillo Ponce de León (1994–2000). These included opening to international markets, industrial restructuring, the state's withdrawal from selected economic sectors, and deep currency devaluations. Both administrations hoped to use the economic crisis as a justification for their changes to the rules of the politico-economic game—including a realignment of forces and the fortification of neoliberalism (Assiz 1996: 20).

These changes to Mexico's economic model did not end the crisis. Administrations have "managed" the situation only by enlisting every available strategy to maintain a facade of equilibrium in Mexico's key economic indicators (inflation, investment, and capitalization)—whatever the cost—in hopes of convincing all onlookers that the country is on the verge of entering the First World. In pursuing this strategy, President Salinas privileged economic concerns over social and political ones. He even went so far as to criticize the former Soviet Union and attribute its decline to the fact that the Russians had

Translation by Sandra del Castillo.

given priority to political liberalization over economic liberalization (Borge 1993).

Heeding the Russian "lesson," Salinas postponed indefinitely any democratization of Mexico's authoritarian political system in order to focus on economic change. This approach presupposes that democratic and political development are subordinate to economic progress. Moreover, it assumes that, because of the political immaturity of the Mexican populace, the administration can stopper or unstopper these processes at will. The resulting economic flux built on political expediency has created a "war economy" in Mexico (Assiz 1996: 20): the country is plagued by indebtedness, an inability to generate revenues, rising unemployment, falling gross domestic product, a skewed concentration of wealth, and strong social polarization. This is the context that gave rise to the Barzón debtors' movement, the tip of an iceberg created when technocrats in the Mexican government made their artificial distinction between economic development, on the one hand, and social and political development, on the other.[1]

The Barzón debtors' organization, which began as a localized group of agriculturalists·and small businessmen caught in a squeeze between falling sales and rising costs, soon transcended its origins to catch the imagination of the Mexican populace at large. Yet the actors involved were all members of one or another of the corporatist "pillars" of the Mexican regime. How did these groups emerge from the core of government-controlled corporatist organizations and free themselves from their complex networks of relationships to stage this powerful challenge to the administration's social and economic policies? This chapter attempts to answer this question by examining the opaque relationship between social movement and political world (see Foweraker 1995: 13).[2]

The chapter examines El Barzón from "below," based on a dialogue with its membership, from the leaders down to the grassroots, supplemented with information from the media and other secondary sources as well as interviews with people outside the movement. The analysis departs from the Gramscian hypothesis that "subaltern classes" have key contributions to make to a national political agenda,

---

[1] The name El Barzón covers a range of groups. These include several that are affiliated with El Barzón Unión, led by Quirino Salas, and others linked with El Barzón Nacional, directed by Maximiano Barbosa. Among them are the Transbarzón, Barzón del Campo, Barzón Metropolitano, Barzón Cristiano, and many others identified by village name, economic sector, or municipality. Some less formal designations reflect the debtors' ideological struggles and interests. Thus the "New" Barzón is identified with more radical elements and with the Party of the Democratic Revolution (PRD), while the "Old" Barzón is linked with more conservative interests and with the Institutional Revolutionary Party (PRI).

[2] For more on the political nature of the credit problem, see Torres and Rodríguez 1994: 75.

although these are not necessarily heeded. The demands of El Barzón are for changes in Mexico's economic model and for improved living standards, two issues that nuance macro-level discussions of the country's political liberalization and put into question whether the central government is the appropriate arena in which to debate the full range of options for political change.

The following discussion comprises four sections. The first reviews the rise of El Barzón, highlighting key conflicts, initiatives, events, and negotiations; it also introduces the movement's leadership, rank and file, and allied social networks. The second section analyzes the political aspects of debtors' movements more generally, based primarily on a historical review supplemented by an ethnographic study of the Barzón and similar groups. The third section examines the emergence and evolution of the debate regarding one's right to adopt a Barzonista stance in a culture of personal fiscal responsibility. The concluding section reflects on El Barzón's impacts in terms of the radicalization and politicization of fractions of the Mexican population.

A Microhistory of El Barzón

A *barzón*, the connecting ring in a yoke for an oxen team, appears in a traditional song from the Mexican Revolution: "*Se me reventó el barzón y la yunta sigue andando,*" or "The yoke is broken, but the team keeps moving on." These lines have long been embraced to describe the situation of many Mexican families. Under President Porfirio Díaz (1876–1880, 1884–1911) they described the living conditions of laborers held in debt peonage to the company store. In 1993 Mexico's agricultural producers adopted the *barzón* as their symbol, casting the country's bankers in the role of the large estate owners of earlier times.[3]

By September 1993, El Barzón had nearly 10,000 members, supported by a wide variety of other debtor groups.[4] Current membership may be as high as two million and includes indebted agricultural producers, credit card holders, householders with mortgages, and small, medium-, and large-sized businessmen in both rural and urban areas.[5]

---

[3] The image of the oxen team was updated to the Barzón's current logo, a tractor.

[4] These eventually included the Asociación Nacional de Usuarios de la Banca, the Asociación Nacional de Tarjetahabientes, the Alianza para la Defensa del Patrimonio Familiar, and the Movimiento Ciudadano "Salvemos Nuestra Casa."

[5] Membership numbers are approximations only. The leader of El Barzón Unión stated that his organization's membership numbered around one million (*Proceso*, May 6, 1996, p. 6). However, after announcing a new support program for debtors, the

The Rise of El Barzón

El Barzón grew out of protest movements that began in the states of Sonora, Chihuahua, Tabasco, and Jalisco in May 1993. These included local demonstrations in Aútlan and Ciudad Guzmán, Jalisco, as well as activities with a higher national profile, including a demonstration in downtown Guadalajara which drew participants from across the state, and a takeover of the international bridge between Ciudad Juárez, Chihuahua, and El Paso, Texas.[6] The movement gained even more visibility with a 52–day tractor blockade in Guadalajara which began in September of that year. This first phase of activities ended with the arrest of El Barzón leaders Maximiano Barbosa and Héctor Madera in November 1993 as they led a caravan of protesters to Mexico City, just as the ruling Institutional Revolutionary Party was announcing Luis Donaldo Colosio as its presidential candidate for 1994.

Rural producers made up the nuclei of the groups that came together to found El Barzón.[7] The Barzón's First National Congress was attended by representatives from twelve Mexican states, all united in the assertion that, under prevailing conditions in Mexico, falling into arrears in loan repayment should not be a mark of disgrace. Much of the debt in the rural sector was directly attributable to the flawed agricultural policies that the federal government had imposed on producers. The situation was aggravated by the Mexican producers' disadvantaged position under the North American Free Trade Agreement (NAFTA), on which they had not even been consulted. Struggling under inflated loan fees and exorbitant interest rates set by bankers and the Ministry of Finance, these debtors declared a moratorium on payments. They then turned their attention to the ballot box and the possibility of electing opposition party candidates as a way to influence government policy. At this point, there was little if any discussion of promoting internal democracy within the organization; instead the emphasis was on incorporating families (wives and children) into El Barzón protests.

Founding members of El Barzón carried their demands for credit policy reform to the nation's bankers and to President Salinas. Hoping

---

Mexican Bankers' Association stated that only 274,000 borrowers (out of some 911,000) had attempted to restructure their debt (*Siglo 21*, May 17, 1996, p. 4).

[6] The following discussion is based on the author's participant observation and on an analysis of more than 2,000 articles published from January 1993 forward in regional dailies (*Siglo 21, El Occidental, El Informador, Ocho Columnas*) and national papers (*El Financiero, La Jornada, Reforma*).

[7] Prominent among them were the Foro Permanente de Sonora and the Frente Democrático Campesino de Chihuahua. Among the first to join in Jalisco were the former municipal president of Gómez Farías, José Ramírez Yáñez, and a group of southern agroproducers.

to forestall further growth of El Barzón (and opposition electoral victories), the federal government launched PROCAMPO, an aid program for rural producers. Soon urban industrialists were demanding that the banking sector accord them the same easing of repayment terms that were being won by agricultural producers in El Barzón. And Finance Minister Guillermo Ortiz, who emerged as the principal moderator between El Barzón and the banks, made his first memorable pronouncement on this issue: he invited the banks to "move from a culture of speculation to one of production." The banking sector responded with its first restructuring of rural producers' debt. Though modest, this restructuring signaled the bankers' recognition of their unfair past practices and their willingness to accept a lower profit margin in the future. However, by proceeding on a case-by-case basis, they also demonstrated their unwillingness to deal with organizations like El Barzón, branding them as politically motivated.

Expansion and Cleavages within Debtors' Organizations

Between January 1994 and March 1995, El Barzón was in its second developmental phase, which included the organization's division into two tendencies, with their respective head offices in Zacatecas and Guadalajara. The break between El Barzón Unión (Zacatecas) and El Barzón Nacional (Guadalajara) was underscored by attacks on each other's leadership in the press, with the two directors accusing one another of partisan politics in support of either the PRI (Barzón Nacional) or the Party of the Democratic Revolution (PRD) (Barzón Unión).[8]

The two groups also differed with regard to their tactics. El Barzón Unión, in the north, became radicalized, as evidenced by the takeover of the Ciudad Juárez–El Paso international bridge by members of the Peasant Democratic Front of Chihuahua (Frente Democrático Campesino de Chihuahua), and a second tractor blockade, this one organized by El Barzón de Zacatecas. In Jalisco, the headquarters of the PRI–leaning El Barzón Nacional, there was a brief period of inactivity punctuated by lightning campaigns against banks and flurries of negotiations with the state and federal governments.

Despite these differences between leaderships and tactics, the two tendencies remained committed to their shared strategic objective. Their unity at this level enabled them to resist efforts by the Ministries of the Interior, Agriculture, and Finance, as well as the media, to co-

---

[8] In fact, Maximiano Barbosa, head of El Barzón Nacional, sought election to the legislature as a PRI candidate, and Juan José Quirino Salas, of El Barzón Unión, sought office on the PRD slate.

opt them or play them off against one another and, in the process, dilute their combined strength.

In this phase, a metamorphosis was under way in both Barzón organizations. El Barzón Unión floated a proposal at a national assembly to convert El Barzón into a political party that could represent agriculturalists nationwide, while Maximiano Barbosa, of El Barzón Nacional, backed the formation of apolitical agricultural associations. Both proposals underwent modifications over time.

El Barzón Unión began targeting urban sectors. Under the leadership of Alfonso Ramírez Cuéllar and Liliana Flores Benavides (a former PRD assemblyman and former PRD representative, respectively), the group's growth in the cities surpassed all expectations. A December 1994 count revealed a dramatic change in the organization's membership profile: 80 percent of the members were small and midsized entrepreneurs, merchants, homeowners, and credit card holders. El Barzón Unión also added 300,000 women to its member base. El Barzón Nacional, meanwhile, was increasingly active politically, becoming involved, for example, in the negotiations and power struggles of the cattlemen's union.

This second phase of the movement's development took place within a chaotic national context shaped by the emergence of the Zapatista Army of National Liberation (EZLN) and the assassination of PRI presidential candidate Luis Donaldo Colosio and his replacement by Ernesto Zedillo. It was also a moment of violent ruptures between rhetoric and practice. In an effort to impose some calm on the troubled waters in which it found itself, El Barzón began to promote democratization within the organization, and these efforts coincided with an increased presence of women as members.

Both factions established civil resistance committees to block bank repossessions. These committees, each tailored to suit its local or regional context, joined with other local groups and mounted coordinated actions that prepared their membership for the long political and legal struggle ahead. Unfortunately, these often ingenious actions lost much of their impact over time; they required a major effort to launch but were becoming easier to repress. This situation suggested that progress in resolving the issue of overdue loans at the national level would be more elusive than previously thought.

The Chiapas uprising in January 1994, spearheaded by the EZLN, renewed El Barzón leaders' energy and optimism. They offered their financial backing to the EZLN, drawing upon monies that otherwise might have gone as interest to the banks. In exchange, the Barzonistas asked Bishop Samuel Ruiz, who was mediating between the EZLN and the federal government, to include the Barzón's list of demands with others to be discussed at the negotiating table. This attempt to ally with the EZLN may well have intensified divisions within El Barzón, because it highlighted the more radical nature of El Barzón Unión.

In addition to giving support to the indigenous uprising in Chiapas, El Barzón Unión was active in urban neighborhoods, especially in Mexico City, where residents who had fallen behind in their mortgage payments were being evicted. These residents joined the cause and significantly increased the scope of El Barzón's repayment moratorium. El Barzón Unión also filed suit over the banks' exorbitant interest rates and placed payments on overdue loans in safekeeping with the courts and the National Credit Bank (NAFIN). They also petitioned the federal Senate and Chamber of Deputies to pass emergency legislation to deal with the country's economic crisis.

During this same period, the Barzón Nacional emphasized the organization's rural origins and pursued its proposal to build a campesino political organization along the lines of a "rural party." In advancing its demands, it resorted both to semi-violent tactics (including the tarring and feathering of a bank lawyer) and to legal channels. It hired the organization's first legal counsel. And it promoted the creation of regional production associations and municipal livestock associations that would be independent of national-level organizations.

At this point, the banks and the federal government presented their second proposal for debt restructuring. But once again this proposal offered debtors few viable options and seemed designed instead to mitigate the financial hardship being felt within the banking sector. El Barzón had made significant organizational advances, and its membership now covered virtually all of Mexico and a broad range of urban and rural sectors. Furthermore, the takeover of the Ciudad Juárez–El Paso bridge by Barzonistas in Chihuahua gave the movement international visibility. This prompted the Barzonistas to take their cause to Washington, D.C., in the belief that much of Mexican policy was developed in the United States.

Regrouping and Redefinition

The third phase of El Barzón's history began in March 1995 with several proposals to reunify the debtors' movement. The culmination came in December 1995 during a legislative session in the Chamber of Deputies, held at the request of El Barzón Unión and legislators from the Party of the Democratic Revolution (PRD), the National Action Party (PAN), and the Labor Party (PT), and even some from the PRI. The outcome of the debates was the formation of a debtors' front encompassing eighteen organizations. What was most notable in this effort was the Barzonistas' success in convening the debate and then convincing a broad range of organizations to abandon their partisan inclinations and work together for a debt moratorium and new rules for the banking system.

Another round of currency devaluations swelled the ranks of El Barzón even more, adding new members in such unlikely locales as Acapulco and Puerto Vallarta. Some of these new affiliates were structured like sectoral organizations, such as the Transbarzón (which grouped transportation workers), the Tortibarzón (tortilla producers), and the Artists' Barzón.

Both Barzón factions continued to grow and to pursue their strategy of building alliances. (Their leaderships also left off attacking each other publicly.) The Barzón Unión approached business organizations (including the Mexican Employers' Confederation, or COPARMEX, and the Private-Sector Coordinating Council, or CCE) and citizen groups like the Foro Ciudadano (Citizen's Forum) as potential allies in a coordinated effort to negotiate a resolution to the overdue loans issue. It even suggested establishing an alternative "economic pact," supported by a broad front of political party members, businessmen, citizens, and the EZLN.

The burgeoning membership of El Barzón Nacional led to the opening of local offices in both rural and urban areas. New rural members included producers of corn and agave, who brought renewed vitality to the organization's activities, culminating in a month-long sit-in in the heart of Guadalajara.

Both factions dismissed the restructuring programs proposed by the bankers as unrealistic. Rejecting the president as an effective mediator, the factions turned instead to members of Congress and to social groups for assistance in resolving their conflict with lenders. The two groups had different readings of the situation, however; El Barzón Unión saw the bankers' proposals as a government-inspired effort to divide the debtors and turn them against one another, whereas El Barzón Nacional saw them simply as unworkable and insufficient.

El Barzón soon stepped up its efforts to organize acts of civil disobedience and to politicize its base. It used videos as a teaching aid to educate the populace about the series of economic decisions that had left twenty-five million Mexicans in poverty, what steps to take to prevent creditors from repossessing their belongings, and how to promote movement solidarity. The organization began to present a more proactive image and to develop organizational democratization. It also made a counter-proposal to establish a tripartite "settlement trust fund," whose oversight committee would include debtors, government officials, and bankers, an approach that economists, journalists, and even bankers admitted held some potential for resolving the debtors' dilemma.

El Barzón next stepped up its blockades of banks, insurance companies, and courthouses. Government reprisals for these blockades included the arrest of some of the Barzonista leadership, and this led, in turn, to a takeover of the offices of the Ministry of the Interior (and later the offices of the Banco de México). This put El Barzón in a somewhat paradoxical situation. At the same time that it was pursuing its legal battle to change the laws regulating the banking industry and seeking alliances with business groups, it was also intensifying its strategy of civil disobedience and finding new ways to frustrate lenders', lawyers', and judges' actions against debtors.

In another paradox, members of El Barzón Nacional sought out regional opportunities for negotiating with opposition governments, like the PAN government in Jalisco. But when it had exhausted these opportunities, it then sought to open discussions with the PRI state governments and the federal government. In one instance, there was an upswelling of support for a group of small merchants about to be evicted from Guadalajara's central market. Because the officials threatening the eviction were members of the PAN, the Barzón defined the attempted evictions as PRI initiatives in PAN clothing.

The most important achievement of this period was the enactment of state laws that declared familial patrimony inalienable. On the issue of outstanding debt, however, officials from the Ministry of Finance and bank representatives refused to recognize the debtor organizations as valid interlocutors. Whatever restructuring proposals they advanced were intended, in fact, to immobilize the debtors and fractionalize their movement. And the federal government refused even to consider modifying its banking system or its development model, an inflexibility that has proven costly to taxpayers. Basically the issue of overdue debt in Mexico was at an impasse.

Toward a Political Characterization of Debtor Organizations

The brief overview offered in the preceding section sets the stage for an in-depth look at the lack of continuity between Barzonist rhetoric and practice. To a degree, these discontinuities emerged when strategies or tactics developed in advance had to be modified once they were put into action.

The following discussion covers tenets of organizational theory that coincide in identifying political strength—especially within opposition or subaltern groups—with an organization's homogeneity and capacity for collective action. Fragmentation connotes weakness. This is an important point in our discussion of El Barzón because, despite its fragmentation into Unión and Nacional, it continued to grow and to ally with existing groups. That is, divisions have not impeded the movement's expansion.[9]

The discussion also addresses some paradoxes in the development of both Barzón factions, including (1) the Barzón Unión's abandonment of its project of creating a national agrarian party in favor of becoming a multisectoral urban/rural front; and (2) the Barzón Nacional's reversal on its proposal to create apolitical and neutral organizations, opting to function instead as a coalition of rural pressure groups.

The Parts Need Not Diminish the Whole

Whether or not an organization carries out joint actions does not always correlate directly or consistently with the gains the organization can achieve or the benefits it can distribute to its membership. Although the debtors' movement pressured hard for government intervention to "put right" Mexico's malfunctioning economic system, these efforts only consolidated and began to produce visible results after the debtors drew a broad range of social sectors into their struggle. Thus any attempt to explain the Barzón's success by giving sole credit to the resources and will concentrated within the organization will miss the mark, because both of these were expressions of a circumstantial and differentiated solidarity.

The tangible benefits that the Barzón was able to deliver to its members include financial savings (payments that were withheld from creditors) and the rescue of personal belongings and property through interventions that halted repossession attempts. Although these achievements did not constitute definitive triumphs, nor did the movement suffer any catastrophic defeats, despite the breakup of some groups and the exit of whole contingents lost to the other section of El Barzón, to other debtors' groups, or to the movement entirely.

If one is attempting to understand the inconsistencies or tensions within the debtors' movement, it is of little use to begin from a utopian or abstract model of internal institutional democracy or to adopt a paradigm that excludes certain types of individual or group behaviors. Whether efforts are united or divided does not, in itself, make them effective or ineffective. Yet it is important to note that any fragmentation within the Barzón was generally attributed to manipulation by a symbolic enemy—the government, the banking sector, stockholders, or Finance Minister Ortiz and other government officials who sought to hold on to power. (These actors did indeed play

---

[9] Laclau (1993: 15) indicates that the multiplication of "public spaces" and referent groups is key to the construction of a radicalized democratic alternative.

on any divisions within the movement to dilute its demands and undercut the impact of its protest actions.) Instead of looking to models, we must develop explanations that reveal how the debtors' programmatic strategy—the right to *"barzonear"*—was forged, how it was reflected in the movement's demands in support of a range of interests, and what important social achievements were attained.

From this perspective, what distinguishes the Barzóns is the juxtaposition of their fragmentary institutional structure with the compounded relevance of their joint actions. Although the arguments expounded by the movement's leadership can appeal to an intellectual or partisan elite, the leaders themselves are also debtors and ordinary people engaged in everyday routines. Therefore, they do not calculate outcomes in the same way that leaders of professional organizations, labor unions, or political parties might do. Instead of a sustained and overarching plan, they lean toward discrete, sporadic interventions that parallel the vehemence with which the movement erupted on the political scene. The daring with which the Barzonistas have taken on Mexico's political and institutional hierarchies may appear irreverent and ingenuous. Yet they have been able to legitimize or delegitimize individuals across the country's power spectrum, while successfully avoiding being drawn into futile battles themselves.

Explaining the Organizational Paradoxes

The Barzonistas' avoidance of organizational models and the sometimes exotic, sometimes commonplace tenor of their demands constitute still other paradoxes in the Barzón experience.

According to the presidents of some Mexican banks, as well as officials such as Finance Minister Ortiz, the Barzonistas represent individual interests, and these cannot be equated with the *national* interests that the Barzonistas claim to represent. But the bankers' and officials' position also reflects their efforts to restrict the Barzón's ability to affiliate with other expressions of civil society that have a stake in the government and governmental institutions. Their arguments identify the Barzonistas as anti-Mexican and incapable of speaking for the majority of the banks' clients. These officials and bankers are marginally tolerant of the Barzonistas, but only in the interest of preserving a facade of democracy and avoiding a higher level of social unrest.

It is highly significant that the Barzonistas have staged many of their protests in places that were previously deemed off limits, the "sacred" precincts reserved to the government or other power groups. The vigor of the movement can be seen in its occupation of the Ministry of the Interior, the Banco de México and other banks, the federal Chamber of Deputies, state and municipal government palaces, and state court houses, as well as luxury hotels where the nation's bankers were convened. Mobilizations that brought massive crowds and tractor brigades into the main squares of Mexico's largest cities also left an indelible image of the Barzón's vitality.

Actions staged by the Barzón run the gamut from amusing and clever to borderline violent: piles of farm produce blocking bank entrances; bank customers presenting checks in the amount of a single peso; marches in reverse to symbolize the "backwardness" of government policies; self-styled fakirs who "sewed" their eyes shut to represent the blindness of government officials and bankers; petitions for economic asylum in foreign consulates; the burning of tractors and credit cards; farm animals brought into the federal Government Palace; lawyers "tarred" with molasses and feathered; and closures of highways and international bridges. These expressions of rural custom and urban practice merged together in a voice of rural and urban solidarity raised in support of a collection of political and economic demands.

These heterogeneous strategies respond to the varied logics—resistance, survival, negotiation, and a search for options—that combine to bring individuals together in groups to confront the authoritarian structure that is undermining their ability to survive. All of them contributed to identify arenas for mobilization and to define the debtors' collective actions.

One key to explaining the Barzón's institutional paradoxes involves two types of structural format. The first is based on the logic of the political system, which, because of its primordial concern with governability and institutionality, cannot countenance an uncontrollable phenomenon such as the emergence of a debtors' group. Recognition of such a phenomenon would imply that the society is in a situation of extreme organizational fragmentation in both its rural and urban sectors. The second is the dynamic that operates within organizations themselves and between similar organizations. This dynamic tends toward interactions that are anti-democratic, authoritarian, exclusionary, and internally and externally conditioning—largely as a result of accumulated political inertias and, in the case of Mexico, exacerbated by a situation of national economic collapse and the resulting political disarray.

Thus the level of organizational success on the issues of overdue loans and declining quality of life itself acts to regulate the internal life of the organization. The fact that the leadership has very little space for maneuver frequently incites the rank and file to exceed the leadership's control. In any case, it is clear that neither Mexican agencies charged with national security nor the experts hired by the bankers for the purpose were able to accurately gauge the breadth, nature, and disposition of the debtors' movement.[10]

Explanations for the paradoxes apparent in the debtors' movement cannot stand on a single factor or a causal link, because the movement has not followed an evolutionary trajectory free from reversals. Clearly there are certain features—specific cultural traits, the predominance of conservative values in certain rural areas, leadership styles, and a sense of opportunity—that help explain why the Barzón Nacional tended toward an organizational style that was relatively less concerned with internal democracy. But this does not mean that we can reject its actions as lacking in strategic coherence. Throughout the history of the Barzón, varied practical and well-reasoned logics have blended to create a diversity of possibilities and circumstances that are reviewed in the following paragraphs.

On a Theory for Collective Action

Reichmann and Fernández Buey (1994) posit the need to combine different theoretical approaches in order to understand the social complexity surrounding post–1968 social movements. And this complexity means that one must include in the analysis the movements' contexts and the nature of their collective action. These authors point to the inadequacy of theories that treat one or another factor of social mobilization in isolation. These approaches focus on factors such as responses to being socially excluded or economically deprived, loss of status, citizens' actions as the outcome of a cost-benefit analysis, contextual peculiarities, a lack of access to resources, the nature of citizen-government relations, cultural customs of power holders and of mobilized social networks, and movement leaders' imagination and skill. Such approaches yield partial explanations at best, but the problem of providing a comprehensive explanation for collective action remains. Ramírez Saiz (1994: 11, 1996: 31), building on work by Melucci and Touraine, suggests that social mobilization be analyzed in terms of three elements: identity, opposition, and totality.

Several identifying characteristics have remained constant throughout El Barzón's development despite internal fragmentation and discord; these include shared interests and an identifiable common enemy. The various groups of Barzonistas continue to self-identify as part of a single body of debtors. All subgroups retain the tractor as their symbol, and all carry the name "El Barzón," even as

---

[10] Journalists from *La Jornada*, *El Financiero*, and *Reforma* reportedly let it be known that the Ministries of the Interior and Finance, some banks, and the Mexican Bankers' Association sponsored studies to identify ways of restricting the growth of debtor groups.

they jockey for political space, argue over strategies, and make their individual claims as the legitimate, rightful carrier of the Barzón tradition.

A review of the history of the Barzón movement confirms that it constructed its collective identity largely through confrontation with its opponents. Given the complexity of interests represented within the organization, there have been occasions when some Barzonistas might have been tempted to replace their identified enemies— bankers and the Ministry of Finance—with a scapegoat, that is, with the other branch of El Barzón or with leaders they considered to be traitors to the cause. To date, this has not happened. Instead, we see a refining and adjusting of strategies in both Barzón organizations. This explains their development along different paths: local-level versus national-level resistance, rural versus urban organizational styles, and different forms of alliance formation, negotiation, and struggles for power.

This leads to two questions: Is El Barzón a "national" organization? And is there a model for alternation implicit in its actions and proposals? In answer to the first question, "national" is not an "institutional" attribute despite such claims by officials pretending to speak for the whole nation or by bankers who see themselves as owners of the country. The pressure that El Barzón brings to bear is constant but it is not uniform, because the organization is pursuing a range of objectives. This is visible in its appropriation of everyday spaces for civil disobedience and the establishment of groups of local intellectuals up and down the country, forming a multitude of focus points nationwide. In this sense, El Barzón's undertakings far exceed any centralized power framework or organizational control structure.

What is most important about El Barzón is not the fact that this organization targets the highest levels of government and the banking sector. Nor is it the strategies of resistance that have been developed. What is most significant is the multiplier effects—one might even say the "educational impacts"—of the actions El Barzón has undertaken.[11] The organization's capacity, its action arena, and its political impact are extended many times over because El Barzón is able to weave together, more or less simultaneously, events ongoing in the farthest corners of Mexico.

---

[11] Laclau argues that "political radicalism will not derive from a subject that embodies what is universal (ideological perfection or purity) … but rather from the expansion and multiplication of fragmentary, partial, and limited subjects that enter into a collective process of decision making" (1993: 14).

The Right to *"Barzonear"*

This author first heard mention of the "right to *barzonear*" at a meeting of women members of El Barzón Unión in August 1995. These women emphasized the need to *"barzonear,"* to carry their message to anyone, anywhere, in an effort to raise awareness and disseminate the aim of their organization. This, simply put, was to defend family patrimony. Under this definition, anyone can be a Barzonista and the organization's potential reach is limitless.

The Barzón slogan—*Debo no niego, pago lo justo,* or "I don't deny that I owe, and I'll pay what is fair"—expresses the reasoned argument collectively held within El Barzón: a debt that had been contracted during Mexico's prolonged economic crisis and whose outstanding balance had risen astronomically as a result of the December 1994 currency devaluation was unpayable, unjust, even unreal. In retaliation, the Barzonistas took aim against the authoritarian economic program that had been imposed by the Salinas and Zedillo administrations.

The "culture of repayment" is another phrase that has appeared and reappeared in recent years. For instance, at the launching of the Alliance for Housing (Alianza para la Vivienda), President Zedillo and representatives of Mexico's banking sector identified the "culture of repayment" as the ethical and institutional underpinning that gives meaning to credit agreements. Moreover, they claimed, it is an indispensable element in the healthy functioning of the financial system and the economy. This understanding, they implied, is both universally valid and without ideological overtones. The "culture of repayment" was also the argument the private sector used to seal its agreement with the Mexican government to dismantle the nationalized banking sector and reprivatize the banks in the early 1990s. And it was this agreement that then opened the door to new rules of the game for setting the price of money and interest rates during the Salinas and Zedillo presidential administrations.

By extension, the culture of repayment became a keystone in Mexico's economic model—expressing the moral exactitude with which Mexico has met its international financial obligations and, from this perspective, constituting a formula for what Mexico as a country should strive to be. By following this logic, the government came to identify the health of the banking sector as a top national priority. It cut no corners in its rescue of the banks, allocating to the rescue package twice the amount set aside in the national budget for the alleviation of poverty.

Antecedents

Arturo Warman (1972) provided a brilliant description of the web of subordination and clientelistic relationships that surrounds thousands of campesino families in Mexico. Warman called these individuals the "favorite sons" of the PRI regimes. It was in Mexico's agrarian regions that the "payment/nonpayment" logic present in El Barzón became politicized. Within clientelistic networks, loans are often extended without any expectation of repayment, and this can include loans from the Mexican government to agricultural producers. In return, the campesinos—whose natural state is presumed to be one of poverty, marginalization, and exploitation—subsidize the urban working class through cheap prices on agricultural goods. And they also cast their votes for the party in power, thereby legitimizing the system of domination imposed from the nation's urban political center.

Mexico's campesinos are well aware that they pay many times over for whatever subsidies they receive and that they get little in return for their votes. The rural population understands full well the politics of money and the humiliation of being "uncreditworthy." They have also learned to distrust legal technicalities. This is the context in which El Barzón took root.

Extending the concept of "the right to barzonear" into the urban setting has generated new definitions, and it has guaranteed wide dissemination—sometimes to an extreme, as in the inclusion of affluent individuals who, while not openly identifying themselves as Barzonistas, do know how to reap benefit from the organization's activities.[12]

This is not to say that El Barzón has no roots in urban Mexico. Collective action has a long history in the poorer neighborhoods of many Mexican cities. Typically, ringing the church bell or setting off a firecracker sufficed to gather residents together to stop an eviction when a unscrupulous property owner raised the rent beyond a tenant's ability to pay. Such situations arose when property owners failed to comprehend the falling incomes and declining living conditions of their employed, underemployed, and unemployed tenants. Community action helped reestablish a semblance of balance in this unequal relationship and gave tenants some time to negotiate a fairer settlement.

---

[12] Such is the case of well-known entrepreneurs who bought bankrupt businesses at bargain prices and then declared a moratorium on their loan payments and joined the debtors' movement.

Some Unanticipated Effects

The Barzón movement poses some problems of definition. Is this an organization comprised solely of people forced to act in their own defense? If so, how does one explain the complex handling of legal issues and the ambiguous character (and real or presumed party affiliation) of civic associations that have allied with it? And what potential does the organization have for participation or for promoting political change? In other words, how can one aggregate all of the ground-breaking initiatives that have resulted, directly or indirectly, from El Barzón's actions and juxtapose them with initiatives pursued by other citizen groups working for national political change?

Regardless of how one answers these questions, it is impossible to ignore what is taking place. El Barzón is an organization that crosses class lines, exerting an especially strong impact on the middle classes, both rural and urban. And by cutting across the corporatist divisions of Mexican society, El Barzón has also redefined the relationship between civil society and government. Furthermore, El Barzón has cast doubt on the viability of Mexico's economic model, and this will have impacts—whether officialdom recognizes it or not—on every discussion about the shape of democracy in Mexico.

Although many proposals regarding this topic are still in an embryonic stage, there has been incredible progress in a surprisingly short time. To hazard predictions as to the future would be unwise, but it is already evident that the government can no longer easily control the arenas in which discussions on democracy are taking place. Perhaps we will never be able to uncover all of the political relations and alliances that form the supporting structure for each debtor organization's struggle tactics. For this reason, allegations will continue to be made that there is an evil hand somewhere in the background, allegations that are generally made to impugn the legitimacy of the movement in general or to disparage specific groups or leaders. Nevertheless, such accusations have not yet succeeded in slowing the growth of the debtor organizations.

El Barzón has unleashed political developments that appear to be irreversible. It has exposed the limitations inherent in Mexico's legal and parliamentary framework. And it has highlighted the ineffectiveness of the courts, which have failed to hear thousands of cases, thereby confirming the urgent need to establish effective checks and balances. Furthermore, El Barzón's determination to resolve issues through local-level negotiation has demonstrated that negotiation can build the social consensus and establish the conditions of governability necessary for reaching solutions that are acceptable to all parties in conflict. In this sense, the Barzón's tactics verify that government pledges of constitutional and other reforms are meaningless if they fail to engage the active involvement of all social sectors. This is certainly true on issues such as the management of capital and the circulation of money, which underlie efforts to resolve the conflicts between debtors, bankers, and the government. Current legislation must be simplified and made more effective; even the bankers themselves have complained that the courts are ineffective. Under current law, there are few restrictions to keep bank employees from conducting informal deals with usurious lenders or other financial intermediaries. The Barzón has implicated a whole range of actors who previously went untouched: law clerks, bank employees, lenders, attorneys, and providers of alternative financing.

The Barzón's tactics, evolving over the course of the organization's activities, have yielded results. The organizational decentralization within the Barzón has raised the possibility of alternative organizational schemes that transcend limited partisan projects. Women have been very visible in the movement: in the case of El Barzón Unión, they have demonstrated their leadership capability and had significant input on strategies and demands. In effect, there has been a convergence of cries from many quarters for a different, more egalitarian Mexico.

By Way of Conclusion

The principal political impacts of the debtors' movement include the explosion of civil disobedience and the range of actions the debtors' took in support of their rights as "Barzonistas." Social struggles reveal the implicit and explicit links between citizen democracy, social democracy, and political democracy; and they expose economic neoliberalism's "neutrality" as a falsehood. To predicate the deepening of democracy on the concession of rights to some and the denial of rights to others is a futile and illusory undertaking. The real exercise of citizens' rights is key to any nation's quality of democratic life. Policy is good policy only to the extent that it improves the living conditions of the majority, and improved living standards are meaningless unless they are accompanied by full citizen inclusion in decision-making processes.

This chapter has discussed three key achievements of El Barzón: (1) the Barzonistas exposed new threats to human and civil rights that lay embedded in the formalities of financial activities, and they established a framework (outside of the formalistic proscriptions of the courts) for defending those rights; (2) they identified a decent living standard for the majority as a paramount social right and underscored the deleterious impacts of the government's policy of fiscal cutbacks; and (3) they opened new spaces for political negotiation around the issue of family patrimony.

These actions blurred the boundaries between "public" and "private," and they redefined citizens' "political rights." The new definition encompasses the radicalization of political democracy as an antidote to exclusion, as well as broadly expanded citizen participation in decision making on policies that affect the citizenry. In this sense, the debtors' struggles for survival foreshadow in many ways the arena for social movements as Mexico enters the twenty-first century.

References

Assiz, Alberto. 1996. "Para mirar un país: supuestos, mapas y hechos." In *¿Devaluación de la política social?* edited by Enrique Valencia Lomelí. Mexico: El Colegio de Jalisco.

Borge, Tomás. 1993. *Salinas: los dilemas de modernidad*. Mexico City: Siglo Veintiuno.

Foweraker, Joe. 1995. *Theorizing Social Movements*. London: Pluto.

Laclau, Ernesto. 1993. *Nuevas reflexiones sobre la revolución de nuestro tiempo*. Buenos Aires: Nueva Visión.

Ramírez Saiz, Juan Manuel. 1994. *Los caminos de la acción colectiva*. Mexico: El Colegio de Jalisco/Instituto Nacional de Antropología e Historia.

———. 1996. "Las teorías sociológicas y la acción colectiva," *Ciudades* 29: 28–40.

Reichmann, Jorge, and Francisco Fernández Buey. 1994. *Redes que dan libertad: introducción a los nuevos movimientos sociales*. Barcelona: Paidós.

Torres, Gabriel, and Guadalupe Rodríguez G. 1994. "El Barzón y Comagro: dos estrategias frente a la modernización neoliberal del campo," *Cuadernos Agrarios* 10: 70–94.

Warman, Arturo. 1972. *Los campesinos: hijos predilectos del régimen*. Mexico City: Nuestro Tiempo.

8

Reaffirming Ethnic Identity and Reconstituting Politics in Oaxaca

Luis Hernández Navarro

"Ayutla Mixe is governed by indigenous customary
practice. No party propaganda allowed." [sign in the
plaza of San Pedro y San Pablo Ayutla Mixe]

Oaxaca held municipal elections on November 12, 1995. What was
especially significant about these elections is that, for the first time in
Oaxaca's recent history, two electoral system were in operation simultaneously: the system of indigenous "customary practice" (*usos y costumbres*) and the system of registered political parties. Of Oaxaca's
570 municipalities, 412 elected their authorities according to customary practice, and 158 according to the rules governing party competition.

These elections marked the first time that the appointment of municipal authorities according to indigenous custom—that is, under the
traditional system of *cargos* and community assemblies, and with no

Much of this chapter is based on work the author conducted while serving as an ad-
viser to the Zapatista Army of National Liberation (EZLN) on indigenous rights and
culture. Other important input came from the National Coordinating Committee of
Coffee Producers' Organizations (CNOC) and the Center for Studies to Promote
Change in Rural Mexico (CECCAM). The author wishes to thank Laura Carlsen,
Adelfo Regino, Aristarco Aquino, Fidel Morales, Miguel Tejero, Josefina Aranda,
Aldo González, Ramón Vera, Eugenio Bermejillo, Hermann Bellinghausen, Gisela
Salinas, Humberto Juárez, Melquiades Rosas, Arturo Cano, Gustavo Esteva, and
Domingo García for their comments and insights. His thanks go as well to the many
Oaxacan indigenous leaders who shared their time and knowledge with him.
Translation by Sandra del Castillo.

political party participation—took place within a legal framework that also made it valid under national law.[1] Previously, municipalities in Oaxaca and other Mexican states with significant indigenous populations could elect their local governments under the system of customary practice, but candidates also had to be registered with a political party (usually the Institutional Revolutionary Party, or PRI) and the ballot had to be secret.

The outcome of this dual electoral system in the 1995 Oaxacan elections was complex and highly controversial. The PRI suffered serious setbacks in municipalities that elected their governments through the party system, even losing control of the capital city. The left-leaning Party of the Democratic Revolution (PRD) gained ground, consolidating its position as the second electoral power in the state; but the right-leaning National Action Party (PAN) also benefited from the PRI's decline in this state where the PAN has traditionally made few inroads. Seen from this perspective, the Oaxacan elections reconfirmed the national trend: the decline of the official PRI party and its increasing difficulties in winning elections. In contrast, the selection of municipal governments under the system of customary practice set a national-level precedent that was taken as a sign of an indigenous movement in triumph. It also set in motion an intense, bitter national debate between those who viewed this event as backsliding on the path to democratization and a concession to populists, and those who viewed it as a step forward in recognizing the pluricultural character of the Mexican nation.

These competing perspectives designate Oaxaca's 1995 elections as an important link in the complex political transition now under way in Mexico. They also identify the state as a laboratory in which to examine the impacts that agreements regarding indigenous rights and culture signed between the federal government and the Zapatista Army of National Liberation (EZLN) exert on Mexico's political institutions.

This electoral context also highlights the profound changes that have taken place in Oaxacan society: the impacts of federal adjustment policies, rising politicization of society, the emergence of human rights groups, the sustained mobilization of community and regional movements, the teachers' labor struggles and network building among communities, and the reaffirmation of ethnic identities that has stimulated the upsurge in political representation without recourse to political parties. The democratization of Oaxacan society—which paradoxically includes its electoral expressions—largely circumvents the prevailing party system. This chapter seeks to explain

---

[1] Under Article 41 of the Mexican Constitution, electoral participation is controlled by political parties.

the origin of this process and to reveal some of its immediate consequences.

The Political Party Path

The primary outcome of the elections conducted through the party system was the collapse of the PRI. Even though officially it won most of the contested municipalities (112, versus 32 for the PRD, 11 for the PAN, and 1 each for the Green Party [PVEM] and the PARMEO [a locally registered variant of the Authentic Party of the Mexican Revolution, or PARM]),[2] it lost in nearly all of the important municipalities, with the exception of Salina Cruz, Tehuantepec, Teotitlán, Cuicatlán, and Huautla. The municipalities won by the PAN, in contrast, are very important: Oaxaca City, Huajuapam, Tuxtepec, and Matías Romero are all leading population and economic centers. The PRD also won important municipalities, including Juchitán, Loma Bonita, Putla, Zimatlán, Etla, Sola de Vega, Nochistlán, Juquila, and Pochutla. The PRI had captured close to 90 percent of the vote in Oaxaca's 1986 elections; after the 1995 elections, it controlled only one-fifth of the state's municipalities; and of these, nearly one-fourth have fewer than 1,000 registered voters.

This collapse of the official party is even more striking when one compares the 1995 results with the PRI's dominance in elections held six years earlier. In 1989, the PRI won 535 municipal presidencies, versus 16 for the PRD, 7 for the Authentic Party of the Mexican Revolution (PARM), only 6 for the PAN, 3 for the Party of the Cardenista Front for National Reconstruction (PFCRN), and 1 for the Socialist Popular Party (PPS). Moreover, the PRI flagged in 1995 despite passage of a law in July 1989 that prohibited opposition parties from running joint candidates, despite irregularities in the voter list, despite the federal government's anti-poverty National Solidarity Program (PRONASOL), and despite a supposed modernization of government.

Further, many of the victories scored by the opposition were only marginally attributable to those parties' ideologies or to voter preference for particular opposition proposals. Although there are some clear cases where opposition parties have a real foothold in specific municipalities (as the PAN in Huajuapam or the PRD in Juchitán), in general the 1995 opposition victories were responses to other motivating factors.

The PAN's electoral victories are attributable to four different sources of party support. First, the PAN triumphed in municipalities

---

[2] These are final results, after various post-electoral conflicts.

where it had spent long years building a base of support. This is true of Huajuapam, a longtime bastion of the National Action Party and a municipality with a well-established pattern of party alternation. Second, the PAN gained ground in the state capital when it invited individuals who were not formally affiliated with the party to run on the PAN ticket. These individuals all had well-developed connections in the community, especially among the middle classes who represented an emerging political elite, and among members of the PRI who had become disillusioned with their own ticket when the state governor imposed a relative as the party's candidate to the municipal presidency. Third, in some municipalities, such as Tuxtepec, the PAN succeeded in attracting to its ranks the old PRI bosses who had been allied to Víctor Bravo Ahuja.[3] And fourth, in still other municipalities, such as San Pablo Huixtepec, the PAN was the party vehicle chosen by local anti-cacique groups, who brought a distinctly working-class flavor to the PAN campaign. In sum, the PAN's election successes in Oaxaca were driven overwhelmingly by local issues, and only in a minute degree by the National Action Party's enhanced profile nationwide.

The PRD, which in 1995 won nearly 30 percent of all votes cast statewide, owed many of its municipal electoral victories to the fact that it had previously established party offices in many areas (throughout much of the Isthmus, for example), to the presence of a strong "cardenista" current (as in the Mixteca),[4] and to alliances with emerging local political groups that see the PRD as both a kindred force and an umbrella organization (this is particularly true of local and regional citizen organizations, some to the left of the PRD). This support tends to subdivide into three independent currents (actors organized, respectively, around the Coalition of Workers, Peasants, and Students of the Isthmus [COCEI], the Democratic Campesino Union [UCD], and a core of veteran Communist Party militants); each current maintains its own organizational offices.

In many of the municipalities where citizens are staging struggles to reclaim power from local political bosses, the electorate relied on the long-standing practice of allying with whichever political party offered them the best terms for representation. In Jalapa de Díaz, this was the Green Party; in Ucila, it was the PFCRN. In other cases, such as Chilchotla, anti-cacique groups opted to register their candidates

---

[3] Bravo Ahuja was governor of Oaxaca between 1968 and 1970 and minister of education from 1970 to 1976. Born in Tuxtepec, he was at the center of a regional political group representing important livestock interests in the state.

[4] This *cardenista* current dated from 1934, when President Lázaro Cárdenas (1934–1940) instituted Mexico's agrarian reform program. It gained renewed vigor in 1988, when Cuauhtémoc Cárdenas, son of the former president, ran—and nearly won—as the National Democratic Front's (FDN) candidate to the Mexican presidency.

with the PRI. In still others, groups presented their initiatives outside of the accepted legal structure. Thus in Huautla, where three officially recognized municipal presidents held office simultaneously for the term ending in 1995, the citizenry presented an independent slate of candidates, despite the fact that such a slate cannot be legally recognized.

Customary Practice: The Oaxacan Experience

In 1995, 412 Oaxacan municipalities elected their local governments according to indigenous customary practice. This in itself was not especially noteworthy; Oaxacan communities had been choosing their leaders according to their own internal rules for years. What was new was that 1995 marked the first time these communities had a legal framework for their actions and the first time their candidates were not required to register under the banner of a political party.

The reform that gave legal recognition to customary practice in the election of municipal authorities was passed by Oaxaca's state legislature on August 30, 1995. In 1986, the state's constitution had been amended to reflect Oaxaca's multiethnic composition. The 1995 reform merely brought the state's electoral law into accord with Articles 16 and 25 of the state constitution. Article 16 recognizes the pluriethnic nature of the state's population and pledges to protect and preserve indigenous communities' forms of social organization; Article 25 protects indigenous traditions and practices regarding the selection of local government. Prior to 1995, these considerations and protections did not extend to the state's electoral laws.

The reforms outlined above are a reflection, in turn, of Mexico's ratification of Convention 169 of the International Labour Organisation, which specifies that "indigenous peoples must have the right to preserve their own customs and institutions, as long as these are not incompatible with the fundamental rights defined by the national judicial system nor with internationally recognized rights." The ratification of the convention in September 1990 and its publication in Mexico's *Diario Oficial de la Federación* on January 24, 1991, acting in conjunction with Article 133 of the Mexican Constitution, elevated these protections to the highest level of national law.

Winning legal recognition of customary practice as a legitimate route for selecting municipal governments, above and outside of the existing legal framework, can be traced to three factors. The first is the persistence of indigenous political and social institutions over time despite the encroachment of national-level institutions for political representation. The second is these communities' struggles to have their practices and institutions recognized within the national framework. The third factor is the temporal intersection of two phenomena: (1) the peasant rebellion in Chiapas in January 1994, led by the Zapatista Army of National Liberation, and its immediate mobilizing impacts in neighboring states like Oaxaca, and (2) the severe and ever-widening breach between the federal government and indigenous populations in this state.

The legislation that gives official recognition to customary practice came only as a result of sustained struggle. Oaxaca's indigenous communities and organizations pressed their demands for autonomy, services, and land for over twenty years. Their efforts were quite noteworthy; eighteen of the nineteen Mixe and Zapotec municipalities of the Sierra (with Yalalag and Guelatao the most prominent among them) coordinated their struggles and joined to form organizations like Services of the Mixe People (SER), the Union of Organizations of the Sierra Juárez (UNOSJO), COMUNALIDAD, and the Union of Indigenous Communities of the Isthmus (UCIRI), among others, which serve simultaneously as issue platforms for local officials and for ideological-political organizations seeking autonomy for indigenous peoples. The linking of these two organizational structures has promoted the entry of relatively younger members of indigenous groups into organizational leaderships, all united in reaffirming indigenous identity as an element of resistance and development.

The reform proposal that later passed into law emerged, after long deliberations, from a group of communities in Oaxaca's Sierra Norte. These communities presented their initiative to the governor-elect in October 1992 at a forum organized by the Mixe. They also demanded that Mexico's official party stop interfering in the appointment of local officials. From that point forward, indigenous groups in the state continued to develop and refine their proposal collaboratively. Their efforts intensified following the armed uprising of the EZLN in 1994.

On April 16, 1994, the federal Congress convened meetings across the country to review the application of Article 4 of the Mexican Constitution. Indigenous groups in Oaxaca refused to attend the meeting convened in Totontepec. In the words of Aldo González, a leader from the Sierra Juárez:

> They gave us only two days' notice. It was all a pretext. In Oaxaca alone, five forums were scheduled on the same day. They called us to meet in Totontepec, which is at least six hours away by truck for people in Villa Alta, Ixtlán, Tlacolula, Choapan, and the Mixe zone. We decided not to participate. It was the only forum in the whole country that did not meet that day. Even the federal deputy for this zone didn't show up (Gijsbers 1996: 39–40).

Later meetings were held in Lachirioag, Yalalag, Atitlán, and Guelatao, but none included government officials. These forums quickly turned into venues for debating the basic rights of indigenous peoples, and these debates further refined the proposal regarding customary practice that was ultimately incorporated into the law passed by the state legislature in August 1995.

This legal initiative, which emerged from the grassroots, was at first opposed by the state government, but eventually the gap between the two was closed. As Zapotec leader Aristarco Aquino, a PRD representative in the state legislature and one of the sponsors of the reform, noted:

> Governor Carrasco says he is a defender of indigenous rights. On March 21, 1994, he proposed a new relationship between the government and indigenous peoples. Yet earlier, when community leaders had offered this same proposal, he opposed it, and then in March he offered it as if he had developed it independently (Gijsbers 1996: 36–37).

The reform bill passed in the legislature despite initial opposition from the PRI and the PAN. The National Action Party, for example, voiced concerns over the need to avoid conferring "fringe" rights, reiterated the need to bring full citizenship to Mexico's indigenous peoples, and stressed the role of political parties as the path to modernization. Government officials insisted that if political parties were prohibited from participating in the political life of indigenous communities, the same restriction should apply to social organizations.

When the official PRI party finally approved the reform, it did so because the alternative was even less attractive. Failing to approve the reform would have prompted many of the indigenous communities to incorporate their platforms and candidate slates under opposition party banners, especially that of the PRD, and the decline of the PRI in indigenous areas would have been exacerbated. That is, the state government approved the legislation giving official recognition to customary practice in order to keep indigenous communities from allying electorally with the opposition.

There are some differences between the initiative that unfolded in the communities and the bill approved in the state legislature. For example, the communities' proposal listed twenty-four reforms; the legislature approved only five. One of the reforms that was voted down was the "community initiative" proposal. This reform would have limited the role of the State Electoral Institute to witnessing the selection of representatives in community assemblies and would have recognized councils of elders as legitimate consultative bodies.[5]

---

[5] For a detail examination of the community proposal, see *Ojarasca*, issue 45.

Partisan interests succeeded in insinuating a number of holes into the legislation as it made its way through the approval process. For example, elected officials can still be registered with political parties even though the parties themselves are excluded from the electoral process; and there is no requirement that authorities chosen in community assemblies be given immediate recognition. Moreover, there is no harmonization of election days; municipal elections are held at any time between September 15 and November 12.

Collective Community Life

When the Oaxacan state legislature gave official recognition to customary practice as a mechanism for selecting municipal authorities, it was only ratifying what already existed in fact. Many Oaxacan communities preserve their indigenous practices and governing institutions, and they privilege these over formal political institutions. Customary practice also provides the basis for conflict resolution within the community, making this system more than a mechanism for appointing authorities. It serves as well as a system for the administration of justice. According to Joel Aquino, a community leader in Yalaltec: "Zapotec and Mixe communities have their own legal system, one that complements rather than contradicts the national legal order" (Gijsbers 1996: 30; see also Díaz Gómez 1995; Stavenhagen 1992; Esteva 1996).

One of the basic characteristics of customary practice as a mechanism for electing authorities is its diversity. Each community has its own rules, developed from its particular experiences. In some communities, selection of leaders converges with the system of cargos, positions that carry particular responsibilities within the community. The cargo system developed during the colonial era, as a result of the merging of Spanish political restructuring policies and preexisting indigenous forms of organization. The *cargo* system is based on positions of civic and religious importance in the community, which are filled on a rotating basis by the men of the town or village. Over time, indigenous groups adapted the *cargo* model to fit their own needs, and variations now exist from community to community. Yet the system operates everywhere as a mechanism providing political representation on a rotating basis. It orders the collective life of the community, and, because it is often closely tied to agricultural cycles, it provides the communal labor that these cycles require. Under the cargo system, authority becomes synonymous with both experience and service. Political parties are completely alien in this context.

In other locales, leadership positions are filled by a show of hands or a more formal vote in community assemblies. In still others, community members select their leaders by consensus arrived at through long processes of negotiation. In the Central Valleys, selections are made by a show of hands or by ballot in general assemblies. In the Costa region, elders compose a list of names, reached through consensus, and submit it for ratification by the general assembly. In the Cañada region, authorities are elected by direct vote. In nearly half of the municipalities, the council of elders proposes candidates to the assembly. Municipal authorities in the Mixteca are chosen through a direct vote. In the Isthmus, community leaders outline the responsibilities that authorities must assume and stress the need for them to abide by the will of the community. In the Sierra, local notables direct the process, proposing candidates for consideration by the assembly (Instituto Estatal Electoral 1996; author's communication with Aristarco Aquino, Aldo González, and Adelfo Regino).

There is also a growing tendency to bring women into the decision-making process. An indigenous woman participating in the women's assembly in Anipa summarized this impetus as follows: "We women want to be included in customary practice, but with a twist. We want the custom to be respect for women."

Two key features of customary practice are its flexibility and its room for innovation, enabling indigenous communities to adapt their response strategies to community issues. This fact was acknowledged during the negotiation of Oaxaca's political-electoral reform:

> The decision is taken to recognize customary practice, by which communities select their authorities. These communities' passionate defense of their territory, culture, and traditions, in combination with their marked isolation, has generated a formidable diversity of governmental forms and electoral procedures. The proposed reform to electoral law takes these factors into consideration, limiting itself to a generic recognition of the validity of customary practice in the election of municipal authorities. If the reform attempted to incorporate the full range of variations in the state and to regulate each one, we would have to develop a set of regulations for each and every community, and this would contradict the spirit of the law, which aims to be general and abstract (Instituto Estatal Electoral 1995: 5).

As noted earlier, political parties have no role in these processes. Under the cargo system, authority is conferred based on tasks accomplished and politics is synonymous with service to the community. Party politics in such a context serves only to divide communities, especially when the parties hold monopoly control over the electoral process. To require that leaders selected by their community be reconfirmed through a vote is redundant. And worse, requiring such confirmation opens the door to vote manipulation and electoral fraud.

The struggle to win recognition of customary practice is part of a larger worldview that has emerged within indigenous communities in Oaxaca and elsewhere. It is generally referred to as communality. Communality is the driving force in the indigenous movement, and it is premised on three basic principles. First, it is the community, the collective, that shapes individual destinies in harmony with an individual's own interests. Second, humans are a part of nature, not its center. The growth of populations and communities is directly linked to respect for the natural world. And third, indigenous peoples must reaffirm their differences and diversity, giving this issue preference over policies to impose strict equality and homogeneity. People are not superior or inferior, just different. A key component of communality is communal power: the people hold the power to take and implement decisions, with core decisions being made in the general assembly and community members obeying the collective mandate. Other central characteristics are communal land tenure and communal labor.[6]

The staying power of customary practice confirms both its value as what Guillermo Bonfil called the "indigenous people's other civilizing matrix" (1987) and its contribution to the survival of indigenous peoples under extremely adverse conditions. According to a member of the Committee for Communal Goods in San Pablo Yagañiza: "We did not invent customary practice, but it is only thanks to customary practice that we have survived" (Gijsbers 1996: 56). His words are both a claim to his right to be different and a claim to a strategy for survival.

The Roots of 1995

Oaxaca's 1995 elections marked the culmination of a complex social interaction that combined the impacts of national adjustment policies, a rupture in the regional system of domination, indigenous groups' demands for autonomy, several rounds of teacher strikes, growing popular concern for human rights, a tradition of community mobilization, and the beginnings of political-military projects promoting practical forms of self-defense within regions. As Moisés Bailón noted:

---

[6] This brief mention of communality is based on a fuller description developed by Adelfo Regino, Mixe representative to the National Indigenous Congress. On this topic, also see Martínez Luna 1993; Díaz Gómez 1988.

> The Oaxacan power structure rests on procedures for po-
> litical mediation and intermediation with the state's major
> populations: urban salaried workers, organized urban
> middle sectors, the poor, and, especially, rural municipali-
> ties. Just as the political boss tries to manipulate the com-
> munity according to his own ends, the indigenous leader
> will recur to his traditional authority structures, his people,
> his language (Bailón 1991: 37).

These mechanisms of intermediation have been eroding at a fast pace in recent years, under the force of grassroots struggles, fragmentation within the traditional political class, and the spread of rural poverty.[7]

One indicator of the political breakdown that has occurred in Oax-aca is the state's human rights situation. Between June 1990 and May 1996, Oaxaca's state government earned the dubious honor of being named in the greatest number of appeals (fifty-six) submitted to Mexico's National Human Rights Commission (CNDH). The state-level commission, for its part, received 939 complaints between June 1995 and June 1996. The Mazatec Community Assembly of Mazatlán Villa de Flores prepared a report on the thirty-plus assassinations of municipal officials and indigenous leaders that had taken place in the state beginning in 1995. The appearance of the Popular Revolutionary Army (EPR) has produced even more violations of human rights:

> The frequency and severity of human rights violations in
> Oaxaca merit special attention from both the state and the
> federal government. Efforts must be undertaken at both
> levels of government to redress past violations and to keep
> these abuses from continuing into the future (Rohde 1996:
> 7).[8]

Several relatively sustained cycles of peasant struggle in Oaxaca began in 1970, centering first on issues of land tenure, and later on demands for an adequate supply of basic foods and for control of the productive process. These mobilizations quickly took on anti-cacique, pro-democracy overtones (see Fox 1992; Moguel 1991; Aranda 1988; Székely and Madrid 1990), and they often evolved into attempts to win control of municipal governments (see Díaz Montes 1992; Barabás and Bartolomé 1986; Hernández and Fox 1994). And, most important, they gave rise to a broad range of regional campesino or-ganizations, to an experienced and embedded leadership, a participa-

---

[7] According to data from the World Bank, the number of rural poor in Oaxaca, Chia-pas, and Guerrero has increased by 24 percent since 1989. For an analysis of the situation in rural Oaxaca and recent World Bank policies, see Fox and Aranda 1996.

[8] For the CNDH's recommendations, see *La Jornada*, October 22, 1996. Concerning the human rights situation in Oaxaca, see Centro de Derechos Humanos 1996.

tory culture intent on recovering its ethnic identity, and a new correlation of forces between the indigenous peasant communities and the
federal government.

Elementary schoolteachers play a key role in Oaxaca's political
and social life. Their mobilizations, which began in 1980, severed
many of the state's traditional mediation arrangements. The teachers
spread their struggle tactics to other sectors, promoted the organization of new social groups, and supported the formation of new political elites. Teachers in support of bilingual education were particularly
effective in networking with indigenous communities.[9] Unfortunately,
the outcome of these efforts has not been uniform. According to
Miguel Bartolomé (1994: 79),

> In many cases, teachers have stimulated the development
> of an organic awareness directed at recovering indigenous
> cultures, thereby playing an important role in the ideologi-
> cal revitalization of these peoples. But in other cases, the
> teachers have become cultural intermediaries, cultural bro-
> kers, at the service of institutional interests.

Oaxaca has a long tradition of associational community life, visible
under normal conditions but also under abnormal conditions such as
migration. This tradition is a key factor in explaining how these communities endure and how they resist federal authority. It is also a
strong element for explaining the enormous importance that municipal governments hold for many of these populations. In their efforts
to withstand continuing onslaughts of modernization, indigenous
peoples in Oaxaca seem to have revitalized and reinforced their civic-
ethnic associationalism as a survival strategy.

As a whole, these factors—along with the upsurge of issues surrounding ethnic identity—appear to have undermined the regional
system of domination and promoted the change in the correlation of
forces that was expressed electorally on November 12, 1995.

Political Representation and Indigenous Peoples

At least one of every ten Mexicans is a member of an indigenous ethnic group. According to a study carried out by the National Indigenous Institute (INI), Mexico's indigenous population totals 8,701,688
in 59 different ethnic groups.[10] Some, like the Mixes, are spatially con-

---

[9] On the teachers' movement in Oaxaca, see Cook 1990, 1996. On the teachers' community network building, see Hernández 1990, 1995.

[10] On Mexico's indigenous groups, see Embriz 1993. For a detailed critique of Embriz's
methodology, see Bartolomé 1996.

centrated; others, like the Nahuas, are dispersed across several states. Some indigenous groups are large; others are represented by a few families only. All live in alarming conditions of extreme poverty and marginality. In Mexico, to be Indian is to be poor. Nearly all municipalities in Mexico that are 90 percent or more indigenous are classified as extremely poor. According to a National Population Council (CONAPO) study based on the 1984 census, more than three-quarters of Mexico's indigenous population lives in 281 municipalities classified as extremely marginalized. Nearly half of the indigenous population is illiterate, versus 12 percent for the national population overall. Nearly half of the indigenous municipalities have neither electricity nor potable water, against national averages of 13 percent and 21 percent, respectively, for these services. In nearly 60 percent of indigenous municipalities, the inhabitants are forced to migrate, although this survival strategy does not necessarily improve their situation. Between 70 and 84 percent of indigenous youngsters under five years of age are malnourished,[11] and the mortality index for this age group is 26 percent, compared to a national figure of 20 percent. Eighty percent of childhood illnesses are infectious diseases associated with malnutrition, anemia, and unsanitary living conditions.

An inescapable correlate of poverty is injustice. In 1993, prior to the appearance of the EZLN in Chiapas, 170 Indians were killed, 18 "disappeared," 367 illegally detained, 3,620 victimized, 21 held in solitary confinement, 410 wounded, 7 kidnapped, and 37 tortured. These violations of human rights are attributable to political repression, land conflicts, and problems in delivering and administering justice. According to Jorge Madrazo Cuéllar, president of the National Human Rights Commission, Mexico's courts fall far short of having the necessary infrastructure—translators and judges knowledgeable in indigenous customary practice—to hear cases involving indigenous individuals (1995: 155).

This situation is directly attributable to the country's failure to recognize indigenous institutions and to indigenous people's lack of political representation in state and federal government. There is no correlation between the size of the indigenous population and the number of indigenous individuals holding posts in government. The number of indigenous individuals in local legislatures and the national Congress is extremely limited, in large part because concentrations of indigenous populations tend not to correspond to electoral districts. The same situation prevails at the municipal level, even in municipalities that are predominantly indigenous, which tend to be governed by urban mestizos.

---

[11] These data are drawn from the *Informe Nacional sobre Seguridad Alimentaria* as reported in *Reforma*, November 1, 1996.

This lack of formal political representation holds serious implications for indigenous groups, and it even extends to government agencies dedicated to indigenous issues. These offices design their policies, implement their programs, identify their beneficiaries, and evaluate the results without involving the populations themselves.

Oaxaca is home to 18.3 percent (3,224,270 individuals) of Mexico's indigenous population. Yet these individuals, forced into migration streams, tend to be scattered throughout nearly all of Mexico and the southern United States. Census data indicate that over 52 percent of Oaxacans speak an indigenous language and belong to one of sixteen ethnic groups (Embriz 1993).[12]

Oaxaca is also the target of one-third of the federal government's programs directed at indigenous groups. The INI has been active in the state since 1954, but, according to Gonzalo Aguirre Beltrán, Mexico's indigenous policies were not policies formulated by indigenous groups for indigenous problems. They were policies imposed by the majority population on groups they designated as "indigenous" (quoted in Díaz-Polanco 1996). The INI's core objective was to convert indigenous peoples into Mexicans, which has had deleterious effects on these communities.

For electoral purposes, Oaxaca is divided into 25 electoral districts comprising 7,210 communities, of which 98 percent are rural. Although the large number of municipalities in Oaxaca offers the indigenous population relatively easier access to political representation than is available in states with fewer municipalities, there are barriers and hurdles that undercut indigenous groups' ability to organize and gain input in shaping the government policies that govern their lives.

Despite this situation, Oaxaca is experiencing significant ethnic vitality, in both its communities and its organizations. For example, a vibrant cultural movement is afoot to preserve indigenous languages and increase the population of speakers (Montemayor 1995). This has also produced a flowering of literature written in indigenous languages.

A new cohort of indigenous leaders has emerged, and the number of indigenous political organizations has multiplied. These organizations use the affirmation of ethnic identity as a basis on which to construct platforms for community action and efforts directed toward alternation in power, and they have allied with one another in broad networks. Organizations like the COCEI and the Frente Democrático de Tlacolula, which give political authority to social organizations active in electoral processes, are becoming more common. Indigenous groups have also formed fronts—like the Frente Cívico Mazateco and

---

[12] According to Bartolomé (1994), this number will soon be reduced to eleven, because several groups are on the brink of extinction.

the earlier Asamblea de Autoridades Mixes—that restore indigenous normative systems. Progressives within the Catholic Church have played a key role in this process (Muro 1994). They have promoted initiatives for indigenous groups' self-government and have helped educate the new indigenous intellectual elite. The holding of municipal elections according to customary practice was a high point in this organizational process; it also marked the beginning of a new phase of struggle.

The Electoral Experience

Municipalities holding elections by customary practice experienced a variety of problems on election day. In approximately 284 of these municipalities, the PRI, capitalizing on its dual identity as both political party and government, tried to register the elected officials as party members. In San Juan Cotzocom, San Antonio Eloxochitlan, and San Cristóbal Lachirioag, locals were able to block this PRI strategy, but in other locales the PRI took the citizenry unawares and succeeded. The party was able to do this primarily because the new reform law had not yet been thoroughly disseminated among indigenous communities.

In Mazatlán, Ayutla, and San Juan Lalana, caciques, collaborating with the PRI and officials, claimed their right to party affiliation, thereby hoping to impede the implementation of customary practice. In San Juan Lalana, several local and regional officials tried to register a PRI slate; when they were blocked, they then attempted to impose their candidates by force. Officials also tried to impose candidates in Ayutla. In Mazatlán, armed PRIistas opposed to the system of customary practice closed down the municipal government for several months (Agresiones n.d.).

In Tenango, a broad coalition of local organizations was unsuccessful in its efforts to hold elections according to customary practice and ultimately had to register its candidates with the PRD. The PRI responded with an aggressive campaign of vote buying and coordinated attacks against the opposition. When the PRI was declared the victor in these elections, the opposition coalition took over the municipal palace and held it for months.

Choosing officials by customary practice is not automatically more democratic than other methods. It can even pave the way for continuing boss rule in communities where the system is not well developed. During the 1995 elections there were reports of government officials telling communities that, because the PRI had "customarily" appointed officeholders in the past, this was the "practice" that should be continued. Yet, despite such cases, many communities used customary practice as a means to achieve transparent self-government and to root out the caciques.[13] There is also some evidence to suggest that in municipalities where women or other groups are traditionally disenfranchised, despite these communities' supposed reliance on customary practice, the vote is not really open and free. In these locales, the PRI routinely "goes to the trouble" of marking the votes in its favor.

Generally speaking, caciques, both Indian and non-Indian, derive their power from their control of economic and political power, but also from their control of government and party functions. They control PRI committees and make use of government agencies for their own benefit. In Oaxaca, they also serve as government representatives, to the point that it is difficult to differentiate between the Institutional Revolutionary Party and the government. Party colors are government colors; party members are members of government. Election campaigns publicize government programs or, at minimum, parallel government policies. When communities elect their local governments through customary practice, they break the symbiotic PRI–government–caciques relationship, something they would be hard pressed to do if working through the party system.

A detailed analysis of community struggles would demonstrate how customary practice has been adapted to include women and youths (as in Tlahuitoltepec), non-Catholics, in roles that carry no religious responsibilities (as in San Pablo Yaganiza), and a broad range of municipal organizations (as in Mazatlán Villa de Flores). Although change has been neither linear nor automatic, the trend is very clear.

It is also important to note that indigenous communities are being subjected to a number of stresses—from both within and without—that tend to undermine their cohesiveness: market forces, government policies and programs, internal social differentiation, and exploitation as "vote repositories" for the PRI. Many of the human rights violations in these communities derive directly from the intertwining of indigenous community and PRI–government.

The Ensuing Debate

Oaxaca's 1995 municipal elections provided a starting point for a debate on the nature and usefulness of mechanisms for political representation based on customary practice. Critics saw them both as a populist weakness and as a path to continued rule by political

---

[13] See, for example, the case of Yalalag (Equipo Pueblo 1988).

bosses.[14] But supporters saw them as an affirmation of their rights and as the route to national democratization.

The debate has now become part of the broader negotiations regarding the relationship between the federal government and indigenous populations that began between the EZLN and the federal government in San Andrés Larráinzar. This is not an item placed on the agenda from above. Quite the opposite. The framework for establishing a new relationship has emerged, forcefully, from the grassroots. It is supported by a vigorous indigenous movement that has gained tremendously in representational and mobilizational capacity since the Zapatistas appeared on the scene in January 1994. It is also supported by international organizations of which Mexico is a member country, which maintain that racial discrimination persists in the country and that the government is failing to curtail this discrimination with appropriate legislation.

Opponents of election by customary practice have advanced an array of arguments. They have called such elections anti-democratic, populist, racist, and pro-cacique. They claim they erode the party system, and they assert that the only legitimate means for electing governments is via direct and secret universal suffrage *and* political parties. Such opinions generally reflect a lack of understanding regarding the value that customary practice holds for indigenous peoples. But customary practice retains its widespread legitimacy within indigenous communities, and it is making a rapid comeback in communities where it had grown weak.

Party System versus Customary Practice

The outcomes of the party system elections, along with some electoral results reached through the customary practice system, provoked serious post-election conflicts. The rout of the PRI sparked a violent response from party militants in the Isthmus. They blocked highways, burned election materials, and took over public buildings—actions usually associated with opposition parties. The COCEI–PRD, for its part, also fed post-electoral frictions, but more as a preemptive strike aimed at opening an alternative negotiating space and assuring that they would not lose control of the Juchitán municipal government.

Violence surged in several municipalities where the PRI tried to steal the elections. One notable incident took place in Mazatlán Villa de Flores, when local PRI partisans launched an armed attack against the opposition. They killed one person in the attack, and they arrested

---

[14] See, for example, the essays by Fernando Escalante in *Vuelta* or those by Sergio Sarmiento and Federico Reyes Heroles in *Reforma*. Defenders of customary practice include Gustavo Esteva, Salomón Nahmad, and Julio Moguel.

and jailed the opposition-party municipal president. Gunmen work-ing for the PRI also threatened the life of the PRD candidate in Putla.

The state legislature had to declare electoral results null and void in ten municipalities, two voting by party system and eight abiding by customary practice. In Santiago Yiaitepec and San Mateo del Mar, the state government appointed municipal administrative councils rather than reschedule elections. Although elections were rescheduled in Asunción Ixtaltepec, these were never held, and this municipality also got a municipal administrative council. A second round of elec-tions in Gueva de Humbolt and Mazatlán Villa de Flores produced victories for the community slates over the PRI.

In general terms, these new governmental "constructions" are based only tangentially on registered political parties. With a small number of exceptions—the PAN in Huajuapam and the PRD in parts of the Isthmus and the Mixteca—parties have few organic links to these new governments. They tend, rather, to give their "stamp of approval" to community candidates in exchange for votes.

Liberal democracy has not empowered indigenous communities to escape the control of political bosses. Quite the opposite. The PRI continues to use indigenous communities to inflate the party's vote totals. If the government uses liberal democracy to defeat customary practice among indigenous populations, it will condemn these peo-ples to a context in which the correlation of forces works very much against them.

This fact has clear repercussions on how politics operates in Oax-aca. Neither local legislatures nor state agencies can serve as vehicles for reaching meaningful political agreements, unless, of course, one aims to preserve a political fiction.

Recognizing customary practice as part of the electoral process is important for a number of reasons. First, it ends the mockery of su-perimposing an official electoral system on indigenous institutions and practices. Second, it curtails the PRI's illegitimate use of indige-nous votes. Third, it opens the door further for indigenous self-government at the municipal level and advances groups' claims to recognition as indigenous peoples.[15] Fourth, it ends the PRI's monop-oly control over elections and opens up the electoral process to the

---

[15] The author understands "indigenous people" as defined in Convention 169 of the International Labour Organisation on Indigenous and Tribal Peoples: According to Article 1, Section b, they "are considered to be indigenous because they are de-scended from populations that inhabited the country or regions that belonged to the country at the time of the Conquest or colonization, or during the establishment of current state boundaries, and that, whatever their legal situation, they retain all or part of their own social, economic, cultural, and political institutions." Article 2 indi-cates that: "The consciousness of a tribal or indigenous identity should be considered as a fundamental criterion for determining to which groups the resolutions of the present Convention apply."

broad spectrum of political and social forces taking shape throughout Mexico. Large sectors of Mexico's population view politics and politicians with suspicion, and the country's political institutions are becoming weaker day by day. At a moment like this, the indigenous tradition that defines politics as service to the community and political representation as responsibility gives these groups the moral strength to rebuild their communities. In the face of "modernization through market shocks," customary practice enables communities to defend themselves and reconstruct their identities.

A far-reaching revamping of political mediation is under way in Oaxaca, and ethnopolitical and community-based civic movements have taken the offensive. Whatever new forms emerge will have to take this new reality into account.

References

Agresiones. n.d. "Agresiones activadas por el grupo armado del PRI y del gobierno del estado en contra del pueblo mazateco de Mazatlán Villa de Flores, como un intento más de frenar el avance de las comunidades por recuperar su poder de decisión y de regresar el poder municipal a la familia caciquil priísta." Report to Interamerican Commission on Human Rights.

Aranda, Josefina, ed. 1988. *Las mujeres en el campo*. Mexico: Instituto de Investigaciones Sociológicas, Universidad Autónoma "Benito Juárez" de Oaxaca.

Bailón, Moisés J. 1991. "Sistema de dominio regional y Juntas de Administración Municipal en Oaxaca." In *Insurgencia democrática: las elecciones locales*, edited by Jorge Alonso and Silvia Gómez Tagle. Guadalajara: Universidad de Guadalajara.

Barabás, Alicia M., and Miguel A. Bartolomé, eds. 1986. *Etnicidad y pluralismo cultural: la dinámica étnica en Oaxaca*. Mexico City: Instituto Nacional de Antropología e Historia.

Bartolomé, Miguel A. 1994. "La represión de la pluralidad. Los derechos indígenas en Oaxaca." In *Derechos indígenas en al actualidad*. Mexico City: Universidad Nacional Autónoma de México.

———. 1996. "De mayoría a minoría," *Crónica Legislativa*, no. 7 (February–March).

Bonfil, Guillermo. 1987. *México profundo: una civilización negada*. Mexico City: Secretaría de Educación Pública/CIESAS.

Centro de Derechos Humanos "Miguel Agustín Pro Juárez." 1996. "La violencia en Oaxaca." Mexico City: Centro, August.

Cook, Maria. 1990. "Organizing Opposition in the Teachers' Movement in Oaxaca." In *Popular Movements and Political Change in Mexico*, edited by Joe Foweraker and Ann L. Craig. Boulder, Colo.: Lynne Rienner, in association with the Center for U.S.–Mexican Studies, University of California, San Diego.

————. 1996. *Organizing Dissent: Unions, the State, and the Democratic Teachers' Movement in Mexico*. University Park: Pennsylvania State University Press.

Díaz Gómez, Floriberto. 1988. "Principios comunitarios y derechos indios," *México Indígena* 25 (September).

————. 1995. "Contribuciones a la discusión sobre derechos fundamentales de los pueblos indígenas." Mexico: SER.

Díaz Montes, Fausto. 1992. *Los municipios: la disputa por el poder local en Oaxaca*. Oaxaca: Instituto de Investigaciones Sociológicas, Universidad Autónoma "Benito Juárez" de Oaxaca.

Díaz-Polanco, Héctor. 1996. "El indigenismo simulador," *La Jornada*, October 28.

Embriz, Arnulfo, ed. 1993. *Indicadores socioeconómicos de los pueblos indígenas de México*. Mexico City: Instituto Nacional Indigenista.

Equipo Pueblo. 1988. "Testimonios indígenas. Yalalag." Mexico: Equipo Pueblo.

Esteva, Gustavo. 1996. "Derecho y pueblos indios: de la pluralidad al pluralismo." Oaxaca, October.

Fox, Jonathan. 1992. *The Politics of Food in Mexico: State Power and Social Mobilization*. Ithaca, N.Y.: Cornell University Press.

Fox Jonathan, and Josefina Aranda. 1996. *Decentralization and Rural Development in Mexico: Community Participation in Oaxaca's Municipal Funds Program*. Monograph Series, no. 42. La Jolla: Center for U.S.–Mexican Studies, University of California, San Diego.

Gijsbers, Wim. 1996. "Usos y costumbres: caciquismo e intolerancia religiosa," *Campo* (Oaxaca).

Hernández, Luis. 1985. "Otra vez en el camino," *Información Obrera* 59 (July).

————. 1990. "Maestros y autogestión: la construcción social de la autonomía." In *De las aulas a las calles*. Información Obrera–Equipo Pueblo.

Hernández, Luis, and Jonathan Fox. 1994. "La difícil democracia de México: los movimientos de base, las ONGs y el gobierno local." In *Nuevas políticas urbanas: las ONG y los gobiernos municipales en la democratización latinoamericana*, edited by Charles A. Reilly. Arlington, Va.: Fundación Interamericana.

Instituto Estatal Electoral de Oaxaca. 1995. "Comentarios a la iniciativa de reformas al código de instituciones políticas y procedimientos electorales del estado de Oaxaca," In "Mesa de Negociación para la Reforma Político-Electoral del Estado de Oaxaca." Mexico: Comisión Especial de Análisis y Propuestas para la Reforma.

————. 1996. "Memoria de los Procesos Electorales de Diputados y Concejales 1995." Mexico: Instituto.

Madrazo Cuéllar, Jorge. 1995. "Derechos humanos, cultura y reforma indígena," *Revista del Senado de la República* 2 (January–March).

Martínez Luna, Jaime. 1993. "¿Es la comunidad nuestra identidad?" In *Movimientos indígenas contemporáneos en México*, edited by Arturo Warman and Arturo Argueta. Mexico City: Universidad Nacional Autónoma de México/Miguel Angel Porrúa.

Moguel, Julio. 1991. "La Coordinadora Estatal de Productores de Café de Oaxaca." In *Cafetaleros: la construcción de la autonomía*, edited by Luis Hernández and Gabriela Ejea. Cuadernos de Desarrollo de Base, no. 3. Mexico.

Montemayor, Carlos. 1995. *Encuentros en Oaxaca*. Mexico City: Aldus.

Muro, Víctor Gabriel. 1994. *Iglesia y movimientos sociales en México, 1972–1987. Los casos de Ciudad Juárez y el Istmo de Tehuantepec*. Mexico: Red Nacional de Investigación Urbana/El Colegio de Michoacán.

Rohde, Clifford C. 1996. *The Rule of Lawlessness in Mexico: Human Rights Violations in the State of Oaxaca*. Minneapolis, Minn.: Minnesota Advocates for Human Rights; and Chicago, Ill.: Heartland Alliance for Human Needs & Human Rights.

Stavenhagen, Rodolfo. 1992. "Los derechos indígenas. Algunos problemas conceptuales." Paper presented at the seminar "Derechos Humanos, Justicia y Sociedad," 1992, Buenos Aires.

Székely, Miguel, and Sergio Madrid. 1990. "La apropiación comunitaria de recursos naturales, un caso de la Sierra Juárez, Oaxaca." In *Recursos naturales, técnica y cultura. Estudios y experiencias para un desarrollo alternativo*, edited by Enrique Leff, Julia Carabias, and Ana Irene Batis. Mexico City: Universidad Nacional Autónoma de México/Secretaría de Desarrollo Urbano y Ecología/United Nations Environmental Program.

9

Zapotec and Mexican: Ethnicity, Militancy, and Democratization in Juchitán, Oaxaca

Jeffrey W. Rubin

In the city of Juchitán in the Isthmus region of Oaxaca, Indian peasants who take legal action to protect their land speak Zapotec in city hall. Teenagers from poor neighborhoods write poetry in Zapotec at the Casa de la Cultura. Women in Juchitán maintain standards of beauty dramatically different from Mexican national ones, donning brightly patterned and embroidered clothing that defies Western norms of color and style. Such norms are also challenged by a flourishing alternative male gender role, with males in varying arrangements of women's dress and body forms dancing with one another at fiestas and playing prominent public roles in work and ritual.

In the 1980s, Juchitán's peasant economy of maize production survived government-sponsored agricultural projects and urban commercialization. The sprawling Zapotec market, consisting of hundreds of women vendors, continues to dominate the space and economy of the center of the city and to constitute the most important lo-

This chapter is based on field research carried out in Juchitán in 1983, 1985, 1986, and 1993, and funded by the Social Science Research Council, the Doherty Foundation, the Inter-American Foundation, the Tinker Foundation (through a grant to the Committee on Latin American and Iberian Studies at Harvard University), and Amherst College. The author is grateful to the Center for U.S.–Mexican Studies and to Wayne Cornelius for providing an inspiring research environment in which to carry out portions of this work, as well as for inviting the author's participation in the Mexico City conference at which the first draft of this chapter was presented. He is also grateful to Vivienne Bennett for discussions about the effects of presidential and gubernatorial cycles on grassroots mobilization.

cal network of information. Zapotec midwives deliver the majority of babies born in Juchitán, and the descendants of Lebanese immigrants wear traditional dress and encourage their university-educated children to continue Zapotec traditions. Altogether, the society forged by Juchitecos provides an example of what "development" might have looked like if indigenous and Western cultures had met on more equal terms: not necessarily a rejection of the "Western" or "modern," or a reinforcing of geographic and cultural borders between local and outside, but rather the creation of multiple modernities by means of non-Western knowledge, language, and style.[1]

A Zapotec political movement, the Coalition of Workers, Peasants, and Students of the Isthmus, or COCEI, has governed Juchitán since 1989. Virtually without precedent among indigenous and leftist political organizations, the COCEI is recognized by the Mexican government as a legitimate and autonomous political force.[2] It administers social welfare funds for the city of 100,000 with widely acknowledged efficiency, promotes Zapotec language and culture, and mobilizes poor people around pressing economic issues. The COCEI secured this right to govern through fifteen years of militant grassroots activism, during which it faced regime-sanctioned killings and military occupation. Since 1989, in contrast, Mexican authorities have respected the results of democratic elections in Juchitán, invested in municipal services, and curbed human rights abuses, outcomes that are particularly noteworthy in light of decades of polarized conflict in nearby Chiapas and Guerrero. By making use of local capacities for cultural resistance and appropriation to construct an organized movement and gain formal political power, the COCEI brought about a complex and uneven regional democratization that involves ongoing negotiation over cultural representation and economic justice.

This democracy includes, but is not limited to, free and fair electoral competition and the transfer of municipal power. The COCEI's actions in Juchitán also contributed to forms of voice and autonomy in churches, marketplaces, teachers' unions, municipal offices, and family courtyards. As a result, poor Juchitecos in the 1990s had greater voice—and could hold those with power more accountable—in more arenas of their lives than they had in the 1960s and 1970s. Juchitecos

---

[1] In viewing Juchitán as a site of alternative forms of development, the author is indebted to Arturo Escobar for his critique of the Western discourse of development and his suggestions for reimagining encounters between Western and "Third World" locations and cultures (Escobar 1995).

[2] The Popular Defense Committee of Durango (CDP) achieved such recognition at approximately the same time as the COCEI, early in the Salinas administration. The armed Zapatista movement in Chiapas seems to have gained a similar status, though its survival continues to be threatened by military occupation and paramilitary violence.

exercised such voice and accountability in their participation in ritual and artistic activity, their relatively unproblematic assertion of their ethnic and gender identities, their capacity to pressure agrarian agencies and labor courts for fair treatment, their ability to solve local problems by local means, their freedom to bring their own language to official offices, their access to complex networks of information, and their influence in municipal governments that repeatedly secured funding from the federal government during periods of national economic crisis.

In this context, the COCEI's internal characteristics and its role as governing party have been tempestuous and contradictory. A nonviolent movement, it has nevertheless incited turbulence and threat. Claiming to be democratic, it has limited dissent and reached decisions nondemocratically, while at the same time reinvigorating electoral competition for public office. As municipal administration, it has paved streets and installed drainage honestly and transparently but neglected to develop new leadership and forward-looking economic programs. Many of the COCEI's historical claims contradict the experiences of ordinary Juchitecos; and despite the COCEI's extensive promotion of images of women's activism, women are excluded from positions of political leadership and artistic innovation in the movement.

The COCEI's internal characteristics thus differ from those of conventional portraits of leftist grassroots movements, including many depictions of the COCEI itself. Such descriptions, which emphasize congruence between the claims of leaders and the experiences of supporters, as well as homogeneity of consciousness among members of a radical movement, are captured in representations of COCEI leaders and the COCEI itself as children of the *pueblo* fighting against oppression. In contrast, the complexity of the COCEI's internal dynamics makes the movement, like the regime itself, the sum of many different, often competing parts.

The path from violence in the streets to multifaceted democracy in Juchitán covered several stages. The COCEI began in the early 1970s as a leftist coalition of workers, peasants, and students in Juchitán and surrounding Isthmus communities. In its first decade, the COCEI organized militant mobilizations of unprecedented size and fervor around issues of land, labor, and urban services, winning partial gains in these areas in the face of violence and military intervention. In 1981, in the context of a national political reform process, the COCEI successfully pressured the Mexican government to recognize the movement's victory in municipal elections, making Juchitán the first and only city in Mexico with a leftist government. This led to two years of radical administration—an unprecedented *ayuntamiento popular*, or people's government—with the COCEI

challenging class inequalities concerning land and labor and bringing the social activities and Zapotec culture of ordinary Juchitecos
to the center of city life. As a result, Juchitán became a symbol and
rallying point for the Left throughout Mexico, its transformed municipal spaces attracting national and international visitors and
publicity.

In 1983, in the face of what newly organized business and political
groups characterized as an escalating regional threat, the COCEI was
thrown out of office by the state legislature and the army. Several
COCEI leaders were imprisoned, and the army established permanent barracks at strategic locations around the city. Armed soldiers
stood guard on the balconies of city hall, maintaining nonstop surveil-
lance over the building and the city's central square for five years.
However, in a mixture of repression and restraint characteristic of the
Mexican regime, military occupation was combined with large-scale
state investment and relative respect for civil liberties (in comparison
with the 1970s).

In this context, the COCEI was able to resume its direct action organizing and electoral campaigning. The movement once again made
successful use of protest mobilizations to gain entry into a coalition
government in Juchitán in 1986, and it has won elections and governed Juchitán since 1989. The COCEI administration of Municipal
President Héctor Sánchez, in office from 1989 to 1992, won universal
praise for its efficiency and honesty in implementing projects of street
paving and drainage with funds from the National Solidarity Program (PRONASOL, the national social welfare initiative). This exemplary competence with regard to public works, a symbolic and practical centerpiece of municipal politics in Juchitán, differentiated the
work of the COCEI government from the disregard and corruption
that had characterized previous Institutional Revolutionary Party
(PRI) administrations.

In addition to public works, the politics of the COCEI in office
demonstrates both the opportunities and challenges that face the Left
when it governs. In late 1993, the last time this author was in Juchitán,
there were perceptible moves to the center on the part of the governing Left, which led to the first grumblings from poor campesinos who
were longtime COCEI supporters. At the same time, these campesinos
pointed not only to the paved streets but to other successful COCEI
mobilization campaigns since 1986 involving credit, insurance settlements, strikes, land invasions, and indemnifications from PEMEX, the
Mexican oil company. Organized dissent within the COCEI also became discernible for the first time in 1993. Groups within the movement challenged the perpetuation of a small group of leaders, along

with the absence of open processes of discussion and decision making.[3]

The internal tensions of radical politics also extended to the COCEI's relationship with the Party of the Democratic Revolution (PRD) when these two leftist organizations clashed over the autonomy of the grassroots movement within the party. And, finally, the COCEI's moves toward moderation, which troubled its longtime supporters, were welcomed by the business community but nevertheless deemed insufficient. While the COCEI negotiated new private-sector investment in Juchitán, some Juchitecos worried that larger state-sponsored plans for new roads and an industrial corridor in the Isthmus would circumvent Juchitán entirely, in retaliation for its democratic successes.

The process of establishing political competition, spaces for voice and autonomy, and opposition government in Juchitán constituted an extraordinary set of political lessons in Mexico. For the Left, Juchitán provided an example of standing up to power through militant grassroots mobilization and *winning*, along with the benefits and limits of combining militancy with negotiation. For regime officials, PRIistas, and regional elites, Juchitán signified the possibility of coexisting with an autonomous and indigenous leftist movement, of a relatively nonviolent path from explosive conflict to "ordinary" politics. Both sets of lessons have been central to the dynamics of the Zapatista uprising in Chiapas, and they will continue to be central to the establishment of spaces for multifaceted democratic activity in Mexico in future years.

How did this extraordinary democratization occur? Most obviously, it resulted from ongoing interaction between a mobilized, militant grassroots movement and a regime characterized by give and take. Scholars of Mexican popular movements have shown such interaction to be central to protest and opposition (Cook 1996; Foweraker and Craig 1990; Hindley and Harvey, this volume), and they have traced the conflicts and alliances between hard-liners and reformists within the state, on the one hand, and organizations and movements in civil society, on the other (Fox 1993, 1994). This chapter will support such views of the state and of state–social movement relations in Mexico by illustrating key periods of interaction between national and regional political phenomena in the course of the COCEI's twenty-three-year history. In so doing, it will highlight the role of presidential and gubernatorial terms in shaping political con-

---

[3] Many of these criticisms were acknowledged publicly for the first time by former COCEI municipal president Leopoldo de Gyves de la Cruz in a speech at the twentieth anniversary celebration for the Casa de la Cultura in Juchitán.

testation and reform.[4] It will further contribute to an already rich literature on popular movements by demonstrating the centrality of violence, militancy, and ethnic culture to the success of democratization in Juchitán.

The chapter then queries why a leftist social movement was so strong in Juchitán, and why it was able to navigate treacherous waters and promote political innovation so successfully, and why there was a local political power structure with the capacity for give and take. In answering these questions, it will show, first, that contestation between the central state and regional forces did not originate with the COCEI but has been a fundamental characteristic of politics in Juchitán since the Mexican Revolution (1910–1917). The very notion of democracy in Juchitán has arisen in different ways in succeeding historical moments, debated and shaped and combined with local political and cultural discourses. Seen in this light, democratization in Juchitán does not signify the importation of a new, outside project in the 1980s or 1990s, but rather the reorienting of electoral participation and discourses of Western democracy that have long been present in regional life.

Second, it will outline the history of Juchitán's strong and politicized Zapotec culture. Juchitecos' ability to organize and sustain a radical political movement grew out of a century-long process of negotiation of political rule that was itself embedded in the construction and reconfiguration of ethnic identity, gender relations, and economic production. These phenomena occurred at the intersection of regional and national political projects, and they linked everyday forms of innovation and resistance to broader and more formal processes of political conflict and transformation. As a result, the process of democratization in Juchitán, as well as the meanings and daily significance of democracy itself, were shaped by such matters as the place of Zapotec culture in Mexican nationalism, reformist critiques of agricultural development projects, the creation of myths and practices of women's autonomy, and the ability of an Indian movement to manipulate threats of violence.

This perspective yields a somewhat different answer to the question of what made democratization possible in Juchitán. The interaction of a strong opposition movement with a complex and flexible (or fractured) state is only part of the story. Juchitán's political and cultural history underscores Juchitecos' relative success in negotiating their separateness and difference from the outside. Juchitán exhibits both a Zapotec ethnicity that constantly fought over and renegotiated its place in the nation, and a regional culture and way of life that forged alternative paths to Western economic development. Democ-

---

[4] For a comparison of the influence of presidential and gubernatorial cycles on popular movements in Juchitán and Monterrey, see Bennett and Rubin 1988.

racy occurred in Juchitán not because Western practices had proceeded apace there, but because Juchitecos exercised control over the
cultural and economic borders linking them to the outside.[5] As a result, much of the normalization[6] characteristic of Western development was avoided in Juchitán, and the intersection of Zapotec and
Mexican cultures produced a hybrid form of modernity (García
Canclini 1989) unusually open to innovation, as well as to dialogue
with Western discourses of democracy. The militancy and disruption
that fostered democracy in Juchitán were thus themselves facilitated
by ethnocultural difference.

Social Movement and Regime

The story of the COCEI's formation and growth—including the organization's direct action mobilizations, its experiences of violent repression, and the solidarity the COCEI fostered among Juchitecos[7]—
occurred in a particular series of national and state political contexts.
Broadly speaking, these can be seen as moments in which state and
national officials fostered or tolerated particular forms of innovation
and empowerment, concurrent with various levels and kinds of repression. At the national level, political openings alternated with repressive policies throughout the 1970s and 1980s. At the state level in
Oaxaca, the conservative postrevolutionary power structure, still in
place in the mid–1970s despite decades of challenge, gave way, in the
course of considerable conflict, to a somewhat more reformist state
politics by the mid–1980s. The COCEI's ability to form, survive, and
gain municipal office—to wield its own cultural and political power
and thereby democratize politics—occurred at the intersection of
these state and national political processes.

   Juchiteco students in Mexico City and Juchitán formed the COCEI
in 1973, during the democratic opening that took place under President Luis Echeverría (1970–1976). At this time, Echeverría responded
to the political crises of the 1960s and early 1970s with a policy of
opening up spaces for opposition political action outside of existing
PRI–affiliated organizations. This move to the left of center at the national level drew on the skills and political commitments of reformers

---

[5] On the centrality of cultural borders with the outside—how they are constructed and
maintained, how fluid they are, who controls them—to the cultural politics of social
movements, see Álvarez, Dagnino, and Escobar 1998.

[6] Normalization here means the social practices—concerning such matters as education, medicine, policing, mental health, agriculture, wage labor, and local culture—
that generally accompany the development of modern states and economies.

[7] For detailed accounts of COCEI activities in the 1970s and 1980s, see Bailón Corres
1987; Campbell 1994; Gutiérrez 1981; Rubin 1997, 1987; Zermeño 1987.

within the state, and it both responded to and fostered peasant, worker, and urban community movements throughout Mexico in the mid-1970s. In initiating such a program, the regime strengthened forces that could potentially take on landowners, industrialists, and parts of the PRI, thus recasting itself as a mediator between Left and Right. While this opening to radicalism and mobilization was clearly an effort to readjust the PRI system and ultimately contain opposition, it also demonstrated the way in which the regime's governing strategy involved ongoing and somewhat flexible interaction with civil society. By way of both repression and creative responses to challenge, the regime provided repeated opportunities for resistance and opposition.

The COCEI gained maneuvering room as federal officials responded to its land claims with a series of findings in the movement's favor (Binford 1985). As the COCEI mobilized thousands of supporters in direct action mobilizations against state rice and sugar mills, private enterprises, large landowners, and the state agrarian bureaucracy, government-sponsored land expropriation and the establishment of a collective ejido appeared likely. Officials of reformist national agencies lent legal and administrative support, along with occasional personnel and equipment, to the COCEI's activist efforts. In this context of partial regime opening and widespread militancy among Juchitecos, the COCEI won battles over labor rights and municipal services and rapidly expanded its political and cultural projects.

These successes were met with ongoing violence on the part of state police and paramilitary groups. This violence was encouraged and at times sponsored by Juchitán's PRIista municipal president and the governor of Oaxaca, Manuel Zárate Aquino, and never criticized, investigated, or curtailed by authorities in Mexico City. Thus, from the beginning, there were two sides to the regime's reformist efforts. Repression was not only an option that dominated politics in particular periods (1977–1980 and 1983–1985) but one that was present during moments of openness as well (1974–1977 and 1980–1983). In this context of ever-present state and private violence, the strategic capacities of COCEI leaders played a key role in broadening spaces for autonomy and negotiation.

In response to the opposition mobilizations of the Echeverría years, including dramatic land occupations and expropriations in Sonora, President José López Portillo (1976–1982) acted to shift the Mexican political economy to the center-right. This initiated a period of "closing down" toward independent oppositions, which in Juchitán meant the abandonment of the promised agrarian reform and reinforcement of the land status quo. In the COCEI's hands, however, the failed land battle became a symbol of the movement's strength and an impetus for further mobilization. The COCEI's continuing militancy in the 1970s and the democratization that resulted a decade later occurred at the intersection of a new national project, the political reform and a decade-long process of challenge to the conservative postrevolutionary elite in Oaxaca.

Beginning in the 1940s, the federal government had repeatedly attempted to challenge the power of the Oaxaca elite by installing "modernizing" governors who would promote infrastructural investment and agricultural development projects. Until the 1980s, these efforts had failed, in the face of multi-class coalitions that supported the elite in opposition to federal economic and political intervention. As recently as the mid–1970s, Echeverría had placed hardliner Manuel Zárate Aquino, a strong supporter of the old elite, in office in Oaxaca.

In the mid–1970s, however, students, peasants, and workers mobilized in and around the state capital, uniting in the Coalition of Workers, Peasants, and Students of Oaxaca (COCEO). The actions of the COCEO and COCEI together brought about growing polarization in the state and increasingly violent repression on the part of Zárate Aquino. The strength of the popular movement and the resulting political crisis led to Zárate Aquino's removal in 1977 by López Portillo and, in 1980, to the appointment of a relative moderate, Pedro Vásquez Colmenares, to the governorship. After continuing political turmoil in Juchitán throughout Vásquez Colmenares's term, including the period of COCEI government and its removal from office by the military in 1983, President Miguel de la Madrid (1982–1988) designated a left-leaning leader of the official Oaxaca peasant movement, Heladio Ramírez, to succeed Vásquez Colmenares in 1986. With the designation of Ramírez, de la Madrid moved simultaneously to resolve political tension in Juchitán and to implement the federal government's long-standing goal of "modernizing" Oaxaca politics.

In 1986 this Oaxaca project intersected with the regime's uneven political reform. After the political and economic "closing down" with which López Portillo had begun his term, he initiated a process of electoral reform, largely as a way of dealing with the grassroots movements that had emerged during the democratic opening.[8] Like Echeverría's democratic opening, the political reform was at once a limiting and controlling move; it signified flexibility on the part of the regime and opportunities for grassroots opposition. Furthermore, this reform originated during Mexico's oil boom years, a period of pros-

---

[8] López Portillo sought to reconnect autonomous activism to electoral politics, and indeed his administration's legalization of leftist parties, modification of electoral procedures, and rhetorical commitment to democratic political competition became the basis for the contestation over electoral rules and democracy that has continued to the present day in Mexico.

perity and change in which reformist officials could envision new economic projects and new forms of political competition.

Elections had long mattered in Juchitán, despite the fact that they were not conducted fairly and the PRI always won. The jockeying for nominations and the ability to bring followers out into the streets were central to the forging of political programs and loyalties and thus to the workings of municipal and state politics. The COCEI had mobilized around elections since its inception, a key strategic move that differentiated the COCEI from other radical movements of the 1970s. COCEI campaigns for municipal office in 1974 and 1977 had won the movement visibility and a formidable claim to local sovereignty. As a result of this electoral participation, furthermore, the COCEI was well poised to take advantage of the new political arena.

In 1979, COCEI leaders debated whether to participate in legislative elections (the first national elections in the political reform period) and whether to acquire legal status in municipal elections by allying with a national party in 1980. Legal status offered participation in the registration process, representation at the polls, and access to grievance procedures. But alliance with a national party also represented a potential loss of independence for an opposition movement, as well as support for a repressive regime. The COCEI's internal debate about whether or not to ally with a national party, as well as whether to participate in state and national elections, was made public in a series of newspaper articles written by two COCEI supporters, one of whom spoke for the dominant COCEI view of nonparticipation, and one of whom, who was also a member of the Mexican Communist Party (PCM), argued for the Communist Party's position of working within the system.

In the debate, the dominant stance within the COCEI was that the organization should reject elections—which were manipulated by the regime—in favor of mass mobilizations that challenged the regime head on. This dominant position, in effect presented as *the* COCEI position, denied in theory what the COCEI had been doing in practice since its formation: combining electoral participation with direct action. In addition, the majority argument rejected just the sort of simultaneous engagement with local *and* national electoral processes that would begin to characterize the COCEI's successful political strategy a year later and would, by the end of the decade, represent the philosophy of much of the Mexican Left.

As a member of the Communist Party, in contrast, Alberto López Morales argued that the political reform provided Juchitecos an opportunity to establish a new form of opposition politics, and he urged the COCEI to ally with a party and participate in legislative elections. López Morales argued that taking elections seriously and trying to pressure the state from within were valid and necessary parts of a revolutionary struggle, alongside mass organizing, the development of consciousness, and attention to pressing problems (*El Satélite* [the local weekly, hereinafter *ES*], April 29, 1979). What López Morales imagined is what indeed occurred in Juchitán in subsequent years: sustained participation in official politics on the part of an independent opposition that continued to act in the interest of its constituents.

A third voice in the debate came from outside the COCEI. A columnist for *El Satélite* spoke for political moderates in Juchitán and put the matter more bluntly: the government had been pushing the COCEI into clandestine activity, and the organization needed to take advantage of the new law to secure legal status. That way, it could mobilize more citizens throughout the Isthmus (*ES*, March 26, 1978). In the COCEI's anti-electoral discourse, in contrast, mass mobilization meant staying out of electoral politics, which did not provide for genuine competition, took energy away from productive activity, and served the interests of elites. The political reform was designed to "strengthen the Mexican political system," as its creators stated explicitly (*ES*, April 15, 1979). Focusing on the dangers of party politics and ignoring its own immersion in municipal elections, the COCEI insisted that "education and organization [for radical politics] can and must take place at the margins of elections" (*ES*, July 22, 1979).

The debate itself, however, illustrates the ambiguity of these margins and represents a dividing line between two different leftist positions. More than a disagreement about electoral participation per se, the debate concerned whether and how a regional grassroots movement would engage with national politics. Before 1979, the COCEI participated in elections in practice but rejected them in theory, and its participation occurred overwhelmingly in the regional context. Beginning in 1980, in contrast, the COCEI not only participated in municipal elections, but it engaged directly with national political actors in the process—allying with a national party and competing in national and state legislative elections.

The COCEI thus forged a path that would be adopted by much of the Mexican and Latin American Left in the 1980s and 1990s—from grassroots politics "at the margins of elections" to grassroots politics publicly engaged with national politics. This path developed in interaction with, but ultimately separate from, the direct action tactics of the land battle in Juchitán and the multifaceted mass mobilizations in Oaxaca. Both of these campaigns achieved great success in organizing and in fostering new forms of political awareness among ordinary people, but they failed to gain significant material or political concessions. It was in the electoral domain that the COCEI forged the capacity to engage with the national regime in the 1980s.

Leftist Government in the 1980s and 1990s

The COCEI won elections in 1981, in alliance with the Mexican Communist Party, and became the only leftist government in Mexico. As a result of this COCEI administration and subsequent events in the course of the decade, peasants and workers and their organizations in Juchitán gained greater influence in regional politics, economy, and cultural life. And, correspondingly, regional and national power holders became more accountable to the majority of the population. The process of transformation and democratization in Juchitán occurred through locally constructed political meanings and the elaboration of alternative cultural projects. When the *ayuntamiento popular* took office in 1981, "[it] symbolized indigenous self-government, an ethnic millennium." On inauguration day, in the words of COCEI leader Mariano Santana, "the streets of Juchitán were adorned with red flowers, and the red flag of the COCEI flew at full mast in the municipal palace. After a long road with many sacrifices and obstacles, we had realized a Zapotec dream: to be the government" (Campbell 1994: 169).

A coincidence of regional and national events made possible the annulment of fraudulent elections held in 1980 and the subsequent COCEI victory. On the national level, the López Portillo administration placed considerable emphasis on newly invigorated electoral competition. Between 1980 and 1983, policy decisions under Presidents López Portillo and de la Madrid permitted opposition victories of the Left and Right in a number of relatively large cities in Mexico. This strategy meant encouraging the electoral participation of the COCEI and possibly tolerating a leftist victory.

National economic and geopolitical factors also influenced this period of political opening in the Isthmus. During the oil boom, it was expected that increased political competition, to the extent that it occurred, would take place in the context of unprecedented industrial and commercial growth. Correspondingly, the national government would possess sufficient fiscal resources to reward multiple constituencies. The political opening also coincided with intense conflict and increasing leftist success in Central America, with Guatemalan refugees fleeing to Mexico in record numbers and regional conflict appearing likely to widen. These economic and geopolitical pressures had conflicting effects on the regime's willingness to accept leftist political participation in the Isthmus. While militant conflict would endanger the regime's economic plans and political control, violent repression in the Isthmus would scare investors and weaken Mexico's foreign policy, which was based on support for leftist movements in Central America.

Locally, the COCEI was strong and able to mobilize considerable mass support in protest activities in 1980. The PRI, meanwhile, was divided, its historical conflict between machine politicians and reformist challengers continuing to fragment the party. In addition, the PRI and its outgoing municipal president were discredited, with accusations of corruption and inefficiency coming from across the political spectrum. In this context, the multi-class nature of Zapotec ethnicity, the COCEI's success in representing the identity of the *pueblo*, and the support that some moderates were exhibiting for radical politics helped set the stage for the PRI's acceptance of a COCEI victory. The sentiment across classes was that it was time to throw the PRI out of office and give the COCEI a chance to govern.

Events at the state level also played a central role in the 1981 opening. Both political and business leaders were in a state of disorganization. Oaxaca's two major business groups were engaged in a struggle for control of the State Federation of Chambers of Commerce and could not act as a unified force against the COCEI. And the new governor, Pedro Vásquez Colmenares, who had just arrived from Mexico City, had no base in Oaxaca politics and was not the preferred candidate of the business elite. Hoping to establish his own political support, Vázquez sought to represent the national political opening at the state level; a repressive approach to Juchitán, likely to provoke violence, would have been both risky and undesirable at the beginning of his term (Bailón Corres 1985).

PRI leaders in Juchitán initially found no effective way to respond to state and national support for the COCEI's victory, which was based on strategies that responded as much to national as to local concerns. By permitting a COCEI victory, the regime hoped to give credence to its claims of democracy, to promote the sort of regional and state-level reform that national authorities had attempted for decades in Oaxaca and the Isthmus, and to weaken the radical movement by "giving the COCEI enough rope to hang itself" (author interview with a Ministry of the Interior official, January 1985). For the latter reason, the formal political opening that brought the COCEI to power was limited and uneven. Despite his ostensible support for the COCEI's right to govern in Juchitán, Vásquez Colmenares cut off much of the municipal budget as soon as the COCEI took office, and both state and federal agencies opposed loans and credits to the *ayuntamiento popular*. In response, the COCEI organized a march from Juchitán to Oaxaca City, pressuring the governor to agree to negotiations before the marchers reached the capital. The municipal budget increased only gradually, and well-publicized pressure tactics of this sort were needed repeatedly to secure the basic necessities of municipal administration.

The 1981 democratic opening was perhaps the most significant event in the COCEI's first decade. Despite harassment and subsequent violent repression, the COCEI's two and a half years in office provided the opportunity for a people's government and secured for the movement a claim to municipal sovereignty and the enduring support of large numbers of Juchitecos.

In office, the COCEI government acted with unprecedented speed to reverse the neglect that Juchitán had suffered under a succession of corrupt PRI administrations. Working with city residents, municipal officials repaired streets, constructed and staffed local health clinics, established a public library, and rebuilt the crumbling city hall. They took on two of the largest local employers—a beer distributor and a Coca Cola bottling plant—and, after bitter strikes, secured higher wages and better benefits for workers.[9] In addition, the COCEI negotiated with state and national authorities to secure agricultural credit and crop insurance settlements for peasant farmers, and it sponsored the invasion of a large tract of government-owned land, where several hundred families built houses.

In 1982, the COCEI participated in congressional elections. This was the first time its leaders agreed to compete for office beyond the municipal level. While the COCEI did not have sufficient support to win a majority seat in the Chamber of Deputies, its candidate gained a place as a member of the Mexican Unified Socialist Party's (PSUM) proportional representation list.[10] This achievement served important symbolic and practical purposes. For COCEI supporters in Juchitán, having a representative in Congress indicated that their movement was strong and successful. In terms of political power and negotiation, a COCEI deputy provided an additional, direct means for the COCEI to publicize its situation in Mexico City, a tactic of continuing importance in limiting the state's use of repression. Participation in national elections in alliance with the PSUM also indicated the COCEI's willingness to acknowledge the usefulness of a national party in furthering grassroots politics.[11]

---

[9] Accounts of the activities of the *ayuntamiento popular* can be found in the Oaxaca weekly *Hora Cero*, 1981–1983; Ornelas Esquinca 1983; Taller 1984.

[10] The PSUM was a direct descendent of the Mexican Communist Party, with which the COCEI had first allied.

[11] In 1985, the COCEI again campaigned for a seat in the federal Chamber of Deputies, in alliance with the PSUM. The COCEI remained the electoral ally of succeeding incarnations of the PSUM, following its merger with other leftist parties in the National Action Party's (PAN) and the Socialist Party's subsequent joining with the backers of Cuauhtémoc Cárdenas to form the Party of the Democratic Revolution. During the 1988 presidential campaign, the COCEI organized large public demonstrations in support of Socialist Party candidate Heberto Castillo and then in support of Cárdenas, in whose favor Castillo withdrew from the race. However, the COCEI's relations with the PRD have been marked by hostility and discord since the COCEI's

In addition to opposing the economic and political privileges of the PRI and its supporters, the *ayuntamiento popular* laid claim to the public spaces of the city, encouraging supporters to make use of areas where they had not previously gathered, such as the square in front of city hall (author interview with Adriana López Monjardín, 1986). The COCEI literally changed the language used in public institutions in a way that simultaneously facilitated people's use of those institutions and reaffirmed their cultural identity: "The PRI forced our people to speak Spanish, whether they could or not, in judicial affairs. Today this policy has been discarded, and Zapotec is spoken in the court-house, police station, and the office of the municipal president" (López Nelio 1993: 234).

COCEI intellectuals affiliated with the Cultural Center published a sophisticated literary magazine that reached national and international audiences. COCEI journalists, along with national and international visitors and reporters, produced commentary not only for foreign audiences but for avid Juchiteco readers as well. Bright red graffiti, posters, and multicolored murals covered city walls, pickup trucks circled the city publicizing COCEI events, and city hall itself was covered with high-colored political banners, including the COCEI's own flag waving from the rooftop (Campbell 1994: 175). COCEI neighborhood committees held weekly meetings to address both neighborhood administrative and judicial issues and the COCEI's ongoing campaigns. Festive and militant demonstrations featured the "expression of a ritual elegance that had previously been available only to the rich through their *velas* [yearly ritual celebrations]" (Campbell 1994: 177). During the *ayuntamiento popular*, the Cultural Center conducted classes and workshops on poetry, painting, and photography, blending Zapotec and outside artistic styles, and it offered political lectures, poetry conferences, films, and art exhibitions (Campbell 1994: 180). The scope of these activities indicated the COCEI's ambition to reshape power relations by fostering resistance and innovation throughout the city's physical and social geography.

During the *ayuntamiento popular*, the COCEI government also emphasized the regional nature of its activities. The COCEI articulated the demands of peasants throughout the Isthmus, organized workers and supported strikes in an independent Isthmus union, and announced its intention to participate in the 1983 municipal elections throughout the region (Bailón Corres 1985: 11). During its time in office, the COCEI invaded agricultural land in at least six different Isthmus towns, and its Union of Indigenous Communities of the Isthmus (UCIRI), which formed in 1983, drew together peasants from

decision to participate in President Salinas's social welfare program, PRONASOL, and the COCEI's insistence on a prominent role in the PRD itself.

twenty towns and began to constitute a powerful force in regional agrarian politics (Campbell 1990: 391–92). While the COCEI was able to keep only a small amount of the land it invaded, these efforts were powerful symbols of the movement's intentions and mobilizational capacities. In all these efforts, furthermore, the COCEI bypassed the traditional power structure of the local PRI and negotiated directly with state and national authorities.

In response to COCEI strength and successes, local PRI politicians and businesspeople formed new groups to fight the movement on the local level and pressure state and national authorities to intervene. The right wing of the PRI organized the Committee for the Defense of the Rights of the People of Juchitán. Unfettered by official constraints, this group waged a virulent anticommunist campaign, invoking the image of Central American–style conflict in the Isthmus and making free use of violence and intimidation. The Committee challenged precisely the animation and politicization of municipal life that the COCEI promoted. In an unsigned pamphlet enumerating the COCEI's "crimes," the Committee described a context in which Salvadorans encouraged Juchitecos to undertake subversive activities and COCEI municipal president Leopoldo de Gyves incited violence over the radio. The local authors of the pamphlet asserted that Juchitán was submerged in "terror and anarchy," that it was a "no-man's-land," a "communist paradise," and a breeding ground for vice and prostitution, where the CIA–agent director of the Cultural Center and COCEI leaders engaged in "bizarre" (homoerotic) sexual acts (*COCEI* 1983: 6, 13ff, 22, 26, 35).

Business leaders in Juchitán also acted against the COCEI in 1983 by electing a new executive committee to head the Chamber of Commerce and turning this organization into a focal point for unified opposition to COCEI demands, with support from state and national business confederations. According to the president of Juchitán's Chamber of Commerce at the time, business groups in the capital and across the state of Oaxaca joined in efforts to oppose the COCEI because they were afraid it would become unstoppable. A national business newsletter characterized the COCEI as "Sandinismo on a smaller scale," and it charged the *ayuntamiento popular* with assassination, guerrilla activity, support for Christian Marxists, and extortion, calling it "the center of [subversive] operations for the entire southeast" (COPARMEX 1983). Even the middle-class moderates who had once supported the COCEI charged the movement with rabble-rousing and called for government to be placed in the hands of the "educated."

By 1983, then, PRI politicians and businesspeople in Juchitán had formed new organizations to oppose the COCEI. In addition, hostility to the COCEI's economic, cultural, and political projects and practices had crystallized among potential supporters as well as opponents. The pressures exerted by these groups coincided with state and national changes. The more conservative Oaxacan business leaders had won control of the State Federation of Chambers of Commerce, and they joined with the Juchitán Chamber of Commerce to organize a business strike in May 1983, enlisting the support of local chambers statewide to pressure the state and federal governments to remove the COCEI from office (Bailón Corres 1985: 12).

In the early 1980s, Isthmus oil production and revenues reached an all-time high, with a trans-Isthmus pipeline bringing crude oil from the northern isthmus to the newly constructed refinery in Salina Cruz. The nearby port city had just been designated one of a handful of priority development poles in Mexico.[12] In addition, the Mexican regime had invested heavily in a trans-Isthmus rail and highway system, which passed alongside Juchitán. In its decisions about recognizing the COCEI's electoral victories and its responses to the COCEI government in office, the regime steered a course between competing dangers: the risk of a militant COCEI in office versus the risk of repression and violence fomenting Central American–style turmoil and in that way scaring off investors. It did this by ousting the militant COCEI from office but refraining from the most brutal forms of repression, which might have engendered increased disruption and violence.

In the summer of 1983, a violent incident provided the state government with a pretext for throwing the COCEI out of office and appointing a PRI administrative council to run the city. When the COCEI refused to leave city hall, federal troops arrived to patrol the streets and set up permanent barracks. In defending and publicizing its claims to public office, the COCEI deployed much the same resources it had used during the *ayuntamiento popular*. The movement drew on local patterns of communication, protest, and ethnic display—as well as national and international networks of support and media attention—to stage an enormous protest demonstration followed by ongoing, nonviolent resistance to the military occupation. After three months, new elections were decided in favor of a young, professional PRI candidate. The army then attacked city hall and removed COCEI supporters. A period of repression followed, during which arrests and beatings of COCEI backers became commonplace.[13]

After several months of severe repression, there emerged a variety of activities that would characterize the regime's subsequent strategy

---

[12] In an apparent repeat of this 1980s effort, President Zedillo unveiled an "Isthmus Megaproject" in July 1996 that would include a railway line, superhighway, and two electricity plants (*Mexpaz* 1996).

[13] Four COCEI leaders, jailed without charges or trial, were named prisoners of conscience by Amnesty International (1986: 47–63).

in Juchitán. These included a public military presence, state investment in municipal services and infrastructure, respect for most civil liberties most of the time, elections that sometimes permitted opposition victories, and reform of the local PRI. Members of the COCEI were gradually and unevenly permitted to exercise their rights to free speech and assembly. While harassment, assault, and imprisonment continued, the military crackdown of 1983 and 1984 sought to intimidate rather than eliminate COCEI leaders and supporters, and paramilitary right-wing violence occurred with less frequency and intensity than in the 1970s.[14]

In May 1986, Mexico City authorities surprised Oaxacans by designating Heladio Ramírez, the most progressive of the precandidates and a longtime supporter of peasant claims within the National Peasants' Confederation (CNC), as the official candidate for governor of Oaxaca. This choice represented a challenge to the conservative economic elite in the state. The designation of Ramírez represented a clear effort on the part of national authorities to recognize some of the claims of opposition groups in Oaxaca and, in the 1980s context, move the state's politics to the left. Ramírez, in turn, chose a young member of the reformist wing of the PRI in Juchitán as candidate for municipal president there, demonstrating the regime's commitment to reform of the local party.

PRI political leaders in Juchitán responded by going to the home of the newly appointed candidate and threatening him and his family. The candidate resigned, and local PRI officials replaced him with a schoolteacher whom they could easily manipulate. The business and professional group in Juchitán, which had allied with Ramírez, then formed its own organization—MIPRI, or the Integrated PRI Movement, but also "my PRI." Supporters of the dissident group refused to back the official candidate and campaigned actively for abstention and for annulment of the elections. Looking ahead, they sought to demonstrate strength before the 1986 elections in order to gain support from the governor for political changes in Juchitán in the future.

The COCEI entered the 1986 municipal elections with the same strong support it had maintained since the 1970s. The number of people voting in Juchitán had increased 84 percent since 1981, a result of efforts on the part of both the PRI and COCEI to mobilize voters and also a clear indication of the increasing centrality of elections to political contestation. The COCEI's candidate, an accountant who taught at the regional Technological Institute, was older and more established professionally than the COCEI's two previous candidates. His campaign emphasized a moderate rather than militant approach,

---

[14] While half of the COCEI's most important leaders were imprisoned, the other half resumed their organizing activities within months, and those in prison were released after a year and a half.

made overtures to the middle class, and promised accords rather than confrontation with business. With Ramírez as the incoming governor, COCEI leaders thought they had a good chance of being allowed to win these elections. They negotiated with Ramírez and his allies repeatedly over electoral rules and procedures and received support for several key demands. As in the first 1980 elections and in 1983, however, the PRI was declared the winner, with 56 percent of the vote,[15] despite evidence of fraud in the preparation of the voter list and voter ID cards.

In response, the COCEI blocked the international Pan American Highway repeatedly. Members of the COCEI also carried out hunger strikes in the federal Congress and the state capital, and staged demonstrations in front of Juchitán's city hall. These actions won the annulment of elections in several towns around Juchitán, providing the first official acknowledgment of regional strength for the COCEI. Pressures continued for annulment of the electoral outcome in Juchitán, with support from the business sector and the new governor. After the COCEI refused to participate in a coalition government headed by the newly elected PRI municipal president, Ramírez named Felipe Martínez López, a Juchiteco sociologist and political moderate who had written a book about the conflict in Juchitán (1985),[16] as municipal administrator. This appointment broke the stalemate and, after lengthy negotiations, the PRI and COCEI agreed to participate in a coalition government, with half the offices in the city government going to each group.

The price the regime paid for the COCEI's apparent adherence to the formal rules of the game after 1986 was recognition of the grassroots movement as a legitimate regional political force, an extraordinary phenomenon in the context of postrevolutionary Mexican politics. This legitimacy was evidenced first by the inclusion of the COCEI in the governing coalition in 1986 and then by recognition of COCEI victories in municipal elections in 1989, 1992, and 1995. In addition, during these years, violence against the COCEI was met with prompt negotiation and arrests, in striking contrast to official tolerance of such violence in the past (Campbell 1990: 415, 424–25).

Partly in exchange for this recognition by the regime and partly out of its own calculations of political strategy, the 1989 COCEI administration agreed to participate in President Salinas's program of *concertación social*. This program offered substantial economic and political support to established oppositions in return for a reduction

---

[15] Official results gave the PRI slightly more than 50 percent in 1980, 48 percent in the subsequent 1981 contest, and 54 percent in 1983.

[16] In the book, Martínez López had argued that the strength of the COCEI arose more from PRI weakness and errors than from an enduring mass base, thus suggesting that reform of the PRI would enable the party to regain support in the city.

of militant tactics, along with public acknowledgment of negotiation and coexistence with the regime. In this way, Salinas's own need to respond to a major regime crisis—the massive grassroots electoral support for Cárdenas in 1988—resulted in a new opportunity for the COCEI, along with the risks attendant to accepting government funds.

Critics of participation in *concertación social*, especially Cárdenas and the opposition Party of the Democratic Revolution, saw the program as a means to weaken the new party. Arguments in favor of the COCEI's participation in "concertation" were similar to those for allying with the Mexican Communist Party in elections a decade earlier: that the COCEI could take advantage of the opportunities and concessions the regime offered while also maintaining its militancy and independence. During the 1989–1992 administration of Municipal President Héctor Sánchez, COCEI leaders used funds from the PRONASOL program to pave streets and install drainage, improving the local infrastructure most relevant to people's daily lives. Furthermore, through efficient management and the use of volunteer labor, the Sánchez administration stretched the development money to pave even more streets than had been funded. As a result, Juchitecos from across the political spectrum praised the honesty and efficiency of the development efforts.

The COCEI's moderation, its presence in office for a third term, its extensive use of government funds, and its close relationship with regime officials all raise questions about the movement's present and future. The COCEI's willingness to negotiate publicly with the Salinas administration solidified the movement's officially acknowledged role as a regional political force, brought continued funding to the COCEI administration, and contributed to the process of formal democratization. At the same time, however, the centralization of power among a small group of leaders and the material comfort enjoyed by those leaders led to growing criticism of internal power relations, as well as accusations of corruption, in the 1990s. Furthermore, the COCEI faced difficult choices concerning cooperation with the central government, conciliation with local middle-class and business groups, and representation of poor Juchitecos during a period of regional economic decline.

In the midst of these crosscurrents, and in striking contrast to its own past and to most places in Mexico, Juchitán exhibited a vibrant democratic politics in the early 1990s, including honest and competitive elections, a responsive administration, efficient administration of social welfare funds, and active and innovative Zapotec cultural institutions.[17] In the face of obstruction on the part of successive Mexican

---

[17] These observations are based on field research in November 1993.

administrations, the COCEI had stimulated political debate, dramatically increased voter turnout, and improved living and working conditions. Juchitecos secured these gains, furthermore, during a period of increasing inequality and considerable manipulation of elections nationwide.

This achievement of democracy in Juchitán demonstrates a number of points that have not been well understood about Mexico in the 1980s and 1990s but that have become increasingly clear in light of the Zapatista uprising in Chiapas and indigenous mobilizations elsewhere: that the PRI and the regime are capable of—as well as resistant to—reform in specific cases; that reform, when it occurs, may depend on the existence of radical, grassroots oppositions and on virtually uncontrolled class conflict; that elections matter, even when they are fraudulent; that participation in elections increases opposition movements' chances for survival; that democratization is related to but quite distinct from elections, and involves political, economic, and cultural arenas; that ethnicity can form the basis of the fiercest and most successful popular resistance to the Mexican regime; that grassroots opposition can be strengthened by images of indigenous explosiveness and actual and potential acts of violence; and, finally, that grassroots movements can survive and grow, can avoid co-optation even as they achieve concessions, and can become recognized regional power holders.

This analysis suggests that democratization in Mexico, to the extent that it occurs, may not be something that is sought and implemented as such by state actors. Rather, democracy may result from the interaction between a regime grappling to maintain power with the tools it has available (including those it improvises) and locations and forms of opposition, including grassroots movements and popular cultures, that challenge the regime in a variety of ways. Contestation over what have long been the currencies of politics—office, land, wages, and ethnic languages and cultures—can at times yield new negotiations and new arrangements of power. In Juchitán today, as in contemporary Mexico generally, these contestations make increasing use of the languages and procedures of elections and democracy.

Region, Ethnicity, and Nation in Juchitán

The history of Juchitán illustrates the distinct and often circuitous pathways by which forms of political voice, economic well-being, and cultural autonomy can be established amidst persistently unequal power relations. As Partha Chatterjee suggested for the regions of India, this and other Mexican regional histories "[contain] in the divergences in their trajectories and rhythms the possibility of a different imagining of nationhood" (1993: 114). Consequently, they also recommend a different imagining of the processes and outcomes of democratization.

The COCEI's battle with the Mexican regime was animated and shaped by Juchitán's such different imaginings, past and present, along with the alternative forms of development they engendered. The path from violence in the 1970s to leftist municipal government in the 1990s involved how the nation was envisioned and negotiated, from Juchitán and from Mexico City, and how it was made the basis for the exercise of rule.

The possibility and pathway of democratization in Juchitán involved such matters as the forging of a Zapotec "domain of sovereignty" (Chatterjee 1993) within the Mexican nation, the articulation of a moderate discourse of development and reform, the building of artistic and intellectual connections between Juchitán and Mexico City, and the creation of myths and practices of Zapotec women's autonomy and innovation. These phenomena interacted with more explicitly "political" forces in the 1970s and 1980s, such as national political openings, international geopolitical pressures, and militant grassroots mobilization. The "art of making" (Escobar 1992: 74) at the heart of democratization in Juchitán thus involved interrelated processes linking past and present, region and regime.

In the second half of the nineteenth century in Juchitán, Zapotec ethnicity defined a multi-class *pueblo* at odds with the outside, making repeated use of violent and nonviolent forms of resistance to evade the economic claims and political impositions of elites in the state capital. After the Mexican Revolution, in contrast, the Zapotec *pueblo* coexisted with the outside, accepting a position—as a "domain of sovereignty"—within the nation rather than defining itself as separate and hostile. Paradoxically, accepting a place within the nation—now a nation that based its legitimacy on recognition of its Indian past— brought benefits that had previously been sought by constructing In- dianness in opposition to Oaxacan and Mexican identities.

The domain of sovereignty in Juchitán signified a configuration of region and nation in which cacique politics could resist outside political forces and shape regional politics in its own fashion. This arrangement involved a particular construction of Zapotec leadership that enabled Zapotec elites to be recognized by ordinary Juchitecos as legitimate political authorities and arbiters of Zapotec style, even as they made successful forays into regional and national economic and artistic activities. Zapotec elites during this period were Indians *and* Mexicans, a flexible identity made possible by the dual dynamics of Zapotec social life and the politics of Mexican nationalism. The domain of sovereignty also meant that economic endeavors in Juchitán remained predominantly, though not exclusively, small scale and local, and that ordinary people could perform daily activities of speech, ritual, and work in ways that distinguished these activities from national Mexican ones. The resulting social and economic relations were not egalitarian, but they were distinctly different in character and internal meaning from the politics and culture of the center.

During this period of coexistence, Juchiteco artists began to make a name for themselves on the national cultural scene. The crossing of borders between regional, ethnic art and national "high" culture—as between Zapotec and Mexican elites—could occur because representations of Indianness coincided with the nationalist identity and political project constructed by the postrevolutionary state. Artistic border-crossing was also a gendered activity. Men produced formal art and through that art represented Zapotec identity to Juchitecos and to the outside. Male artists spoke with recognized public authority. They developed their narratives and visions in cantinas and workshops, and they portrayed Zapotec culture as consisting of traditions that had existed locally "from time immemorial" and that were exclusively indigenous. In this way, male Juchiteco artists acted to keep the outside out of Zapotec historical and cultural narratives.

In contrast, Juchiteca women brought in, modified, and made use of economic and cultural practices from outside the city. Furthermore, before the construction of a dam and irrigation district in the Isthmus in the 1960s, much of the women's activity of appropriation and reconfiguration occurred in the absence of men, who left for months at a time to find work or, earlier, to fight in the nineteenth-century rebellions and later in the Mexican Revolution. Women thus acted with authority in daily life in a gendered domain of sovereignty within the geographic and cultural one, developing local practices in courtyards and markets. Women's authority was fortified by myths of Juchitecas' power and sexuality. This discourse, produced by nineteenth-century male European travelers and twentieth-century Mexican artists and journalists, many of them female, was reinforced by Juchiteco men and women in local art, ritual practices, and daily banter. These representations of women's power responded to and in turn fortified the various ways in which women had unusual room for maneuver in Juchitán. They also hid from view many processes of violence and exclusion, shared with women elsewhere in Mexico, that Juchitecas experienced in powerful and enduring forms.

In the 1960s, the domain of sovereignty in Juchitán was both continued and reshaped as it intersected in new ways with the national economy and state and as Juchitecos confronted the need for new regional political forms. Government agencies brought outside economic practices into the Isthmus through the construction of the irrigation district and various agroindustrial projects. As they experienced the interaction of the Zapotec domain of sovereignty and national economic changes, Zapotec elites themselves acted to bring more of the national economy and culture into Juchitán, pressing for further industrialization and for urban forms of architecture, communication, commerce, and education. Yet Zapotec elites also sought to maintain for themselves legitimate leadership status. They wanted to rework the domain of sovereignty—its interrelations of economy, ethnicity, and nation—on their own terms, including considerable borrowing from discourses of Western democracy. Elites mobilized Juchitecos politically to do this around issues of private property and clean government.[18]

But by this time Zapotec culture had also changed in response to outside influence, particularly the critical student and intellectual perspectives of the 1960s. As a result, the local culture infused art and representation with new social and political content related to class and a critical stance toward the regime. The barbarism and difference that had traditionally been attributed to Juchitán took on new, explicitly political content at the same time that the cultural and political domain of sovereignty was experiencing new strains and as ordinary people's lives were disrupted by development projects and commercialization. In this context, as students and intellectuals politicized Zapotec art in new ways, moderates among Juchitán's educated elite and middle class produced a powerful critique of the state's development policies and political practices. They did so simultaneously as insiders and outsiders. Juchiteco moderates fiercely denounced the corruption and inefficiency of state agencies and the absence of democracy within the PRI, even as they argued for a better, reformed PRI that could lead the city to clean government and economic prosperity. Moderates defended the integrity and needs of the Zapotec *pueblo*, to which they belonged, even as they sometimes joined outside planners in decrying local cultural practices as incompatible with development.

Despite its ambivalence, the vehemence of this indigenous critique of outside economic policies aptly characterized the combination of mobilization and exclusion experienced by Juchiteco students, peasants, and workers in the 1960s. The confluence of politicized artistic culture, economic critique, and changing daily experience contributed to the formation and strength of the COCEI in the 1970s and 1980s. During these years, Zapotec men's artistic representations were effective in bringing outside political support, as well as in scaring authorities with images of Indian fierceness. The COCEI made use of

---

[18] In the early 1960s local landowners mobilized widespread multi-class support, including the region's campesinos, to oppose a presidential decree designating Juchitán's newly irrigated lands as an ejido. In 1971, reformers who broke with the PRI gained municipal office on a platform of cleaning up both the PRI and the regional agrarian bureaucracy.

the myths of matriarchy in Juchitán to construct an easily identifiable, alluring, and frightening iconography to represent the radical political movement to the outside. These representations also became, for many women activists and scholars and for ordinary Juchitecas, the image of women in the COCEI. At the same time, Juchitecas themselves, through cultural practices quite distinct from those that the male artists and political leaders described, fostered the daily cultural richness and flexibility that could sustain radical politics over time, in the face of fierce repression and steep familial conflicts and losses.

The construction of gender and sexuality that took shape in the domain of sovereignty functioned both to reinforce and to resist structures of power. The alternative male gender role in Juchitán, called *muxe*,[19] was largely invisible in the COCEI's public politics, and many *muxe* allied with the PRI in the 1980s, thereby linking prominent Zapotec cultural practices to PRI political authority. But *muxe* identity also embodied the kinds of cultural difference, experimentation, and display that have both sustained Zapotec culture and empowered the COCEI's radical politics. Similarly, women's identity—their physical presence, verbal boldness, self-confidence, and margins of sexual freedom—have both upheld and challenged dominant power relations. Juchiteca identity provided a vocabulary of forthrightness and militancy that directly facilitated radical mobilization. But the characteristics attributed to Juchitecas also lent an eroticism and allure to social life as it existed, thereby enhancing both the usefulness and seductiveness of the regime's political authority.

In its depictions of gender roles and sexuality—as in other arenas such as militancy, claims about the origins of political activism, and absence of internal democracy—the COCEI promotes representations of local life that correspond to some aspects of the worldviews of Juchitecos, while at the same time the movement coexists with, and relies on, quite different, less homogeneous, and far more contested daily practices. Despite the costs of some of these (mis)representations—such as the continuing exclusion of women from positions of political power, the lack of attention to women's domestic and occupational subordination, and the exclusion of a prominent

---

[19] Males publicly identified in both Zapotec and Spanish by the Zapotec word *muxe* play a prominent role, distinct from those of both females and other males, in economic and ritual activity. Boys often take up this identity in adolescence and go on to perform economic roles associated with women, such as food preparation and marketing, to reside in their mothers' houses, and to dress in ways that are partly, though not entirely, associated with women. *Muxe* also play particular public roles in the division of labor at fiestas, where they sit among women and dance as women while exhibiting body forms, dress, and adornment that mix common "male" and "female" characteristics. At the same time, prominent men rumored to be homosexual who do not adopt the *muxe* identity are spoken of pejoratively, and there is strong public sentiment against either men or women living together as couples.

form of male social life from artistic discourse—the COCEI's ongoing strength derived in part from its ability to balance (mis)representation and respect for daily practice.[20]

Democratization in Juchitán

The separateness and internal complexity of the regional, Zapotec activities that constituted the domain of sovereignty in Juchitán thus provided the terrain on which oppositional activities would be shaped—and strengthened and limited—during the fierce, class-based battles of the 1970s and 1980s. In the 1970s, as the COCEI organized a class-based opposition, the *pueblo* again defined itself in opposition to outside authority, as it had in the nineteenth century, but this time in opposition to the Zapotec elite as well. Since then, Juchitán has become a striking example of an enduring and multifaceted democratic space within a system of domination. In contested and changing ways, the path from polarization to transformation brought fair elections, opposition government, new opportunities for alternative linguistic and cultural elaboration, spaces for dissent and democracy in labor unions and community associations, and protection for small-scale agriculture.

This politics is explosive and exclusionary, even as it is competitive and open ended. Indeed, multifaceted democracy was secured in Juchitán through the combination of locally mediated discourses of Western democracy and ongoing mobilization at the borders of violence. In Juchitán, the economic and social complexity of a rural city, the strategic importance of a development zone, and the domestic politics of an unevenly liberalizing regime intersected. Enduring militancy resulted in significant part from the COCEI's ability to claim control of the meanings and practices of Zapotec ethnicity for a poor people's movement in such a location. Through a flexible and changing mixture of Leninist and what are sometimes called "new social movement" practices,[21] the COCEI sustained activism and forged innovative opposition practices, including leftist participation in elections and an extensive Zapotec cultural project. What the COCEI achieved, however, was not so much a new inclusion of Indians in the nation (a process that has accelerated dramatically since the Zapatista rebellion in Chiapas) but rather the opportunity for poor Juchitecos to be included within the quasi-democratic maneuverings of the Mexican regime. In the 1980s, a new form of entry into the na-

---

[20] For a discussion of ambiguity and contradiction in the COCEI's internal practices, see Rubin 1998.

[21] By new social movement practices is meant such attributes as internal democracy, nonviolence, gender equality, and openness to coalition building.

tion and a corresponding expansion of the benefits of citizenship could occur through the discourses and practices of electoral competition. By virtue of being frightening and "unknown" Indians, Juchitecos achieved a new version of the 1930s–1950s domain of sovereignty *and* a new level of involvement with Western democracy. At this juncture of democracy and difference, new power relations were forged.

As a result of their Zapotec past and their experiences with Mexico's turbulent student movements, COCEI leaders not only spoke Zapotec, but they spoke the language of the regime as well. The COCEI survived because its leaders consistently took advantage of the ambivalence and conflict within the regime regarding reform or repression as political strategies. COCEI leaders knew when and how to provoke, retreat, and negotiate.

The vocal and influential group of political moderates in Juchitán consistently recognized the reasonableness of many of the COCEI's claims. Moderates spoke in a language of open political competition, civil rights, and economic development (though their commitment to these goals varied and they had little success in achieving them). By being willing to question the system in fundamental and increasingly radical ways and to speak in defense of the Zapotec *pueblo*, moderates themselves outlined much of the COCEI's later agenda. In the 1970s, when the COCEI faced regime intransigence and violence, moderates defended the integrity of the Zapotec movement and the justness of its claims. However, when the COCEI governed Juchitán in the early 1980s and pursued the radical goals it had previously championed, moderates opposed the leftist movement, charging that it fostered violence and anarchy. When the COCEI was removed from power, moderates made use of the political views they had articulated in preceding decades to ally with the regime in support of democracy in Juchitán and reform of the local PRI, a strategy they believed would bring a reinvigorated official party to power through fair elections. Two local cultures of politics thus interacted in Juchitán in the process of democratization, both with dual origins in the mid-century domain of sovereignty and in Mexican politics.

The *ayuntamiento popular* galvanized peasant and worker support for the COCEI at the same time that it alienated middle-class Juchitecos and businesspeople. The *ayuntamiento popular* fostered militant class conflict and governed in favor of COCEI supporters, treating others with hostility and arbitrariness. It also defended and celebrated the popular culture of the poor, including aspects of Zapotec daily life that middle classes and elites rejected as obstacles to "decency" and development. In contrast, the COCEI's stance during the 1986 coalition government and the subsequent, democratically elected COCEI administrations was more conciliatory.

Such a shift underscores the usefulness of moderation in democratic politics. However, the trajectory of conflict and democratic accommodation in Juchitán suggests as well that militancy and hostility were important steps in the path to leftist government—and that multifaceted and enduring democracy was achieved in Juchitán because the establishment of Western democratic norms was only one of a variety of goals for moderates and the COCEI alike. Discourses and practices of Western democracy emerged among different Juchitecos in different decades, embedded in local meanings and local methods of disruption. Moderates debated the meaning of democracy and weighed it against the notion of an official party during campaigns for internal PRI primaries in the 1960s. The COCEI forged democratic electoral practices on the ground since its inception, even as it rejected them in theory and refused them internally. It was thus Juchitán's own complex discourse of democracy, combined with mobilization and government at the borders of violence, that impassioned supporters, frightened opponents, and brought democratic transformation. Disruption may be equally crucial to the vitality of democracy itself. As COCEI leaders age and COCEI administrations balance mobilization and conciliation, the organization's own past poses a key question for leftist government in systems of unequal power relations: where can spaces be forged, in or out of elected government, for the militancy and disruption that may be necessary to reinforce and deepen democratic politics?

Democracy and Difference

In Juchitán, militancy and disruption were facilitated by difference. Democracy occurred not because Western cultural and economic practices proceeded apace, but because the outside was kept out in significant ways and the normalization characteristic of Western development was avoided. Juchitán's domain of sovereignty, like those described by Chatterjee (1993: 75) in India, served "to resist the sway of the modern institutions of disciplinary power."[22] As a result, the intersection of Zapotec and Mexican cultures and economies produced a hybrid form of modernity unusually open to innovation. The links between hybridity, difference, and innovation are evident in Juchitán not only in the physical and ritual panorama of the city, but also in the stunning alternatives of gender, sexuality, and language there. In Stuart Hall's words, "this notion of hybridity is very different from the old internationalist grand narrative, from the superfici-

---

[22] These institutions, such as schools, hospitals, police forces, and government bureaucracies, regulate the normalization described in note 6.

ality of old style pluralism where no boundaries are crossed" (1993: 362).

In Juchitán, boundaries are crossed in the strength and forthrightness of women and the myths describing them, in midwives who make use of doctors to maintain their own prestige and wealth, and in the unabashed mixture of typically male and female clothing, bodily appearance, and demeanor among *muxe* males in public places. In Juchitán, women are not harassed in the streets, babies are born at home or in midwives' courtyards, and males in women's dress dance with other males in women's dress at public fiestas. In all of these locations, furthermore, and in businesses and government as well, Juchitecos' rich and playful use of a "barbarous" indigenous language establishes yet another border with the rest of urban Mexico.

Juxtapositions of "unruliness" and discipline, of "nature" and technology in Juchitán are not only or primarily the results of poverty but of preference and sensibility and identity. If the encounter between Western and indigenous cultures and economies had occurred on less unequal terms, the twentieth century very possibly would not have been a period of "appropriate" technology and "sustainable" development, but one in which the uses, values, and paths of economic and social change would have been more grounded in local needs and commitments. Thus Juchitecos pursue forthrightly—indeed celebrate—the habits that modernizers decry. The COCEI's experiences in the last two decades demonstrate the possibility of being radical and taking on the regime, of governing and managing budgets, while simultaneously resisting the language of economic development and cultural normalization. This does not imply unilateral rejection of the benefits of new technologies or the possibility of profit. Juchitecos disagree vehemently among themselves about how much of the outside to embrace and on what terms. Juchitecos' forthrightness with strangers and engagement with multiple economies and cultures bring satisfaction and autonomy. Furthermore, they confer an ability to stand up to, and even ridicule and dismiss, Western assumptions.

Juchitán does not provide a recipe for democratization. Rather, it demonstrates the embeddedness of democracy in particular cultural and historical forms at the regional level. At the end of the twentieth century, Juchitán offers the paradoxical lesson that the persistence and elaboration of difference can foster the establishment of multifaceted democracy. Difference does not make democracy happen nor necessarily pave its way. But in Juchitán the intersection of an open-ended modernity with Western democratic discourse has indeed produced unprecedented democratic innovation. To approach the analysis of democracy this way—through the place of region in the nation and through alternative pathways of development—is thus not to ignore democratic procedures. Rather, it is to recognize that much of the inequality and violence that democratic procedures obscure—and that have come increasingly to characterize situations of democratic transition in Latin America—can be seen and negotiated in these other arenas.

Over time, the voice and autonomy of Zapotec ethnicity has been articulated in contestation with Mexican nationalism, and the economic survival and relative prosperity of Juchitecos have been articulated in contestation with Western development. Western democratic discourse has been essential for democratization in Juchitán not as a "universal" political theory, imposed or imported from without, but always "insist[ing] on specificity, on conjuncture" (Hall 1988: 46). The negotiated position of region in nation and the boundary-crossing hybridity of development have given Juchitecos considerable margin for maneuver in their encounters with Western modernity. Through the Zapotec modernity and democratic discourses they constructed, Juchitecos formed and empowered the COCEI and achieved democratization.

References

Álvarez, Sonia E., Evelina Dagnino, and Arturo Escobar, eds. 1998. *Cultures of Politics/Politics of Cultures: Revisioning Latin American Social Movements.* Boulder, Colo.: Westview.

Amnesty International. 1986. *Mexico: Human Rights in Rural Areas.* London: Amnesty International.

Bailón Corres, Moisés. 1985. "El desconocimiento del ayuntamiento de la COCEI," *Guchachi' Reza* 23.

―――. 1987. "Coyote atrapa a conejo: poder regional y lucha popular. El desconocimiento del ayuntamiento de Juchitán en 1983." In *Juchitán: límites de una experiencia democrática,* edited by Moisés J. Bailón Corres and Sergio Zermeño. Mexico City: Instituto de Investigaciones Sociales, Universidad Nacional Autónoma de México.

Bennett, Vivienne, and Jeffrey Rubin. 1988. "How Popular Movements Shape the State: Radical Oppositions in Juchitán and Monterrey, Mexico, 1973–1987." Paper presented at the Fourteenth International Congress of the Latin American Studies Association, New Orleans.

Binford, Leigh. 1985. "Political Conflict and Land Tenure in the Mexican Isthmus of Tehuantepec," *Journal of Latin American Studies* 17.

Campbell, Howard. 1990. "Zapotec Ethnic Politics and the Politics of Culture in Juchitán, Oaxaca (1350–1990)." Ph.D. dissertation, University of Wisconsin-Madison.

―――. 1994. *Zapotec Renaissance: Ethnic Politics and Cultural Revivalism in Southern Mexico.* Albuquerque: University of New Mexico Press.

Chatterjee, Partha. 1993. *The Nation and Its Fragments: Colonial and Postcolonial Histories.* Princeton, N.J.: Princeton University Press.

COCEI: Este es tu obra. 1983. Also entitled ¡*Juchitán: un pueblo que clama justicia!* Juchitán.

Cook, Maria Lorena. 1996. *Organizing Dissent: Unions, the State, and the Democratic Teachers' Movement in Mexico.* University Park: Pennsylvania State University Press.

COPARMEX (Confederación Patronal de la República Mexicana). 1983. "Juchitán, algo más que una presidencia municipal," *Hechos de la Semana* 36 (August 2–8).

Escobar, Arturo. 1992. "Culture, Economics, and Politics in Latin American Social Movements Theory and Research." In *The Making of Social Movements in Latin America: Identity, Strategy, and Democracy,* edited by Arturo Escobar and Sonia E. Álvarez. Boulder, Colo.: Westview.

————. 1995. *Encountering Development: The Making and Unmaking of the Third World.* Princeton, N.J.: Princeton University Press.

Foweraker, Joe, and Ann L. Craig, eds. 1990. *Popular Movements and Political Change in Mexico.* Boulder, Colo.: Lynne Rienner, in association with the Center for U.S.–Mexican Studies.

Fox, Jonathan. 1993. *The Politics of Food in Mexico: State Power and Social Mobilization.* Ithaca, N.Y.: Cornell University Press.

————. 1994. "The Difficult Transition from Clientelism to Citizenship: Lessons from Mexico," *World Politics* 46 (2): 151–84.

García Canclini, Néstor. 1989. *Culturas híbridas: estrategias para entrar y salir de la modernidad.* Mexico City: Grijalbo.

Gutiérrez, Roberto J. 1981. "Juchitán, municipio comunista," *A: análisis histórico y sociedad mexicana* 2 (4): 251–80.

Hall, Stuart. 1988. "New Ethnicities." Black Film, British Cinema.

————. 1993. "Culture, Community, Nation," *Cultural Studies* 7 (3): 349–63.

López Nelio, Daniel. 1993. "Interview with Daniel López Nelio." In *Zapotec Struggles: Histories, Politics, and Representations from Juchitán, Oaxaca,* edited by Howard Campbell et al. Washington, D.C.: Smithsonian Institution Press.

Martínez López, Felipe. 1985. *El crepúsculo del poder: Juchitán, Oaxaca 1980–1982.* Oaxaca: Instituto de Investigaciones Sociales, Universidad Autónoma "Benito Juárez" de Oaxaca.

Mexpaz. 1996. "Heartbeat of Mexico," August 1.

Ornelas Esquinca, Marco Antonio. 1983. "Juchitán, ayuntamiento popular." Bachelor's thesis, Instituto Tecnológico Autónomo de México.

Rubin, Jeffrey W. 1987. "State Policies, Leftist Oppositions, and Municipal Elections: The Case of the COCEI in Juchitán." In *Electoral Patterns and Perspectives in Mexico,* edited by Arturo Alvarado. La Jolla: Center for U.S.–Mexican Studies, University of California, San Diego.

————. 1997. *Decentering the Regime: Ethnicity, Radicalism, and Democracy in Juchitán, Mexico.* Durham, N.C.: Duke University Press.

————. 1998. "Ambiguity and Contradiction in a Radical Popular Movement." In *Cultures of Politics/Politics of Cultures: Revisioning Latin American Social Movements,* edited by Sonia E. Álvarez, Evelina Dagnino, and Arturo Escobar. Boulder, Colo.: Westview.

Taller de Investigación Sociológica, Universidad Nacional Autónoma de México. 1984. "Juchitán: el fin de la ilusión." In *Oaxaca: una lucha reciente: 1960–83*. Mexico City: Nueva Sociología.

Zermeño, Sergio. 1987. "Juchitán, la cólera del régimen." In *Juchitán: límites de una experiencia democrática*, edited by Moisés J. Bailón Corres and Sergio Zermeño. Mexico City: Instituto de Investigaciones Sociales, Universidad Nacional Autónoma de México.

10

Indigenous Mobilization, Development, and Democratization in Guerrero: The Nahua People vs. the Tetelcingo Dam

Jane Hindley

On September 4, 1990, the Mexican government notified the International Labour Organisation (ILO) that domestic procedures for ratifying ILO Convention 169 on Indigenous and Tribal Peoples were complete (Gómez 1991: 22). Mexico's swift ratification of the new convention was clearly shaped by the context of the buildup to the 1992 Quincentenary and the increasingly visible mobilizations of indigenous peoples internationally. It should be seen both as part of President Carlos Salinas de Gortari's (1988–1994) sustained effort to demonstrate to external audiences his commitment toward Mexico's indigenous peoples and as part of a broader preemptive reform program (Coleman and Davis 1982) designed to assuage critics and contain discontent domestically (Hindley 1996). Nevertheless, Convention 169 represented a substantive rupture with long-standing indigenist orthodoxies, and it established a new normative frame-

This chapter is based on ethnographic research and forms part of the author's doctoral project, "Indigenous Mobilisation, Development and Political Reform in Mexico: The Struggle of the Nahua People of the Upper Balsas, Guerrero." The author would like to thank the Centro de Investigaciones y Estudios Superiores en Antropología Social (CIESAS–México), the Center for U.S.–Mexican Studies at the University of California, San Diego, and the Economic and Social Research Council (UK) for supporting this research. Thanks are also due to the Fuller Bequest Fund, Department of Sociology, University of Essex, and the Ford Foundation for facilitating travel to the Local Politics and Democratization Workshop in Mexico City. Finally, the author is grateful to the many people from the Upper Balsas who shared their thoughts and documents, and to Andy Wroe and Andrew Canessa for their comments on this piece.

work for relations between states and indigenous peoples. It formally reversed assimilationist policies toward indigenous peoples and placed an obligation on states to recognize their collective cultural, economic, political, and social rights. In this respect, Convention 169 constituted a potential political opening and a legal grounding for the historic claims of indigenous movements that national governments respect their specific rights and identities (see Hindley 1996).

This chapter examines the history of one regional indigenous movement that capitalized on this political opening and mobilized under the rubric of Convention 169, challenging exclusionary state planning and asserting their rights as indigenous people to inclusion in decision making regarding a state project that had drastic consequences for their lives. It provides an account of the mobilization of the Nahuas of the Upper Balsas, Guerrero, against a Federal Electricity Commission (CFE) project to build a large-scale hydroelectric dam on their ancestral lands. It traces the war of position (Gramsci 1991) carried out by the Nahuas in local, state, and federal spaces of decision making in order to get satisfaction of their fundamental demand—"No to the San Juan Tetelcingo dam!"

It should be emphasized that when the Nahuas started to mobilize against the Tetelcingo dam, they found no accounts of successful resistance to large-scale dams in Mexico. Their mobilization thus constitutes an important precedent for future rural and indigenous peoples facing the same threat. Moreover, it should also be stressed that the exclusions inscribed in the CFE's Tetelcingo project are common to a general program of large-scale dam construction implemented across the South, including Mexico, since the 1950s (Adams 1990; Bartolomé and Barabás 1990). The most important are the exclusion of local social considerations, and the exclusion of local people from the planning process and decision to construct and from such projects' projected benefits. Decisions are generally in the hands of powerful state corporations, like the CFE, that are accountable only to national governments. In Mexico, local people have generally been informed once decisions have been taken and sanctioned by the federal government, usually after construction has begun. Dealings with local people over relocation have been mediated by vertically accountable local power holders and bureaucrats within the corporatist system and the ruling Institutional Revolutionary Party (PRI), as well as by anthropologists and the National Indigenous Institute (INI). The deployment of the army has also been a general characteristic of dam relocations (Bartolomé and Barabás 1990).

There is no doubt that the Nahuas' challenge to these exclusions and mediations was facilitated both by the specific opening toward indigenous peoples outlined above and by the general liberalization of the Mexican political system in recent years (Loaeza 1994). Indeed, the effects of such macropolitical changes are visible in the emergence of grassroots, anti-dam protest movements during the same period in other Latin American countries, most notably Brazil (Hall 1994). It is clear that the proliferation of independent actors, nongovernmental organizations (NGOs), and opposition parties, along with the expansion of spaces available for the expression of dissent in civil society, shaped the terrain on which the Nahuas' struggle took place. Thus their mobilization occurred within a quite different political opportunity structure from those facing rural and indigenous peoples in past cases of large-scale dam projects in Mexico. However, for the purposes of this chapter, and in order to concentrate on the process of mobilization at the grassroots, the process of liberalization is assumed.[1]

The main objective here is to describe and analyze the micropolitics of mobilization at each stage of the Nahuas' struggle against the dam. The chapter focuses on the internal organization of the movement, processes of decision making and strategic choice, the role of leaders, and the specific contributions of different allies—all in response to calls for more detailed attention to be paid to these internal dimensions of popular struggle (Craig 1990; Fox 1990; Hellman 1994). Such attention is a means to evaluate claims that popular movements contribute to processes of democratization, not only by challenging exclusionary state/government decision making and structures of representation, but also by engendering democratic practices and citizens. Moreover, in this case it facilitates understanding of how, through mobilization, the Nahuas constructed new regional indigenous political identities and the grounds for long-term political change in their region. In the wake of the Zapatista opening, these identities have become the basis for the Nahuas' current negotiations over the creation of a new indigenous municipality and an autonomous indigenous region.

Informing the People

The CFE's Tetelcingo project dates from 1959, when explorations to ascertain the hydroelectric potential of the Balsas basin began (García Calvario and Riva Palacios 1990). Yet at no time from 1959 onward did the CFE officially inform the Nahua towns located within the "reservoir area" about its plan to build a large-scale hydroelectric dam to meet increasing national demand for electricity. It seems that,

---

[1] The liberalization process has been well analyzed and documented by other scholars. See, for example, Cornelius, Gentleman, and Smith 1989; Cook, Middlebrook, and Molinar Horcasitas 1994.

over thirty years of intermittent geological and geographical survey missions, deliberate efforts were made to avoid contact with the towns and to conceal the character of the CFE project. In San Agustín Oapan, for example, people recall being told by surveyors in the early 1980s that the government was planning "an irrigation project"; in another town, informants remember riverside survey posts appearing mysteriously overnight. Moreover, the CFE's preliminary social study was prepared without any visits to the towns or consultations with local townspeople and their authorities. Instead, it seems to have been compiled from an ad hoc collection of existing government statistics, which are notoriously unreliable for rural and indigenous areas. For example, the study suggests the dam would "affect" fifteen towns with a total population of 16,051 (García Calvario and Riva Palacios 1990: 26), apparently based on figures derived from the 1980 national campaign to eradicate malaria, which grossly underestimated the real numbers involved. The CFE's strategies to keep the local population misinformed or uninformed were generally successful. During the 1970s and 1980s, vague rumors about a dam circulated in several towns, and a few outsiders tried to raise the alarm. But even in these communities, warnings and rumors seem to have induced little but skepticism, which, ironically, is best explained by prevailing cynicism toward the government: "the government always promises, but it never delivers."

The catalyst that radically transformed this situation came in the summer of 1990 when low-level CFE representatives asked anthropologist and local expert Eustaquio Celestino Solís to collaborate on the relocation project. In this capacity, Celestino obtained copies of CFE documents that provided clear evidence of the CFE's intentions for the area. They indicated that geological and technical studies for the dam were complete, and they included a timetable for the project's different phases. Preliminary construction was to begin in early 1991, major construction would commence in early 1992, and the sluice gates would close in 1996. The relocation of the affected towns was to be determined between August 1990 and October 1991 and completed by 1994. The documents also contained maps showing the proposed reservoir, the towns to be flooded, and sites for their relocation, including Celestino's hometown of Xalitla. Communities would be moved from their location on the river plain, where the best agricultural lands are located, to new towns on the stony mountains above. In the process, some communities with long histories of intercommunal conflict were to be merged.

The acquisition of these documents marked the beginning of the war of position within the "reservoir area" between the forces of resistance and the government.[2] For the forces of resistance (at this point, Celestino and a few confidants in Xalitla) this meant two things. First, it involved persuading local people of the reality of the CFE's plans, convincing them that the consequences of the dam would be disastrous, and gaining consent for the project of resistance. Second, and conversely, it entailed preventing the entry of vertically accountable government agents propounding the supposed benefits of the dam to the people and engineering consent for its construction.

To understand the first steps taken by the forces of resistance and the concrete form that the war of position was to assume, it is necessary first to understand the historical and sociopolitical configurations within the "reservoir area" in September 1990. All the threatened towns shared a common Nahua identity and relatively strong independent town government based on the indigenous *cargo* system, which is structured around the principles of direct democracy (for male citizens). But the "reservoir area," which extended over seventy kilometers along the Balsas River, did not coincide with either an "organic region" or an existing unit of collective political representation or action. The towns fell within two historically distinct, adjacent Nahua regions, separated by a deep gorge and with no direct links. Political configurations and the recent political histories of these two regions were quite different.

In the Nahua region upriver (the Copalillo region), ethnic boundaries coincided with political boundaries, and all the threatened towns shared collective political representation within the municipality of Copalillo. Here, after over ten years of political struggle against PRI *caciquismo* (bossism) culminating with democratic elections in December 1989, the municipality was governed by the opposition Revolutionary Workers' Party (PRT) (Estrada Guadalupe 1988). By contrast, in the region closest to the dam site (the western region) the Nahua towns shared no unit of collective political representation, although strong social, religious, and economic intertown networks existed. These towns were divided among five municipalities, and the towns to be flooded, among three: Huitzuco de Figueroa, Mártir de Cuilapan, and Tepecoacuilco, all held by the PRI and governed from mestizo towns outside the region. Here there was no history of regional political struggle, the penetration of opposition parties was weak, and relations between the Nahua towns and their municipal authorities were characterized by neglect and marginalization rather than tight cacique control.

---

[2] Here, war of position should be understood as a double-sided process whereby each side attempts to gain support for its political project and actively prevent the other side from doing so (Gramsci 1991).

These different political configurations, together with an understanding of the tactics that state and ruling party actors commonly deploy to prevent the emergence of popular dissent, clearly shaped the first step in the war of position and the strategies adopted for informing the people about the dam. In the Copalillo region, Celestino's first contacts were with the PRT indigenous municipal authorities. Their immediate response was to protest against the dam publicly in the press—a protest that elicited the first affirmation from the state government that the dam was to go ahead (*Excélsior*, August 28, 1990, p. 1). The Copalillo authorities then took on the task of informing the threatened towns within their jurisdiction.

By contrast, Celestino deliberately avoided the municipal authorities in the western region, who, being from the PRI, would simply comply with orders from above. Instead he went directly to the political authorities of the towns, initially the *comisarios municipales* (mayors) of Oapan and Xalitla. Oapan was the first town to express public opposition to the CFE project and rebuff government attempts to penetrate the western region. On September 18, 1990, the Oapan general assembly refused visiting engineers from the Ministry of Agriculture (SARH) permission to perform studies for the dam. Underscoring their refusal, the assembly signed an official act of noncompliance expressing unanimous opposition to the CFE project. At the same time, the townswomen began a religious vigil that would continue until late December. Additionally, the Oapan *comisario* set about informing the towns upriver, sending out citizens' commissions to speak to their authorities, all of whom returned messages of opposition to the dam.

In the meantime, Celestino and a few other professionals from Xalitla began surveying the broader terrain of struggle, seeking out information on both the Tetelcingo project and large-scale dams in general. At the federal offices of the INI, they were told the dam was under study but that no notification had come from the CFE regarding approval of the project. In contrast, at the Department of Highway Safety (Protección y Vialidad), a lawyer from the region confidently assured them that the dam was approved and budgeted—and offered his services for compensation claims. Celestino and his companions also visited Mezcala, the nearest community to Xalitla downriver on the Balsas, which had been relocated by the CFE for the Caracol dam in 1986. There they heard of the miseries of relocation: the CFE's broken promises, badly built houses, lack of compensation payments, and a host of other problems. This equation of relocation with disaster would be confirmed by further empirical evidence obtained later, the most notable being a video documenting tragic experiences among the Chinantec people who were moved from Oaxaca to Veracruz to make way for the Cerro de Oro dam in the 1970s and 1980s.

The Consejo de Pueblos Nahuas del Alto Balsas

The differences between the two regions clearly explain why the focus of the war of position in the "reservoir area" was to be the western region. In the Copalillo region, the collective representation of the Nahua towns' resistance was assured within the formal political system by the indigenous PRT municipal authorities. In the western region, the challenge was to create an independent organization to represent the towns against the dam and prevent the PRI and mestizo municipal authorities from claiming their formal prerogative of representing the people while acting on orders from above.

On October 1, 1990, after the initial process of circulating information about the CFE project was complete, the first intertown assembly of indigenous authorities took place in Xalitla. It was attended by *comisarios* from fourteen towns in the two regions and the municipal government representative (*síndico*) of Copalillo. Uninvited representatives from opposition parties and officials from the state INI, the National Institute of Anthropology and History (INAH), and the SARH also turned up. These officials attempted to dissuade those assembled from the path of resistance with the argument that "the dam was still under study and nothing had been decided, so there was nothing to worry about," and with veiled threats about the consequences of resisting the government. These arguments and threats were to comprise the official version offered repeatedly through mid–February 1991. In an assertion of independence, the Nahuas asked all outsiders to leave, and the meeting ended with the first collective intertown declaration of unanimous opposition to the dam, signed by all authorities present. A second assembly was set for October 21 in Oapan.

Several hundred townspeople and *comisarios* from seventeen towns attended the Oapan assembly. For the majority, this was the first time they had witnessed outright public defiance of their municipal authorities. The *síndico* from Copalillo and professionals and teachers from Xalitla and other towns successfully contested efforts by the PRI municipal presidents of Tepecoacuilco and Apango and a municipal official from Huitzuco to convince those assembled that representation of the towns' interests was safe in their hands. This defiance of the PRI authorities constituted one of the founding moments of the resistance movement. Instead, the professionals proposed that an autonomous regional committee be formed, to represent the towns threatened by the dam. They also asserted the legality of such a move on the basis of the towns' indigenous identities and their rights as indigenous peoples to self-representation.

The legality of the new Regional Committee constituted in Oapan was reaffirmed in its organizational structure. The positions of authority on the first of its four tiers were all occupied by *comisarios*, recognized by the government and the people themselves as legitimate representatives of the people of each town. This tier was composed of ten offices: a general secretary and the secretaries of organization, acts and agreements, press and propaganda, and finance, each with a deputy. In practice, their role as moral authorities was largely symbolic, primarily because of the obstacles to performing the functions assigned; for example, there was no telephone in the hometown of the secretary of press and propaganda. This symbolic function was also evident in the election of the *comisario* of San Juan Tetelcingo as general secretary.

The second tier comprised delegates (*comisionados*), a small group of individuals who became the driving force of the movement. The group included the university-educated municipal leaders from Copalillo and other professionals, mostly from Xalitla, who worked outside the region and were well versed in national and state politics.

At the level of the third tier, each town assembly was to organize a support committee to ensure effective linkage between the existing town political organization and the new intertown council. In Oapan the support committee was incorporated as a new tier of the *cargo* system; officers were elected annually and assigned specific responsibilities for assisting the *comisario* in dam-related protest events. By contrast, the San Juan Tetelcingo support committee ensured their town was represented at protest actions despite the reluctance of its successive *comisarios*. In several towns, support committees were never organized, and in some cases this reflected apathy; in others, as in San Miguel Tecuiciapan, it was thought redundant, given that the town assembly had reached consensus about resisting the dam.

Finally, the fourth tier proposed the establishment of national and international support committees, assigning sympathetic outsiders a role within the movement. A few outsiders—mainly academics from Mexico City and from the Autonomous University of Guerrero—were present at the Oapan assembly. One who was notable by his absence was Arturo Warman, director of the federal INI; on the basis of his reputation as a defender of indigenous rights, he had been specifically invited to show his support and provide "truthful information" about the dam.

The assemblies in Xalitla and Oapan in the western region were followed by a third in Tlalcozotitlán, in the Copalillo region, on November 17, 1990. The location was chosen for its proximity to the Olmec ceremonial site of Teopantecuanitlán, which was also to be flooded. This assembly was attended by two CFE engineers who repeated official assurances that the dam was only under study and thus should not cause alarm, until heckles from the floor prompted them to depart.

By this time, the Regional Committee had gathered fresh evidence that the dam had been approved and that the project was moving forward. These included a state planning document referring to the INAH's rescue excavation of Teopantecuanitlán that had been unearthed by the Copalillo municipal authorities; photographs of deep tunnels in the hillsides on either side of the river at the dam site, taken by a commission from Xalitla; reports from Oapan about strangers surveying streets and houses; and information that the CFE had contracted laborers to work at the dam site.

With these reports in hand, the Regional Committee took a number of important decisions. First, after hearing that the delegation sent to Chilpancingo (the state capital) had been unsuccessful in securing an appointment with the governor, it was agreed that a demonstration would be held to back up this request. The demonstration would be supported by PRT local deputy María Garfías Marín and timed to coincide with a demonstration that the PRT popular umbrella organization (UGOCEP) had already planned for November 28. Second, in the absence of the San Juan Tetelcingo *comisario*, whose municipal president had apparently dissuaded him from attending, the members elected a new general secretary: Sixto Cabañas, a teacher from Oapan. Third, the organization was renamed. Up to this point, some documents referred to the Regional Committee of Indigenous Towns of the Balsas, others to the Regional Committee of Nahua Towns. From the Tlalcozotitlán assembly onward, it would be known as the Council of Nahua Communities of the Upper Balsas (Consejo de Pueblos Nahuas del Alto Balsas, or CPNAB). With the adoption of this name the alliance between the towns of the two regions was sealed and a new regional indigenous identity established.

Rituals of Petitioning

The establishment of the CPNAB challenged the representative prerogatives of the PRI municipal presidents and discredited their public efforts—like those of low-level CFE and state officials—to persuade the townspeople to accept or ignore the dam.[3] Yet defying and discrediting such actors in the towns was a very different matter from gaining access to power holders in positions higher up in the political system in order to make regional opposition to the dam visible.

In this regard, the demonstration, over a thousand strong, held by the PRT/UGOCEP in November 28, 1990, provided the Nahuas with an important platform from which to launch their campaign at the

---

[3] Such pro-dam actors, CPNAB leaders argued, were simply obeying political orders from above out of self-interest—in accordance with the logic of clientelism.

ple, and appealed to the president's benevolence and paternalism: "We have decided to bring our vigorous protest against the CFE project directly to you, Mr. President, because we know of your government's strong commitment to the defense of ourselves, Mexico's indigenous groups." While containing no explicit reference to rights, the petition ended by framing the conflict within the context of the president's pluralist discourse and the international political conjuncture:

> Mr. President, our towns are very well known, not just in the Mexican Republic but also in many foreign countries around the world, for our bark paintings and our artisanship in producing pottery, wooden masks, handwoven hammocks, and other craft items. We have given much to our country, to the point that one of our bark paintings now appears on television with the words, "México se pinta solo," showing that our art is considered part of the patrimony of all Mexicans. How is it possible that Mexico, and the government over which you preside, should celebrate the Quincentenary of the discovery of America with a project that would destroy a region of the most authentic Mexican culture?

This petition, like the letter to Ruiz Massieu, was delivered with accompanying materials—in this case, the ILO documents and a brief letter stating that if a reply were not received by the end of December, the CPNAB would be forced to adopt alternative courses of action.

Also like the letter to Ruiz Massieu, the petition to Salinas ensured that the CPNAB could later demonstrate its good efforts to resolve its demands first through existing channels of representation. Both petitions were a means to establish the existence, and the political autonomy, of the CPNAB and should be seen as important rituals in the process of nonviolent mobilization. They laid the groundwork for the subsequent war of position against state and federal authorities.

Consolidating Resistance in the Upper Balsas

Three days after visiting Iguala, Salinas presented to the Mexican Congress his proposal to reform Article 4 of the Mexican Constitution so as to recognize the "pluricultural composition of the Mexican nation." The first feature report on the Nahuas' struggle to appear in the national press (an article by Martha García in *El Nacional*, December 12, 1990) made explicit the contradictions between the proposed amendment and the threat of ethnocide facing the Nahuas as a result of the government's dam policy. These contradictions were also underlined in the first published commentary on the CPNAB; the

author, Daniel Cazés, suggested the matter be taken up by the recently created National Human Rights Commission (CNDH) (*La Jornada*, December 22, 1990). These articles marked the initial results of
the CPNAB's war of position against the federal authorities. Nevertheless, from early December 1990 to late January 1991, the focus of
struggle continued to be the western region.

In the second half of December, three general assemblies were
held in three different towns in the western region, along with the
first "solidarity and information" roadblock on the Mexico-Acapulco
highway. These assemblies were a crucial part of a strategy to consolidate consensus against the dam at the grassroots. In part, they
were a response to continuing government efforts to dismember and
silence the movement.[5] But the assemblies were also a recognition that
in towns where they had not been held, the towns' articulation to the
CPNAB had been via the town authorities or, in exceptional cases like
San Francisco Ozomotlan, via one or two committed individuals. If
the movement were to be successful, it had to be based on a clear understanding of the dam's consequences and the possibilities for effective grassroots resistance, not least to ensure that the *comisarios*, the
obvious targets for co-optation, were held accountable by their citizens.

Assemblies generally lasted between four and six hours and had a
standard form. The date and place were set at the previous assembly,
and relevant town authorities were requested to make appropriate
preparations. Delegates set the agenda in a preparatory meeting.
Upon arriving, delegates set up the CPNAB's banner, CFE maps
showing the "reservoir area" and relocation sites, and photos of protest actions and copies of press reports. They then joined town
authorities in calling all the townspeople—including women and
children—and registering the arrival of delegations from other towns
and allies from outside the region. Assemblies commenced with in-
troductions of the CPNAB secretaries, *comisarios*, municipal authorities, and outsiders. Elections of officers to oversee procedure (chair,
secretary, vote counters) then took place.

Speeches generally opened with accounts of the CPNAB's formation and internal organization, affirming its non-party, indigenous
identity. They then moved on to explain the implications of the CFE
project: the loss of lives and the flooding of towns, houses, churches,
and agricultural lands, but also the inviability of resettling the communities on stony, mountainous sites that had no sources of water.
These predictions were reinforced with a video of the Chinantec relo-

---

[5] The most overt examples of government efforts include letters from the president of
Tepecoacuilco summoning *comisarios* to discuss the dam, and the intimidating presence of the army in Xalitla for three days in mid–December, supposedly to investi-
gate drugs and cattle theft.

Though general assemblies continued, the focus of the campaign shifted from then on.

Campaigning in Mexico City

By late January 1991, the CPNAB had established a political presence in the region. Yet it had failed to break the official line that the dam was "still under study," despite contrary empirical evidence and CFE press statements in other contexts that construction would commence shortly (see, for example, *La Jornada*, January 23, 1991, p. 27). Nor had the CPNAB gained government recognition as a "valid interlocutor," a crucial step in any grassroots struggle in Mexico. The next phase in the war of position was to take demands to the federal authorities in Mexico City; the target was the INI.

The INI had not replied to the Nahuas' October letter requesting information and support. In their few press statements, INI functionaries had simply repeated the official version, which for CPNAB leaders seemed to corroborate INI complicity with the CFE. The urgency of challenging the INI lay in the suspicion that, as the state agency responsible for indigenous matters, the INI would claim the role of representing the Nahuas in negotiations between federal agencies. Given the INI's lack of autonomy and its subordinate position within the federal state apparatus, this would mean negotiating the terms of relocation, not the cancellation of the project. At the same time, the obvious contradictions between the INI's newly established program promoting indigenous rights and its refusal to respond to, or recognize, the CPNAB (along with its past and current role in dam relocations) provided strategic political leverage for the CPNAB.

For this phase the CPNAB leaders adopted strategies based on a realistic appraisal of the forces lined up against them and the socio-economic obstacles to establishing a mass presence in the capital city. Strategies aimed to maximize the CPNAB's voice and to emphasize the organization's autonomy and the morality, legality, and justice of its demands. Initial plans, ratified at the December general assemblies, included a hunger strike and an overture to the environmental pressure group of prominent Mexican intellectuals (the Grupo de los Cien), both timed to coincide with the annual pilgrimage from Xalitla to the national shrine of the Virgin of Guadalupe in Mexico City. These strategies depended on obtaining press coverage, a major stumbling block for an unknown regional organization at a time when "indigenous issues" were generally outside the news agenda. Attracting the press would be up to the CPNAB delegates and the three journalists on the support committee.

The national media campaign was launched on February 8, 1991, with the publication of an exclusive interview with INI director Arturo Warman in *El Nacional*. This was Warman's first public statement on the situation in the Upper Balsas; in it he interpreted the Nahuas' protests as a result of "miscommunications" with the state government and CFE. This interview provided a clear reference point for contestations, the first of which appeared the very same day in *El Universal*.

On February 9, a CPNAB delegation marched from the Basilica of the Virgin of Guadalupe on the outskirts of Mexico City to the Zócalo (the capital city's main square). They held a press conference, and Merenciano Máximo, of Xalitla, began a hunger strike with hunger strikers from another regional indigenous organization, the National Coordinating Committee of Indigenous Peoples (CNPI). The hunger strike provided the CPNAB's campaign with a dramatic anchor point and ensured day-to-day coverage in *La Jornada*. However, such protests by obscure rural organizations are common and do not guarantee response from government or state agencies. So in order to amplify press coverage, the CPNAB support committee journalists organized an exhibition of Claro's photos from the Upper Balsas at the gallery of the Unión de Vecinos y Damnificados—one of Mexico City's strongest popular organizations. Press attendance at the opening on February 11 was assured by the organizers' personal contacts. As a result, as the campaign proceeded, feature articles on the Nahuas' struggle proliferated in the national press.

On February 13, the INI's position began to shift. Jesús Rubiell, head of social development, declared that the dam would not be built for another two years and that the INI was prepared to meet with the CPNAB, send a team to assess the "real situation" in the Upper Balsas, and set up projects for the towns (*La Jornada*, February 13, 1991, p. 21). The CPNAB retorted that in two years time the Nahuas would be in the same position (*La Jornada*, February 14, 1991, p. 27). An appointment with the INI was set for Monday, February 18, and the CPNAB used the intervening days to strengthen its bargaining hand. Merenciano Máximo continued his hunger strike, while the CPNAB and the CNPI secured publication of a letter to President Salinas on the editorial page of *La Jornada*, in which they denounced "bureaucratism" and the violation of their rights by government officials.

The CPNAB's trump card was reserved for the day of the meeting. A full-page protest letter signed by CPNAB officeholders, members of the national support committee, and the Grupo de los Cien appeared in *La Jornada*. It laid out in very forthright fashion all the reasons for the CPNAB's opposition to the dam. The first section detailed the disastrous impacts the dam would have on the people of the region; the

GEA researchers who could provide a technical-environmental critique of the CFE project.[8]

The CPNAB consolidated its reach regionally by organizing general assemblies in towns where none had been held previously. Asserting the CPNAB's political presence continued to be of paramount importance. For example, after anonymous visitors attempted to intimidate and bribe the Xalitla *comisario* in late June 1991, the CPNAB organized a Solidarity Forum in Xalitla on July 28 to demonstrate the strength of its strategic alliances and capacity for organization. Opposition parties, academics, and environmental, indigenous, and popular organizations all publicly pledged their support to the Nahuas' cause. But the strongest mark was made by engineer Carlos Pérez Aguirre, who outlined the technical inviability of the Tetelcingo project. Because Pérez Aguirre was a member of the PRI and a former secretary of public works and urban development for Guerrero, he could not be dismissed as a member of the "professional opposition."[9]

During this period the CPNAB also started to link up with the broader indigenous movement, an alliance that later enabled it to capitalize on the historic conjuncture of the Quincentenary. In late April a coordinator from the Mexican Council of Five Hundred Years of Indigenous and Popular Resistance (CM500ARI) attended a CPNAB general assembly and invited CPNAB members to participate in the national coordinating council. One outcome of this alliance was that on September 12, 1991, CPNAB delegates joined forces with leaders of other indigenous organizations in Guerrero to form the Guerrero Council of 500 Years of Indian and Popular Resistance (Consejo Guerrerense de Quinientos Años de Resistencia Indígena y Popular, or Consejo Guerrerense)—the first statewide indigenous organization independent of political parties. Additionally, membership of the CM500ARI opened opportunities to take the Nahuas' campaign to international forums and thereby extend the CPNAB's networks with international NGOs.

The CPNAB's alliances with the converging indigenous movement defined the organization's place in the long-term struggle to gain effective recognition for indigenous rights in Mexico. In the short term they spurred decisions to extend the exercise of these rights in the region. At the CPNAB's first anniversary celebrations in October 1991, the general assembly approved a proposal that the CPNAB ex-

---

[8] Such critiques were presented at the first national conference held on the social impact of large-scale dams and a later seminar on regional development convened by the CPNAB at the Autonomous University of Guerrero. These conferences enabled CPNAB delegates to extend their networks to academics.

[9] The night before the forum Governor Ruiz Massieu telephoned Pérez Aguirre to request that he not attend the forum. Pérez later learned that President Salinas had discussed his speech at a meeting in Los Pinos, the presidential residence.

pand its representative role beyond the original remit of campaigning against the dam and take on the task of representing the Nahua towns in relation to general problems. A sign of increasing political confidence, this proposal was also a response to contingent events in the western region. First, a cholera epidemic reached the region in September, killing at least forty-five people. Officials denied that there was a health crisis, and it was only through the CPNAB delegates' repeated efforts that health teams were finally sent in. Second, the recent arrival of the Mexican Petroleum Company (PEMEX) for exploratory drilling and of Ingenieros Civiles Asociados (ICA) to construct a bridge over the Balsas River for the new Cuernavaca-Acapulco highway was creating unprecedented disruption. In the absence of responsive municipal government, some towns had invited the CPNAB to negotiate with these companies on their behalf.

The CPNAB Blockade in Oapan

Between late October 1991 and early January 1992, the CPNAB made little progress in its campaign against construction of the Tetelcingo dam. It had not conducted direct negotiations with either the state or the federal government. Even its negotiations with the INI had shrunk to the details of the alternative development project, on which Warman had requested revisions in December. The INI seemed to have become a buffer between the movement and the political system, deflecting conflict away from government. But there was also a loss of momentum within the movement. Constant innovation is difficult. The "news value" of the Nahuas' story appeared exhausted, and the CPNAB seemed prepared to bide its time until the Quincentenary to press its agenda directly with the federal government. Nevertheless, a series of little-publicized events occurred during this period which in late January 1992 were to culminate in the CPNAB's most intensive grassroots mobilization: a nineteen-day roadblock in Oapan. Led by CPNAB general secretary Sixto Cabañas, this would break the political impasse and open up direct negotiations with the state government.

The focal point of the resistance shifted to Oapan because of perceptions there that the incursion of ICA and PEMEX was having deleterious impacts on regional space and society. The townspeople saw the companies' activities as blatant evidence of social injustice for a number of reasons. First, they contrasted the speed with which the companies were able to set up camps with services versus the lack of municipal services in their town.[10] Second, they noted that neither

---

[10] The Oapan comisario that year received no materials from the municipal authorities

The political authorities' first attempt to resolve the conflict came on February 8, 1992, two weeks after the start of the roadblock and simultaneous with another roadblock on the Mexico-Acapulco highway. Óscar Bárcenas, municipal president of Tepecoacuilco, summoned the *comisarios* from the CPNAB towns under his jurisdiction and offered the Oapan *comisario* a number of public works along with a letter from the state government canceling the dam. The Oapan assembly rejected this offer outright—based on Bárcenas's record of acting with impunity and on evidence that the letter was a classic deception, carrying a December date and lacking a reference number.

A second summons came the next day via PRD federal deputy García Castro; it directed the CPNAB to meet with Governor Ruiz Massieu the next morning. With only four days remaining before his fifth annual government report, Ruiz Massieu informed the CPNAB that he had appointed his secretary of government to mediate negotiations with ICA, scheduled to begin on the following Wednesday. There, the CPNAB would receive an official letter canceling the San Juan Tetelcingo dam—but only for one year, the duration of Ruiz Massieu's term in office.

On February, 13, 1992, Ruiz Massieu publicly announced his cancellation of the dam in his annual report. Meanwhile, the Oapan blockade was lifted when ICA started paving the road through the western region, thereby meeting the petitioners' first demand. After nearly a year and a half of struggle, the CPNAB had finally obtained recognition as a "legitimate interlocutor" and won its main demand from the state government. Additionally, it had extended its role to include negotiating for services. The war of position in the state had been won—provisionally; the final stage of the campaign was to obtain ratification of Ruiz Massieu's "cancellation" from the president.

The Quincentenary

From the beginning of the mobilization, the Quincentenary had shaped the CPNAB campaign and provided some leverage for articulating the Nahuas' demands with the federal government. Yet the government's symbolic demonstrations of commitment to indigenous peoples internationally and domestically were channeled into cultural events and managed to avoid dealing with the economic and political legacies of the Conquest or the demands of grassroots movements (Hindley 1996). Meeting with indigenous political or economic organizations was not on the official agenda. It was only through mobilization in alliance with the broader indigenous movement that the CPNAB had the opportunity to present its demand directly to the president on October 13, 1992.

By June 1992, the strategic opportunities offered by participation in the CM500ARI had proven their worth. CPNAB delegate Marcelino Díaz became one of four CM500ARI coordinators responsible for organizing the Quincentenary protests.[15] The plan was to organize marches from Mexico's different indigenous regions under the shared banner of the March of Indigenous Dignity and Resistance. These would converge in Mexico City on October 11 in order to contest the official celebrations on October 12. In the meantime, the CM500ARI would seek an appointment with the president, hoping that Salinas, anxious to show his commitment to indigenous peoples, would not refuse.

This plan appeared to be the perfect vehicle for the CPNAB to gain access to the president and obtain the cancellation of the dam project. Implementing the plan was far from straightforward, however. The CM500ARI had never taken on the task of mobilization. And the CPNAB had held no general assemblies or direct protest actions between the end of the ICA blockade in early February and mid–June, when the march was planned. The CPNAB's primary focus had turned to weekly negotiations with the state government and ICA over the blockade petition. Threats of renewed mobilization sometimes surfaced to strengthen their bargaining position, but the negotiations had become routinized. This transformation of relations with state government came accompanied by shifts in the region's political atmosphere. Following Ruiz Massieu's "cancellation" of the dam, the main collective events had been acts of celebration. As Martha García noted, in their town fiestas and everyday behaviors the Nahua townspeople were expressing their view that the dam threat had been lifted.[16]

A further obstacle to the Quincentenary plan was the deepening factional conflict among CPNAB delegates. Díaz and his confidants advocated remobilization. Others argued that continuing negotiations with the state government and negotiations with the INI over the alternative development project was the most appropriate strategic path for the CPNAB.

However, new evidence emerged that strengthened Díaz's position. The new INI director, Guillermo Espinosa, informed the CPNAB that he had been unable to obtain documents from the CFE or from the president that ratified the governor's cancellation. Therefore, he

---

[15] As a participant in the CM500ARI, Marcelino Díaz attended the Non-Governmental Conference on Environment and Development in Paris, the World Indigenous Conference on Environment, Development and Territory, and the NGO Global Forum in Rio de Janeiro.

[16] Projects embodying faith in the future, like building houses and getting married, that had been postponed due to the profound anxieties and uncertainty provoked by the CFE project were resumed (*Ojarasca*, May 1992: 13–14).

could pursue their petition no further (CPNAB Assembly Minutes, June 23, 1992). Subsequently, Leonardo Rodríguez Alcaine, national head of the Electrical Workers' Union (SUTERM), announced that, "regardless of who may be hurt, who may be displeased, the San Juan Tetelcingo dam is going to be built" (*Uno Más Uno*, August 14, 1992, p. 29). This declaration by one of the most interested parties confirmed the importance of the march and the urgency of obtaining a presidential cancellation.

Because some of the CPNAB leadership continued to oppose the march, in late August Díaz and his allies decided to put the matter directly to the towns. They visited each town in the western region to explain the march and ask for support. At the general assembly in San Juan Tetelcingo in early September, the Copalillo authorities, who generally remained neutral in the factional conflicts, came out in support of Díaz and swayed the balance in favor of the march. The CPNAB towns would participate, along with the other organizations in the Consejo Guerrerense.

The March of Indigenous Resistance and Dignity that left Chilpancingo on October 3, 1992, had an inauspicious beginning. It was planned to draw support from other popular sectors and coincide with a teachers' rally. But a storm scattered the demonstrators, leaving the small contingent of seventy-two indigenous marchers unsupported: Amuzgos from the Costa Chica, Tlapanecos and Nahuas from La Montaña, and a few individuals from the CPNAB. Others would join later, however. In Xalitla 250 people were incorporated from Nahua towns in the western region, and a delegation of 50 from Copalillo joined up in Iguala.[17] Not all the towns participated, but most did, making the CPNAB the strongest force under the Consejo Guerrerense's umbrella. Along the way, popular organizations, ecclesiastical base communities, and the PRD provided the marchers with food and shelter. On reaching Mexico City on October 11, the marchers numbered over seven hundred and represented the four principal indigenous peoples of Guerrero: Amuzgos, Mixtecos, Nahuas, and Tlapanecos.

The convergence of marches from different states was planned to maximize the symbolic significance of the protest and the media attention it attracted. That afternoon the Guerrero marchers were welcomed by the ecclesiastical base communities and met with indigenous contingents from all over the country in the Plaza of the Three Cultures in Tlatelolco, the site of the last indigenous resistance to Cortés. Originally conceived as a rally to mourn the assaults and vio-

---

[17] The Upper Balsas delegations were organized in diverse ways: in Copalillo by the municipal authorities; in the western region by the towns authorities, some adopting a relay rotation system and others marching all the way.

lations of the Conquest, it seems to have turned into an indigenous fiesta, complete with performances of dance and music. After the rally, the marchers proceeded to the Basilica of the Virgin of Guadalupe, where they slept. The following morning they attended a special mass held in recognition of the inextricable relationship between colonization and evangelization, during which progressive priests asked forgiveness for the violations of the past. Present also were journalists from the national and foreign media who followed the several thousand indigenous protesters to the Zócalo, where approximately 200,000 people were gathered for the popular fiesta.

It was to this audience of journalists that the two indigenous speakers—Marcelino Díaz from Guerrero, and Carlos Díaz Torres from Oaxaca—directed their speeches. Their message also went out to the Mexican government: they demanded an appointment with the president and announced that they would not leave until it was granted. It was only at 11 PM, as the marchers were preparing to spend the night in the Zócalo, that the leaders received a reply: the president would meet with indigenous representatives in the presidential residence the next morning.

The magnitude of the Nahuas' problem and the fact that Marcelino Díaz was one of the march's organizers assured the CPNAB access to the meeting—and to the president. As Díaz later recounted, after a brief introduction, he went straight to the question of the Tetelcingo dam:

> I have here a document [Ruiz Massieu's cancellation letter]. The president will recall that on December 4, 1990, we met in Iguala, Guerrero, and we raised this matter. You agreed to send us a reply within twenty days, but we've heard nothing since. [At this point, Díaz notes, Salinas said, "Ah, yes," making it clear that he did remember.] On February 12, 1992, we were told that you ordered the governor to issue a document stating that the San Juan Tetelcingo dam has been totally canceled. [Díaz then turned to look at Salinas, who nodded as if to say, "yes, that's true."] Mr. President, if it's true that you agree, I beg you to ratify, in this same document, that the San Juan Tetelcingo dam is totally canceled.

Then, given that the president had confirmed this understanding in the presence of forty-four indigenous delegates from all over the country, Díaz reports that he crossed the ten meters between them and said: "Here is a pen." Salinas responded that he had his own pen and then signed the document, or rather, as Díaz notes, "a copy of the document; it should have been the original signed by the governor."

At the end of the meeting Salinas instructed Carlos Rojas (head of SEDESOL, the Ministry of Social Development) and the INI director to deal with the package of four hundred demands presented by the indigenous organizations. He also made his position about the CFE project clear:

> I was always up to date on the matter of the San Juan Tetelcingo dam. I want to tell you that the San Juan Tetelcingo is canceled, at least for the remainder of my term. Now you all must demonstrate, with the proposals that have been put forward on other occasions, that your proposal is viable. Perhaps you want to contact the CFE to inform them that I've reached this judgment.

The president's "cancellation," like Ruiz Massieu's, would not be binding on his successor. Nor was it recognized by the CFE, which viewed it as merely a "suspension." Yet this meeting with Salinas marks the culmination of the war of position to stop the dam. By January 1995, the time that the CPNAB had set for remobilizing and taking its demands to the new president, macropolitical events had intervened to ensure that the Tetelcingo dam would not be built. The Zapatista uprising in January 1994 and the economic crisis of late December of that year and the subsequent deep recession transformed the political and economic environment on which the implementation of the project had depended.

The final seal of closure on the remobilization against the dam came from an unexpected quarter. In November 1994, four years after the CPNAB had written to the International Labour Organisation, an ILO request came for "more up to date information about the San Juan Tetelcingo dam." In June 1995, CPNAB leaders received a photocopied page from the "Observations on Ratified Conventions" section of the ILO's 1995 *Report of the Committee of Experts on the Application of Conventions and Recommendations*. The third point on this page reads as follows:

> Articles 4 and 7 (environment and development). The Commission takes note with interest that the San Juan Tetelcingo hydroelectric project was canceled on October 13th, 1992, by the President of the Republic and the State Governor of Guerrero, due to the fact that it was not beneficial to the communities of the region. Noting that this action was taken due to a resolution adopted by the Consejo de Pueblos Nahuas del Alto Balsas (ILO 1995).

Conclusions

The Nahuas' mobilization against the Tetelcingo dam led to a popular democratic outcome to the conflict over the future of this region. However, this popular democratic outcome, understood as the inclusion of the local people's demands in the decision-making process, should not be confused with a democratizing impact on government or state policy. The government's resolutions—the INI's "suspension" and Ruiz Massieu's and Salinas's "cancellations"—were open ended and contingent. The cancellations were clearly shaped by prevailing political conjunctures. Thus, although the Nahuas framed their demand under the rubric of indigenous rights, this demand was conceded as a pragmatic response to mobilization. In sum, these political resolutions bore all the hallmarks of a liberalized authoritarian regime as defined by Loaeza (1994). Regarding state policies of dam construction, the CFE never officially recognized the "cancellation" of the Tetelcingo project, much less the grounds raised by the Nahua opposition for rethinking general policy.

In this respect, the importance of the Nahuas' struggle as a precedent for future rural and indigenous peoples facing the same threat lies in its demonstration effect. The mobilization showed that resistance to large-scale dams can succeed in Mexico. It revealed how political liberalization had undermined the authoritarian conditions on which previous dam construction had rested; the press, opposition political parties, and environmental NGOs all played a critical role in protecting the movement and preventing the suffocation of organized dissent by forces favoring the dam. For indigenous peoples, the Nahuas' campaign also showed how indigenous rights could be deployed to contest the utilitarian logic of discourses legitimizing dams in the name of "national development." The fact that CPNAB leaders have told the story of their "great mobilization" in countless forums on rural and indigenous matters around Mexico means that this precedent is likely to inform the terrain on which future struggles against such projects occur.

At the same time, our focus on the micropolitics of mobilization has shown how the movement in the Upper Balsas was organized, how strategy was defined and decided, and what the leadership's central role was at each stage of the struggle. The following points are worth reemphasizing. The CPNAB was initially constructed by articulating the existing units of indigenous government and democratically elected indigenous leaders to the project of resistance against the dam. In the Copalillo region, it was constituted through the municipal authorities and town *comisarios*; in the western region, it was through town *comisarios* and consolidated at the grassroots through assemblies held in the different towns. Although leadership of the movement was formally conferred through elections of *comisarios*, in practice it was the delegates participating on a voluntary basis who emerged as the de facto leaders. It was this small group of professionals who assessed the terrain of struggle and defined strategic choices at each point of the mobilization. They were responsible for contacting strategic allies, identifying the potential political resources such allies might contribute, and selecting which allies to deploy at different stages of the struggle. However, approval for the implementation of strategy was sought from the CPNAB general assemblies, which were usually attended by the majority of *comisarios* as well as the people from the specific town where each was held. When strategy involved mass participation, it was generally town *comisarios* and assemblies that organized delegations (with the support of municipal authorities in the Copalillo region). The blockade in Oapan, initially conceived as an action to win concessions on specific demands, was an exception to this.

There is little doubt that by demonstrating the effectiveness of collective organization and the possibility of challenging the local, state, and federal governments, mobilization against the dam created a solid basis for long-term political change in the Upper Balsas. The mobilization contributed to the local peoples' sense of citizenship and to their understanding of the broader political changes occurring in Mexican society. It recast long-standing relations of political exclusion: those between towns and their municipal/state authorities in the western region; and those within towns, such as taboos about women's participation in political activities. Moreover, the collective political identities constituted during the campaign against the dam have become the basis of negotiations over the creation of an indigenous municipality in the western region and the definition of the Upper Balsas as an autonomous indigenous region.

If such projects signify an assertion of the desirability of autonomous indigenous government over the neglectful and unaccountable mestizo–PRI government, they are also a means to democratize the CPNAB itself. Between 1992 and 1994, rivalries between delegates led to the division of the CPNAB into two competing organizations. This division was directly related to conflicts generated by the disjuncture between the CPNAB's formal and de facto leadership; the delegates were subject to neither formal mechanisms of accountability nor clear rules for ensuring the circulation of leadership or the resolution of disputes over strategic choices. The indigenous municipality and autonomous region would institutionalize such mechanisms and rules. If these political projects succeed, it will then be possible to speak of the democratization of local politics.

References

Adams, W.M. 1990. *Green Development: Environment and Sustainability in the Third World.* London: Routledge

Bartolomé, M., and Alicia Barabás. 1990. *La Presa Cerro de Oro y el Ingeniero Gran Dios.* Mexico City: Instituto Nacional Indigenista.

Coleman, Kenneth M., and Charles L. Davis. 1983. "Pre-emptive Reform and the Mexican Working Class," *Latin American Research Review* 18: 3–32.

Cook, Maria Lorena, Kevin J. Middlebrook, and Juan Molinar Horcasitas, eds. 1994. *The Politics of Economic Restructuring: State-Society Relations and Regime Change in Mexico.* Contemporary Perspectives in U.S.–Mexican Studies, no. 7. La Jolla: Center for U.S.–Mexican Studies, University of California, San Diego.

Cornelius, Wayne A., Judith Gentleman, and Peter H. Smith, eds. 1989. *Mexico's Alternative Political Futures.* Monograph Series, no. 30. La Jolla: Center for U.S.–Mexican Studies, University of California, San Diego.

Craig, Ann. 1990. "Institutional Context and Popular Strategies." In *Popular Movements and Political Change in Mexico*, edited by Joe Foweraker and Ann L. Craig. Boulder, Colo.: Lynne Rienner, in association with the Center for U.S.–Mexican Studies, University of California, San Diego.

Estrada Castañón, Alba Teresa. 1994. *Guerrero: sociedad, economía, política, cultura.* Mexico City: Universidad Nacional Autónoma de México.

Estrada Guadalupe, Sabino. 1988. "El ayuntamiento popular y las alternativas de desarrollo en Copalillo, Guerrero." Bachelor's thesis, Universidad Nacional Autónoma de México.

Fox, Jonathan, ed. 1990. *The Challenge of Rural Democratisation: Perspectives from Latin America and the Philippines.* London: Frank Cass.

García Calvario, Marco, and Ricardo Riva Palacios. 1990. *Ingeniería geológica del proyecto hidroeléctrico San Juan Tetelcingo, Río Balsas, Estado de Guerrero, México.* Cuernavaca: Comisión Federal de Electricidad.

Gómez, Magdalena. 1991. *Derechos indígenas: lectura comentada del Convenio 169 de la Organización Internacional del Trabajo.* Mexico City: Instituto Nacional Indigenista.

Gramsci, Antonio. 1991. *Selections from the Prison Notebooks.* London: Lawrence and Wishart.

Hall, Anthony. 1994. "Grassroots Action for Resettlement Planning: Brazil and Beyond," *World Development* 22 (12): 1793–1809.

Hellman, Judith Adler. 1994. "Mexican Movements, Clientelism, and the Process of Democratization," *Latin American Perspectives* 81 (21): 124–42.

Hindley, Jane. 1996. "Towards a Pluricultural Nation: *Indigenismo* and the Reform of Article 4." In *Dismantling the Mexican State*, edited by Rob Aitken, Nikki Craske, Gareth A. Jones, and David E. Stansfield. London: Macmillan.

Hobsbawm, Eric. 1973. "Peasants and Politics," *Journal of Peasant Studies* 1 (1): 3–22.

ILO (International Labour Organisation). 1995. *Report of the Committee of Experts on the Application of Conventions and Recommendations.* Geneva: International Labour Office.

Loaeza, Soledad. 1994. "Political Liberalization and Uncertainty in Mexico."
    In *The Politics of Economic Restructuring: State-Society Relations and Regime
    Change in Mexico,* edited by Maria Lorena Cook, Kevin J. Middlebrook,
    and Juan Molinar Horcasitas. La Jolla: Center for U.S.–Mexican Studies,
    University of California, San Diego.
Scott, James C. 1990. *Domination and the Arts of Resistance. Hidden Transcripts.*
    New Haven, Conn.: Yale University Press.

11

Resisting Neoliberalism, Constructing Citizenship: Indigenous Movements in Chiapas

Neil Harvey

The growing interest in the relationship between local politics and democratization is an important corrective to those studies that take the nation-state as the principal unit of analysis. A regional perspective can shed light on the different ways in which broader changes associated with neoliberal economic restructuring and political reform are affected by regional dynamics. This chapter examines how indigenous organizations in Chiapas, including, of course, the Zapatista Army of National Liberation (EZLN), have been shaped by the profound economic and political transition initiated in Mexico in the early 1980s. In turn, these struggles have also shaped the transition itself, by inserting new demands, actors, and meanings into national (and even international) debates concerning democracy and development.

In this respect, it is important to consider how, in the case of Chiapas, long-standing material grievances have been articulated within a discourse of civil and political rights. However, the emergence of a democratic discourse should not lead to an uncritical reading of the struggles for voice. The public expression of indigenous demands within the discourse of citizenship and human rights is but one possible path of engaging the political system. The presence of other

The author would like to thank Héctor Díaz Polanco, Todd Eisenstadt, Rosalva Aída Hernández Castillo, Jane Hindley, and Shannan Mattiace for their helpful comments on earlier draft versions of this chapter.

armed groups, most notably the Popular Revolutionary Army (EPR), is a clear indication that the Zapatistas' discourse of democratization is not the only one that moves people to rebel against social injustice and repression. There are also many ambiguities in how citizenship is being constructed in Mexico by different social movements, governmental actors, the media, and intellectuals.

Rather than assuming a unilinear path toward citizenship, this chapter brings out the complex process of negotiating a concept of citizenship that acts as a unifying point for diverse projects of the indigenous population. Citizenship is therefore defined not solely in terms of a set of universal traits (the equal rights of all subjects within a state) but as the articulating principle around which a plurality of social groups and individuals challenge different forms of domination by adhering to the ethical and political ideals of equality and liberty (Mouffe 1993: 84). The Zapatistas' search for "words that others might understand" is an example of this articulation.[1] It should be noted that the content of this political project is not constrained by the individualist assumptions of liberal democracy. By bringing together numerous struggles against discrimination and authoritarianism, the EZLN is proposing a unique form of what Laclau and Mouffe have termed "radical democratic citizenship" (Laclau and Mouffe 1985; Mouffe 1993).

But is radical democratic citizenship a theoretically valid proposition in the capitalist periphery? Laclau and Mouffe would say no. For them, radical democracy, which involves the articulation of an infinite number of subject positions through a democratic "chain of equivalence," is contingent on the prior historical fact of liberal democracy. That is, radical democracy cannot emerge out of authoritarianism, but only as the extension of the democratic revolution that was initiated by the Enlightenment. This project is not constrained by the hegemony of bourgeois liberalism but is open to radical transformation through the struggles of diverse social movements around multiple points of antagonism. In contrast, in Third World countries, Laclau and Mouffe argue that the political field has traditionally been divided more clearly in binary oppositions, for example, between peasants and landlords, people and oligarchy, nation and imperialism, proletariat and bourgeoisie (Laclau and Mouffe 1985: 131). Social agents therefore occupy *popular subject positions*, in contrast to the *democratic subject positions* occupied by the social movements in advanced industrial societies.

---

[1] "The men and women of the EZLN, the faceless ones, the ones who walk in the night and who belong to mountains, have sought words that other men and women could understand. And so they say: First. - We demand that there be free and democratic elections" (CCRI–Ejército Zapatista de Liberación Nacional, February 1994, cited in Dussel 1995: 54).

This distinction has been criticized by Escobar (1992: 79) on the grounds that it invokes a necessary "threshold" of democratic values *before* social movements can engage in the struggle for radical democracy. As a result, it implies a teleology that is akin to that of other theories of modernization and development and fails to see the implications of its own argument. The case of Chiapas brings out these implications more fully. Unless we believe that agents in "Third World" struggles are somehow more unified than in the "First World," then the articulation of multiple subject positions through democratic discourse is entirely possible and consistent with the extension of the democratic revolution. Just as the struggles of minorities in liberal capitalist societies bring new meanings to democratic discourse, so do those of popular movements in Latin America. This is not to deny that democratic struggles face greater obstacles where the historical precedent is authoritarianism rather than liberalism, but nor does it rule out culturally specific constructions of radical democratic citizenship in which the assertion of indigenous identities is inseparable from the modern task of democratization.

We should therefore think of radical democracy not solely in terms of the expansion of the discursive hegemony of a set of universal ethico-political values, but as the practical appropriation and transformation of these values by democratic subjects. This process will inevitably entail local specificities that may appear as contradictory for the democratic ideal. However, it would be just as contradictory, as well as politically dangerous, to ignore history and culture for the sake of abstract rather than concrete expressions of democratic aspirations. In the words of an indigenous woman speaking at a forum in Chiapas in 1994, "we women demand respect in order to live without suffering attacks, discrimination, and repression, affirming our roots and reconstructing the history and identity of our peoples" (Convención Estatal 1994).

In Mexico, indigenous movements have sought to occupy a new space from which they can influence the country's political transition. The demand for the autonomous self-government of indigenous peoples, which was seen as peripheral prior to 1994, has become an important contribution to democratization in Mexico. The Zapatista uprising created the possibility for a new type of democracy in which conditions are created for "the effective equality and mutual respect of diverse sociocultural groups" (Díaz Polanco 1992: 162). Although we cannot predict the final outcome of the talks between the EZLN and the Mexican government, we can say that the rights of indigenous peoples constitute a key component in the reformulation of the Mexican political system. As such, they are articulated not as expressions of popular subject positions but as democratic subject positions.

This analysis finds parallels with recent work on the role of social movements in forcing democratic openings in Latin America. For example, Lehmann (1990) argues that the new social movements that emerged during the dictatorships in Brazil and Chile tended to turn more on questions of citizenship and fair treatment than on the seizure of state power and the subsequent transformation of class relations. Similarly, Foweraker (1990) has argued that popular movements in Mexico during the 1980s constituted a wedge that may force a democratic opening, not because of their economic demands but because they challenge the government's corruption, clientelism, and arbitrary use of power. This does not, of course, abandon the task of transforming class relations and economic inequalities, but it does approach that task with a different strategy to those of the guerrilla insurgencies of the 1960s and 1970s. Central to this strategy is the insistence on rights as citizens. However, the demand for rights does not necessarily find a satisfactory home in the individualist parameters of liberal philosophy. In fact, as indigenous people are discovering, the meaning of rights is far from self-evident and instead tends to emerge only through political struggle.

This theme is also echoed by the contributors to the volume edited by Jelin and Hershberg (1996a) on human rights and citizenship in Latin America. As Jelin puts it, the challenge for analysis is to document the social processes through which citizenship is constructed, "that is, the ways in which the formally defined subjects of law actually become such—in social practices, institutional systems and cultural representations" (Jelin 1996: 101). These authors are right to question the neat evolution of civil, political, and social rights that T.H. Marshall (1964) saw as the almost inevitable consequence of modernization in England. In its place we need to pay closer attention to the process whereby citizenship emerges as the contingent outcome of struggles against discrimination, poverty, and inequality. In the context of indigenous struggles we must also note that access to universal, individual rights cannot be guaranteed without positive steps to eliminate racism (Stavenhagen 1996: 147).

This chapter attempts to explain the emergence of indigenous political projects and points to what are its main implications for democratization in Mexico. In order to understand the significance of popular mobilization in Chiapas, it is argued that we need to understand the linkages between local and national processes of political change—specifically, how the changes initiated by the federal government during the 1980s unintentionally opened up spaces in which indigenous organizations were able to insert their demands through an oppositional discourse of democratization. The meaning of democracy and citizenship will continue to define the parameters of political struggle in Mexico for some time. It is therefore useful to highlight the contested nature of the current transition in Mexico in these terms.

The chapter is divided into three sections. The first discusses the implications of neoliberalism for the political tasks of controlling and mediating popular demands—that is, for the overall reproduction of Mexico's authoritarian regime. The concept of "third-order change" (taken from Hall 1993) is introduced to describe the shift toward neoliberal policy making and to underscore the distinctively *political* challenges that this type of change implies.

The following section examines how the new *indigenista* thinking was elaborated within the neoliberal policy paradigm, and how it resulted in the unsatisfactory reform of Article 4 of the Mexican Constitution in 1990. This section makes reference to the existence of a "post-indigenista" thinking that has enabled convergence around the need for deeper changes in Article 4. The final section discusses the indigenous organizations' own "transition" in terms of the evolution of their demands toward the goal of autonomy. The chapter concludes by reflecting on the culturally contingent nature of political identities in the Zapatistas' own formulation of "radical democratic citizenship."

Third-order Change and the Problem of Mediations

The evolution of the indigenous movement in Chiapas should be understood in the context of the shift in macroeconomic policy that has been pursued by the Mexican regime since 1982. In particular we need to understand the problems that this shift created for the mediation of popular demands through the institutions of the state. In fact, in Chiapas it was the crisis of traditional patterns of mediation that opened the way for a more open-ended (and often violent) process of struggle to redefine the "rules of the game," a process that is still far from over.

It is analytically useful to focus our attention on mediations for two reasons. First, we avoid reifying either the state or society as autonomous unified actors, and, second, we assert the dynamic and political nature of policy making rather than its static or rationalistic basis. Mediations can be understood as the forms of intervention in the political arena that seek to legitimize policies that promote a particular strategy of capital accumulation. In capitalist societies they are designed to shape the political terrain on which class and other social struggles take place, enabling the long-term reproduction of capitalist relations of production and exchange (Foweraker 1982). However, they are political and ideological strategies that are open to contestation from many sources and, as such, are never fully secure. Although this open-endedness of political struggle is a permanent feature of postrevolutionary Mexico, the nationalist and populist legacy provided sufficient political capital for the regime to define the main policies of rural modernization between the 1930s and the 1970s. This is not to deny the incompleteness of the state's hegemonic project or to say that resistance from below was absent in this period. However, if we are to consider macroeconomic policy and the guiding principles of rural modernization, we must also recognize the political fact that nationalism and populism held sway for close to four decades, a unique achievement in the Latin American context.

Our concern here is with the contradictions that arise when tried and trusted forms of mediation are gradually abandoned and new ones are introduced. During the last twenty years many regimes have embarked on similar processes of restructuring with greater or lesser degrees of disruption. It is therefore useful to discuss Mexico in this context.

Following O'Donnell (1979), we can say that the comparative stability of the postrevolutionary Mexican state emerged from the successful articulation of certain expressions of *lo nacional* and *lo popular*. The former strategy constructed a sense of national independence (particularly vis-à-vis the United States), while the latter sought to legitimize programs of distributive justice (for example, agrarian reform). The third type of mediation of which O'Donnell speaks—that of the legal definition of individual rights and responsibilities (modern citizenship)—existed in the written constitution but was violated in daily practice. In sum, liberal citizenship existed as an idea, but the principal linkages between officialdom and people were always *lo nacional* and *lo popular*.

It was therefore somewhat inevitable that the economic crisis and neoliberal restructuring of the 1980s would test and eventually break the power of such mediations. The program of economic restructuring took as its guide the exigencies of transnational capital. Not to restructure would leave Mexico out in the cold, the argument went. The crisis demanded trade liberalization, fewer restrictions on foreign capital, less protection for uncompetitive domestic producers, and privatization of state-owned companies. The restructuring amounted to what Hall (1993) has termed third-order change, or a shift in "policy paradigm." It was not limited to minor adjustments of available policy instruments (first-order changes) nor even more efficient use of those instruments (second-order changes), but was a redirection of the goals of economic policy. Whereas first- and second-order changes can take place within the limited sphere of governmental institutions, a shift in policy paradigm inevitably spills over into the political sphere of parties and interest groups. Nor can the debates be confined to the legislature and peak organizations (in Mexico, the federal Congress and its acceptance of various "pacts" since 1987). The influence of other actors who operate independently of the legislature and the Institutional Revolutionary Party (PRI) can be seen, at one level, in the increasing autonomy of financial institutions, and at another, in the struggles of numerous popular organizations and nongovernmental organizations (NGOs) for voice within the political sphere. Nor are these actors restricted by national boundaries. International pressures from such institutions as the World Bank and the International Monetary Fund are well known. For the case that concerns us, the role of international human rights law and the prominence of ethnicity worldwide are additional factors that intervene in contesting the terms of new policy paradigms.

Third-order change cannot be guided by purely technocratic modes of decision making. This is important to note because the technocratic view points precisely in the opposite direction, toward a policy-making process insulated from the "rent-seeking" activities of interest groups and political parties. This was the way that President Carlos Salinas de Gortari (1988–1994) approached the challenge of third-order change. Instead of negotiating suitable compromises, the regime drew up its reforms and then presented them for approval from a compliant Congress. The recalcitrants who insisted on more public debate on such key policy issues as the North American Free Trade Agreement (NAFTA) and the reforms to constitutional Article 27 were marginalized (Aguilar Zinser 1993; Calva 1993).

It is here that Hall's analysis is most penetrating. Third-order change assumes a much more ambitious task than fine-tuning the established policy paradigm. As a result it requires a sociological and political understanding of the points of support and resistance, rather than a blind faith in its own inherent merit. This type of change requires, in sum, a series of new mediations to control and manage the process of transition from above because, after all, this was a shift engineered by elites and for elites. This was the problem that faced Salinas, just as it has faced leaders as diverse as Felipe González, Margaret Thatcher, Boris Yeltsin, and Carlos Saúl Menem. Salinas's administration appeared to be based on a new level of public acceptance, but this was more often than not due to the effective publicity campaigns surrounding the National Solidarity Program (PRONASOL) and the illusory benefits of an overvalued peso. As the Chiapas uprising would reveal, the dismantling of *lo nacional* and *lo popular* was not replaced by a sufficiently secure mediation of citizenship.

Referring to the Southern Cone, O'Donnell spoke of the "nostalgia for democracy" as a powerful motive for elites to eventually disassociate themselves from irresponsible dictatorships. It was simply impossible to return to the mediations of nationalism and populism, and so the holding of elections and the return of Congress appeared at-

tractive, especially because the brutal repression of the Left had reduced the threat from that quarter. But in Mexico, where the high
point of regime legitimacy lay not in appeals to liberal democracy but
to anti-imperialism and revolutionary nationalism, the search for new
mediations from the perspective of the state has been far more problematic.

If the transition in Mexico lacks any democratic precedent, and if
the new policy paradigm weakens the effectiveness of appeals to *lo
nacional* and *lo popular*, what linkages or mediations can take their
place? In Mexico, the Salinas administration invested heavily in dismantling precisely those linkages that appealed to those who voted
for Cuauhtémoc Cárdenas in 1988—nationalism and populism. However, the slow pace of political reform was a function of the rapid
pace of economic reform, because the mediations that Salinas sought
were not to be found in the ballot box but in PRONASOL and NAFTA.
The new citizenship sought by Salinas's social liberalism was that of
the productive and cooperative individual whose demands on the
state could be expected to simply "wither away" as the self-reliant
community and the market took over. Citizenship was defined less by
individual rights (still less by collective rights) and more by the rem-
nants of populism, linked to a modernized utilitarian concept of
negative freedom—the absence of constraints on the individual's
freedom to pursue self-interest. The only problem was that, for the
vast majority of the population, material conditions did not favor
such liberty, and nowhere was this more evident than in Chiapas. The
response from the state was to rely on tried and trusted mechanisms
of political control (repression, imprisonment, draconian reforms to
the state penal code), which only compounded the frustration and
anger felt by indigenous and campesino organizations.

Jorge Alonso, writing in 1992 of the "New Mexican State," argued
that, rather than enhance the liberal notion of citizenship, the Salinas
administration appeared determined to suppress it wherever and
whenever it threatened to become a reality (Alonso 1992: 45). How
can we talk of appeals based on notions of citizenship when the
names of thousands of real citizens are shaved from the electoral roll,
and when they are replaced by fictitious or repeated names? Alonso
correctly concluded that the new Mexican state was still being fought
over, and it was to the popular sectors that we must look if the new
state was to be any more democratic than its predecessors. This theme
was echoed by González Casanova, who warned of a transition toward a "democracy without options": a neoliberal regime in which
the new policy paradigm would be effectively insulated against serious public debate (González Casanova 1992). Alonso was also correct
in predicting the costs of not finding new forms of mediation: violent
actions that cannot be completely suppressed, leading to persistent

crises of governability (1992: 46). A more hopeful scenario would emerge from the successful articulation of popular demands in a broad convergence around the principles of democracy and respect for pluralism. In sum, the state proved incapable of leading the transition to democracy and instead fell back on the oldest of all the political mediations available: presidentialism.

From the New Indigenismo to Post-Indigenismo

The current debates and struggles over indigenous peoples' rights cannot be understood independently of the third-order change to which we have been referring. What is particularly important is that we avoid reifying the state in this process. The weakening of earlier forms of mediation and the search for new ones created a set of contradictions that became most apparent in the various constitutional reforms approved during the Salinas administration. The area of indigenous issues was no exception. If we keep the ambiguous and essentially open-ended nature of policy implementation in mind, then we can more fully appreciate the strategic opportunity for indigenous organizations to insert themselves and their demands in the political system and thereby, as Foweraker has demonstrated, transform the shape of the legal and institutional terrain where political struggle takes place (Foweraker 1990, 1993).

During the 1980s and early 1990s Mexico undoubtedly saw the emergence of a new, indigenista policy paradigm. The old assimilationist models that trace their roots to Vasconcelos appear to have finally been abandoned, at least in rhetoric. The minimal accord reached between the EZLN and the government on indigenous rights and culture may be seen as the most complete recognition of this change, one that will potentially lead to further modifications of the legal and institutional terrain. But this is not the same as saying that the new, post-indigenista paradigm is a creation of the state. Instead, it is the result of struggle to redefine relations between indigenous peoples and the state, a struggle that independent indigenous organizations were able to influence to a degree not previously contemplated.

Several observers have noted that indigenous issues were given greater attention by the Salinas administration (Díaz Polanco 1992; Fox 1994a; Hindley 1996; Sarmiento 1991). For example, the budget of the National Indigenous Institute (INI) was increased eighteen-fold during the first half of Salinas's six-year term (Fox 1994a: 188), and local INI officers began to work more closely with independent grassroots organizations, such as the Oaxaca State Coffee Producers' Network (CEPCO) and the Independent Front of Indigenous Peoples of Chiapas (FIPI) (Hindley 1996; Fox 1994b).

What factors explain this sudden interest in the most marginalized sector of Mexican society? More importantly, how did indigenous organizations transform this process through their strategic political interventions? According to Díaz Polanco, the shift in government strategy began in the early 1980s with the realization that it was better to absorb ethnic differences than to suppress them. The techniques of power had to be more subtle and less violent, geared to a long-term project of remaking "national culture" in which indigenous people would take their place *as equals*, but *not as different*. The distinctive features of third-order change began to reveal themselves: a radical shift in how the "indigenous problem" was conceptualized; the salience given to notions of grassroots "participation" in development programs; the stress on individual human rights; and, most importantly, the long-term goal of constructing a harmonious polity.

Far from being an exclusionary ideology, the new *indigenismo* sought to include all peoples and provide them with the same rights and access to justice, irrespective of their ethnicity. However, as Hindley has argued, the new policies spoke of justice, not of rights, in the belief that rights were already established in law and the real issue was the procurement of justice. This interpretation not only ignored the social and economic factors that prevented indigenous peoples from access to justice, but it also reproduced the authority of the state (and specifically the executive) over the acceptable practices of indigenous peoples. Such neocolonial pretensions were fully consistent with neoliberal economics; and, believing that the philosophical questions had been solved, Salinas immediately proceeded to implement a set of reforms that would alter the legal and institutional terrain for subsequent struggles, including the one that most reflected his administration's shortcomings—the Zapatista uprising.[2]

The most significant of these reforms turned out to be the modifications to Article 4 of the Constitution.[3] The paragraph that was fi-

---

[2] Salinas's reforms are discussed by Díaz Polanco (1992: 164–70) and Hindley (1996). Besides the increase in the INI's budget, the reforms included the appointment of the prominent anthropologist Arturo Warman as head of INI (January 1989), the creation of a new National Justice Commission for Indigenous Peoples (April 1989), and ratification of the International Labour Organisation Convention 169 (August 1990). Salinas also saw that there were easy short-term benefits to be gained from portraying his government as a defender of indigenous rights. International forums, such as the first Iberoamerican Summit in Guadalajara in 1991, were ideal opportunities to present an internationally agreeable picture in the run-up to the Quincentenary and, of course, NAFTA.

[3] We can also include the reforms to Article 27 in this discussion. For reasons of space, the reader is referred to Moguel 1992 for an analysis of how the ejido reform fitted into the *transición salinista*, or what we have been calling "third-order change."

nally inserted and approved by Congress made reference, for the first time, to the pluricultural nature of the Mexican nation. It did not go beyond this to specify the collective rights that real indigenous people were demanding. In fact, the "consultation" that the new INI organized was simply a sham exercise which excluded those voices not aligned with the government. However, the reform to Article 4 generated much criticism from those people whom it was intended to assist. The issue would now be whether or not the space would be used to transform the political character of Article 4 and, subsequently, its regulatory law. This was a question that could only be answered in practice and depended on the strategic inventiveness of indigenous organizations and their leadership.

Prior to the Zapatista uprising, one of the most outspoken proponents of a "post-indigenista" Mexico was Margarito Xib Ruiz Hernández, a Tojolobal Indian from Chiapas and leader of the FIPI. Since the mid–1970s Ruiz had been an active member of one of the most important independent campesino movements in Chiapas, the Independent Confederation of Agricultural Workers and Peasants (CIOAC). In 1988 he became a federal deputy of the Mexican Socialist Party (PMS) under Mexico's rules of proportional representation. In the Chamber of Deputies, Ruiz argued in vain for more far-reaching reforms to Article 4, concluding that what was at stake was not an "indigenous problem" but a problem with indigenismo as a set of assumptions, institutions, and practices (Ruiz Hernández 1993).[4]

Although Ruiz commended the openness of PRONASOL's Regional Solidarity Funds toward independent organizations in Chiapas (including FIPI), he remained critical of the economistic approach and argued for broader, democratically managed regional development plans instead of numerous, disconnected micro-projects. Interestingly, Ruiz also noted the speed with which the government responds to maintain the initiative in setting policy agendas. Almost in parallel with the independent activities of nongovernmental organizations (NGOs), he saw the emergence of new "governmental nongovernmental organizations" (GNGOs), such as the Trust Fund to Support Indigenous Peoples and Organizations (Fideicomiso para el Apoyo a los Pueblos y Organizaciones Indígenas).

Ruiz was also fully aware that the indigenous organizations were not automatically more effective instruments simply because of their social rather than institutional origin. Many lacked the technical and administrative skills (not to mention the financial resources) that the GNGOs commanded. This constituted a central challenge for indige-

---

[4] Ruiz was also a member of the coordinating committee of the Mexican Council of 500 Years of Resistance (Consejo Mexicano 500 Años de Resistencia Indígena, Popular y Negra), which coordinated protests and demands of a wide range of indigenous and popular organizations in the context of the Quincentenary in 1992.

nous organizations if they were to increase their negotiating capacity while maintaining a distinctive set of political demands for autonomous, regional self-government.[5] The goal of the indigenous movements was therefore to establish an entire chapter of collective rights within a new Article 4. These rights would reflect the provisions of international laws to which the Mexican government is a signatory, in particular Convention 169 of the International Labour Organisation, which recognizes collective economic, political, social, and cultural rights of indigenous peoples (Hindley 1996: 231–32).

The "post-indigenista" view was finally given its chance by the Zapatista uprising. Although the early communiqués did not specify the ethnic demands of the EZLN, it was not long before the question of autonomy was posed. Of the thirty-four demands presented to the government in February 1994, the following referred specifically to indigenous people: the creation of an independent indigenous radio station; the mandating of compulsory indigenous languages for primary through university education; respect for indigenous culture and tradition; an end to discrimination against indigenous people; the granting of indigenous autonomy; the administration of their own courts by indigenous communities; the criminalization of forced expulsion from communities by government-backed caciques and allowing the expelled to be able to return; and, finally, the establishment of maternity clinics, day-care centers, nutritious food programs, *nixtamal* and tortilla mills, and training programs for indigenous women.

The attempt to separate local from national reforms (combined with the government's shift to a hard-line position following the assassination of Luis Donaldo Colosio, presidential candidate of the ruling party in March 1993) led the EZLN to reject the official response and instead turn its attention to building networks of grassroots support within civil society. It was in this context that the contacts with other indigenous leaders and organizations developed. Contesting Salinas's reform to Article 4 had provided a point of convergence which indigenous organizations were now fully able to exploit. The economic struggles for land, credit, and fair prices, while necessary to build regional organizations, were increasingly articulated in a cultural-political discourse of indigenous autonomy. In Chiapas, the declaration of autonomous pluriethnic regions in late

---

[5] In an interview with the author in January 1992, Ruiz explained how post-indigenista thinking was indispensable for a true process of democratization in Mexico. Although, as Díaz Polanco noted (1992: 148), national political parties and movements had begun to see the democratic value of pluralist respect for difference, in practice there was still a long way to go in overcoming racism or implementing ethnic-blind structures and practices. Similarly, the electoral system did not allow for the true representation of Mexico's pluriethnic composition.

1994 set the stage for a new period of mobilization to protest the illegitimacy of the new state government. These events are discussed in more detail below, but here it is important to note that, just as with Article 27, Salinas's reforms in the area of indigenous affairs rebounded on the government with an extraordinary force, obliging it to finally do what it felt it could avoid in 1989: begin to negotiate with independent indigenous organizations a more meaningful reform of the legal and institutional terrain.

Campesino Movements, Indigenous Autonomy, and Citizenship

One of the principal demands of the EZLN is that indigenous peoples should have political autonomy to make decisions affecting their own economic, social, and cultural development. This demand draws from a prior history of popular movements that have aspired to varying degrees of autonomy from existing political parties, unions, and governmental bodies. It also extends the concept of autonomy in ways that are discussed below.

How has autonomy been understood by campesino and indigenous organizations in Mexico? Since the early 1970s a new type of organization emerged throughout the country from complex and uneven processes of state reform and social mobilization (Fox 1992; Harvey 1990a; Moguel, Hernández, and Botey 1992; Otero 1989; Rello 1990). New movements resulted from the limited capacity of the official National Peasants' Confederation (CNC) to influence agrarian and rural policy, the emergence of new regional campesino leaders, and the increase in state intervention in ejido-sector agriculture during the administration of Luis Echeverría (1970–1976). As the federal government began to create new producer organizations "from above," new spaces opened up for campesino mobilization, particularly in regions like Chiapas where authoritarian elites monopolized access to land, credit, and marketing services. This vertical pattern of mobilization was soon contested as members of the new organizations demanded greater accountability from federal agencies and more autonomy in directing their internal affairs.[6] In this sense, the

---

[6] Two of the most common types of organization created in the 1970s were the Union of Ejidos (UE) and the Rural Collective Interest Association (ARIC). Both are simply formal, juridical categories and in practice vary widely in their size, objectives, and performance. The official rationale was to modernize the ejido sector by unifying similar or adjacent ejidos in larger productive units. The UE is made up of two or more ejidos and is known as a "second-level" organization. The ARIC refers to the union of two or more Unions of Ejidos and is known as a "third-level" organization in the social sector.

struggle for new forms of rural representation can be understood as the struggle for the democratic right of associational autonomy, which, in the definition of Fox (1994b: 152), "allows citizens to organize in defense of their own interests and identities without fear of external intervention or punishment."

Under the José López Portillo administration (1976–1982), repression of land struggles became more common and production-related demands appeared to offer a more viable basis for campesino mobilization. The struggle for autonomous campesino control of the production process began to take root in several regions, including Sonora, Nayarit, Hidalgo, Puebla, and Chiapas (Moguel and Robles 1990: 436–50). The capacity to establish autonomous control over the Unions of Ejidos and the Rural Collective Interest Association (ARIC) varied according to two main factors: the extent of community-level mobilization from below, and the willingness and capacity of state actors to provide an opening from above. This process, which Fox (1994b) has characterized as the "difficult transition from clientelism to citizenship," implied political conflict with local bosses tied to the traditional apparatus of the ruling PRI in remote rural districts. In most cases the transition toward associational autonomy was blocked by authoritarian governors or shifts within the federal government which weakened the hand of reformists.

During the Miguel de la Madrid government (1982–1988), functionaries close to Salinas (then head of the Ministry of Planning and Budget) attempted to open up spaces at the regional level for autonomously managed producer groups. This proved relatively successful where the support of the governor was forthcoming, as in Guerrero under Cervantes Delgado (1981–1987) but had more ambiguous effects where associational autonomy was seen as more threatening and even subversive. This was the case in Chiapas under the governorship of General Absalón Castellanos Domínguez (1982–1988) when dozens of opposition activists were arrested, imprisoned, or killed (Amnesty International 1986; Benjamin 1989; Harvey 1990b). The repression was not solely directed at the radical Left, as dissident groups within the CNC found out to their cost when demonstrating for higher guaranteed prices for corn in 1986 (Hernández 1994: 28).

Despite the limited success of associational autonomy in practice, the idea remained appealing, both as an aspiration for campesino organizations and as a means of legitimizing the reform of the state. As with the new indigenismo, Salinas was quick to perceive the potential of a discourse that upheld the autonomy of campesinos to determine their own future by freeing them from the deadweight of corrupt and bureaucratic state agencies. The state would revise its functions by shifting reduced resources into targeted social programs, and it would encourage co-responsibility from the citizenry in their implementation. This was the political strategy behind PRONASOL, which appeared to be relatively successful in containing dissent while the new policy paradigm was being implemented. In other words, it appeared that a new, less burdensome form of mediation had begun to show its worth.

However, respect for associational autonomy depended on much more than Salinas's rhetorical support for "social liberalism," and this is where political organization and strategy come in. Indeed, many observers began critically to assess the scope of campesino autonomy in the context of neoliberal restructuring and the withdrawal of the state (Bartra 1991; García de León 1989). It is worth referring briefly to the coffee sector in order to illustrate this debate in the case of Chiapas.

Three Unions of Ejidos were created in the Lacandon rain forest and Central Highlands in 1976. With the urging of catechists and Maoist advisers, they joined together in 1980 as a third-level organization, the Union of Ejido Unions and Solidary Peasant Groups of Chiapas (UU), later formalized as ARIC–Union of Ejido Unions in March 1988 (Harvey 1992). In terms of the prospects for associational autonomy, the high point for the Union of Ejido Unions was in the period 1979–1982, during the governorship of Juan Sabines Gutiérrez. Although Sabines did not actively promote this new organization, his government did not attempt to repress it either. Perhaps this was because it was seen as less confrontational and less threatening in its demands than the more radical groups of land petitioners who were engaged in violent struggles with ranchers and plantation owners.[7]

As it was, one of the main instruments of campesino autonomy—official approval for a self-managed credit union—was won after a series of mobilizations in 1981, which the governor failed to stop. However, this victory was marred by an internal dispute between advisers, which led to a split in the organization. The main point of disagreement concerned the way in which the Pajal Ya Kac'Tic Credit Union was set up without the full participation of the members of the different Unions of Ejidos. One of the advisers had a close relationship with key figures in the federal government and negotiated the terms of approval of the Credit Union without the full knowledge of most of the communities. This style of leadership was seen as compromising the autonomy of the Union of Ejido Unions and the consensual forms of indigenous democracy, in which all members are allowed to voice their opinions. The split resulted in a much weaker

---

[7] The most active (and most repressed) were the Emiliano Zapata Peasant Organization (OCEZ) in the central and border municipalities of Venustiano Carranza, Independencia, La Trinitaria, Chicomuselo, and Frontera Comalapa; and the Independent Central of Agricultural Workers and Peasants (CIOAC) in the northern highland municipalities of Simojovel, El Bosque, Jitotol, and Pueblo Nuevo.

organization and a gradual decline in participation during the 1980s. It would eventually leave the Zapatistas' armed option as a more attractive alternative, particularly to the younger generation who viewed the end of land reform as the final straw.

Parallel to the formation of the EZLN in 1989–1993, other organizations began to express material demands in new political discourses. The demands for economic autonomy were overtaken in these years by struggles for human rights and cultural identity. The protagonism of the Catholic Diocese of San Cristóbal on human rights issues and the projects of Xi'Nich, FIPI, and, eventually, the EZLN transcended the productivist discourse of groups such as the ARIC–Union of Ejido Unions. In the highlands, new organizations of nonconformist Indians demanded an end to expulsions from their communities and the right to return to their homes. Rather than ignore economic problems, these organizations worked to recast them in a more overtly political and cultural struggle against the threat of permanent exclusion and poverty.[8]

The main initiative of the Salinas government in Chiapas was PRONASOL. However, although Chiapas received more funds than any other state, resources were insufficient and most of the funding was allocated to social welfare and public works, with only 12 percent given in support of productive projects of *ejidatarios*. In addition, each project had a low investment ceiling, allowing the government to reach a larger population with small projects but reducing their overall social and regional impact. Although Chiapas ranked first in the number of local solidarity committees (ostensibly a sign of the program's political success), most of these participated in basic infrastructure and social welfare projects of short duration, or—as in the case of Municipal Funds—were very tightly controlled by local political bosses (Moguel 1994).

PRONASOL was also manipulated by the state governor, Patrocinio González Garrido. The program to support subsistence farmers with interest-free loans was controlled not by a community or regional board as in other states, but by the governor's office, allowing him to reward political friends in the PRI and CNC (Cano 1994). A state-level Ministry of Community Participation, staffed by loyal PRI and

---

[8] In the spring of 1992 over four hundred people from five ethnic groups and eighteen municipalities marched from Palenque to Mexico City to demand solutions to social and agrarian demands (Robles 1992). The "march of the ants," known by the Chol term "Xi'Nich," had a great impact on national public opinion regarding the plight of indigenous people. The march came at a time when Salinas was proclaiming the new indigenismo in domestic and international forums, and its arrival in Mexico City coincided with the officially sponsored International Indigenous Dance Festival. What was significant was the salience of demands of an ethnic and political nature, which would be taken up by the EZLN in 1994. On the struggles of the expelled communities, see Morquecho 1994.

CNC leaders, was set up in early 1992 in an effort to institutionalize these arrangements. In contrast to Oaxaca, the governor also dismissed officials who attempted to support local independent organizations. For example, in 1990 the regional director of the National Indigenous Institute in Las Margaritas was forced to resign after assisting the Union of Ejidos of the Rain Forest (Unión de Ejidos de la Selva, one of the member organizations of the ARIC–Union of Ejido Unions) in its efforts to gain PRONASOL funding to purchase a coffee-processing plant from the Mexican Coffee Institute (INMECAFÉ). Then in March 1992 three top INI officials in Chiapas were arrested: the state director, and the regional director and treasurer for the Tzeltal area. They were falsely accused of corruption in the use of funds to support small-scale livestock activities of the ARIC–Union of Ejido Unions in Ocosingo and Chilón (Harvey 1994: 19).

The absence of associational autonomy in Chiapas was highlighted by the vulnerability of even partial attempts to bypass local elites through INI and PRONASOL. The preparation of an armed rebellion occurred precisely in the context of political repression and exclusion in the Lacandon rain forest and Central Highlands. The goal of autonomy, linked since its inception to matters of production, credit, and marketing, had proven elusive amid the general context of macroeconomic reform and internal fragmentation. The scope of autonomy was also seen as too economistic and lacking a clear political focus. When the coffee cooperatives of the ARIC–Union of Ejido Unions began to unravel after 1989, the armed option became more attractive, particularly to younger ejido members whose access to land was abruptly canceled out by Salinas's reforms to Article 27 of the Constitution (Harvey 1994).

The Zapatista uprising provided the region's organizations with the opportunity to retake disputed land through direct action. The formation of the State Council of Indigenous and Peasant Organizations (CEOIC) in January 1994 represented the unification of most of the agrarian movements in the state. Their struggles were not confined to land-related issues and instead became part of the broader popular mobilization in Chiapas, particularly after the fraudulent gubernatorial elections in August 1994.[9]

---

[9] The identification of sectoral and political goals became evident in CEOIC in June after the failure of talks with the state government to resolve land disputes. At a meeting held in Ocosingo in early July, leaders of the more independent organizations expressed their frustration at the time lost in negotiations. They also supported the EZLN in its call for a government of transition, a new constituent assembly, and the writing of a new constitution. Those leaders who took a more official line rejected this position, and CEOIC effectively split into two camps: CEOIC–Official and CEOIC–Independent. From this point on, the CEOIC–Official became an integral part of AEDPCH, a coalition of popular organizations, most of which gave their support to Amado Avendaño, the candidate of "civil society" (though registered by

After the August elections, the main goal was to prevent PRI candidate Eduardo Robledo Rincón from taking office. Land invasions now fitted into a more general civic insurgency that also included the occupation of town halls and the proclamation of rebel governments in "autonomous pluriethnic regions" in several parts of the state (Burguete Cal y Mayor 1995). With the imposition of Robledo, CEOIC (in line with the position of the Democratic State Assembly of the Chiapanecan People , or AEDPCH) refused to recognize the state government. In this situation the channels for negotiating land claims were restricted to the federal government, whose February 1995 offensive placed CEOIC and other Zapatista sympathizers at a clear disadvantage.

This period was marked by increasing violence against campesino movements associated with CEOIC. In September 1994 a leader of the Party of the Democratic Revolution (PRD) was assassinated in Jaltenango la Paz. In the same month police evicted campesinos from private estates in Suchiate, carried out house searches in La Trinitaria, and impeded a meeting of the Emiliano Zapata Peasant Organization (OCEZ) in Chicomuselo. The civic insurgency called for by AEDPCH began on November 20 with the occupation of nine town halls and five road blockades. A march in Comitán was violently dispersed by police fire and tear gas, leaving four people seriously wounded.[10]

It was in this context that the CEOIC began negotiations with Dante Delgado Rennauro, the federal government's representative for social and development programs in Chiapas. The talks did not produce significant results, and CEOIC leaders viewed Dante Delgado as part of the government's more general counter-insurgency plan for Chiapas. Access to resources and the solution of land disputes, which by May 1995 had increased to over one thousand cases representing ninety thousand hectares, was politically conditioned, forcing communities to make their allegiances known. The military presence in areas outside the zone of conflict, such as Marqués de Comillas, was

---

the PRD) for the state governorship in August 1994. All future references to CEOIC in this paper are in fact references to CEOIC–Independent.

[10] One of the most ominous signs was the presence of white guards in evictions of land and town halls. In May 1995 the National Human Rights Commission (CNDH) called for an investigation into the killing of six people in southern Chiapas on January 10, 1995. On that date campesinos taking part in the civic insurgency of AEDPCH peacefully occupied the town hall in Chicomuselo. They were violently evicted by police assisted by white guards and local landowners. In addition to the six dead, several others were injured, including the parish priest and a nun shot at in their church. Further cases of violent evictions and killings were reported in April and May 1995 in the municipalities of Salto de Agua, Venustiano Carranza, Suchiate, and Jaltenango. The expulsion of three foreign priests from the Diocese of San Cristóbal in late June was also in response to the unfounded allegations made by local bosses in Sabanilla, Yajalón, and Venustiano Carranza.

also designed to intimidate oppositional movements from pursuing their agrarian and social demands. Not only were political activists identified as Zapatistas, but so was anyone associated with community organization, such as health promoters.[11]

At the same time that peace talks began to address the issues of indigenous rights in November 1995, there was an increase in the number of violent evictions of disputed lands. In early October, Interior Minister Emilio Chauyffet met with leaders of the ranchers' associations and promised that land invaders would be evicted following the October 15 municipal elections. The negotiations between the federal government and the Zapatistas at San Andrés Larráinzar were, in the words of one commentator, "the eye of the hurricane," as reports of detentions, beatings, and killings came in from around the state (Hernández 1995). Representatives of AEDPCH informed the negotiators gathered in San Andrés that their talks with Dante Delgado had broken down due to the lack of solutions to their agrarian demands. They also read out a litany of violent actions against members of popular organizations in 1995 which included 860 arrests, 50 evictions, and 40 politically motivated killings (Bellinghausen 1995).[12]

The San Andrés talks on indigenous rights and culture reached a minimum accord on January 18, 1996, which was subsequently ratified by the EZLN bases and signed by the two delegations four weeks later. This was the first signed agreement since the January 1994 rebellion and should be seen as a partial advance in the redefinition of Mexico as a pluriethnic nation. It calls for reforms to Articles 4 and 115 of the Constitution that would allow for the redrawing of municipal boundaries and the recognition of the right of indigenous people to compete for public office independently of national political parties. At the state level, similar reforms would be implemented with the goal of increasing political representation of indigenous people in the local congress. In addition, a state-level Law of Justice and Agrarian Development would be drawn up, and a special committee would be created to discuss the agrarian problems in Chiapas, with the participation of representatives of the EZLN, other indigenous

---

[11] Author interviews with members of the Independent Regional Peasant Movement, MOCRI, June 1995 and July 1996.

[12] Agreements to resolve over two thousand land conflicts in Chiapas were signed between the federal government and sixty-nine campesino organizations (official and independent) in February 1996. The government agreed to distribute sixty thousand hectares to the independent organizations represented in AEDPCH. According to a leader of AEDPCH, only five thousand hectares had been distributed by July 1996 (*La Jornada*, July 8, 1996). The February accord was immediately followed by the violent eviction of campesinos from disputed lands in the municipalities of Pichucalco, Nicolás Ruiz, and Venustiano Carranza, in which several people were killed and others injured.

and campesino organizations, and government ministries. This body would also be responsible for drawing up a census of land tenure in the state (*La Jornada*, February 15, 1996).

While these agreements were seen by the EZLN as a step forward, other groups within the indigenous movement (particularly the FIPI) saw them as limited by the lack of legal recognition for the regional autonomy of indigenous peoples. This would have permitted indigenous people greater control over the use of land and natural resources in their traditional territories by establishing pluriethnic autonomous regions as a "fourth level" of government, alongside the current federal, state, and municipal levels. This limitation reflected not only the government's unwillingness to meet this demand but also the differences between sectors of the indigenous movement and Zapatista advisers over the extent to which the issue should be pressed in the political conjuncture of early 1996.

Regional autonomy remains an important goal within the national indigenous movement, but its success will depend on the interplay between internal discussions and the political context in which this demand is formulated. The heterogeneous nature of the indigenous movement is reflected in internal disputes over the meaning of autonomy. The goal of pluriethnic regional autonomy is only one of several projects that are being fought over within the indigenous movement. Others emphasize community-level or municipal-level autonomy. Some advisers of the EZLN also warn against the possible re-regulation by the state of indigenous norms and traditions under the guise of respect for autonomy.[13]

We must also bear in mind that the political context shifted significantly in the period between November 1995 and January 1996. During the first round of talks, the government negotiators were more open to the idea of indigenous peoples' regional autonomy. This position changed radically when the team of reformist advisers from the INI was replaced for the second round by hard-liners from the Chiapas state government. Military maneuvers close to Zapatista bases in late December were another ominous sign of a shift in the government's position prior to the final round of talks. The continued militarization of Chiapas and the hardening of the government's position on each of the issues to be negotiated at San Andrés may even lead to

---

[13] These debates have been developed within the National Indigenous Assembly for Autonomy (ANIPA), a grouping of various regional organizations of indigenous people that drew up proposals for constitutional reforms during 1995. The January 1996 forum gave birth to a broader initiative to continue the debates beyond constitutional issues and to ensure implementation of the San Andrés accords. This initiative became known as the Permanent National Indigenous Forum (Foro Nacional Indígena Permanente).

a breakdown of the entire peace process. At the very least, it reduces the possibility of any serious reforms in the short term.

Conclusions

The relationship between indigenous organizations and democratization in Mexico must take into account the political effects of economic crisis and neoliberal adjustment. The argument is not that popular movements are simply responding to economic hardship, but rather that they are contesting the political and ideological hegemony that underpins neoliberal economics. This is primarily a political struggle over the terms of inclusion and exclusion in the new post–NAFTA Mexico. It has therefore forced indigenous organizations to engage in the struggles to define citizenship and democracy in both theory and practice, in law and politics. The emergence of new organizations and leaders greatly undermined the capacity of the regime to maintain its traditional alliances in the local and regional networks of power. At the same time, the content and pace of neoliberal reform could not be decided by technical criteria of economic management. They are inherently political and therefore open to contestation. The intensity and outcome of this struggle will vary across cases, but its very scope and open-endedness potentially allow for a greater amount of public intervention than changes within more consolidated paradigms.

It is precisely because third-order change spills over into the public sphere that Salinas felt it necessary to maintain tight control over the content of the most crucial policy initiatives, of which NAFTA was the cornerstone. However, the weakening of the traditional mediations of nationalism and populism left his administration open to the charge that the poor were simply dispensable in this new model. To counter such charges, PRONASOL was given great publicity and indigenismo was elevated to new heights, but these reforms were ad hoc strategies to overcome short-term legitimacy problems. As Hindley put it, the feverish activity at INI gave the impression that "something was being done" (Hindley 1996: 243). Yet it is also important to remember that this activity provided the new organizations and leaders with spaces in which they could assert their different goals under the common banner of citizenship and democracy. This point is supported by the fact that much of this debate has revolved precisely around that section of the Constitution that aims to define who the citizens are—Article 4.

It should not be assumed that this struggle will be resolved in favor of popular or indigenous notions of citizenship and democracy. The failure of the peace talks in San Andrés to achieve more than a minimal accord demonstrates the scale of the problems that indige-

nous organizations face. The apparent ambivalence of the government to the success of the peace talks, combined with the rise of violent attacks against Zapatista sympathizers, is also an indicator of the
reluctance to reconsider the direction of economic policy and the
scope of political reform. As a result, it appears that lo nacional and lo
popular are not being replaced by citizenship and democracy, but by a
neoliberal authoritarian state.

It is worth noting that one of the principal features of such a state
is its absence or weakness in regions where powerful private elites
dispense their own brand of justice. Imagining a three-colored map
designating the presence of legitimate and efficient state institutions,
O'Donnell (1993) ranked such regions as "blue" (high state presence),
"green" (middle), and "brown" (low). Chiapas has long been a "brown
area," despite the proliferation of federal and state agencies, because
the real power is exercised through extra-legal means, including private armies ("white guards"). O'Donnell's proposed solution involves
the strengthening of social and political institutions, but he recognizes
that this is a difficult proposition because the current political crisis
has led to a loss of faith in social cooperation, solidarity, and civic
commitment among large portions of the population. It is here that
indigenous organizations have had at least some success, in creating a
national movement in which the aspirations of democracy and citizenship have become the "articulating principles" for diverse subject
positions.

However, the articulating principles of a radical democratic citizenship are unlikely, in practice, to be abstract, universal notions of
equality and liberty. While equality and liberty are entirely appropriate goals for any democratic movement, the actual political construction of such a project is far more complex and contradictory than
this implies. At the same time, however, the contradictions do not
mean that the struggle to redefine citizenship and democracy is only
present at a discursive level among small groups of leaders, advisers,
and academics. This struggle takes place first and foremost on a daily
basis, in communities, ejidos, unions, schools, churches, and many
other sites. The public expression of these struggles emerges from
shared meanings around the nature of the struggles themselves and
are not automatically represented as democratic struggles, just as
material struggles are not always understood as class struggles. In
thinking about the emergence of democratic discourse in Mexico, we
therefore need to pay close attention to the collective nature of developing new expressions of political consciousness. The result may not
be consistent with liberal democratic notions of citizenship, but it will
be a more authentic representation of the current redefinition of citizenship by popular movements, including indigenous peoples' organizations. This method of analysis shares the view that identities

are relational, cultural, historical and contingent, rather than reducible to individual preferences for discursively appealing but ultimately abstract concepts (Foweraker 1994; Nash 1995; Tilly 1995).

The implications of this analysis for the current political process in Chiapas are not insignificant. At stake is the reordering of political mediations through the democratization of a legal and institutional terrain that has historically discriminated against the indigenous population. But can such a reform be divorced from the structural discrimination to which the Indians have been subjected since the Conquest? That is, can democratization be furthered through legal changes alone, or do these changes presuppose economic and social reforms that effectively enfranchise all citizens and therefore make democratic politics possible? This question has long been a source of debate in comparative politics and has recently reappeared in the literature on transitions from authoritarian rule in Latin America (Anglade 1994; Karl 1990; Lipset 1959). Part of this issue revolves around the need to construct democratic institutions, particularly in the judiciary and legal system, that are able to process the diverse demands of social agents through accountable and responsible mechanisms (Jelin 1996: 111–14; Jelin and Hershberg 1996b: 223). Yet even these changes will not address the social and economic inequalities that led to the Zapatista uprising. In fact, for the EPR guerrillas, the Zapatistas' negotiation strategy has failed to win any meaningful concessions from the government. However, there is even less evidence that sporadic acts of guerrilla violence would be more successful. The actions of the EPR have instead been met by greater repression of popular movement activists and by the militarization of more areas of the country. In contrast, the EZLN and the national indigenous movement have sought to frame economic demands within the discourse of citizenship and democracy. The question becomes not simply the "right to life" as a universal human right but the right to decide the content of that life—one that inevitably requires changes in the current economic model and political system, and one that the Zapatistas have attempted to articulate through their own version of radical democratic citizenship.

References

Aguilar Zinser, Adolfo. 1993. "Authoritarianism and North American Free Trade: The Debate in Mexico." In *The Political Economy of North American Free Trade*, edited by Ricardo Grinspun and Maxwell A. Cameron. New York: St. Martin's Press.

Alonso, Jorge. 1992. "Introducción. Cuestionar al Estado." In *El nuevo Estado mexicano*. Vol. 1. Mexico City: Universidad de Guadalajara/Centro de Investigaciones y Estudios Superiores en Antropología Social/Planeta.

Amnesty International. 1986. *Mexico: Human Rights in Rural Areas. Exchange of Documents with the Mexican Government on Human Rights Violations in Oaxaca and Chiapas.* London: Amnesty International.

Anglade, Christian. 1994. "Democracy and the Rule of Law in Latin America." In *Developing Democracy: Comparative Research in Honour of J.F.P. Blondel*, edited by Ian Budge and David McKay. London: Sage.

Bartra, Armando. 1991. "Pros, contras y asegunes de la apropiación del proceso productivo: organizaciones rurales de productores," *El Cotidiano* 39 (January–February): 46–52.

Bellinghausen, Hermann. 1995. "Causaron 'baja' en las pláticas las huestes del Instituto Nacional Indigenista," *La Jornada*, November 15.

Benjamin, Tom. 1989. *A Rich Land, a Poor People: Politics and Society in Modern Chiapas.* Albuquerque: University of New Mexico Press.

Burguete Cal y Mayor, Araceli. 1995. "Autonomía indígena: un camino hacia la paz," *Revista Memoria* 75 (March): 19–24.

Calva, José Luis. 1993. *La disputa por la tierra: la reforma del Artículo 27 y la nueva Ley Agraria.* Mexico City: Fontamara.

Cano, Arturo. 1994. "Lo más delgado del hilo: Pronasol en Chiapas," *Reforma* 28 (January): 3–7.

Convención Estatal de Mujeres Chiapanecas. 1994. *Escribiendo nuestra historia.* San Cristóbal de las Casas, Chiapas: Convención.

Díaz Polanco, Héctor. 1992. "El Estado y los indígenas." In *El nuevo Estado mexicano.* Vol. 1. Mexico City: Universidad de Guadalajara/Centro de Investigaciones y Estudios Superiores en Antropología Social/Planeta.

Dussel, Enrique. 1995. "Ethical Sense of the 1995 Maya Rebellion in Chiapas," *Journal of Hispanic/Latino Theology* 2 (3): 41–56.

Escobar, Arturo. 1992. "Culture, Politics and Economics in Latin American Social Movements Theory and Research." In *The Making of Social Movements in Latin America: Identity, Strategy and Democracy*, edited by Arturo Escobar and Sonia Álvarez. Boulder, Colo.: Westview.

Foweraker, Joe. 1982. "Accumulation and Authoritarianism on the Pioneer Frontier of Brazil," *Journal of Peasant Studies* 10 (1): 95–117.

———. 1990. "Popular Movements and Political Change in Mexico." In *Popular Movements and Political Change in Mexico*, edited by Joe Foweraker and Ann Craig. Boulder, Colo.: Lynne Rienner.

———. 1993. *Popular Mobilization in Mexico: The Teachers' Movement, 1977–87.* Cambridge: Cambridge University Press.

———. 1994. "Popular Political Organization and Democratization: A Comparison of Spain and Mexico." In *Developing Democracy: Comparative Research in Honour of J.F.P. Blondel*, edited by Ian Budge and David McKay. London: Sage.

Fox, Jonathan. 1992. *The Politics of Food in Mexico: State Power and Social Mobilization.* Ithaca, N.Y.: Cornell University Press.

———. 1994a. "Targeting the Poorest: The Role of the National Indigenous Institute in Mexico's Solidarity Program." In *Transforming State-Society Relations in Mexico: The National Solidarity Strategy*, edited by Wayne A. Cornelius, Ann L. Craig, and Jonathan Fox. La Jolla: Center for U.S.–Mexican Studies, University of California, San Diego.

————. 1994b. "The Difficult Transition from Clientelism to Citizenship," *World Politics* 46 (January): 151–84.

García de León, Antonio. 1989. "Encrucijada rural: el movimiento campesino ante las modernidades," *Cuadernos Políticos* 58 (September–December): 29–40.

González Casanova, Pablo. 1992. "México: ¿hacia una democracia sin opciones?" In *El nuevo Estado mexicano*. Vol. 1. Mexico City: Universidad de Guadalajara/Centro de Investigaciones y Estudios Superiores en Antropología Social/Planeta.

Hall, Peter. 1993. "Policy Paradigms, Social Learning and the State," *Comparative Politics* 25 (3): 275–87.

Harvey, Neil. 1990a. "The New Agrarian Movement in Mexico, 1979–1990." Institute of Latin America Studies Research Paper No. 23. London: University of London.

————. 1990b. "Peasant Strategies and Corporatism in Chiapas." In *Popular Movements and Political Change in Mexico*, edited by Joe Foweraker and Ann Craig. Boulder, Colo.: Lynne Rienner.

————. 1992. "La Unión de Uniones y los retos políticos del desarrollo de base." In *Autonomía y nuevos sujetos sociales en el desarrollo rural*, edited by Julio Moguel, Carlota Botey, and Luis Hernández. Mexico City: Siglo Veintiuno/Centro de Estudios Históricos del Agrarismo en México.

————. 1994. *Rebellion in Chiapas: Rural Reforms, Campesino Radicalism, and the Limits to Salinismo*. Transformation of Rural Mexico Series, no. 5. La Jolla: Center for U.S.–Mexican Studies, University of California, San Diego.

Hernández, Luis. 1994. "The Mobilization of Corn Producers: From the Struggle for Fair Prices to Integrated Rural Development." In *Economic Restructuring and Rural Subsistence in Mexico: Corn and the Crisis of the 1980s*, edited by Cynthia Hewitt de Alcántara. La Jolla: Center for U.S.–Mexican Studies, University of California, San Diego/United Nations Research Institute for Social Development.

————. 1995. "San Andrés: el ojo del huracán," *La Jornada* 21 (November).

Hindley, Jane. 1996. "Towards a Pluricultural Nation: The Limits of *Indigenismo* and Article 4." In *Dismantling the Mexican State?* edited by Rob Aitken et al. London: Macmillan.

Jelin, Elizabeth. 1996. "Citizenship Revisited: Solidarity, Responsibility and Rights." In *Constructing Democracy: Human Rights, Citizenship and Society in Latin America*, edited by Elizabeth Jelin and Eric Hershberg. Boulder, Colo.: Westview.

Jelin, Elizabeth and Eric Hershberg, eds. 1996a. *Constructing Democracy: Human Rights, Citizenship and Society in Latin America*. Boulder: Westview.

Jelin, Elizabeth and Eric Hershberg. 1996b. "Convergence and Diversity: Reflections on Human Rights." In *Constructing Democracy: Human Rights, Citizenship and Society in Latin America*, edited by Elizabeth Jelin and Eric Hershberg. Boulder: Westview.

Karl, Terry L. 1990. "Dilemmas of Democratization in Latin America," *Comparative Politics* 23 (1): 1–21.

Laclau, Ernesto, and Chantal Mouffe. 1985. *Hegemony and Socialist Strategy: Towards a Radical Democratic Politics*. London: Verso.

Lehmann, David. 1990. *Democracy and Development in Latin America: Economics, Politics and Religion in the Post-war Period*. Philadelphia, Penn.: Temple University Press.

Lipset, Seymour Martin. 1959. "Some Social Requisites of Democracy: Economic Development and Political Legitimacy," *American Political Science Review* 53: 69–105.

Marshall, T.H. 1964. *Citizenship and Social Democracy*. New York: Doubleday.

Moguel, Julio. 1992. "Reforma constitucional y luchas agrarias en el marco de la transición salinista." In *Autonomía y nuevos sujetos sociales en el desarrollo rural*, edited by Julio Moguel, Carlota Botey, and Luis Hernández. Mexico City: Siglo Veintiuno/Centro de Estudios Históricos del Agrarismo en México.

———. 1994. "Chiapas y el PRONASOL," *La Jornada del Campo* (supplement of *La Jornada*), January 25.

Moguel, Julio, Luis Hernández, and Carlota Botey, eds. 1992. *Autonomía y los nuevos sujetos en el desarrollo rural*. Mexico City: Siglo Veintiuno/Centro de Estudios Históricos del Agrarismo en México.

Moguel, Julio, and Rosario Robles. 1990. "Los nuevos movimientos rurales, por la tierra y por la apropiación del ciclo productivo." In *Historia de la cuestión agraria mexicana: los tiempos de la crisis*. Vol. 9, Part 2, edited by Julio Moguel. Mexico City: Siglo Veintiuno/Centro de Estudios Históricos del Agrarismo en México.

Morquecho, Gaspar. 1994. "Expulsiones en los Altos de Chiapas." In *Movimiento campesino en Chiapas: expulsiones, ideología y lucha por la tierra*. San Cristóbal de las Casas, Chiapas: DESMI, A.C.

Mouffe, Chantal. 1993. *The Return of the Political*. London: Verso.

Nash, June. 1995. "The Reassertion of Indigenous Identity: Mayan Responses to State Intervention in Chiapas," *Latin American Research Review* 30 (3): 7–41.

O'Donnell, Guillermo. 1979. "Tensions in the Bureaucratic-Authoritarian State and the Question of Democracy." In *The New Authoritarianism in Latin America*, edited by David Collier. Princeton, N.J.: Princeton University Press.

———. 1993. "On the State, Democratization and Some Conceptual Problems: A Latin American View with Glances at Some Postcommunist Countries," *World Development* 21 (8): 1355–69.

Otero, Gerardo. 1989. "The New Agrarian Movement: Self-Managed, Democratic Production," *Latin American Perspectives* 16 (4): 28–59.

Rello, Fernando, ed. 1990. *Las organizaciones de los productores rurales en México*. Mexico City: Facultad de Economía, Universidad Nacional Autónoma de México.

Robles, Rosario. 1992. "Xi'Nich: la marcha por la paz y la dignidad," *Campo Uno* (supplement of *Uno Más Uno*), April 27.

Ruiz Hernández, Margarito. 1993. "Todo indigenismo es lo mismo," *Ojarasca* 17 (February): 30–36.

Sarmiento, Sergio. 1991. "Movimiento indio y modernización," *Cuadernos Agrarios* (nueva época) 2: 90–113.

Stavenhagen, Rodolfo. 1996. "Indigenous Rights: Some Conceptual Problems." In *Constructing Democracy: Human Rights, Citizenship and Society in*

Latin America, edited by Elizabeth Jelin and Eric Hershberg. Boulder, Colo.: Westview.

Tilly, Charles. 1995. "Citizenship, Identity and Social History," *International Review of Social History* 40, Supplement 3: 1–17.

PART IV

Center-Periphery Conflicts:

Implications for Democratization

12

Electoral Federalism or Abdication of Presidential Authority? Gubernatorial Elections in Tabasco

Todd A. Eisenstadt

On January 18, 1995, local leaders of the Institutional Revolutionary Party (PRI) in a remote state in Mexico launched perhaps the most direct challenge ever to the country's ruling party since its pre–World War II consolidation. The "Rebellion of the PRIistas" in Tabasco remains one of the strongest indications of the breakdown of the PRI's internal discipline in the 1990s. The actual revolt—consisting of social disturbances, and sometimes even fisticuffs between PRI and opposition leaders—lasted only about three days. Yet some four years after the rebellion, the underlying cause of the revolt has not been resolved: the questionable November 20, 1994, election of Roberto Madrazo as governor of Tabasco, reputedly through extensive fraud.

President Ernesto Zedillo (1994–2000) and other national PRI leaders failed in their bid to remove Madrazo peacefully. Tabasco's corrupt local political bosses prevailed, and for a brief moment their extensive social mobilizations rendered Tabasco ungovernable. Not only were they able to turn aside questions about the governor's legitimacy, local supporters brought into question the effectiveness of the Zedillo administration itself. Unlike his predecessor, Carlos Salinas de Gortari (1988–1994), who named interim governors at will, Zedillo has been unable to challenge the independent power bases of

The author would like to thank Kathleen Bruhn, Jorge Buendía, Wayne Cornelius, and Jane Hindley for their comments.

governors like Roberto Madrazo in Tabasco and Rubén Figueroa in Guerrero,[1] despite Zedillo's strong emphasis on the rule of law and "the new federalism."

The fact that Zedillo was not the instrumental force in determining who would serve as governor of Tabasco could be taken to mean that he respected the democratic expression of Tabasco's citizenry (or at least a vocal portion of that citizenry). It could also be viewed as a successful application of the "new federalism"—that is, giving local and state governments the autonomy and responsibility largely to govern themselves. A more pessimistic interpretation, the one adopted in this chapter, is that Madrazo's continuation in power demonstrates a failure on the part of the federal government to uphold the rule of law.

The Rebellion of the PRIistas was not an instance of local politics and democratization in action; rather, it was a demonstration of the maneuverings of a local authoritarian political machine trying to hold on to power, even as the national government was trying to wrest power away. Zedillo and his team fell far short in their efforts to discipline the Madrazo political machine, offering discomforting evidence both of the local "holes" in Mexico's recent democratic opening and of the ways that local political bosses have used Zedillo's "new federalism" as a cloak to shield themselves from sanctions for their unethical activities. The lasting significance of the Tabasco uprising lies in the fact that it demonstrated that a few well-positioned local bosses with sufficient resources can defy national policies without fear of reprisal.

This chapter chronicles the Rebellion of the PRIistas, analyzing its structural and circumstantial causes. More importantly, it assesses the mobilization as a crucial expression of failed coordination between the national PRI and local party bosses. The national PRI's objective was to smooth relations with an angry opposition and to ensure nationwide governability for the incoming president. The Tabasco PRI wanted only to perpetuate its long-standing local monopoly.

---

[1] The prosecution of Governor Rubén Figueroa of Guerrero offers a particularly grim example of the limits of Zedillo's legalism. The federal attorney general and the Mexican Supreme Court determined that Figueroa was implicated in the police slaying of seventeen peasants at Aguas Blancas in July 1995. Yet jurisdiction to apply sanctions against governors resides with the state legislatures and the Guerrero legislature did not hold Figueroa accountable (González Oropeza 1996). More recently, Zedillo removed governors in Chiapas and Morelos, in ongoing but as yet unsuccessful efforts to rein in authoritarian abuses in these "hot spots."

From Discretionary Power to Legalism

The Zedillo administration has been characterized by its strong emphasis on the rule of law, that is, the need to abide by decisions taken within the procedural domain specified in the Mexican Constitution and subsidiary legal codes (see, for example, Alcocer 1996). In long-standing democracies, the rule of law is self-evident; the need to abide by established legal codes is taken for granted. This is not the case in Mexico, particularly in conflictive realms like that of electoral politics, where disputes often have been resolved through informal ("extralegal") political negotiations. However, severe economic crisis has weakened the Mexican presidency and curtailed the president's public mandate, including his power to resolve conflicts among constituents through the strategic channeling of government and party resources.

This is a marked break from the past. During the PRI's sixty-eight years of uninterrupted domination at the federal level, the president had unlimited control over the distribution of largesse. Zedillo's predecessor, Carlos Salinas, embraced the rule of law in word, but he often negotiated the outcomes of gubernatorial elections with little regard for state electoral codes' provisions regarding the legal procedures for challenging controversial electoral outcomes.[2] Rather, Salinas and his advisers often based their determination of the "winners" in state and local races on other factors. These included the strength of the losing party's post-electoral mobilizations, that party's national coalition and blackmail potential,[3] what the losing party might be willing to exchange for a favorable post-electoral settlement, and whether proclaimed PRI gubernatorial victors (and their federal allies) could withstand the political instability that might result from opposition mobilizations. In effect, ballot counts were less important than the *national* political circumstances of the losing opposition party contesting a *local* race.

This subordination of local political ends to national political means was acknowledged by national and local political leaders alike. For example, Arturo Núñez, undersecretary in the Ministry of the Interior (Gobernación) and former director of the Federal Electoral Institute (IFE), noted that, although he himself had never been in-

---

[2] Salinas named interim governors to "fill in" for declared victors on seventeen occasions—most notably, in San Luis Potosí in 1991, Guanajuato, 1991, and Michoacán, 1992. It was estimated that, at any time, 20 percent of Mexico's sitting governors had not been elected to the office (Grayson 1994).

[3] These are Sartori's terms (1976: 122–23). Coalition potential refers to the potential for alliance formation, while blackmail potential is one party's capacity for undermining the objectives of another party.

volved in "horse trading," the PRI may well have conceded electoral victories to the National Action Party (PAN) in exchange for that party's support of PRI initiatives, such as constitutional amendments on land reform and Church-state relations, and for PAN certification of Zedillo's victory in 1994 (author interview, August 1996). Núñez reported that such a quid-pro-quo logic pervades PRI–PAN relations and has been a hallmark of state-opposition relations during Mexico's democratic transition. High-ranking PAN officials like Juan Miguel Alcántara, national coordinator of local PAN legislators, also acknowledge this pattern of interparty collaboration, which dates from 1988 (author interview, June 1996).[4] Carlos Castillo Peraza, national president of the PAN from 1992 to 1996, specified that, although there was no systematic "instruction manual" on post-electoral negotiations, party leaders took several factors into account: the closeness of the official results, the local configuration of forces, the willingness of the federal government to negotiate, available evidence of electoral fraud, and "the prevailing international situation" (author interview, August 1996). It is worth noting that only some of these factors are directly related to the outcome of the election. For PAN negotiators, losing elections at the ballot box but then "recovering" them at the post-electoral bargaining table required a shrewd assessment of what they could demand and what they would concede in exchange for a chance to govern.[5]

The Party of the Democratic Revolution (PRD), the PRI's strongest challenger in Tabasco, was less experienced than the PAN in conducting post-electoral negotiations, for three reasons. First, the PRD, a leftist party with a strong peasant and urban blue-collar constituency, is very loosely organized and lacks the discipline necessary to

---

[4] More specifically, Alcántara traced the PRI's recognition of the PAN as its "chosen opposition interlocutor" to the moment when the PAN's charismatic 1988 presidential candidate, Manuel Clouthier, accepted Salinas's victory. The PRD's candidate, Cuauhtémoc Cárdenas, refused to accept Salinas as the legitimately elected president after the close, controversial, and tainted election, thus setting the stage for PRI–PAN cooperation and PRI–PRD animosity.

[5] Such was the case with the Guanajuato governorship in 1991 and municipal presidency races in Mérida in 1993 and Monterrey in 1994. Depending on one's interpretation, the appeals chamber of the Nuevo León electoral court was justified in overturning the PRI's "victory" in Monterrey and "granting" the office of municipal president to the PAN, *or* this was a case of post-electoral negotiations "whitewashed" by the national PRI and PAN, who pressured the electoral court judges to "give" the election to the PAN. In exchange, the national PAN would accept the results of the concurrent presidential election. After weighing the evidence, this author takes the second position, which is also that of many Monterrey politicos and most of the regional media (see Eisenstadt 1998a). In contrast, Mérida offers a clear-cut case of "laundering" post-electoral negotiations through electoral institutions.

"deliver" on quid-pro-quo promises to the federal PRI–government in exchange for local post-electoral concessions. Second, unlike the more powerful PAN, the PRD has little to offer the federal government.[6] Third, under the taciturn leadership of Cuauhtémoc Cárdenas, Salinas's political enemy since Cárdenas almost bested Salinas in the 1988 presidential election, the PRD has steadfastly refused to negotiate with a federal government it considers illegitimate. Andrés Manuel López Obrador, leader of the PRD in Tabasco, was one of the few leaders in his party who had adopted a PAN–style post-electoral negotiating strategy, reclaiming three 1991 municipal presidency races at the post-electoral bargaining table. Named national PRD president in July 1996, López Obrador soon showed himself to be a more flexible leader than Cárdenas. He softened his party's position on the legitimacy of the Salinas presidency, and thereby forced the PRI to offer concessions to the PRD, as it traditionally has done with the PAN.

Zedillo's dilemma in Tabasco, then, was how to shift from the Salinas strategy of informal political bargaining to resolve post-electoral conflicts ("the political path") to a formal "judicial path" more consistent with his priority of fortifying Mexico's rule of law. The differences between these two paths can be best illustrated through example. The starkest instance of a "political path" resolution was the 1991 Guanajuato governor's race (see Prud'homme, this volume). The PRI candidate was declared the winner in that election, but PAN mobilizations prevented him from taking office. Subsequent negotiations between the PRI and PAN at the national level caused Salinas to intervene, naming the first PAN interim governor. While the judicial path seems to work at the federal level,[7] such institutional success clearly has not fully "trickled down" to the local level. The Tabasco case is further evidence of this fact.

Prior to the mid–1990s, local PRI elites were generally able to turn local electoral courts to their own purposes. However, the 1996 reforms to the Mexican Constitution granted the Federal Electoral Tribunal, which is much less susceptible to local interest group pressures, the authority to review local electoral court decisions. Over the

---

[6] The right-leaning PAN, which commands a sizable minority of seats in the Chamber of Deputies, frequently legitimizes PRI legislative initiatives. The PAN, largely composed of middle-class professionals, was the party the federal government used to give bipartisan credibility to its programs, and only one opposition party was really needed to eliminate the image of a monopolistic PRI–government forcing its initiatives through the PRI–dominated Congress.

[7] At the federal level, eight congressional races have been overturned, recalled, or annulled, one in 1991 and seven in 1994. For more on the contrast between the judicial effectiveness of the Federal Electoral Tribunal and the ineffectiveness of the state courts, see Eisenstadt 1998b.

last two years, the Federal Electoral Tribunal has heard hundreds of local appeals and reversed municipal presidency victories in several small municipalities.[8] However, the court's reversal of these electoral outcomes was more a symbolic display of authority than a real challenge to the PRI–government power structure, especially when compared to the dozens of post-electoral negotiations outside the law involving governorships and important cities like Monterrey and Mérida.

An analysis of the Tabasco case will demonstrate the interplay of interests that prompted the PRD to "appeal" to the national PRI after failing at the voting booth and in the state's electoral court. If Zedillo's inexperienced team had been able to follow through on its intention to unseat Governor-elect Madrazo, the political path would have prevailed. Zedillo and his team were not up to the task, however, and Madrazo remains in office.

It is impossible to determine the precise alignment of forces that prompted Zedillo's tactical switch from rejecting Madrazo to accepting him as the winner of the Tabasco election. The Rebellion of the PRIistas, the first major crisis of his administration, certainly played a role. In subsequent post-electoral conflicts—such as the 1995 gubernatorial races in Guanajuato, Jalisco, and Yucatán—Zedillo adhered strictly to his advocacy of the rule of law, thereby staving off opposition arguments for "political path" resolutions.

The post-electoral conflict in Tabasco was part of a broader transitional context in which Mexico's principal opposition parties saw a dramatic increase in the range of instruments with which to contest electoral results.[9] The "formal" judicial path for contesting power began to yield occasional favorable results, and opposition parties complemented these victories with others won through traditional "informal" bargaining strategies.

When it closed off the option of extra-legal negotiation, the federal government may have reinforced the traditional political spaces for sovereign political development by the states (that is, "the new federalism"), a result applauded by many traditional PRI governors.[10] Or, as the critics contend, in closing off the political resolution option, the Zedillo administration may have institutionalized a new "feudal" order within the states, allowing governors to perpetuate electoral

---

[8] These include Tepetlaoxtoc, México State; Santa Catarina, San Luis Potosí; and Aconchi, Sonora.

[9] When electoral commissions and courts were set up starting in the late 1980s, opposition parties and the PRI realized that the credibility of these institutions depended on the parties' compliance with their dictates. This new arsenal of options empowered opposition political parties at the expense of the PRI–government.

[10] See, for example, Moreno's (1995) interview with Puebla governor Manuel Bartlett.

fraud and corruption with impunity.[11] The latter interpretation applies especially in states traditionally known for rampant electoral fraud.[12] By this logic, merely abiding by the law is insufficient. Citizens must abide by fair laws that enforce a just regime built on equitable electoral laws, and the state's electoral institutions must comply with them. Whichever interpretation of the new legalism is correct, the federal PRI–government is paying a high price for its policy of pursuing only judicial path resolution of post-electoral disputes.[13]

The ongoing normative debate, as applied to the case of Tabasco, is whether—from the perspective of Tabasco's and Mexico's democratic transition—it is more harmful to let stand the biased results of compromised electoral institutions or to undermine these institutions by disregarding them and pursuing more discretionary, but ultimately more equitable, political path decisions. The following sections discuss how Zedillo and the national PRI came to find themselves in this political predicament, where the policy failed, and what may be the implications of this short-term failure for democratic institution building in Mexico's regions.

Zedillo's Dilemma

The threat of post-electoral conflict was in the air long before the election for the governorship of Tabasco took place on November 20,

---

[11] See critics from both sides of the opposition, such as López Obrador (1995: 187), who names Bartlett, Patricio Chirinos of Veracruz, Rubén Figueroa of Guerrero, Madrazo, and Víctor Cervera Pacheco of Yucatán among the "tramplers of individual and political rights of citizens in the name of federalism." The PAN, in its call for central government intervention in resolving post-electoral disputes in the 1995 Yucatán governor's race, also criticized the "*caciquismo*" of local PRI elites and called on Zedillo to prove his democratic mettle by intervening in both Tabasco and Yucatán (PAN 1995).

[12] Such practices are illegal in Zedillo's more abstract and normative terms. The rich terminology describing Mexico's dozens of ways of perpetrating electoral fraud is legendary. Electoral fraud operatives are called "*mapaches*" (raccoons). They are known to inflate vote tallies through a wide assortment of practices, including "*tacos de votos*"(vote stuffing), "*operación tamale*" (small breakfast bribes to voters), "shaving" the electoral list, "*carruseles*" (vans of partisans who travel from polling place to polling place to vote multiple times), and "*ratón loco*" (the "crazy mouse" tactic in which a known opposition sympathizers' polling station is changed at the last minute to inconvenience these voters to the point that they do not vote).

[13] In 1995, the PRI conceded gubernatorial defeats in Baja California, Guanajuato, and Jalisco, in accordance with the new rules of the game which included abiding by electoral institutions' strict reporting and certification of results. In November 1996 the PRI accepted another major defeat, losing almost all important municipalities in the country's most populous state, México.

1994. The federal government's role in that election embraced two apparently incompatible objectives: assuring equitable elections and assuring a peaceful transition. Given the local polarization of forces, it was basically a "no win" situation. If Zedillo decided not to intervene and Tabasco's electoral institutions (the State Electoral Commission, or CEE, and the State Electoral Tribunal, TEE) proved unable to resolve the post-electoral conflict credibly, Zedillo risked losing the cooperation of the PRD in national-level dialogues on federal electoral reform. Of even more immediate importance, Zedillo's inauguration was slated for December 1, 1994, the precise moment when any post-electoral mobilization by the PRD in Tabasco would be fully engaged in disrupting social peace.

Another crucial implication of the Tabasco election regards the impact that perceptions of instability have on foreign direct investment. The post-electoral mobilization came just one month after a sharp devaluation of the peso, which had undercut international investor confidence in the Mexican economy and exacerbated the ensuing recession. Any further political mobilization in southern Mexico would undermine what scant investor confidence remained.

Yet if Zedillo and the federal government stepped in to mediate the post-electoral dispute in Tabasco informally, they would reestablish the Salinas administration's pattern of the federal government intervening in state affairs to resolve opposition party grievances through extra-legal channels.[14] Under Salinas, such arbitrary interventions undermined the development of independent electoral institutions at the regional and local levels and, in more general terms, countermanded the development of the rule of law.

From the outset, the Tabasco election was much more than an exercise in local politics and democratization. It was the first critical test of an incoming president's political will. Zedillo's dilemma was eventually resolved in favor of legalism, but only after the new administration realized that it lacked the political weight to impose a resolution. The administration's initial indecisiveness opened a post-electoral bargaining space that the PRD is still trying to fill.

How the federal and state authorities ultimately handled the Tabasco post-electoral conflict offers a textbook case in how *not* to resolve such disputes. Local electoral authorities did not have either the autonomy or the power to resolve the deep-seated sociopolitical con-

---

[14] A decision by the president to intervene formally, dissolving the federal pact and imposing an interim governor, was unlikely because it represented the most interventionist course of all. Although such a "dissolution of powers" was practiced widely in the 1920s and 1930s (González Oropeza 1996: 239–50), this practice had become much less common by the 1970s, when laws governing violations of state sovereignty were tightened.

flict. Federal authorities did have such power and could easily have overridden local judicial resolutions, but they "backed off" in their efforts to generate a political compromise when it became clear that their proposed solutions carried untenably high political costs. Thus all the costs of a "political path" resolution accrued to the federal government. Four years after the Tabasco gubernatorial race, there is still widespread consensus that exorbitant levels of campaign spending won the election for the PRI candidate. This was confirmed by the federal Attorney General's Office, and the case was prosecuted before the Mexican Supreme Court. The Court decided, however, that the allegations fell outside its jurisdiction; in Tabasco, meanwhile, Madrazo was found innocent of charges of illegal campaign spending and was allowed to remain in office.

A year of calm followed the findings in Madrazo's favor, but the controversy regained a place on the national agenda in March 1998 when Representative Santiago Creel launched impeachment proceedings against the governor.[15] Although it is extremely unlikely that the impeachment proceedings will move forward in the Chamber of Deputies or Senate, the new investigation has resurrected questions about Madrazo's character midway through his term. While Mexico's protracted democratic transition has been full of electoral fraud scandals, none other has festered in the public debate for three years. The following section explains why Tabasco's Rebellion of the PRIistas has remained so controversial.

The Rise of a Worthy Opponent: Tabasco's PRD

Until the late 1980s or early 1990s, Tabasco, a poor agricultural backwater, was PRI country.[16] The discovery of Mexico's huge petroleum deposits served to accelerate the flow of tremendous amounts of money—and corruption—into the state, changing both the economic and the political landscape. In 1987, when an important fraction of the national PRI leadership defected from their party to create the National Democratic Front (FDN, forerunner to the PRD), a similar shift took place in Tabasco. The state PRI's finance director, Andrés Manuel López Obrador, and several other young leaders broke ranks

---

[15] Creel, a former "citizen counselor" in the Federal Electoral Commission, had run successfully as a PAN candidate to the Mexican Congress, where he headed the committee charged with oversight of public officials.

[16] The state's most celebrated native son was Carlos Madrazo, governor from 1959 to 1964, national PRI president in 1964–1965, and father of Roberto Madrazo. Ironically, Madrazo Sr. was famous for his visionary, but failed, efforts to democratize candidate selection within the PRI.

with their party. López Obrador had worked as the state government's chief liaison with remote indigenous communities in the mid–1980s, where he had acquired a loyal following. These communities formed his constituency when he split with his mentor, Governor Enrique González Pedrero, to run as the FDN gubernatorial candidate in 1988.

PRI candidate Salvador Neme Castillo won that election, but the 1988 vote was almost certainly manipulated in his favor.[17] The November 17, 1991, midterm elections were also suspicious. Press accounts report that PRD candidates were unfairly denied registry, the voter list was flawed, ballots were not always kept under electoral authorities' control, and isolated incidents of violence occurred (Curzio Gutiérrez 1995: 76–80). Despite what seemed to be a high turnout among PRD supporters in key local enclaves, the PRI was declared the winner in each of the state's seventeen municipalities.

The PRD was certain that it had carried the vote in at least three municipal races: in Cárdenas, Nacajuca, and Macuspana (López Obrador 1995: 117). Two days after the election, López Obrador expressed his grievances, extra-legally, to Minister of the Interior Fernando Gutiérrez Barrios. When Gutiérrez Barrios refused to annul the PRI's "victory" in the Cárdenas race, López Obrador determined that it was time to escalate the conflict to the national level: "we knew that if we stayed in Tabasco, confrontation would be inevitable" (López Obrador 1995: 118).

Inspired by the "Dignity March" of opposition gubernatorial candidate Salvador Nava in San Luis Potosí earlier in 1991 (see Calvillo, this volume), López Obrador and hundreds of supporters launched an "Exodus for Democracy." As their caravan neared Mexico City on foot, offers for a post-electoral settlement began arriving from the Ministry of the Interior. In its best offer, the Ministry agreed to annul the Cárdenas election and grant the PRD three plurinominal seats in the state legislature. López Obrador read the government's offer as an attempt to divide the PRD because, although the federal government was ready to accept PRD governance of Cárdenas, this would not be under the leadership of the PRD's candidate to the municipal presidency, Carlos Alberto Wilson. The caravan arrived in Mexico City on January 11, 1992, and set up headquarters in the Zócalo, the gargantuan square in front of Government Palace (López Obrador 1995: 119–22).

---

[17] Neme's administration was characterized by nepotism, corruption, and discord between factions of the Tabasco PRI and between party leaders at the state and national levels (Curzio Gutiérrez 1995: 65–67). Neme resigned his office in 1991 to assume a federal government post, leaving the governorship to Manuel Gurría Ordóñez.

Once in Mexico City, López Obrador saw his negotiating position grow stronger, aided by the government's concern for its public image while debates were ongoing for the North American Free Trade Agreement (NAFTA) (author interview, January 1996). The PRD also benefited from the international spotlight focused on Mexico for the signing of the El Salvador peace accords in Mexico City on January 12, 1992. Minister Gutiérrez Barrios began to soften his stance, and the Salinas administration finally accepted political path resolutions for all three contested municipalities, as well as in three post-electoral conflicts in the neighboring state of Veracruz. In exchange, participants in the Exodus for Democracy agreed to vacate the Zócalo and return home (López Obrador 1995: 122–26).

The 1991 post-electoral negotiation was the PRD's first bargaining victory,[18] and it set the parameters for López Obrador's pursuit of local electoral justice at the national level in 1994. The 1991 incident was also notable as a victory for the more pragmatic side of the national PRD, led by Porfirio Muñoz Ledo, over the party faction led by the PRD's founder and its 1988 and 1994 presidential candidate, Cuauhtémoc Cárdenas.

"Opaque Transparency" in the 1994 Elections

Tabasco's 1994 gubernatorial race took on a high national profile as the federal government tried to gauge the state's potential for post-electoral upheaval. PRI activists allege that the federal government sought to impose a weak candidate as the PRI's choice for the governorship in order to placate the PRD—and effectively concede the race beforehand. Infuriated local PRI and business leaders blocked the imposition and took candidate selection into their own hands. According to Pedro Jiménez León, now majority leader of the Tabasco legislature, the local PRI leadership named Madrazo as their gubernatorial candidate against the wishes of the party's national leadership, which wanted to avoid post-electoral tensions at all costs. "But we decided that even if the National Executive Committee of the PRI wanted to impose another candidate, we Tabasqueños would still back Madrazo and then wait and see what happened" (author interview, January 1996). The local PRI announced their candidate choice in June.

Jiménez León reported that negotiations were ongoing in Mexico City throughout the summer of 1994 in an effort to ensure a transpar-

---

[18] Other PRD post-electoral bargaining victories would follow, such as in local races in Michoacán in 1992 and Chiapas in 1995, but these were largely local matters with federal oversight but no direct federal negotiating participation.

ent election. Moreover, he asserted that Madrazo had offered to negotiate an electoral reform in consultation with all parties' gubernatorial candidates, "putting everything on the table" on the understanding that, if an agreement were reached, the electoral outcome
would be respected. In an effort to involve the federal government,
López Obrador asked Beatriz Paredes, an undersecretary at the Ministry of the Interior, to mediate. Several meetings were held, attended
by Paredes and by state and national representatives from the PRI
and PAN, but the PRD boycotted. State-level PRI leaders feared that
López Obrador was "betting it all" on post-electoral conflict, despite
guarantees from presidential candidate Zedillo that his administration would not sacrifice Madrazo, if elected, in post-electoral negotiations.

According to Jiménez León, Zedillo conveyed this same message
to López Obrador: "If I succumb to these pressures, the opposition
parties are going to be pestering throughout my entire term. Furthermore, how would I be able to face the voters if I do not respect the
result of their election?"

Whatever the precise terms of the center-region dialogue, it is clear
from the accounts of Jiménez León and López Obrador that one existed and that, even prior to the election, the national PRI leadership
and the Tabasco PRI were two separate actors. The national PRI's
primary goal was to maintain governability and contain local conflict,
even if this meant sacrificing the PRI candidate. The local PRI, on the
other hand, had invested heavily in a Madrazo victory as the means
for retaining control of PEMEX, the national oil company and Tabasco's cash cow. A López Obrador victory was entirely unacceptable
to most of Tabasco's middle and upper classes—even if it defused
political conflicts at the broader, national level—because López Obrador's redistributive policies threatened their very livelihoods.

By most accounts, the pre-electoral playing field was severely
tilted in favor of Madrazo, with unprecedented disparities in campaign spending and extremely biased media coverage.[19] It was also

---

[19] According to a content analysis of September and October articles in Tabasco's five
major newspapers, Madrazo received 54 percent of the mentions; López Obrador, 22
percent; Juan José Rodríguez Prats of the PAN, 10 percent; and other candidates, 14
percent. These percentages bear no resemblance to the level of popular support for
the candidates, even as reported in the official results. If one discounts López
Obrador's 53 percent of candidate mentions in the sole pro–PRD newspaper, *La
Verdad del Sureste*, he slips to 17 percent. Television coverage was even more slanted.
Madrazo received 53 percent of the coverage in Tabasco's two major news
programs; Rodríguez Prats received 22 percent, López Obrador, 16 percent, and
"other," 9 percent (Comité de Derechos Humanos/Academia Mexicana 1994: 10, 24).
PRI campaign records indicate that the party spent close to U.S.$50 million, many
times the legal limit. While this information was not made public until after the

characterized by the kinds of improprieties, or apparent improprieties, that have been legislated out of electoral codes in other states, such as a partisan State Electoral Commission.[20] The election itself suffered from only isolated incidents of violence and few overt irregularities. Yet there is evidence of foul play.[21] For example, the PRD intercepted telephone conversations on the afternoon of November 20, 1994, in which local and national PRI leaders assessed voter turnout and affirmed the need to "get out the vote."[22] That evening, a mysterious blackout crashed the computer on which vote tallies were being run. Before the power went out, the vote count in the gubernatorial race totaled over 468,000. When the lights came back on, the total had dropped by almost 20,000 votes (López Obrador 1995: 166; López 1994a: 64).

Early Success of the PRD's "Mixed Path" Strategy

Tabasco's PRD leadership immediately challenged the official results, which gave 56 percent of the vote to the PRI and 37 percent to the PRD. It presented a multitude of "complaints of nonconformity" to the State Electoral Tribunal. Twenty of these were rejected on techni-

---

election, there were visible indications of high spending prior to the election, including newspaper ads that alone would have exceeded campaign limits (López Obrador 1995: 158; López 1994c: 76). The Comité de Derechos Humanos de Tabasco (1994) also reported over sixty verified cases of Tabasco officials trying to purchase or barter votes.

[20] Rafael López Cruz, the PRD's representative on the CEE, repeatedly objected to the partisan histories of his fellow CEE members (especially the supposedly nonpartisan "citizen counselors"), and to the partisan and economic commitments of the magistrates of Tabasco's State Electoral Tribunal (author interview, January 1996). His suspicions may have been justified, at least regarding the CEE; at least two high-ranking CEE officials were subsequently named to the Supreme Court by Governor Madrazo. Even if they were named for their impartiality or judicial wisdom, many Tabasco electoral officials consider their promotions inappropriate (author interview with State Electoral Tribunal magistrate Emiliano Jiménez Pérez, January 1996).

[21] The most obvious watchdog for election day irregularities *should have been* the Special Prosecutor for Electoral Crimes (FEPADE). Tabasco was among the first states to have such an institution, which paralleled the federal-level office of the same name. However, of the thirty-seven electoral crimes alleged to have taken place, only three resulted in criminal investigations and all of these were trivial misdemeanors (author interview with José Antonio Ovis Pedrero, Tabasco special prosecutor for electoral crimes, January 1996). Critics dismissed the Tabasco FEPADE as an immature institution founded on the eve of the election for "cosmetic" purposes only (author interview with López Cruz).

[22] These conversations, taped by the PRD, were subsequently authenticated and transcribed in the national press. See Áviles 1994.

cal grounds, without any consideration of their merits, because they lacked the signature of the filer (López 1994c). In the end, the TEE did not nullify results from even a single ballot box.[23]

Moreover, the TEE judges accused the complainants of submitting "carbon copy" allegations, using forms on which one need only indicate the relevant ballot box number and then check the particular incident off from a list of possible violations. The "carbon copy" nature of the complaints purportedly could lead to a lack of correspondence between the grievance presented and the facts offered as evidence (author interview with Emiliano Jiménez Pérez, magistrate in Tabasco's electoral tribunal, January 1996).

The lawyer for the PRD defended the practice of submitting "check list complaints"; this form was needed, he argued, because most complainants were campesinos with little or no formal education. He added that, regardless of these mass-produced complaints, the TEE judges had no excuse for producing "carbon copy" resolutions, some of which began by addressing one election and ended up discussing another if the judge failed to erase completely the underlying "master text" (author interview with Rafael López Cruz, president of the PRD in Tabasco, January 1996). State magistrate Emiliano Jiménez Pérez responded that the TEE indeed did resolve identical complaints with identical resolutions: not to do so would have been a miscarriage of justice. The TEE magistrate also cut through all the technical arguments from electoral authorities and the political parties when he announced that "a resolution by the State Electoral Tribunal is definitive."[24]

This put a quick end to PRD efforts to pursue the judicial path. Yet these efforts did serve an important purpose. As López Obrador insisted, all judicial path options had to be exhausted before he and his supporters escalated to the political path: "Whatever we do, it will be construed as acting outside the law, so we must proceed through

---

[23] This angered López Cruz, who asked how he and his legal team could have filed sufficient complaints before the Federal Electoral Tribunal to win the annulment of nearly 20 percent of the ballot boxes in several congressional races, only to be accused, four months later, of sloppiness in their filing of state election complaints. Federal Electoral Tribunal records demonstrate that Tabasco's PRD had indeed filed several successful complaints relating to the August 1994 federal elections. Seven of the fourteen complaints filed by López Cruz and his team were deemed "founded" or "partially founded," which was much higher than the overall success rate of 21 percent for complaints filed for that election. The Tabasco PRD complaints prompted the TFE to annul almost 60,000 votes under legal criteria and operating procedures much more strict than those in effect at the state level (TFE 1995: 464 ff.).

[24] Unlike federal electoral laws governing post-electoral conflict resolution, and unlike the electoral codes of most Mexican states, in Tabasco there is no higher court to which the PRD could appeal.

strict legal channels to avoid these criticisms. We must follow this legal course, even as we mobilize the citizenry, and even knowing that legal recourse ultimately does not work" (author interview).

The PRD's recourse to the political path involved mobilizations similar to those that López Obrador had employed successfully in 1991. This time around, the tactics of political negotiation backed by social mobilization involved a "Caravan for Democracy" which left Tabasco for Mexico City on November 24, 1994.

Mexico City was in the international spotlight once again, a fact that the PRD activists tried to turn to their advantage. This time the event was Zedillo's inauguration, scheduled to take place in the Zócalo on December 1. Esteban Moctezuma Barragán, slated to become Zedillo's minister of the interior, promised that if the Tabasco activists would leave the Zócalo, he would meet with López Obrador that same day; furthermore, he seemed willing to consider annulling both the gubernatorial and municipal elections in Tabasco if the PRD could demonstrate that irregularities had affected tallies from 20 percent of the ballot boxes, a baseline stipulated in the state's electoral law (López Obrador 1995: 170). Moctezuma reportedly asked Santiago Creel and José Agustín Ortiz Pinchetti[25] to serve as mediators in the relocation of the demonstrators, an additional step in efforts to avert a confrontation between members of the military who would parade at the inauguration and the hundreds of Tabasco protesters. Although Moctezuma and López Obrador did not reach an agreement, the PRD demonstrators relocated to the Plaza of the Revolution, where they remained until Moctezuma asked Creel and Ortiz Pinchetti to conduct an investigation into the Tabasco elections. They agreed to conduct such an assessment on the condition that both the PRD and federal government were agreed to it and that there was a willingness to seek a political solution" (author interview with Creel, February 1996).

Creel and Ortiz Pinchetti based their report on a macro-level analysis of 439 ballot boxes and a micro-level analysis of a subsample of 63 ballot boxes. They found two widespread irregularities which, although not decisive in every ballot box, did form a pattern. One was the "last minute" substitutions of precinct officials;[26] the other, dis-

---

[25] Like Creel, Ortiz Pinchetti had also been an electoral ombudsman.

[26] Under both federal and state electoral codes, each precinct (or set of ballot boxes) is to be presided over by four citizens randomly selected from voting lists and trained by the CEE. Each of the political parties is allowed to have one official representative present the whole day, and it is these representatives who must sign protests if they intend to prosecute irregularities with electoral authorities. When CEE–appointed and trained precinct officials fail to show up (not an uncommon occurrence), voters are to be randomly selected as they come to vote and deputized into these positions

parities between ballot counts at precinct and district levels.[27] Compelling irregularities appeared in about 78 percent of the micro audits, and procedural irregularities (mainly the substitution of precinct officials, but also the receipt of balloting materials outside the legal time frame) were found in well over half of the larger sample.[28] "Contrast this," the report recommended, "with the fact that not even one ballot box was annulled in the judicial proceedings. This raises ethical, juridical, and political questions about whether there was compliance with the principle of impartiality that should govern every electoral process."[29]

Although it abided by the rules of the judicial path (the burden of proving fraud in 20 percent of the ballot boxes), the electoral audit was strictly an extra-legal exercise and carried no legal weight in Tabasco. In general terms, the report corroborated the PRD's complaints and supported the national PRD's insistence on a political resolution of the post-electoral conflict in Tabasco (and, secondarily, in Veracruz and Chiapas).

Such a political resolution became the precondition for negotiating any "definitive" electoral reform with the Zedillo administration. On January 17, 1995, the national leaderships of all the major parties met at the Los Pinos presidential residence and signed a sort of "letter of

---

by CEE officials. Wholesale "no-shows," as in Tabasco, are not a cause of annulment according to the electoral code, but such patterns may raise suspicions.

[27] Error in ballot counting is a cause for annulment under both the federal and Tabasco electoral codes. Creel and Ortiz Pinchetti used several equations to account for all ballots. Furthermore, the IFE ombudsmen analyzed whether any differences detected were determinant (whether they affected enough votes so as to alter the race), checked how many of the precinct counts failed to report these crucial numbers, and determined whether "adjustments" were made in the district-wide computer counts (when compared to the precinct-by-precinct results).

[28] PRI senator and then-national PRI president María de los Angeles Moreno criticized Creel and Ortiz Pinchetti's methodology. She cited bias in their sample, which was selected from ballot boxes reported by the PRD to have irregularities, rather than from the universe of all ballot boxes in the election (author interview with Moreno, February 1996).

[29] The final report, concluded in mid–January, was leaked to Reforma and printed on January 29, 1995. According to Creel, all parties had agreed not to release the report to the press. Only after the Tabasco PRI reportedly released a falsified version which reported that no widespread irregularities had been found did Creel and Ortiz Pinchetti release the actual report (author interview).

What is notable regarding the Creel–Ortiz Pinchetti effort is that it enjoyed full cooperation from the national-level PRI and from the Tabasco PRI and PRD, which furnished copies of their precinct reports, as well as from the Ministry of the Interior, which sponsored the undertaking. Moreno said there was no explicit understanding that the findings would be binding (author interview), but Moctezuma's top aide, Undersecretary Luis Maldonado Venegas, stated that the parties had agreed to make the Creel–Ortíz Pinchetti report binding (author interview, August 1996).

intent" to address electoral reform as soon as pending regional post-electoral disputes were resolved. The implication in the Pact of Los Pinos was that Madrazo would be sacrificed—either asked to resign or subjected to a recall election. But this option remained unacceptable to Tabasco's PRI.

The Rebellion of the PRIistas

While national party leaders debated alternative political options, tensions mounted within the Tabasco PRI. Jiménez León, leader of the state legislature, insisted that the legislature would refuse to accept Madrazo's resignation, if tendered. When reminded that a governor could be removed at the discretion of the president, Jiménez León responded that "the president does not live in Tabasco." Only state residents, he claimed, understood that any replacement for Madrazo would be no more than a puppet controlled by López Obrador, and that Madrazo's ouster would allow Tabasco's oil wealth to fall into "enemy hands."

The Tabasco Congress met on January 17, 1995, to discuss the possible repercussions if the legislators proceeded with their planned act of insubordination. Among the likely consequences they anticipated was the federal government's temporary suspension of the state's right of self-governance until order could be restored. Consciously mimicking PRD tactics, the insurgent PRI activists shut themselves up in Villahermosa's Pino Suárez Library, and from there they organized roadblocks, statewide work stoppages, and takeovers of radio and television stations, all under the banner of "the new federalism." On January 18, all PRI members of the state congress vowed that they would relinquish office before accepting Madrazo's resignation. Antagonism between the PRI and PRD heightened (Abreu Ayala 1995: 138; author interview with Raúl Lezema Moo, state congressional deputy, January 1996). The PRI–led resistance organized business leaders,[30] ranchers, merchants, and PRI legislators in the Tabasco

---

[30] According to press accounts, many of these business leaders were linked by friendship and kinship into a long-standing political-economic elite said to include two of Madrazo's cousins (Carlos Madrazo Cadena, director of Tabasco's COPARMEX, and Manuel Felipe Ordóñez Galán, president of the Tabasco Construction Consortium), as well as former governor Mario Trujillo García (two of whose daughters are in Madrazo's cabinet), Gonzalo Quintana Guiordano (president of the CEE that certified Madrazo's election), several other former governors and their families, and a hierarchical business network leading back to career public official and business entrepreneur Carlos Hank González in Mexico City.

Many Tabasqueños explained that identifying these political, familial, and business linkages is key to understanding politics in Tabasco and understanding

Civic Front (FCT). And local PRI legislators forcibly removed hundreds of PRD activists from Villahermosa's main square, where they were blocking entry to the state congress (author interview with Lezema Moo).

When Manuel Ramos Gorrión, regional coordinator of the national PRI, came to the Pino Suárez Library stating that Madrazo wanted the Tabasco PRI to accept his resignation, the state's legislative leaders refused to believe that the message really came from Madrazo. Moreover, they were angered by the national PRI leadership's defeatist attitude. On January 19, national PRI president María de los Angeles Moreno contacted Jiménez León. Although there are conflicting accounts regarding the purpose of this call, Jiménez León interpreted it as a signal that the national party had abandoned Madrazo (author interview).

Tabasco's PRI leaders then contacted all party members in the state's federal congressional delegation and pressed them to side with the local PRI against Mexico City; most did. In fact, all PRI senators and deputies from Tabasco participated in a meeting at the Ministry of the Interior at which Moreno and other national party leaders reiterated their support for Madrazo (Marí and Irízar 1995). Subsequent lobbying efforts were made on Madrazo's behalf by the PRI's national congressional leadership and several stalwart PRI governors, led by Puebla's Manuel Bartlett (see Riva Palacio 1995). Regardless of what lay behind the reversal, it was clear by January 21, 1995, that the national PRI had changed its position and that Madrazo was "safe."

The PRD's Finale?

In lieu of forcing Madrazo's resignation, the Ministry of the Interior proposed that the parties try to reach a negotiated settlement. When these discussions did not lead anywhere, López Obrador accused Minister Moctezuma of holding out the promise of a political path resolution solely to dislodge the PRD demonstrators from the Zócalo in time for Zedillo's inauguration ceremony. He further accused Moctezuma of exploiting the federal government's promise to stand by the Creel–Ortíz Pinchetti report to distract the PRD while order was being restored in time for Madrazo's return to Tabasco.

López Obrador and his supporters responded with civil disobedience. They refused to pay bills for public services, and they stopped

---

why this entire "dynasty of the establishment" was at stake in the battle over Madrazo's governorship (author interviews). For more on these linkages, see Delgado and Guzmán 1995.

paying the interest due on bank loans and credit card debt. They boy-cotted products made or distributed by "antidemocratic" businesses. When police detained the PRD municipal president of Cárdenas in March 1995, PRD activists organized a march to Mexico City. There they engaged in civil disobedience at the stock exchange, at the At-torney General's Office, at PEMEX headquarters, and at the Banco de México. Initially these acts were largely symbolic because they lacked any compelling new evidence for reopening dialogue with the federal government—until a dozen boxes of PRI campaign receipts from the 1994 Tabasco governor's race mysteriously appeared at the PRD's "base camp" on the Zócalo.[31]

These documents, deemed authentic first by journalists and later by the federal Attorney General's Office, showed that, far from spending 3.7 million (old) pesos on his campaign, Madrazo had ac-tually spent Mex\$237 billion, more than the U.S.\$50 million that Bill Clinton spent on his 1992 presidential campaign. The PRD filed a formal complaint against Madrazo and dozens of his supporters with the Attorney General's Office in June 1995. In August, Madrazo filed a counter-complaint before the Supreme Court, arguing on constitu-tional grounds that campaign spending in Tabasco races was an in-ternal state matter and beyond the scope of federal jurisdiction.

In January 1996, the Supreme Court was still deliberating. In-censed at the delay and at Madrazo's continuation in office—as well as the environmental damage that PEMEX was doing to lands worked by Tabasco's small farmers and peasants—López Obrador convened another PRD protest. This time, PRD activists blockaded oil wells, causing PEMEX to lose about U.S.\$500,000 per day. On February 8, federal police and military officers were called in to arrest some twenty activists, and on February 9 the federal attorney general is-sued arrest warrants for dozens more PRD activists, including López Obrador and several other party leaders. The Ministry of the Interior justified the federal government's "strong arm" tactics in Tabasco in terms of the urgent need to restore the rule of law in the state.

"Uncivil Disobedience" and Center-Region Relations

Zedillo did not fare well in his efforts to reduce the heat on his young administration. But there was no easy resolution, especially on the heels of Salinas's arbitrary concessions to any opposition party that could show mobilizational capacity and coalition potential. Abiding

---

[31] There are numerous press accounts about the mysterious boxes. López Obrador himself offers a credible depiction of the episode (1995: 211–37).

by formal legalist policies implied a break with both Salinas's long-standing policy and with the Zedillo administration's own early signals. Reopening negotiations in a political path resolution implied subjugating the law to political expediency—and making deals with "lawbreakers" in the PRD.

To be fair to the federal government, it must be noted that in Tabasco, as in other hardship states, there has long been a confluence of poverty, ecological degradation, inequitable patterns of land tenure, and the appropriation of economic and political power by a small elite through exclusionary politics and corruption. Yet had there been more consistency in the handling of the post-electoral conflict with the PRD, this could have gone some way toward a partial resolution of these long-term problems. Instead, the dangerous stalemate between the PRD and PRI in Tabasco was only prolonged.

"New federalism" aside, the real problem seems to be that Zedillo, Moctezuma, and others did indeed wish to remove Madrazo, but they could not do so. When they failed to muster the necessary political muscle, they tried to disguise this failure as respect for the "new federalism." In fact, Zedillo simply lacked the political acumen needed to force the justifiable removal of an unfairly elected governor without alienating the Tabasco PRI.

The success of the Rebellion of the PRIistas seemed to bolster several of Mexico's more democratically deficient local political machines.[32] This suggests that, had Zedillo been able to discipline Madrazo, his action might have reinforced a "rule of law" norm for gubernatorial conduct nationwide. The new federalism was supposed to end discretionary federal interventions in local affairs, not to end federal monitoring of state governors. Controversial electoral outcomes in the wake of the Tabasco rebellion suggest that some of the PRI's more traditional governors, like Manuel Bartlett in Puebla and Víctor Cervera Pacheco in Yucatán, continue to take electoral matters into their own hands.[33]

The post-electoral negotiations in Tabasco also highlighted the PRD's lack of experience. López Obrador clearly possessed sufficient

---

[32] Note, for example, the Figueroa administration's human rights abuses in Guerrero (note 1).

[33] The PAN accused Bartlett of "fixing" a Puebla electoral tribunal verdict so as to reclaim the PRI's 1995 municipal presidency victory in Huejotzingo. While Bartlett denied this, the author's analysis of Puebla electoral tribunal verdicts demonstrates a pattern of anti–PAN irregularities. Despite much internal dissent, the national PRI conceded the Huejotzingo municipal presidency to the PAN months later (see Eisenstadt 1998b). Cervera was accused, also by the PAN, of extending his "get out the vote" tactics to include bribes and the rigging of the state's electoral institutions in his favor.

savvy to negotiate simultaneously with the federal government and the state PRI, despite his less than moderate stance. But the national PRD was largely absent from the bargaining table. The internal struggle at the national level between pragmatist Muñoz Ledo and ideologue Cárdenas effectively undermined the national PRD's ability to lobby the federal government.

The most crucial lesson of Tabasco for local politics and democratization, however, is the level of harm that results from the Ministry of the Interior's inconsistent application of "rule of law" standards. When Moctezuma offered to annul Tabasco's gubernatorial election if López Obrador could prove fraud in 20 percent of the ballot boxes *and* if he relocated the demonstrators, he was using judicial criteria, but in the political realm. In other words, he was devaluing the norms of justice. Implicit in his offer was the acknowledgment that the judicial path was the most valid but that electoral authorities in Tabasco were incapable of pursuing this mode of resolution fairly. This compromise represents the worst of both paths, trying to apply justice, but as one more discretionary use (or abuse) of presidential authority.[34]

If a country is to promote confidence that the rule of law will prevail, it must have a regime of credible enforcement institutions. Mexico has not yet fully developed such a regime.[35] Because such institutions have been manipulated in the past for political ends, the federal government's invocation of them today rings hollow. The federal government appears to be using the "rule of law argument" when it suits and discarding it in favor of political bargaining when that approach seems to offer more advantage. The shift in the federal government's position regarding Madrazo demonstrates that it is not above putting the law at the disposition of everyday politics. Then how can it credibly invoke the "rule of law" to justify its actions?

It is clear from the foregoing discussion that the Rebellion of the PRIistas, the first-ever full-scale breakdown of party discipline, certainly played a part in reversing the federal government's and the national PRI's position on the Tabasco governorship. If, henceforth, the federal government maintains a strictly legal posture, it may be able to avert such intense political conflicts in the future, which, as Creel noted, do "spill over" into national-level negotiations, such as the debates on electoral reform.

---

[34] This should not be confused with a "mixed path" resolution, where actors intent on using the judicial path for political ends abide by its dictates, but only until such proceedings reach the limits of their usefulness.

[35] Such a regime is notably absent in Tabasco. A sophisticated regime of post-electoral dispute resolution has evolved at the federal level since 1988 but has not yet reached all states and localities (see Eisenstadt 1998a).

Indeed, the Tabasco crisis was perhaps just the most dramatic regional demonstration to date of the crisis in the national PRI.[36] Four years after the 1994 Tabasco gubernatorial election, the state's post-electoral conflict still stands as the most open defiance of the national PRI leadership by local PRI leaders. The post-electoral conflict also coincided with the first open breaches within the party about how best to serve its long-term interests. Zedillo—with his overtures to the PRD, recognition of opposition victories, and tolerance of reforms aimed at leveling the federal electoral playing field—seems to represent the moderate side of the party. This faction recognizes that the era of PRI hegemony is over, and it favors long-term implementation of the rule of law despite the short-term electoral losses that may result. Zedillo's opponents, the "Syndicate of Governors" led by hardline regional bosses like Madrazo and Puebla's Bartlett, meanwhile, remain inclined to exploit whatever advantages they can to maintain control, regardless of whether their maneuvers undermine efforts to establish a lasting legal order.

As mentioned above, the reformers' main legal weapon may be the new Federal Electoral Tribunal, which is as yet largely untested. However, neither the Electoral Tribunal nor the newly created post of special prosecutor for electoral crimes, within the Attorney General's Office, has jurisdiction to prosecute the worst remaining type of electoral fraud: the pre-election channeling of public resources for partisan ends.[37] Moreover, as the PRI grows ever less disciplined, electoral laws may have only limited effects on the most retrograde caciques. New rules are needed within the PRI that spell out the rewards for candidates who play by the rules and win, and the sanctions for those who perpetrate electoral fraud.

If Zedillo continues his post-Tabasco pattern of adjudicating electoral dispute and is able to stave off the victory-deprived PRI, then

---

[36] Other evidence of the increasing schisms between the president and his party include the reemergence of old-time party bosses (at the expense of Zedillo's modernizers) at the PRI's 16th National Assembly in September 1996, and the PRI congressional leadership's last-minute dumping of Zedillo's "rule of law" showpiece: the first federal electoral reform agreed to by all three major parties. Fearing more electoral defeats in 1997, the PRI majority in the Chamber of Deputies jettisoned Zedillo's hard-fought consensus reform in November 1996, in favor of their own initiative which maintained the PRI's overwhelming advantage in campaign financing. For further observations about recent erosions of Mexican presidential power, see Weldon 1997; on the demise of the PRI, see Craig and Cornelius 1995.

[37] The media have begun to expose the most flagrant of these violations. Examples abound from the heavily contested 1988 governors' races. In Veracruz, the PRI's candidate was caught raffling checks from PEMEX (Jiménez 1998). In Tamaulipas, the PRI candidate was found to have used the Matamoros Water Department's budget to cover personal expenses (Guerrero 1998).

Tabasco stands to become a watershed: a critical case in which one of the most sacrosanct "prerogatives" of Mexican presidentialism—the president's right to remove governors at will and replace them with his own supporters, without electoral "certification—was violated.[38] A more likely outcome is that, despite Zedillo's intentions, the new federalism will create regional power vacuums akin to those that exist at the national level, with machine bosses moving to fill these local spaces whenever they can. Given their extensive local networks, these old-time bosses can only be removed at great cost, and they will not go quietly.

There are signs, however, that the Zedillo administration may be reorienting its policy away from addressing a second-order symptom, excessive federal intervention in state and local matters, and toward resolving the first-order problem, the lack of strong federal watchdog institutions to regulate democratization's backsliders: the electoral institutions in a number of states. In a move that is quite aggressive by Mexican standards, Zedillo empowered the Supreme Court with extended judicial review capabilities in 1994. Although institutional barriers still block efforts to hold some hard-core lawbreakers accountable (González Oropeza 1996), in the electoral realm at least, national monitoring of local processes has been codified and hopefully will be reinforced by the Federal Electoral Tribunal.[39] The high political costs already incurred in the political resolution of Tabasco's 1994 election make it unlikely that the case will be reopened under Mexico's new regime of electoral justice (although the Chamber of Deputies was still considering impeaching Madrazo in mid–1998).[40]

The objectives of the PRIista "rebels" were hardly democratic. But the Rebellion of the PRIistas did manage to shift the locus of discretionary decision making from the center to the periphery. Zedillo has succeeded in decentralizing authority, but he has not been able to curb abuses of authority, especially at the regional level. At the very least, the Rebellion of the PRIistas may have decentralized research on the "new federalism," if not on decision-making processes themselves. Scholars of the new federalism's democratic, and authoritarian, uses may finally glean their evidence not just in the Ministry of the Interior in Mexico City but also in the local archives of Villahermosa's Pino Suárez Library.

---

[38] This widely held tenet of Mexican politics was "codified" by Luis Javier Garrido (1989).

[39] For a preliminary assessment of these reforms in practice, see Eisenstadt 1998b.

[40] For the record, there has still been no test case of the Federal Electoral Tribunal's new jurisdiction over local and state elections where constitutional violations are alleged, and legal scholars continue to argue that the 1994 race in Tabasco would have been an effective litmus test.

References

Abreu Ayala, Arturo E. 1995. *Madrazos en "El Trópico."* Villahermosa: Abreu Ayala.

Alcocer, Jorge V. 1996. "Ernesto Zedillo: presidente fuerte; presidencia democrática," *Voz y Voto* 36 (February): 4–12.

Áviles, Jaime. 1994. "Inflar la votación, orden en una grabación telefónica, denuncia—Marchará López Obrador al DF para demandar la anulación de las elecciones," *El Financiero*, November 22.

Comité de Derechos Humanos de Tabasco. 1994. *Informe de compra y coacción del voto previo a la jornada electoral en Tabasco.* Villahermosa: Comité.

Comité de Derechos Humanos de Tabasco/Academia Mexicana de Derechos Humanos. 1994. *Análisis de contenido electoral de cinco diarios y dos noticiarios de televisión del estado de Tabasco, noviembre de 1994.* Villahermosa: Comité.

Craig, Ann L., and Wayne A. Cornelius. 1995. "Houses Divided: Political Reform in Mexico." In *Building Democratic Institutions: Party Systems in Latin America*, edited by Scott Mainwaring and Timothy R. Scully. Stanford, Calif.: Stanford University Press.

Curzio Gutiérrez, Leonardo. 1995. *Tabasco: sociedad, economía, política y cultura.* Mexico City: Universidad Nacional Autónoma de México.

Delgado, Álvaro, and Armando Guzmán. 1995. "El quien es quien de los pudientes tabasqueños que retuvieron la 'inversion lambda Madrazo'," *Proceso*, January 30, pp. 28–33.

Eisenstadt, Todd A. 1998a. "Courting Democracy in Mexico: Party Strategies, Electoral Institution-Building, and Political Opening." Ph.D. dissertation, University of California, San Diego.

———. 1998b. "Electoral Justice in Mexico: From Oxymoron to Legal Norm in Less Than a Decade." Working Paper, Carter Center of Emory University. Atlanta, Ga.: Carter Center.

Garrido, Luis Javier. 1989. "The Crisis of *Presidencialismo*." In *Mexico's Alternative Political Futures*, edited by Wayne A. Cornelius, Judith Gentleman, and Peter H. Smith. La Jolla: Center for U.S.–Mexican Studies, University of California, San Diego.

González Oropeza, Manuel. 1996. "La irresponsabilidad de los gobernadores en México." Paper presented at the conference "New Federalism, State and Local Government in Mexico." Mexican Center, University of Texas at Austin, October 26.

Grayson, George W. 1994. *A Guide to the 1994 Mexican Presidential Election.* Washington, D.C.: Center for Strategic and International Studies.

Guerrero, Roberto. 1998. "Usan dinero municipal Yarrington y Cavazos," *Reforma*, June 7.

Jiménez, Sandra Isabel. 1998. "Rifan en mitin del PRI cheques de PEMEX," *Reforma*, May 24.

López, René Alberto. 1994a. "Cifras contradictorias y otro apagón en el Instituto Electoral," *La Jornada*, November 22.

———. 1994b. "Pudo ser una elección diferente; el priísmo lo impidió, dice el panista," *La Jornada*, November 19.

———. 1994c. "Desechó el TEE de Tabasco todas las impugnaciones," *La Jornada*, December 10.

López Obrador, Andrés Manuel. 1995. *Entre la historia y la esperanza—corrupción y lucha democrática en Tabasco*. Mexico City: Grijalbo.

Marí, Carlos, and Guadalupe Irízar. 1995. "No permitirán dimisión de Madrazo Pintado—amenazan priístas formar otro partido," *Reforma*, January 19.

Moreno, Daniel. 1995. "Quieren amordazar a los gobernadores," *Enfoque*, November 5.

PAN (Partido Acción Nacional). 1995. *The Democratic Plea of PAN in Yucatan*. Mexico City: PAN.

Riva Palacio, Raymundo. 1995. "Rebelión en la granja," *Reforma*, January 23.

Sartori, Giovanni. 1976. *Parties and Party Systems: A Framework for Analysis*. New York: Cambridge University Press.

TFE (Tribunal Federal Electoral). 1995. *Memoria 1994, Vol. II*. Mexico City: TFE.

Weldon, Jeffrey A. 1997. "The Political Sources of *Presidencialismo* in Mexico." In *Presidentialism and Democracy in Latin America*, edited by Scott Mainwaring and Matthew Soberg Shugart. New York: Cambridge University Press.

13

After the State Withdraws: Neoliberalism and Subnational Authoritarian Regimes in Mexico

Richard Snyder

In their efforts to understand the prospects for democratization in contemporary Mexico, students of Mexican politics have increasingly focused on subnational political arenas. This focus seems appropriate given the "outside-in" quality of Mexico's democratization process, which has been characterized by gradual accumulation of opposition party victories at the state and municipal levels. Indeed, most of the recent attention scholars have devoted to subnational politics centers on opposition governments in states such as Baja California, Chihuahua, and Michoacán (see, for example, Guillén López 1993; Rodríguez and Ward 1994; and the essays by various authors in Rodríguez and Ward 1995).

Research in Mexico for this chapter was supported by a National Science Foundation Graduate Fellowship, a Fulbright Fellowship from the Institute for International Education, and by grants from the Institute for the Study of World Politics and the Ejido Reform Research Project of the Center for U.S.–Mexican Studies at the University of California, San Diego. This chapter was written while the author was a Visiting Research Fellow at the Center for U.S.–Mexican Studies. He wishes to acknowledge the generous help of the many campesinos, rural development workers, and state and federal government officials in Mexico who shared their experiences and trusted his pledge of confidentiality. For helpful comments and suggestions on this material, the author thanks Ruth Berins Collier, David Collier, Wayne Cornelius, Peter Evans, Jonathan Fox, Stephan Haggard, Judy Harper, Luis Hernández, Robert Kaufman, Juan Linz, James Mahoney, Kevin Middlebrook, Gerardo Munck, Elizabeth Perry, David Samuels, Matthew Shugart and the members of the Center for U.S.–Mexican Studies' 1997 Writers Colloquium.

Unfortunately, this enthusiasm for studying newly democratic subnational regimes has not been matched by comparable interest in Mexico's incumbent subnational authoritarian regimes. Although scholars increasingly recognize that political regimes with distinct dynamics exist at the state level in Mexico, we lack a nuanced understanding of varied types of subnational authoritarian regimes.[1]

This lack of understanding is troubling for two reasons. First, broadly comparative work on political regime change has convincingly shown that the characteristics of the previous nondemocratic regime have profound implications for subsequent democratization processes (see, for example, Huntington 1991; Linz and Stepan 1996; Munck 1998; see also Snyder and Mahoney n.d.). Hence Mexico's state- and municipal-level opposition governments may confront distinct challenges depending on the kinds of subnational authoritarian regimes that precede them. Students of democratization in Mexico should thus be cautious not to "jump the gun" by focusing their full attention on new, subnational democratic regimes before adequately understanding the different types of prior subnational regimes from which they emerged.

Second, subnational authoritarian regimes may be here to stay and may even proliferate. As this analysis seeks to show, neoliberal—or market-oriented—economic reforms at the national level can contribute to the maintenance and strengthening of subnational authoritarian regimes. Rather than unleashing market forces, the withdrawal of federal government parastatal enterprises and economic supports may instead trigger "reregulation" projects through which incumbent authoritarian elites seek to generate rents and resources to help achieve their political goals.[2] This study focuses on the deregulation of Mexico's most important agricultural export industry (the coffee sector), showing how authoritarian state governors sought to control policy vacuums resulting from economic liberalization. As we shall see, national neoliberal reforms created fresh political opportunities for the governors of Mexico's coffee-producing states to expand their authority and bases of support.

The first section of this chapter analyzes the deregulation of the coffee sector, exploring the different reregulation projects launched by state governments. It shows how the withdrawal of the parastatal Mexican Coffee Institute (INMECAFÉ) presented governors with opportunities to strengthen their support bases by allying either with the

---

[1] The few analyses that consider subnational authoritarian regimes in the Mexican context include Fox 1994a, 1994b, 1996; and Rubin 1996. Rubin focuses on the cultural dimensions of power, de-emphasizing political institutions.

[2] This understanding of regulation as a tool that political incumbents may employ to generate the "resources by which to govern" draws especially on Bates 1983. On reregulation, see Vogel 1996; Snyder 1999.

mass of "newly available" small producers let loose by the dismantling of INMECAFÉ's organizational grid, or, alternatively, with the
traditional coffee oligarchy. By generating divisible benefits and targetable material rewards, reregulation served as a powerful tool for
helping governors forge such alliances.

The next section focuses on governors and state-level politics in
Mexico, highlighting how variations in both the internal and external
dimensions of subnational power lead to regimes with distinct dynamics at the state level. Based on these variations, a typology of subnational authoritarian regimes is developed that helps explain varied
reregulation projects launched by subnational elites in response to
national neoliberal reforms.

In the following section, a comparative analysis of three of Mexico's most important coffee-producing states illustrates how neoliberal reforms created opportunities for strengthening subnational
authoritarian regimes. In the states of Oaxaca and Guerrero, governors responded to INMECAFÉ's withdrawal by attempting to resurrect
weakened corporatist frameworks of interest representation in order
to assert political control over small producers previously organized
by the parastatal. In the state of Chiapas, by contrast, the governor
sought to win the support of powerful local elites by helping reestablish their traditional monopoly control of coffee processing and marketing. These variations resulted largely from differences in the kinds
of regimes that existed in these states when INMECAFÉ withdrew.

A concluding section discusses the implications of Mexico's federal political system for explaining the country's ongoing political and
economic transformation. The comparative study of state politics offers a powerful yet underutilized methodological tool for understanding this transformation.

The Politics of Reregulation in the Coffee Sector

In 1989, after two decades of extensive intervention in production and
marketing of coffee, which is one of Mexico's important sources of
foreign exchange, INMECAFÉ gradually began to withdraw.[3] This
process of withdrawal was part of a larger policy package of neoliberal economic reforms intended to stimulate economic growth by
reducing government intervention in the economy and increasing the
role of market forces. In the coffee sector, this national policy initiative

---

[3] Between 1970 and 1989, coffee accounted for an average of 5.1 percent of the total value
of Mexico's exports and 34 percent of the total value of agricultural exports Approximately 3 million Mexicans derive some part of their income from the coffee sector (Díaz
Cárdenas et al. 1991: 67). For a comprehensive overview of Mexico's coffee sector, see
Santoyo Cortés, Díaz Cárdenas, and Rodríguez Padrón 1994.

entailed INMECAFÉ's liquidation over a four-year period, which meant eliminating production supports, regulated prices, and public-sector control over marketing channels for the vast majority of Mexico's 300,000 small coffee producers.[4] In sum, these economic reforms were intended to replace state intervention with unfettered market forces, reorienting coffee producers toward free market signals and away from government regulatory agencies.

INMECAFÉ's withdrawal, however, did not have the effects envisioned by its neoliberal architects. In the wake of INMECAFÉ's disappearance, Mexico's coffee producers did not find themselves face to face with free markets. Rather, they confronted a new and in many ways more complex regulatory environment composed of multiple actors that had entered the breach opened by the old parastatal's withdrawal. These actors, which included other federal agencies, the governments of Mexico's coffee-producing states, and grassroots producer organizations, competed to control the institutionalized domains of policy interaction—or "policy spaces"—vacated by INMECAFÉ's withdrawal. Most notably, INMECAFÉ's dismantling created new opportunities for state governments to become involved in market regulation and sectoral policy making, triggering a decentering of policy arenas from Mexico City to the capitals of the coffee-producing states.

Rather than leading to unregulated markets, then, neoliberal economic reforms in the coffee sector unleashed a complex process of shifting policy arenas and institution building that resulted in a variety of new, regulated market structures. This reregulation process was driven by political struggle among state governments, federal agencies, and producer organizations to control the emerging policy arenas and define how coffee markets would be reorganized in the wake of INMECAFÉ's exit.

The governments of Mexico's coffee-producing states sought to use reregulation as a tool for building political support, launching a variety of reregulation projects to occupy the policy spaces vacated by INMECAFÉ's withdrawal.[5] Some state governments saw INMECAFÉ's departure as an opportunity to resurrect weakened corporatist institutions of political control in the coffee sector and launched *neocorporatist* projects[6] intended to monopolize interest representation in the

---

[4] Small producers are defined as those with few than twenty hectares of land (roughly fifty acres).

[5] State-level reregulation projects were not limited to the coffee sector. For example, such projects were also launched by the state government of Jalisco in the fertilizer and tequila sectors. On these cases see Guerrero Anaya n.d.; Torres 1998.

[6] These projects were "neo" in that they were subnational initiatives to resurrect traditional mechanisms of controlled interest group representation in the context of the decay of old, national-level corporatist institutions.

hands of "official" coffee producer organizations formally affiliated with the ruling Institutional Revolutionary Party (PRI). These projects sought to incorporate into new, authoritarian frameworks of interest representation the thousands of small coffee producers who had previously been organized by INMECAFÉ and were being let loose by its dismantling.

Neocorporatist projects consisted of efforts to transfer INMECAFÉ's resources (such as its agroindustrial infrastructure) exclusively to official coffee producer organizations and to construct new institutions for economic governance that excluded independent organizations not affiliated with the PRI. In some cases, such as the state of Guerrero, neocorporatist projects included outright repression of independent organizations and blatant efforts to co-opt their leadership. Such measures were intended to force these organizations to renounce their independent status and affiliate with the PRI's National Peasants' Confederation (CNC).

Other state governments treated INMECAFÉ's withdrawal as an opportunity to build support among traditional societal elites and pursued *crony capitalist* projects intended to create economic rents for the coffee oligarchy.[7] These projects sought to turn the clock back to the period preceding INMECAFÉ's intervention, when local elites had dominated the coffee economy. In contrast to neocorporatist projects, which focused on creating new frameworks of controlled interest representation for small producers, crony capitalist projects focused on resurrecting monopoly control of coffee processing and marketing by local elites.

Crony capitalist projects entailed efforts to create marketing boards and other regulatory institutions managed by the coffee oligarchy. The government of Chiapas, for example, sought to grant prominent members of the oligarchy control over distribution of licenses to export coffee from the state. In addition to creating an important source of rents and corruption, this new regulatory power would have enabled these elites to block efforts by small producer cooperatives to enter export markets, forcing them to sell at exploitatively low prices to elite-owned exporting firms.

To explain these diverse responses by state governments to INMECAFÉ's withdrawal, we need to explore the varied dynamics of subnational authoritarian regimes. As we shall see, different types of regimes yielded distinct reregulation projects.

---

[7] The term "crony capitalism" is commonly used to describe the political economy of Ferdinand Marcos's neopatrimonial dictatorship in the Philippines. See Thompson 1996: 183.

Governors and State Politics in Mexico

Until recently, Mexico's governors shared two important attributes: they were affiliated with the PRI, and, despite the ritual of gubernatorial elections, they were "appointed" by the president. Since the 1940s, with few exceptions, Mexico's governors have been clients in a highly centralized patronage system dominated by the president, who, in addition to appointing governors, also frequently dismissed them (Martínez Assad and Arreola Ayala 1987). Hence governors depended upon presidential favor both for their initial arrival to and continued occupation of their posts. Because the constitutions of Mexico's states prohibited governors from seeking reelection, most viewed their positions as pit-stops on a career trajectory leading back to federal government office. This perception further strengthened incentives for personal loyalty to actors at the center of the political system.

This personalization of power was duplicated, often in an exaggerated fashion, at the state level, and governors frequently behaved like arbitrary dictators. The small size of most state governments contributed to the personalization of power by limiting space for autonomous bureaucratic public-sector institutions to operate. Municipal presidents (the equivalent of town mayors), although formally elected, were virtually "employees" of the governor, chosen by him and removable at his discretion.[8]

Top-down, presidential selection of governors meant that the road to the state house almost always passed through Mexico City, which frequently resulted in governors whom local political elites viewed as illegitimate, imposed "viceroys." Many governors entered office lacking power bases within their states. Their subsequent inabilities to either subdue or accommodate local political groups (an inability frequently reinforced by the exclusionary, arbitrary tendencies of personalistic rule) led to the failure of many governors to complete their terms.[9]

The weak, provisional substitutes who typically replaced these fallen "constitutional" governors lacked the authority to govern and propose policy initiatives, contributing to a pattern of ongoing instability and paralysis of state politics. This pattern is exemplified vividly by the cases of Chiapas, where only 21 percent of the state's 160 governors have been constitutional, and Guerrero, where just six gov-

---

[8] As one municipal president vividly put it, "Most municipal presidents have just one constituency—the governor" (author interview, Guerrero, December 1995).

[9] The dismissal of incumbent governors, although in reality almost always a personal decision by the president, was prescribed by an elaborate set of formal constitutional rules. See González Oropeza 1987.

ernors have completed their full terms since 1917.[10] Political paralysis and instability at the state level reinforced the political system's overall tendency toward centralization at the federal level.

In sum, federalism in Mexico has, until recently, been a thin institutional gloss on an extensive patron-client network radiating outward from the presidency to the state houses. The distinct levels of Mexico's federal system, rather than representing autonomous spheres of authority, have functioned instead as nodes linking national patrons to subnational clients. The first cracks in this structure of patronage federalism began to appear in the early 1980s, when opposition parties began to win control of select municipalities (López Monjardín 1986). However, it was not until 1989, when an opposition candidate won the governorship of Baja California, that the patronage ties traditionally linking governors to the president began to unravel.

As of 1997, none of Mexico's major coffee-producing states had been governed by opposition parties. Hence the subnational regimes analyzed here are products of the old personalistic, centralized system. Despite the characteristics of presidential appointment and personalization of power shared by these authoritarian regimes, their dynamics varied significantly due to differences in both the internal and external dimensions of power. These differences offer a basis for building a typology of subnational authoritarian regimes. This typology allows us to link incumbents' choices of neocorporatist or crony capitalist reregulation projects to broader regime dynamics, thus helping to explain the diverse strategic responses by state governments to INMECAFÉ's withdrawal.

Internal Dimensions of Subnational Power

Subnational regimes can be differentiated in terms of governors' varied power bases within their states and distinct styles of leadership.

THE IMPOSITION DILEMMA

Because most governors achieve office through presidential designation and have prior career trajectories centered in Mexico City, they typically begin their terms as "outsiders," with weak support bases inside their states. Although the imperative of building support coalitions confronts most new governors, they respond differently to this "imposition dilemma."

---

[10] In its 170–year history, the state of Chiapas has thus had an average of approximately one governor per year. The data for Chiapas are from Castro Aguilar 1995: 41. The data for Guerrero are from Estrada Castañón 1994a: 75. See also Rodríguez Saldaña 1992.

Some choose to ally with traditional local elites. For example, the governor of Puebla, Mariano Piña Olaya (1987–1993), sought the support of the city of Puebla's commercial elites, launching a wave of repression against an urban street vendors' movement that threatened their business interests. Alternatively, a new governor may challenge traditional elites by allying with popular-sector groups and/or promoting new, nontraditional elites. For example, the governor of Oaxaca, Heladio Ramírez López (1986–1992), sought to build a support coalition based in the campesino sector. His government met with staunch opposition from private-sector elites, as vividly expressed in prominent local newspapers which described Ramírez's election as a "black night for Oaxaca" and denounced him as a "delirious leftist" (*Noticias*, April 1 and 2, 1986).

Governors' coalition-building strategies are shaped by a host of complex factors, including programmatic goals, perceptions of the balance of power between competing local groups, electoral conjunctures, links to political factions at the center, and their social ties within the state. Regardless of their motives for choosing different strategies, the distinct ways governors seek to manage the imposition dilemma lead to variations in the dynamics of subnational regimes.

LEADERSHIP STYLES

The extreme personalization and centralization of power characterizing state governments also contributes to varied subnational regime dynamics. Factors such as the governor's negotiating style, policy preferences, and ideological orientation critically shape state politics. For example, whether a governor prefers negotiation or repression to manage opposition, or favors market-oriented or statist solutions to economic problems strongly influences the parameters of the political system at the state level. To understand the logic of a subnational regime, then, we must address the question, "*Who* is the governor?"

Extreme personalization of power also frequently results in the fusion of government (the governor and his political team) and state institutions (the bureaucratic and legal institutions of the public sector). This fusion explains why the duration of many subnational regimes corresponds to the periods during which specific governors hold office.[11]

---

[11] The fusion of government and state institutions also justifies using the concept "regime," rather than "government," to characterize the varied roles of governors in Mexican politics.

External Dimensions of Subnational Power

Variations in subnational regimes are also linked to factors external to the state-level political arena, such as presidential missions, the timing of elections, and the nature of governors' ties to national-level elites.

PRESIDENTIAL MISSIONS

Some governors achieve office by being selected for a specific presidential mission, such as clamping down on local opposition groups regarded as national security threats or implementing political reforms to stabilize a volatile state. Not all governors receive such mandates; however, these mandates have defining effects on the regimes of those who do.

For example, General Absalón Castellanos Domínguez (1982–1988), who governed the southern border state of Chiapas, was assigned the task of managing national security concerns stemming from extreme political and social instability in Mexico's Central American neighbors. His regime was one of the most repressive in modern Mexico. Similarly, Rubén Figueroa Figueroa (1975–1981) was chosen to pacify the problematic state of Guerrero, where two armed guerrilla movements had organized at the end of the 1960s. Figueroa's regime, like Castellanos's, was characterized by extraordinary levels of repression: according to one peasant organizer imprisoned by Figueroa, "For the governor, two people talking in public was a riot" (author interview, Guerrero, December 1995).

By contrast, Figueroa's successor, Alejandro Cervantes Delgado (1981–1987), was chosen to implement a reformist program to relegitimate Guerrero's political system after Figueroa's hard-line tactics. Cervantes's regime combined tolerance of opposition groups with participatory public works projects.

THE TIMING OF ELECTIONS

Temporal disjunctures between presidential and gubernatorial elections also contribute to variations across subnational regimes. These disjunctures result in "out-of-phase" governors who remain in office after the presidents who appointed them have completed their terms. These holdover governors may have ideological and policy orientations that have been displaced at the national level. They coexist with "in-phase" governors, who were appointed by the incumbent president and usually reflect his policy preferences.

Diversity among subnational regimes due to electoral phasing is most pronounced after presidential successions characterized by major policy reorientations, such as in 1982, when Miguel de la Madrid replaced José López Portillo and launched neoliberal economic reforms. In the wake of that succession, non-neoliberal enclaves persisted in places like Guerrero and Michoacán, where governors appointed by López Portillo (such as Cervantes in Guerrero and Cuauhtémoc Cárdenas Solórzano (1980–1986) in Michoacán) resisted the new president's neoliberal policies and instead pursued the old, statist economic model.

LINKS TO THE CENTER

Varied relations between governors and competing national political groups also differentiate types of subnational regimes. Even during the "golden years" of PRI hegemony, when the only opposition parties were "satellites" created to cast the illusion of political competition, the national regime was characterized by a limited pluralism: behind the PRI's monolithic image, diverse factions and policy currents competed for control and advantage.[12] By virtue of the requisite passage through Mexico City to reach a governorship, governors typically acquired affiliation with a national political group. In fact, their appointments often represented quotas of power distributed by the president to such groups.

Governors' ties to groups at the center still shape state politics in important ways. Since most governors[13] seek to use their positions as launching pads to high-level federal office (ideally a cabinet-level position), their governance strategies are shaped by requirements of loyalty to the national elites with whom they are affiliated and upon whose support their future career prospects depend. Such loyalty requirements range from adopting specific positions on economic or social policy issues to repressing local organizations affiliated with rival national groups.

The shifting fortunes of national political groups also critically influence political dynamics in states governed by their affiliates. The degree to which a group holds influence in strategic federal ministries or with the president strongly affects the resources available to governors linked to it. Hence governors' abilities to pursue political projects and policy initiatives often depend on the standing of their groups at the center. For example, personal links between Governor Cervantes's team in Guerrero and federal officials in the Ministry of

---

[12] Purcell and Purcell 1980. On competing policy currents, see Fox 1993.

[13] With the exception of those older politicians for whom the governorship represents the culmination of their political careers.

Planning and Budget (SPP) were crucial for securing the resources that fueled Cervantes's populist public works projects.

A national group's weakening (for example, by falling out of presidential favor) often means cuts in federal resources for governors affiliated with it, which can severely limit their room for maneuver and strain internal alliances. By contrast, a national group's strengthening can yield a bubble of fresh resources, potentially altering subnational regime dynamics by opening new possibilities for governors to reshape and expand their support bases (for example, by using public resources to reach out to previously excluded groups). Thus a critical starting point for understanding subnational regime dynamics is to identify the national group with which the governor is linked.

A Typology of Subnational Authoritarian Regimes

Based on variations in governors' internal and external power bases, we can identify three distinct types of subnational regimes: populist authoritarianism, traditional authoritarianism, and modernizing authoritarianism.[14]

POPULIST AUTHORITARIANISM

Populist governors seek to manage the imposition dilemma by allying with popular-sector groups, such as workers and peasants. These governors typically pursue social and economic reforms intended to benefit these groups and, hence, often face strong resistance from local elites.

With regard to leadership style, populist governors prefer negotiation to confrontation, and they frequently make "populist gestures." For example, Ramírez of Oaxaca frequently invoked his "peasant upbringing" and his "indigenous mother." To his bodyguards' dismay, the governor once swam fully clothed across a river to accept an impromptu invitation from a peasant to visit a village that had not been included in his itinerary! In Guerrero, Cervantes

---

[14] This discussion, which is limited to three regime types, obviously does not exhaust the full range of possible types that could be derived from the five dimensions introduced above. The goal, however, is not to engage in a deductive exercise in concept formation, it is instead to distinguish types of subnational regimes relevant for understanding contemporary Mexican politics. Hence the discussion focuses on three types with readily identifiable empirical referents in the Mexican context.

made a point of eating frequently with peasants, and he commonly consulted taxi drivers about his performance.[15]

Leaders of populist regimes seek, as one governor put it, "to bring the state closer to the people" (author interview, Mexico City, April 1995). This goal is usually pursued by constructing new government institutions and launching public works projects. For example, during the mid–1980s, when public-sector enterprises were being dismantled and privatized at the national level, Cervantes's administration created twenty-eight new state government enterprises in Guerrero (Estrada Castañón 1994a: 51). And while public investment declined precipitously at the national level, it expanded dramatically in Oaxaca during Ramírez's term, as the governor sought to fulfill his pledge to "put a public work in every community."[16]

Because the economic orientations of subnational populist regimes after 1981 were clearly out of phase with the neoliberal project dominant at the national level, we might expect these regimes to have been linked to marginal national groups and, hence, to have received little external support. Rather than representing residual quotas of power for marginal national groups or backwaters overlooked by the president, however, populist regimes often received direct presidential support.

For example, Ramírez was handpicked to govern Oaxaca by Carlos Salinas de Gortari. In 1986, when serving as secretary of the powerful SPP and already being viewed as a possible presidential candidate, Salinas secured Ramírez's nomination despite strong opposition from the local PRI machine. Salinas and other national elites perceived Ramírez as the kind of leader needed to restore political stability in Oaxaca, which had been wracked by waves of civil unrest and mobilization since the early 1970s.[17] They recognized that Oaxaca warranted a political project (that is, Echeverría-style populism) that was neither desirable, nor fiscally possible, at the national level. After Salinas became president, his direct support for Ramírez helped the governor secure the resources he needed to implement his populist

---

[15] Many political incumbents try to make these kinds of gestures, and it is common for governors to invoke Mexico's indigenous roots by donning traditional garb and posing for photographs with indigenous communities, typically in front of historic temples or pyramids. However, populist governors have a genuine zest for such moments and seek them out with a greater frequency than do their nonpopulist counterparts.

[16] The quote is from Moguel and Aranda 1992: 178. Between 1986 and 1991, public spending by the government of Oaxaca increased 56.9 percent in real terms (Gobierno del Estado 1992a: 56).

[17] On Oaxaca's political and social turbulence during this period, see Martínez Vásquez 1990.

agenda.[18] The case of Ramírez's regime thus illustrates how subnational populist regimes that emerged after the national regime's turn to neoliberalism may, in fact, be deliberate products of that national regime, rather than residual holdovers from a prior political epoch.

Cervantes's populist regime in Guerrero, by contrast, was more a product of temporal disjuncture between presidential and gubernatorial elections. Cervantes had been appointed at the end of López Portillo's term, just before the neoliberal policy shift orchestrated by de la Madrid. However, even after his presidential patron had left office, Cervantes successfully secured federal government resources for his populist projects. To explain the maintenance of this subnational populist regime in the context of national neoliberal policies, we need to consider federal government elites' perceptions of state-level political dynamics. These elites (especially high-ranking SPP officials) viewed Guerrero, like Oaxaca, as a "problem state" (it had, after all, experienced two guerrilla movements during the previous decade) and felt that looser limits on public spending were required to govern in such a context. According to one top aide to Cervantes, the governor effectively used the threat of renewed instability to secure federal resources for his development programs, politely explaining to recalcitrant federal officials that he could not be responsible for the consequences if they refused his request for funds (author interview, Mexico City, May 1995).

How did populist regimes respond to national neoliberal reforms? The fiscal austerity imposed by such reforms stimulated many populist regimes to seek innovations in social service delivery. For example, populist governments fashioned new social programs that reduced the public sector's fiscal load by increasing the participation of program beneficiaries. One former governor thus observed that the national economic crisis of the 1980s and related budget cuts were actually blessings in disguise, because they led to more efficient and participatory social programs (author interview, Cuernavaca, July 1995). Throughout the 1980s, populist governors in states such as Guerrero, Oaxaca, Tabasco, Tlaxcala, Michoacán, and Quintana Roo launched a slew of new community development programs based on the idea of "co-responsibility" between government and citizens.[19] Many of these state-level initiatives were subsequently adopted at the national level by the National Solidarity Program (PRONASOL) (on PRONASOL, see Cornelius, Craig, and Fox 1994a).

---

[18] Salinas's friendship with Ramírez, which began when the former was an undergraduate at the National Autonomous University of Mexico (UNAM) and participated in a student debate club founded by Ramírez, also helps explain Salinas's support for Ramírez.

[19] Some of these experiences are summarized in the chapters on these states in González Casanova and Cadena Roa 1994.

Populist regimes also responded to neoliberal reforms by building new public institutions to fill policy areas abandoned by federal government agencies. As exemplified by Ramírez's neocorporatist project to organize Oaxaca's small coffee producers, which will be analyzed below, these new institutions were often intended to incorporate popular-sector groups being let loose by the dismantling of federal institutions like INMECAFÉ.[20]

TRADITIONAL AUTHORITARIANISM

Traditional authoritarian regimes seek to manage the imposition dilemma by allying with local elites. The governors of such regimes may have family ties to these elites, which both ameliorates the imposition dilemma and helps predict how it is resolved. For example, the governor of Chiapas, Absalón Castellanos Domínguez, belonged to a prominent family with huge landholdings and extensive interests in the lumber industry near the city bearing the family name: Comitán de Domínguez. The family of Rubén Figueroa Figueroa and his son, Rubén Figueroa Alcocer, forms the core of one of Guerrero's two most important elite groups. Such family ties connect these governors (who are often not the first governor to bear the family name) to long-standing political "dynasties" established by local elites, hence giving them elements of "traditional legitimacy" in the Weberian sense (Weber 1968).

Traditional regimes seek to shield local elites from both redistributive challenges "from below" (for example, from grassroots producer organizations) and competitive challenges "from outside" (as from external capital, whether international or domestic). In exchange for such protection, these elites, who usually control local clientelist networks and paramilitary forces, help maintain political stability and deliver votes to the PRI on election day.

The leadership styles of governors who lead traditional regimes differ dramatically from those of their populist counterparts. For example, rather than swimming across rivers to visit indigenous, peasant communities, as did Ramírez in Oaxaca, Guerrero's Figueroa would arrive in a helicopter and descend, with a pistol on his hip, slinging racist slurs. Traditional regimes tend to be extremely intolerant of groups not affiliated with official government-sponsored organizations, which usually leads to abysmal human rights records.

In terms of external power bases, these regimes are linked to hardline PRI factions opposed to both political and economic liberalization. However, like populist regimes, traditional regimes are not nec-

---

[20] Such neocorporatist projects also sought to pre-empt or defeat organizing efforts by groups not linked to the PRI.

essarily residual backwaters overlooked by the dominant national-level elites who support political and economic reform. As noted above, Castellanos Domínguez was charged with the presidential mission of managing security threats on Mexico's southern border. Furthermore, because of their ties to local elites, the governors who lead traditional regimes may play crucial roles securing votes for the PRI in national elections. Traditional regimes help protect the ruling party's "rural vote reserves," where "everyone—including the dead—votes for the PRI." These vote reserves can have decisive impacts on national elections, as illustrated by the presidential election of 1988, when rural districts tipped the national electoral balance toward the PRI. Hence traditional authoritarian enclaves can be understood as contributing to the PRI's national-level modernizing project by helping secure the political support and stability necessary for that project to proceed (Fox 1994a, 1994b).

Neoliberal economic reforms might be expected to threaten the maintenance of traditional authoritarian regimes, because the local elites who form their core support base usually engage in inefficient economic activities (such as low-technology exploitation of primary products like lumber, cattle, and coffee). Rather than leading to competitive markets that jeopardize the economic standing of these elites and thereby undermine the stability of traditional regimes, neoliberal reforms can instead create welcome opportunities to reconstruct local monopolies weakened or displaced by prior federal government intervention. To put it bluntly, neoliberal reforms get the federal government off local elites' backs, allowing them to return to "business as usual," which often means enjoying monopoly control over regional markets, with the state government's protection.[21] In the wake of neoliberal reforms, then, traditional authoritarian regimes may be able to strengthen themselves by launching crony capitalist reregulation projects that help local elites reassert their economic hegemony.

MODERNIZING AUTHORITARIANISM

Modernizing authoritarian regimes face greater difficulty managing the imposition dilemma than do populist or traditional regimes. This

---

[21] In the coffee sector, one of the principal justifications for INMECAFÉ's expanded role in the early 1970s was precisely to break the grip of local elite intermediaries over small producers by opening alternative marketing channels. Although the degree to which INMECAFÉ actually displaced these elites varied considerably across Mexico's coffee-producing regions, from their point of view the parastatal represented at the very least another palm to be greased and, in many cases, a major competitor that seriously reduced profits. Hence the parastatal's withdrawal created the attractive possibility for coffee-sector elites to revive their old roles as uncontested intermediaries between small producers and external markets.

difficulty stems from the lack of a natural constituency for their economic projects, which focus on opening the local economy to external
investment. On the one hand, traditional elites are likely to feel
threatened by such efforts to attract external investment, which they
may view as a dangerous challenge to their monopoly control over
local markets. On the other hand, the kinds of investment opportunities attractive to outside capital (such as tropical fruit enclaves, tourism, luxury shopping malls, and superhighway toll roads) offer few
direct benefits to popular-sector groups.

The most likely potential support base for modernizing regimes is
the urban middle class, which has the consumption power to enjoy
amenities such as shopping malls and video rental stores. However,
this middle class represents just a small percentage of the population
in most Mexican states. A second potential beneficiary of modernizing projects is the local, "comprador" bourgeoisie, which provides
services and support to external investors. However, in the case of
tourist enclaves, such as Acapulco and Ixtapa in Guerrero, the opportunities for such groups were limited by the preferences of the outside
firms that invested in these areas to import supplies (for example,
seafood and tropical fruits for tourist consumption) from other states,
rather than purchase them locally. Their economic projects thus create
tough coalition-building challenges for modernizing regimes.[22]

A third group that benefits directly from economic modernization
comprises government officials who reap profits through bribes and
kickbacks from external investors. For example, the governor of Guerrero, José Francisco Ruiz Massieu (1987–1993), and the governor of
Chiapas, José Patrocinio González Blanco (1988–1993), reportedly
amassed fortunes by channeling public contracts for highway and
tourist infrastructure projects to companies in which they held ownership stakes.

Most modernizing governors during the late 1980s and early 1990s
were linked closely to President Salinas's inner circle, and hence they
anticipated rapid promotion to top-level federal government posts.[23]
To maintain the momentum of their career trajectories, these governors had to deliver their expected quotas of electoral support for their
party and president. They thus faced especially strong pressures to
overcome the coalition-building challenges described above.

The tensions created by the contradictory goals of implementing
an economic strategy that benefits a narrow segment of the population, on the one hand, and mobilizing political support, on the other,

---

[22] The coalitional challenges posed by neoliberal reforms is a theme emphasized by Collier
(1992) with regard to the national regime's relationship with industrial labor.

[23] Such governors did advance rapidly: after completing his term, Ruiz Massieu was appointed president of the PRI; and in 1993, during the last year of his term as governor,
González was promoted to the prestigious post of secretary of the interior.

lead modernizing regimes to react to opposition in an extremely repressive, almost paranoid fashion. For example, Ruiz Massieu, a highly respected scholar of public law whose image of tolerance and sophistication led many to expect he would deepen the political opening begun by his populist predecessor (Cervantes), instead embarked on a campaign to crush organized groups not officially linked to the PRI. During Ruiz Massieu's tenure, government-sanctioned violence against members of political opposition parties was commonplace, as reflected in the large number of assassinated PRD supporters (see note 45).

Caught between an economic project with limited potential for mobilizing political support and the imperative of securing votes, modernizing regimes (in addition to employing repression) tend sooner or later to reach out to traditional elites and/or popular-sector groups affiliated with the PRI's corporatist confederations. Modernizing regimes are thus unstable amalgams, with strong tendencies to evolve into traditional or populist regimes, especially around election time.

Modernizing regimes treated INMECAFÉ's withdrawal as an opportunity to broaden their narrow support bases by strengthening ties with traditional elites or, alternatively, with popular-sector groups. In Chiapas, Governor González launched a crony capitalist project to build support among the coffee oligarchy. González's economic project had marginalized these elites by focusing on nontraditional exports, such as tropical fruits and rubber. INMECAFÉ's withdrawal provided a chance for him to secure their political support by helping reestablish their traditional hegemony over coffee processing and marketing. In Guerrero, by contrast, traditional elites had a weak influence in the coffee sector, having been displaced by agrarian reforms in the late 1930s. Ruiz Massieu thus focused exclusively on reestablishing the CNC's monopoly control over representation of small producers, launching a neocorporatist project intended to crush a powerful independent producer movement.

Regimes and Reregulation in Oaxaca, Guerrero, and Chiapas

This section analyzes how subnational regimes in Oaxaca, Guerrero, and Chiapas responded to INMECAFÉ's withdrawal.[24] In all three states, governors launched reregulation projects to occupy the policy areas vacated by INMECAFÉ's exit. These reregulation projects varied,

---

[24] For an expanded analysis of these cases, which also includes the state of Puebla, see Snyder 1997.

however: in Oaxaca and Guerrero, governors pursued neocorporatist projects focused on mobilizing mass support for the regime by strengthening the PRI's peasant confederation; in Chiapas, the governor launched a crony capitalist project intended to bolster elite support by delivering economic rents to the coffee oligarchy. As we shall see, differences in regime type help explain these distinct reregulation projects.

Populism and Neocorporatist Reregulation: Oaxaca

Heladio Ramírez López was a curious choice as the PRI's candidate in Oaxaca's gubernatorial election of 1986. Ramírez's political career had taken off in the early 1970s with the support of close advisers to President Luis Echeverría (1970–1976), and his political vision and policy preferences had been forged in the mold of the statist-populist policies dominant at that time. His policy orientations were thus strongly at odds with the neoliberal, technocratic approach characterizing de la Madrid's presidency. This technocratic orientation was reflected in de la Madrid's marked preference for gubernatorial candidates with strong administrative credentials.[25] Ramírez, by contrast, was a career politician with modest administrative experience.[26]

Ramírez's choice of advisers reflected his ideological formation. His team of advisers included several professors from the National Autonomous University of Mexico's Department of Economics, whose faculty was known for its structuralist, statist orientation.[27] Their policy perspectives were a far cry from those of the typically foreign-trained, neoliberal economists who advised the president. As one of Ramírez's advisers put it, "We were taboo for the neoliberals. They thought we were from a premodern epoch" (author interview, Oaxaca, June 1995).

In addition to academics who rejected the prevailing neoliberal orthodoxy, Ramírez's circle of advisers included prominent individuals who had held high-level federal government posts during Echeverría's administration. Fausto Cantú Peña, whom Ramírez invited to supervise policy for the coffee sector, had served as INMECAFÉ's director under Echeverría. Augusto Gómez Villanueva, who

---

[25] De la Madrid's preference for technocrats as governors is illustrated by his choice of gubernatorial candidates such as the following: Rodolfo Félix Valdés in Sonora; former secretary of energy, mines, and parastatal industry Francisco Labastida Ochoa in Sinaloa; and, in Michoacán, former secretary of agrarian reform José Luis Martínez Villicaña (Yescas Martínez 1991: 29).

[26] On Ramírez's career trajectory, see Camp 1995: 575.

[27] For example, Armando Labra, who advised the governor on social policy, and David Colmenares Páramo, who served as secretary of the treasury.

advised Ramírez on rural policy issues, had directed the federal Department of Agrarian Affairs and Colonization during Echeverría's administration. They brought to Ramírez's government considerable hands-on experience administering populist policies.

These advisers' vision of the public sector's appropriate role in Oaxaca was articulated by the doctrine of social liberalism and the related concept of the "social rule of law" (*estado social de derecho*).[28] This doctrine justified government regulation to promote social and economic welfare. As stated in the official document summarizing the "legal framework" for Ramírez's regime, the social rule of law sought to "overcome the limitations of classical, individualistic liberalism, which was characterized by state abstention, by means of dynamic state activity that ... promotes social justice and welfare." The document criticizes perspectives that view the state's role as limited to contract enforcement and protection of individual rights, because such perspectives are "imbued with a liberal, individualistic philosophy that paralyzes [the state's] activity and minimizes its role." Ramírez's government is described as "permeated by the ideology of social liberalism" and characterized by an ongoing quest for "increasing state intervention" in order to "coordinate and harmonize [Oaxaca's] diverse interest groups" and "redistribute goods and services according to the necessities of each [of Oaxaca's] regions" (Gobierno del Estado 1992b: 18; 1992c: 249).

Their efforts to reform the constitution of Oaxaca in order to codify government responsibility for economic management and development indicate that Ramírez and his advisers took this rhetoric seriously. The reform of Article 20 of the state constitution affirmed the public sector's role as "rector" of economic development and granted it power to take measures necessary to promote Oaxaca's economic and social development. This constitutional reform delegated broad responsibilities to the public sector, stipulating that "the state will plan, implement, coordinate, and orient local economic activity and carry out the regulation and promotion of those activities corresponding to the public interest" (Gobierno del Estado: 1992b: 45–46).

In addition to a State Coffee Council, which is analyzed below, new public institutions for economic management created during Ramírez's tenure included a parastatal to coordinate highway and airport infrastructure construction (Caminos y Aeropistas de Oaxaca), as well as a State Council to supervise the lumber sector (Consejo Forestal y de la Fauna Silvestre del Estado de Oaxaca). Although the

---

[28] The concept of "social liberalism" was in vogue at the national level after President Salinas introduced it during his second State of the Nation address on November 1, 1989. See Cornelius, Craig, and Fox 1994b: n. 1. See Villarreal 1993 for a fuller elaboration. The concept of social rule of law, however, seems to have been developed by Ramírez's team.

total number of such instances of "state building" in Oaxaca was small (only four or five), the surprising fact is that *any* new agencies for government intervention in the economy were formed, given increasing national-level efforts during this period to reduce the public sector's role and dismantle government institutions.

FINANCING PERIPHERAL POPULISM

An important difference between Oaxaca's "peripheral populism" during the 1980s and Mexico's national populism of the 1970s is that the former existed in an overall context of shrinking public budgets and growing fiscal restraints.[29] How could subnational populist policies during the late 1980s be reconciled with the national budget cutting mandated by neoliberal reforms?

Although its overall budget contracted due to neoliberal austerity measures, Mexico's federal government reallocated resources in the late 1980s in such a manner that some states actually received more than they had before the shift to neoliberalism. In Oaxaca, federal funds increased so dramatically during the late 1980s that the state government was literally awash in resources. During the second half of Ramírez's administration, Oaxaca's government actually received more federal money than it could spend and was forced to return billions of pesos to the federal government (author interviews, Mexico City, May 1995; *Extra de Oaxaca* 1990). In 1989, for example, the government of Oaxaca refunded 3 billion of 21 billion pesos authorized by the federal government for social development projects, because it lacked the administrative capacity to program and spend the money.

Between 1986 and 1991, public spending by the government of Oaxaca increased 56.9 percent in real terms (Gobierno del Estado 1992a: 56). Federal government investment in Oaxaca grew at the remarkable rate of 60 percent annually between 1988 and 1991, and by 1992 total federal investment in Oaxaca had expanded to six times its 1986 level.[30] These federal resources fueled construction of highly visible public works. Such works proliferated notably after the presidential election of 1988. Preferred projects included medical clinics, roads, and drinking water systems, as well as remodeling of schools and municipal government buildings.

The fiscal surplus that sustained this social spending can be explained by several factors. First, Ramírez was extremely adept at lob-

---

[29] Between 1988 and 1992, overall public spending as a percentage of GNP fell from 28.7 percent to 18.0 percent (INEGI 1994: 273).

[30] Gobierno del Estado 1992a: 19. During the period 1982–1992, average real growth in federal *participaciones* in Oaxaca exceeded that of any other state (Díaz Cayeros 1995: 95).

bying federal government agencies. The extensive personal contacts with key federal officials that Ramírez had cultivated through three decades of political activity in Mexico City and his negotiating skills partially account for his success at the appropriations game. Much of the explanation for this success, however, has to do with Ramírez's close friendship with Carlos Salinas since the early 1960s. According to one of Ramírez's top advisers, Salinas's personal confidence in his capabilities afforded the governor crucial leverage in his negotiations with federal bureaucrats who controlled the planning and budgeting process (author interview, Oaxaca, December 1994).

Ramírez's greatest success lobbying for federal resources was undoubtedly the special status Oaxaca achieved within PRONASOL. Oaxaca became a showcase for PRONASOL, receiving more funds from the program than any other state (Consejo Consultivo 1994: table A6).

In addition to Oaxaca's expanded share of the federal budget, a major increase in World Bank lending to Mexico for antipoverty and environmental projects also explains the ability of Ramírez's government to sustain populist spending in the context of national fiscal austerity. For the five-year period 1986–1990, only 8.6 percent of the World Bank's U.S.$9.9 billion lending commitments to Mexico was allocated to poverty-targeted loans. During 1991–1995, although total lending fell slightly to $8.4 billion, the share allocated to antipoverty lending rose to 27.9 percent (Fox and Aranda 1996: xi–xx). Oaxaca was one of the main beneficiaries of this shift in lending practices. The World Bank's social-sector strategy for Mexico, which included large loans for basic health, education, and community infrastructure, specifically targeted Oaxaca.[31] The World Bank's special interest in Oaxaca was publicized through a visit by its president, Barber Conable, to the state in January 1990. After Conable's visit, Ramírez announced with great fanfare the launching of a World Bank–funded, 1.5 billion peso social development plan to be implemented during the three remaining years of his term (*Extra de Oaxaca*, January 18, 1990).

ORGANIZING FOR PRODUCTION? NEOCORPORATISM IN THE COUNTRYSIDE

In rural Oaxaca, Ramírez's government focused on promoting peasant unions, a task that the governor had mastered during his tenure as the CNC's secretary of union affairs in the early 1980s. Oaxaca experienced a veritable explosion of official rural organizations. The overall organizational scheme was structured around branches of production and based on a three-tiered hierarchy: first-level organizations, such as ejidos and agrarian communities, were incorporated

---

[31] In addition to three other states: Hidalgo, Chiapas, and Guerrero (Fox and Aranda 1996: xi-xx).

into second-level Unions of Ejidos (UEs); Unions of Ejidos were grouped into third-level, state-wide Rural Collective Interest Associations (ARICs) (Gobierno del Estado 1992c: 55–59). ARICs performed a dual function, serving both as collective marketing boards and as sectoral peak organizations, which monopolized interest intermediation for each agricultural production branch. Between 1986 and 1992, nine ARICs were created, and the total number of Unions of Ejidos increased tenfold, from nine to ninety.[32]

This organizing campaign, dubbed "the agricultural revolution through peasant organization," was touted by Ramírez's government as a rural development strategy that would yield substantial increases in agricultural productivity (Gobierno del Estado 1992c: 49). Not surprisingly, given Ramírez's political formation, this strategy of promoting second- and third-level organizations around production branches was developed in the mid–1970s, during Echeverría's presidency (Fox and Gordillo 1989: 142–43). Despite the colorful rhetoric of promoting economic development that surrounded Oaxaca's rural organizing campaign,[33] this project, like Echeverría's before it, was a top-down effort to revitalize corporatist mechanisms of state-controlled interest representation.

Ramírez's government repeated an earlier practice, established during Echeverría's administration, of compulsory incorporation of rural communities into the new second- and third-level organizations. The ARICs and Unions of Ejidos in Oaxaca fostered many of the same abuses of power that had characterized the earlier, Echeverría-era projects.[34] These new organizations were usually characterized by mismanagement of resources, and often by outright fraud and corruption. According to one federal government official who worked in Oaxaca during Ramírez's administration, many of the Unions of Ejidos were literally created overnight and served mainly as "legal shells" to secure funds for corrupt CNC leaders. From his frequent dealings with the coffee-sector ARIC, he concluded that its leadership's main objective was "to steal money" by obtaining fraudulent bank loans (author interview, December 1995).

These new, state-sponsored organizations did not merely line the pockets of corrupt officials, however; they also served as tools for attempting to block expansion of producer organizations not affiliated with the PRI. When these independent organizations sought to form

---

[32] There had been no ARICs in Oaxaca previously. See Gobierno del Estado 1992c: 56.

[33] For example, Ramírez's proclamation that "Organization makes possible the miracle of transforming the weak into the strong and the campesinos can achieve what they never could have individually" (Gobierno del Estado de Oaxaca 1989: 26).

[34] According to Fox (1993: 58), "the size and technical sophistication of these projects made bureaucratic control easier, creating many opportunities for political and economic abuse of power."

their own Unions of Ejidos, in order to take advantage of special financing opportunities available to such unions, they often found they had been preempted by a CNC–affiliated union (Aranda Bezaury 1992: 91).

In sum, despite rhetorical claims of igniting an "agricultural revolution," Ramírez's organizing campaign was more an effort to reassert state control over rural interest group representation in the context of a growing threat from independent producer organizations. The campaign's success in this respect was limited, especially in the coffee sector, where independent organizations expanded considerably during Ramírez's tenure. In the end, perhaps the campaign's most concrete achievement was to create fresh opportunities for illicit enrichment by CNC and National Rural Credit Bank (BANRURAL) officials.

Given his regime's overall focus on reviving mechanisms of controlled rural interest representation, it is not surprising that Ramírez responded to INMECAFÉ's withdrawal by launching a neocorporatist reregulation project to occupy the domains of policy interaction and interest mediation vacated by the federal parastatal. As illustrated by the rural organizing campaign, Ramírez's populist regime sought to leave no political space unfilled. This imperative was especially strong in the coffee sector. Coffee was the state's most important agricultural activity, making a crucial contribution to the livelihoods of approximately 300,000 of the state's 3 million residents, and independent grassroots organizations had made their strongest advances in this sector.

Hence, for Ramírez the challenge presented by INMECAFÉ's withdrawal was clear: build a new set of institutions under state government control to encapsulate small coffee producers, thereby stemming the spread of independent organizations. For this task, Fausto Cantú Peña, the architect of national coffee-sector policy under Ramírez's political mentor, President Echeverría, was the natural choice.

REREGULATING THE COFFEE SECTOR

In late 1988, after several frustrating months writing unanswered letters to Mexico's president-elect, Carlos Salinas de Gortari, suggesting how to formulate national policy for the coffee sector, Cantú accepted an invitation from the governor of Oaxaca to design its coffee-sector policy. Cantú, who had directed INMECAFÉ during the mid–1970s, was a relic from a bygone period of nationalist-populist policies. He had orchestrated INMECAFÉ's transformation from a small agency with limited capacities for economic intervention to a giant parastatal with more than seven thousand employees. To the neoliberal technocrats who advised Salinas, Cantú represented the worst excesses of the statist policies of the 1970s: bloated, corrupt bureaucracy; a leviathan, paternalistic state; and irrational, anti-market government intervention. Hence Cantú should not have been surprised by Salinas's cold response to his letters.[35]

In Oaxaca, as we have seen, things were different. Governor Ramírez welcomed individuals like Cantú, whose nationalist ideologies and vocations for state building were out of step with the national trend of neoliberalism and state shrinking. Cantú's vision for Oaxaca's coffee sector was to build a new set of centralized government institutions to coordinate policy making and coffee marketing. These regulatory institutions would be accompanied by corporatist mechanisms of controlled interest representation to manage producer demands. In short, he sought to create a mini–INMECAFÉ, resurrecting on a smaller, subnational scale the regulatory scheme he had fashioned at the national level fifteen years earlier and which was now being dismantled by neoliberal technocrats.

In February 1989, Ramírez held a forum to unveil legislation Cantú had drafted proposing a "law for the promotion and integral development of coffee production in the state of Oaxaca" (see Cantú Peña 1989). Although this event was officially called the First Statewide Forum for Study, Analysis, and Training about Coffee Production, its purpose was less to stimulate analysis and study than to demonstrate the coffee sector's support for the governor's project. According to several participants, the Forum was intended as a "political show" staged mainly for invited representatives of various federal government agencies. One participant described the Forum as "pre-cooked," pointing out that the official book, which supposedly summarized the conference's conclusions, had been prepared beforehand! (author interviews, Oaxaca, December 1994).

The core of Cantú's proposal consisted of a provision to establish a State Coffee Council. This new state government agency was to be given control of export quotas and financing for Oaxaca's coffee sector.[36] In addition to fueling corruption by INMECAFÉ officials, government control of export quotas had traditionally served as an instrument for sustaining the CNC's monopoly grip over representation of small coffee producers: producer organizations not affiliated with the CNC were frequently denied export permits. Government-controlled financing had functioned in the past as a mechanism for forcing pro-

---

[35] For Cantú Peña's economic orientation as expressed in his own words, see the interviews in Carbot 1989: 369–81.

[36] State control of export quotas and financing were part of the proposed "Fund to Guaranty and Defend Coffee Production." According to the original proposal, the Fund, which would serve as the Coffee Council's "marketing and financing arm," would "administer the quotas corresponding to the production of coffee in Oaxaca" and would "manage and secure financial credits" for the sector. See Cantú Peña 1989.

ducers to sell at below-market prices to INMECAFÉ, which offered advance credits in exchange for the producers' commitments to repay the credit "in kind" with their harvests (Hernández Navarro and Célis Callejas 1994). According to a document justifying Oaxaca's independent small producer organizations' opposition to State Coffee Council control of financing, "[Cantú's proposal] would create a financial instrument—to control the money—that would be directed by a single individual, one not be chosen by the producers" (CEPCO 1989).

As envisioned by Cantú, the Coffee Council's nine-member executive committee would include just two representatives of producers—the secretary general of the CNC's Agrarian Leagues and the president of the CNPP's State Confederation of Small Property Owners—both members of the official, corporatist framework.[37] The rest of the committee would be made up by state and federal government officials, with the governor serving as the committee's president (Cantú Peña 1989: 13).

Cantú's neocorporatist project was challenged by a powerful independent producer movement whose support base in the sector proved much stronger than that of the official, CNC–affiliated organizations, which Cantú had hoped to make the exclusive representatives of Oaxaca's small producers. In the face of opposition from these independent organizations, the governor's penchant for conciliation facilitated a negotiated outcome. Under Ramírez's guidance, the independent organizations were incorporated into the new State Coffee Council, laying the foundations for participatory institutions of sectoral governance in Oaxaca's coffee sector.[38]

Hence Cantú's neocorporatist project resulted in a curious institutional amalgam that corresponded neither to the state-controlled policy arena he had envisioned nor to the unregulated, free markets advocated by neoliberal technocrats in Mexico City. Instead, his project yielded a new institutional framework for economic governance through which independent and official organizations collaborated with Oaxaca's government to improve the welfare of small producers.

Neocorporatist Reregulation in the Context of a Modernizing Regime: Guerrero

Although the governor of Guerrero at the time of INMECAFÉ's withdrawal, José Francisco Ruiz Massieu, like his counterpart in Oaxaca,

---

[37] The CNPP was the PRI's National Confederation of Small Property Owners.

[38] The positive effects of these institutions for sectoral governance on producers' welfare and ability to compete in global markets are analyzed in Snyder n.d.

launched a neocorporatist reregulation project, his modernizing regime differed dramatically from Ramírez's populist regime. The contrasting leadership styles and internal power bases of these two regimes led to important variations in how neocorporatist projects were
implemented in Oaxaca and Guerrero. While both governors shared
the goal of revitalizing corporatist frameworks of controlled interest
representation, they employed distinct tactics to achieve this objective. Ramírez sought to negotiate with independent organizations and
ultimately chose to include them within the new regulatory institutions created by his government. Ruiz Massieu, on the other hand,
favored repression and exclusion against organizations not affiliated
with the PRI's peasant confederation. These differences underscore
the importance of subnational regime type for explaining how governors responded to political opportunities presented by national-level
neoliberal reforms.

REGIME CHANGE IN GUERRERO: FROM POPULISM TO "MODERNIZATION"

The transfer of power on April 1, 1987, from Alejandro Cervantes
Delgado to José Francisco Ruiz Massieu marked the transition from a
populist to a modernizing authoritarian regime in Guerrero. In contrast to Cervantes, a seasoned politician nearing the end of his career
when he became governor, Ruiz Massieu was a young rising star
within the PRI. Given his youth (he was elected governor at the age of
forty) and ambition, Ruiz Massieu looked forward to securing a top
national-level political position upon completing his term.[39] He knew
that a key prerequisite for sustaining the momentum of his promising
career trajectory would be a successful term as governor—the principal measures of which would be his ability to maintain political stability and deliver his quota of votes for his party. Ruiz Massieu's economic strategy—which eliminated the participatory community
development programs launched by his predecessor and focused instead on promoting external investment in Guerrero's tourist enclaves—would complicate these two tasks.

Ruiz Massieu was a technocrat. He had never held elected office
before becoming governor.[40] Indeed, Ruiz Massieu's principal professional achievements had not even been in politics: he was a scholar of

---

[39] The election in 1988 of his brother-in-law, Carlos Salinas de Gortari, to the presidency
surely served to strengthen such expectations. Ruiz Massieu had established close political ties with Salinas since his undergraduate studies at the UNAM's School of Law
(Camp 1995: 641).

[40] This paragraphs draws on Estrada Castañón 1994a: 141; Camp 1995: 632–33; and author
interviews with state and federal government officials who worked in Guerrero during
the 1980s and early 1990s.

public administration and democratic theory, winner of the prestigious National Prize in Public Administration in 1979. Ruiz Massieu had held no major party positions, nor had he served in any of the PRI's corporatist confederations.[41] The only post he had held in Guerrero prior to becoming governor was a brief stint as secretary general of government during the last year of Rubén Figueroa's administration. In 1983, Ruiz Massieu was appointed subsecretary of planning for the federal Ministry of Health and Welfare (SSA), a position he held until he became governor.

In contrast to Ramírez, Ruiz Massieu was very much in step with the neoliberal policy prescriptions dominant at the national level. He understood Mexico's ongoing economic crisis as a product of the failure of populist policies pursued during the 1970s (Estrada Castañón 1994b: 104). For Ruiz Massieu, the solution to this crisis was "economic modernization," which began with drastic shrinking of the public sector.

According to Estrada Castañón (1994a: 142), "The first stage of Ruiz Massieu's administration was characterized by the almost orthodox application of the IMF measures promoted at the national level." During his initial two years as governor, in what he referred to as the "reining in of the public sector," Ruiz Massieu cut the number of state-owned enterprises from thirty-six to seventeen and fired hundreds of public-sector employees. His government introduced computerized systems in all areas of public administration in order to make further personnel cuts (Estrada Castañón 1994a: 142–43; López Hernández 1988: 75). Ruiz Massieu also eliminated the system of participatory planning and rural development programs created by Cervantes.[42]

Ruiz Massieu's economic development strategy focused on attracting private investment (both foreign and domestic) to the three tourist enclaves that formed Guerrero's "Triangle of the Sun": Acapulco, Taxco, and Ixtapa-Zihuatanejo. Rather than implementing a large number of small-scale development projects, such as rural schools and community recreation centers, as had Cervantes, Ruiz Massieu concentrated public investment in a handful of grandiose "megaprojects" intended to attract large amounts of foreign capital. These megaprojects included a luxury condominium and shopping

---

[41] He had served briefly as subsecretary general of regional coordination for the PRI's policy think tank, the Institute of Economic, Political, and Social Studies (IEPES) (1981–1982) and was subsequently appointed to the Institute's advisory board (1983–1986).

[42] López Hernández 1988: 76–77. One area of the public sector that received increased investment was the state's repressive apparatus. Public security forces were granted larger budgets and supplied with modern equipment, and police personnel received up to 300 percent increases in salaries between 1987 and 1990, which was justified as necessary to combat narco-trafficking (Estrada Castañón 1994a: 144).

complex in Acapulco (Punta Diamante) and a new superhighway from Cuernavaca to Acapulco. The extremely high tolls charged by the private-sector consortium that managed this superhighway excluded the bulk of Guerrero's population from using it. As one peasant leader bluntly remarked, "[Ruiz Massieu] only cared about Acapulco. He didn't give a damn about the rest of Guerrero" (author interview, Mexico City, May 1995).

During Ruiz Massieu's administration, the partnerships between government and poor communities that had characterized Cervantes's populist regime were replaced by joint ventures between government and large, private construction firms. Given the huge scale of investment required by Ruiz Massieu's megaprojects, few local businesses had the resources to participate. Hence national and, more often, multinational enterprises benefited most from these projects. Close advisers to the governor, as well as the governor himself, reportedly received large kickbacks from these firms and owned large shares of their stock.

The scarce attention Ruiz Massieu's government devoted to rural development focused on a handful of sectors attractive to foreign multinational corporations. For example, the "Filo Mayor" highway project was intended to facilitate exploitation of Guerrero's vast forest and lumber resources by national and foreign firms. Transnational agribusinesses, which had invested in Guerrero's melon industry, were the principal beneficiaries of a project to renovate and expand irrigation facilities in the Tierra Caliente region. Traditional crops such as corn, sesame, and coffee were neglected.

THE REGIME'S WEAK INTERNAL POWER BASE

Ruiz Massieu entered office with virtually no local support base. The leadership of the PRI machine in Guerrero had not even considered him a candidate for the governorship. His nomination had been largely a fluke: the result of a decision by his mentor, Secretary of Health and Welfare Guillermo Soberón Acevedo, to decline the nomination himself and propose Ruiz Massieu instead.[43] With the exception of his one-year stint in Guerrero's state government in the early 1980s, Ruiz Massieu had spent his entire adult life in Mexico City. Hence he faced an especially acute imposition dilemma. His economic policies intensified this dilemma because they mostly benefited a small group of business interests located outside Guerrero.

---

[43] Estrada Castañón 1994a: 141. Ruiz Massieu's family ties to the then-secretary of planning and budgeting, Carlos Salinas, also probably played a role in his nomination.

To resolve this dilemma, Ruiz Massieu pursued a two-pronged strategy, which combined efforts to strengthen the PRI's corporatist confederations (especially the CNC) with repression of both partisan opposition groups and independent societal organizations not affiliated with the ruling party. In a stark reversal of the image of tolerance and sophistication that this respected scholar of public law had cultivated prior to taking office, Ruiz Massieu was quick to unleash security forces against groups ranging from urban squatters to supporters of opposition parties. The lofty rhetoric of "the politics of ideas and facts," which had marked his inaugural speech, was soon replaced by threatening declarations, such as the following: "Those who come looking for a fight will get blood and problems, because the government of Guerrero is strong and ready to fight."[44] During Ruiz Massieu's tenure, violence against members of political opposition groups reached new heights, as reflected in the large number of assassinations of PRD supporters.[45]

In addition to employing repressive measures against opposition groups, Ruiz Massieu, like his more tolerant counterpart in Oaxaca, also sought to channel economic benefits to the PRI's corporatist confederations. Their monopoly control over rural interest representation in Guerrero had been severely weakened by the proliferation of autonomous producer organizations during Cervantes's term. In an effort to revive the corporatist framework of controlled interest representation, Ruiz Massieu's government pumped resources into the CNC, which received generous distributions of subsidized credit and fertilizer (Estrada Castañón 1994a: 92–93, 144; Calderón Mólgora 1994: 77). Ruiz Massieu also worked to ensure that CNC–affiliated organizations were the exclusive beneficiaries of the dismantling of state and federal government enterprises. He thus sought to guarantee that only CNC organizations received parastatal infrastructure transferred to producers. Furthermore, as illustrated by his treatment of the Alfredo V. Bonfil Union of Ejidos analyzed below, Ruiz Massieu employed a combination of coercion and co-optation against independent campesino organizations in order to force them to affiliate with the CNC.

---

[44] Quoted in Estrada Castañón 1994a: 143. This statement was made just after the strongly contested presidential elections of 1988.

[45] According to a report by the Pro Juárez Center, a human rights NGO, between 1989 and 1995, 222 murders occurred in Guerrero. Of a total of 538 reported cases of human rights violations in Guerrero during this period, 187 were reported by PRD members. According to the Center's report, "Repression has been focused primarily against members and sympathizers of the PRD in the context of electoral and post-electoral processes." See Elizalde 1995; Gil Olmos 1995. "Normal" rural violence (stemming from factors such as blood feuds and drunken brawls), rather than politically-motivated assassinations, probably accounts for a portion of the deaths.

Neocorporatist Reregulation and the Modernizing Regime

Although Ruiz Massieu and Ramírez both focused on rejuvenating the CNC, the two governors' neocorporatist projects differed in important respects. These differences reflect the distinct political regimes behind the reregulation projects.

First, due to his neoliberal policy orientation, Ruiz Massieu focused less on constructing new regulatory institutions than did Ramírez. Ruiz Massieu did not surround himself with advisers of nationalist-populist persuasion: "state-builders" like Fausto Cantú Peña were not welcome in Guerrero. Although Ruiz Massieu did eventually propose a new state government agency to fill the policy domains vacated by INMECAFÉ, this agency, in contrast to Oaxaca's State Coffee Council, never received funding.

Second, Ruiz Massieu's modernizing regime was much more prone to violence than Ramírez's populist regime, which tended to prefer negotiated, peaceful solutions to political conflicts. Consequently, the costs to producer organizations of choosing to oppose the governor's neocorporatist project were significantly greater in Guerrero than in Oaxaca.

Ruiz Massieu's treatment of Guerrero's most important independent organization of small coffee producers—the Alfredo V. Bonfil Union of Ejidos —illustrates his neocorporatist tactics. Just months after entering office, his government launched a campaign to pressure and blackmail the Union's leadership to affiliate with the CNC. With a combination of bribes and threats, CNC infiltrators—who received personnel, vehicles, and money from Ruiz Massieu's government—attempted to co-opt the Union's rank and file. As one of the Union's leaders put it, "the governor entered office with his sword drawn" (author interview, Guerrero, December 1995).

The struggle to defend the Union's autonomy focused on internal elections to renew its leadership scheduled for August 1987.[46] The CNC infiltrators sought to buy votes in exchange for credentials offering benefits such as free medical assistance and life-insurance payments. They informed the Union's rank and file that the governor had already decided the CNC's candidate would be the Union's new president, threatening that all access to government support would be cut off if the membership voted against him.

In the weeks prior to the elections, CNC cadres attempted to bribe delegates from the Union's constituent ejidos. Just five days before the elections, eleven of the twenty-two delegates were invited to attend a "training course" at a luxurious hotel in the state of Morelos. Ruiz Massieu met personally with the delegates and strongly "recommended" that they vote for the CNC slate if they wanted their

---

[46] The following discussion draws on Cobo and Paz Paredes 1991: 60–63.

ejidos to continue receiving government assistance. Each delegate was given a wad of money, presented as a cash scholarship to support their children's' education. The elections resulted in the victory of the CNC's slate, which received the votes of twelve of the twenty-two delegates.

When the defeated "democratic current" regrouped and formed a new independent organization (the Coalition of Ejidos of the Costa Grande), Ruiz Massieu's government refused to grant it legal recognition (Paz Paredes and Cobo 1992: 128). In 1990, after the process of INMECAFÉ's dismantling had begun, the state government blocked the Coalition's attempt to purchase the parastatal's offices and dry-processing infrastructure.[47] Despite the fact that INMECAFÉ's national director supported the sale and had planned an elaborate ceremony (to which President Salinas had been invited) to transfer these facilities to the Coalition, Ruiz Massieu sought instead to force the infrastructure's transfer to the Alfredo V. Bonfil Union of Ejidos (now under CNC control), even though it could not offer a bid comparable to the Coalition's.

After months of delays, an agreement was finally reached. The accord stipulated that the state government, the Alfredo V. Bonfil Union, and the Coalition would jointly purchase INMECAFÉ's facilities. As a result of foot-dragging by the CNC, however, the agreement soon collapsed. In the end, the Coalition was forced to build new offices and processing facilities, and the CNC became the sole owner of INMECAFÉ's former infrastructure. Ruiz Massieu's attacks against the independent producer movement left a legacy of politicization and polarization in Guerrero's coffee sector that severely hindered subsequent efforts to construct institutions for economic governance.

Modernization and Crony Capitalist Reregulation: Chiapas

In Oaxaca and Guerrero, governors treated INMECAFÉ's dismantling as an opportunity to build support among peasant coffee producers. As we have seen, they launched neocorporatist reregulation projects intended to strengthen frameworks of controlled mass interest intermediation. In Chiapas, by contrast, the governor viewed the parastatal's exit as a chance to win political support from traditional societal elites, and thus he launched a crony capitalist reregulation project to resurrect the oligarchy's monopoly control of the coffee economy. The governor's choice of a crony capitalist project can be explained in part by the political support dilemma faced by his modernizing regime.

---

[47] This and the following paragraph are based on interviews with members of the Coalition in Atoyac, Guerrero, December 1995, as well as on Cobo and Paz Paredes 1991: 68.

He sought to manage this dilemma by cozying up to the oligarchy in order to take advantage of the local patron-client networks and paramilitary forces it controlled.

THE MODERNIZING REGIME IN CHIAPAS

José Patrocinio González Blanco (1988–1993) established a modernizing authoritarian regime in Chiapas. Like Ruiz Massieu, González had close family and political ties to President Salinas and supported the president's project of market-oriented reform and economic modernization. His economic strategy combined privatization of government-owned enterprises[48] with promotion of large-scale, external investment in sectors such as tourism, urban consumer goods and services, and nontraditional agricultural exports.

González's proximity to the president also led him to anticipate rapid promotion to a top-level federal government post.[49] He thus confronted the same dilemma as Ruiz Massieu: reconciling an economic strategy that benefited a narrow segment of the population with the need to mobilize political support and preserve stability in order to maintain the momentum of his strong career trajectory. González sought to manage this support dilemma through a combination of repression against autonomous societal organizations and selective alliances with both the traditional oligarchy (that is, large landowners and merchants whose wealth was based in cattle, timber, and coffee) and clientelist, old-guard factions of the PRI's corporatist confederations.[50]

In contrast to governors like Ramírez and Cervantes, who were first-generation politicians from humble backgrounds, González came from a family extremely well established within the national political elite. His father, Salomón González Blanco, had served as secretary of labor under two presidents (Adolfo López Mateos and Gustavo Díaz Ordaz) and had even been considered a possible presidential candidate himself in 1963. At the end of his political career, González Blanco had been interim governor of Chiapas (1978–1980).

González's marriage to Patricia Ortiz Salinas extended and strengthened his inherited ties to the national political elite. Ortiz Sa-

---

[48] Most notably, his government privatized the Chiapas Forestry Corporation (CORFO) and the Pujiltic sugar mill (Harvey 1994: 9).

[49] An expectation realized in late 1992, four years into González's six-year term, when Salinas offered him the cabinet-level position of secretary of the interior—an offer that he quickly accepted. He held this position until early 1994, when the Zapatista uprising led to his dismissal.

[50] On internal divisions within the CNC between reformist, productivist factions and traditional, clientelist groups, see Mackinlay 1996.

linas was the niece of Raúl Salinas Lozano, who had served alongside González's father in President López Mateos' cabinet (as secretary of industry and commerce). She was also the cousin of President Carlos Salinas de Gortari. Her father, Antonio Ortiz Mena, had been considered a candidate for Mexico's presidency in 1970 and had subsequently served as president of the Inter-American Development Bank (1971–1988). During the first two years of Salinas's presidency, he was director general of the National Bank of Mexico (BANAMEX), one of Mexico's most important commercial banks (Camp 1995: 528–29).

Of the governors of Mexico's major coffee-producing states when INMECAFÉ withdrew, González clearly had the most extensive connections to national political and economic groups. These connections critically shaped the dynamics of his regime. Given González's close family ties to the president, he, more than most governors, had cause to believe the governorship would be a stepping-stone for swift promotion to a high-level federal government post. Of course, any such promotion would be contingent on successfully performing the minimal tasks expected of all PRI governors: delivering his quota of votes for the ruling party and maintaining political stability.

González's ties to national business groups, however, created strong incentives for him to pursue economic policies that complicated these tasks. Through his network of contacts in Mexico City, González had established links with politically influential financial and business elites, who sought to exploit the natural resources of Chiapas by investing in the tourist and tropical fruit industries. González's government catered to these interests, focusing on providing them a favorable investment climate. This economic development strategy, however, offered little to the state's predominantly poor, rural inhabitants, whose livelihoods depended on traditional crops such as corn and beans. Nor did this development strategy benefit the traditional oligarchy, whose wealth was concentrated in coffee and cattle.

To attract external investment to the tourist industry, González's government focused on promoting a cluster of natural and archaeological tourist destinations which formed the so-called Mayan Route. New luxury hotels were built, including a five-star establishment conspicuously situated at a principal entrance to the state capital. At another major entrance to the capital city, the state government constructed a gigantic center for the performing arts.

In addition to hotels and cultural centers, a flurry of new retail stores and shopping malls appeared in the capital city. These commercial establishments often carried luxury goods beyond the reach of the vast majority of the population. Such ventures were financed by national business groups from outside Chiapas (including the Chedraui group, led by Antonio Chedraui Obeso, from Veracruz).

State government officials, including González himself, were reported to have received kickbacks and bribes from the construction of these projects.[51] With the exception of a small segment of the population (the urban middle and upper classes), this investment in tourism and retail consumer goods benefited a narrow set of external interests and their local business partners. Shopping malls, cultural centers, and five-star hotels did little to address the needs of the impoverished majority of one of Mexico's poorest states.[52]

"MAIZE, THE CROP OF FAILURE": MODERNIZING THE COUNTRYSIDE

González's rural development strategy focused on promoting large-scale commercial agriculture in the state's tropical fruit and citrus enclave—the Soconusco region. Export crops, such as banana, mango, melon, and citric fruits, received special attention (Harvey 1994: 7; González Esponda and Pólito Barrios 1995: 112). González's government launched a major infrastructure improvement project to upgrade the Soconusco's principal port facility, Puerto Madero, through which most of the state's banana production was shipped.[53] Large agribusiness export firms were the principal beneficiaries of these public works, which helped lower their transportation costs and reduce shipment delays.

González reportedly had a personal stake in the profits of these agribusiness firms. He was identified as a business partner of multimillionaire Carlos Cabal Peniche, who owned Fresh Del Monte Produce (a former subsidiary of Del Monte Foods, which Cabal Peniche had purchased in the late 1980s).[54] Cabal Peniche had an extensive network of political contacts, which included President Salinas, his secretary of agriculture, Carlos Hank González, and numerous governors. He used this network to help build a vast business empire rooted in exports of tropical fruits (especially bananas) from Chiapas, Tabasco, and Yucatán. Indeed, Cabal Peniche had explicitly men-

---

[51] González was reportedly a business associate of Chedraui's through their shared partnership with banker and owner of Del Monte foods Carlos Cabal Peniche (Albarrán de Alba 1994; Ravelo 1994; Puig 1994).

[52] For figures on poverty and marginalization in Chiapas, see Legorreta Díaz 1995.

[53] Mota Marín 1994: 338–39. Banana production doubled between 1989 and 1992 (Ceceña and Barreda 1995: 84).

[54] Several former governors of Tabasco and Salinas's secretary of agriculture, Carlos Hank González, where also mentioned as business associates of Cabal Peniche (Albarrán de Alba 1994). In an interview with the *Wall Street Journal*, published in September 1994, Cabal Peniche boasted that he had numerous former governors as business partners (Puig 1994: 13). Before his indictment in late 1994 on charges of violating banking regulations, Cabal Peniche had been heralded as an "exemplary entrepreneur" by President Salinas and his secretary of commerce, Jaime Serra Puche (Puig 1994: 6).

tioned upgrading Puerto Madero in Chiapas as part of his "business plan," which envisioned a "corridor of ports" across southern Mexico to facilitate his business activities (Ravelo 1994: 17).

This responsiveness of González's government to the needs of agribusiness conglomerates contrasted sharply with its neglect of the hundreds of thousands of campesinos who grew traditional crops, such as maize and beans. Although González's government took modest steps to improve the welfare of small producers by promoting nontraditional cash crops such as rubber, tobacco, peanuts, soybeans, sorghum, and safflower, such initiatives targeted relatively well-off small producers in the Soconusco region. For example, the sixteen ejidos in Chiapas that produced soybeans were all located in the Soconusco, where 10 percent of ejidos had access to irrigation, as opposed to 4.1 percent of ejidos in Chiapas as a whole (Harvey 1994: 7–8). Tobacco production was also confined to the Soconusco enclave.

Despite the fact that Chiapas produced more maize than any other Mexican state, production of this crop received virtually no state government support.[55] Since 1987, maize productivity in Chiapas had fallen precipitously (as it had across Mexico) as producers confronted higher input costs, falling prices, and reduced access to credit (Harvey 1994: 11). González ignored the increasingly difficult situation faced by most campesinos, as indicated by his crass dismissal of maize as "the crop of failure."

In contrast to Ramírez in Oaxaca, who launched a massive campaign of organizing and public investment in the countryside, González sought first and foremost to attend to the needs of external agribusiness firms. Like Ruiz Massieu in Guerrero, González faced the challenge of reconciling an exclusionary development strategy with the political imperatives of maintaining stability and delivering his quota of votes for his party.

Like his counterpart in Guerrero, González sought to achieve these political objectives in part by repressing societal organizations not affiliated with the PRI. During the initial months of his administration, several prominent members of independent campesino organizations were assassinated, including two of the state's most important campesino leaders.[56] In the municipality of Pijijiapan, local police ambushed a group of peasants, killing eight and wounding five.[57] Although González himself may not have personally ordered the at-

---

[55] In 1990, over 166,000 ejidatarios in Chiapas (91 percent of the state's total) produced maize.

[56] For the governor's own account of the assassination of these two leaders, see the interview in Rojas 1995: 53–56.

[57] Pólito and González Esponda 1996: 209–10; Harvey 1994: 22. The Centro Fray Bartolomé de las Casas documented numerous abuses of human rights by state police against campesino organizations (Rojas 1995: 140–41, 203–205).

tacks, he did nothing to punish those responsible for them or to prevent future incidents.

González's government thus quickly established a reputation for employing heavy-handed tactics against peasant organizations. According to Hernández Navarro (1994: 59), "Practically all democratic campesino organizations active in the state had some of their members in prison."[58] A generalized climate of violence reigned across Chiapas, as suggested by one review of the human rights situation five months after González entered office, which reported twenty-six assassinations since the beginning of his term (Legorreta Díaz 1994: 141).

In addition to fostering and exploiting this climate of fear and violence to deter opposition, González sought to build political support by allying with segments of the landed oligarchy. The waves of land reform that swept most other states in the wake of the Mexican Revolution had had a relatively limited impact in Chiapas.[59] In 1990, the traditional landed elite continued to play a key role across much of rural Chiapas. The oligarchy initially viewed González with suspicion, regarding him as yet another outsider imposed by the federal government.[60] The governor's obvious preference for external investors and his neglect of traditional export sectors (coffee, beef, and lumber) confirmed their doubts.

Given the political support dilemmas he faced, however, González could ill afford to alienate the oligarchy. These elites dominated key patron-client networks across rural Chiapas and often had personal mercenary forces ("white guards") at their disposal. Although their grip on rural Chiapas had been weakened since the 1970s by campesino organizations, these elites still controlled on-the-ground "carrots and sticks" in many regions. For González, who had entered office with few local bases of support, allying with these elites offered a solution to the problems of maintaining stability and securing his quota of votes for the PRI.

INMECAFÉ's withdrawal created an attractive opportunity for González to gain the oligarchy's support by reregulating coffee markets to its advantage. The elites who traditionally dominated coffee processing and marketing in Chiapas had been partially displaced by INMECAFÉ, which provided small producers alternative channels for

---

[58] See Pólito and González Esponda 1996 on government violence against peasant organizations in Chiapas.

[59] On the landed elite's ability to avoid the "federal *agrarista* threat," see García de León 1985: 175–218.

[60] Indeed, members of this elite employed a slang term, "*pichichi*"—*pinche chilango chiapaneco* (lousy Chiapan from Mexico City)—to refer to politicians who, like González, had spent most of their careers outside the state. Author interviews with members of the oligarchy, Chiapas, October 1995.

securing production inputs and marketing their crops. The parastatal's dismantling thus offered a welcome chance for the oligarchies to reassert their hegemony. González's crony capitalist project was intended to win their political support by helping them achieve this goal.

COZYING UP TO THE OLIGARCHY: THE SPECIAL SUBCOMMITTEE FOR COFFEE PRODUCTION AND MARKETING

In March 1989, González's government created a Special Subcommittee for Coffee Production and Marketing. The Subcommittee, which was formed under the auspices of the Planning Committee for State Development (COPLADE), would spearhead the state government's crony capitalist project.

The Subcommittee's composition clearly signaled its mission. González appointed Esteban Figueroa Aramoni as the Subcommittee's coordinator. Figueroa, a close friend of the governor, owned a major coffee-exporting firm. The Subcommittee's deputy coordinator, Gabriel Orantes Balbuena, belonged to a prominent elite family (the Orantes), which owned extensive coffee plantations and processing facilities in the Jaltenango region.[61] The Subcommittee also had five representatives of large-scale producers and agroindustrial firms, including the leaders of the coffee industry's three most important private-sector associations: the Regional Agricultural Union of Coffee Producers Tacaná, based in the Soconusco region; the Union of Producers, Industrialists, and Exporters of Coffee of the Yajalón Region, located in northern Chiapas; and Coffee Agroindustries of Chiapas, which drew its membership from across the state (Subcomité Especial 1989a).

By contrast, the Subcommittee included just three representatives for the more than seventy thousand small producers in Chiapas. All three belonged to the CNC and were old-guard leaders linked to clientelist factions of the official peasant confederation. Producer organizations *not* affiliated with the ruling party had no formal representation on the Subcommittee.

The Subcommittee held its first meeting on March 7, 1989. The minutes of this and subsequent meetings clearly reveal its primary objective: reestablishing local elite hegemony over coffee exporting and processing after twenty years of competition from INMECAFÉ. The

---

[61] See *La República en Chiapas*, October 10, 1994, for an interview with a member of the Orantes family. The coffee oligarchy in Chiapas combined extensive landholdings with ownership of processing and other agroindustrial facilities. It was thus a "commercialized-landed" elite.

principal tool for achieving this goal would be regulation of coffee exports via export quotas and licenses.

At the Subcommittee's initial sessions, members focused on wresting control of export quotas from INMECAFÉ. In a letter sent to the governor in April 1989, the Subcommittee expressed its dissatisfaction with INMECAFÉ's handling of export quotas (Subcomité Especial 1989b). They complained that INMECAFÉ had consistently undermeasured Chiapas's production of export-quality coffee and had failed to grant local firms their fair share of national export quotas. To rectify this problem, the Subcommittee proposed a "state register of exporters" which it would manage and upon which INMECAFÉ's distribution of export quotas would be based (Subcomité Especial 1989c).

After the rupture of the International Coffee Agreement (ICA) in July 1989, which caused the immediate collapse of the national export quota system, the Subcommittee sought to establish autonomous power to issue export licenses at the state level. The Subcommittee proposed that to export coffee from Chiapas, firms should be required to secure licenses issued by the state government (Subcomité Especial 1989d). In addition to creating an important source of rents and corruption, this new regulatory power would allow the Subcommittee to block efforts by small producer cooperatives to export directly instead of selling to elite-controlled exporting firms. Ironically, the Subcommittee justified its efforts to establish a new system of export licenses by claiming that this regulatory power would protect the interests of small producers, allowing the Subcommittee to "exclude speculators [and] coyotes" from local markets.[62]

In addition to controlling export licenses, the Subcommittee also sought to promote what it called "direct links" between small producers and private-sector exporters (Subcomité Especial n.d.). The Subcommittee proposed that "the group of exporters-industrialists" should protect small producers' welfare by providing them marketing assistance. As one document put it, "We consider that the best way to help the small producer would be, among other things, establishing contacts with the various exporters, with the obligation on the part of the exporters to provide administrative, financial, and marketing assistance ... in order to help [the small producers] realize their own exporting in the future" (Subcomité Especial n.d.). The document made no mention, however, of promoting ongoing efforts by many small producers to control marketing and production through autonomous, producer-owned cooperatives.

In a perverse twist on the increasingly popular campesino strategy of "appropriating the production process," the Subcommittee thus

---

[62] Subcomité Especial 1989d. "Coyote" is a derogatory term for an exploitative middleman.

cast private-sector exporters and agroindustrialists as small producers' principal allies in their struggle to control coffee processing and marketing. Presumably through charity or noblesse oblige, the agroindustrial elite would willingly cede control of these activities to small producers. Despite such rhetorical nods to the welfare of small producers, the Subcommittee's true objectives were described more accurately by a member of a grassroots producer cooperative: "Producers should produce, exporters should export" (author interview, Chiapas, October 1995).

The Subcommittee's efforts to promote direct marketing relations between small producers and private-sector exporters generated little enthusiasm among the former. An earlier scam by the government of Absalón Castellanos Domínguez had left small producers wary of state government–sponsored export schemes.[63] As one farmer put it, no one wanted to risk delivering their coffee on consignment, or for a small advance, to a "den of thieves" (author interview, Chiapas, October 1995).

Furthermore, the Subcommittee lacked funding. Mexico's extreme fiscal centralization severely limited the size of most state government budgets, and in 1989 the principal government agencies with money to spend in Chiapas's coffee sector were the federal National Indigenous Institute (INI) and PRONASOL. These two agencies were in the process of launching a joint national program to help small coffee producers cope with both a global price crash and INMECAFÉ's withdrawal.[64] INI and PRONASOL officials in Chiapas were not inclined to support initiatives intended to benefit wealthy private-sector elites. Rather than aiding the Subcommittee, these federal agencies backed an alternative marketing project launched by small producer organizations. This alternative project further weakened incentives for small producers to participate in the kinds of direct links with private exporters proposed by the Subcommittee.

By the end of the harvest of 1989–1990, the Subcommittee's efforts to promote such links had clearly failed. Through the rest of 1990, the Subcommittee functioned as little more than an advocate through which private-sector firms lodged complaints about petty corruption by local government officials (Subcomité Especial 1990). At the end of 1990, the Subcommittee was disbanded. The governor's crony capitalist project had been thwarted by an alliance between grassroots producer organizations and reformist federal government officials.

---

[63] In 1985, thousands of small coffee producers had delivered their harvests on consignment to the state government's newly created State Coffee Commission. Most were never paid. For Castellanos Domínguez's efforts to justify the Coffee Commission, see Rojas 1995: 35.

[64] For an overview of the INI–PRONASOL program, see INI–Solidaridad 1994. For a more critical appraisal, see Hernández Navarro and Célis Callejas 1994.

Mexico's Double-edged Federalism

Federalism has had a complex, contradictory impact on the prospects for democratic change in contemporary Mexico. On the one hand, federal institutional arrangements have enabled political opposition parties to achieve important victories at the state and local levels. Although it is by no means certain whether accumulation of such victories will eventually result in national regime change, the increasing number of subnational jurisdictions governed by opposition parties has posed a major challenge to the ruling party's hegemony.[65]

On the other hand, federalism has also benefited hard-line, anti-democratic elites within the PRI by facilitating the maintenance and strengthening of subnational authoritarian regimes. In an effort to appease such hard-line groups, reformist national-level incumbents have at times pursued a strategy of "selective feudalization," allowing regional authoritarian forces free rein at the subnational level.[66]

Furthermore, as this analysis has shown, neoliberal economic reforms have created additional opportunities for subnational authoritarian elites to expand their authority and broaden their support bases. As we have seen, INMECAFÉ's withdrawal triggered reregulation projects through which the governors of Mexico's coffee-producing states sought to generate rents and resources to help achieve their political goals. Rather than serving as a wedge for opposition groups to force national regime change by accumulating subnational victories, Mexico's federal institutional arrangements may contribute instead to the preservation and proliferation of authoritarian enclaves.

Despite the highly centralized character of Mexico's political system, federalism has enabled subnational elites to establish independent power bases, resulting in regimes with distinct dynamics at the state level. This chapter has identified three kinds of subnational authoritarian regimes: populist, traditional, and modernizing. As we have seen, the varied dynamics of these regimes help explain the dif-

---

[65] Indeed, the possibility for opposition groups to win at the subnational level may ultimately *slow* the pace of national-level democratization by deflecting direct challenges to the national regime. Hence the democratic opposition may fizzle out on the periphery, exhausting itself by chipping away at the incumbent regime's edges without ever reaching the center. On Mexican federalism and democratization, see Lujambio 1994. On the complex relationship between federalism and democratization more generally, see Linz 1996.

[66] Examples of selective feudalization include recent state governments in Tabasco, Guerrero, and Puebla.

ferent reregulation projects launched by incumbent authoritarian elites in response to neoliberal reforms.[67]

In Oaxaca and Guerrero, governors launched neocorporatist reregulation projects intended to build support among small producers. The contrasting leadership styles and coalitional bases of the populist regime in Oaxaca and the modernizing regime in Guerrero led to important differences in how neocorporatist projects were implemented: Oaxaca's government sought to negotiate with autonomous producer organizations not affiliated with the PRI; Guerrero's government favored repression against such groups. In the case of Chiapas, by contrast, the governor pursued a crony capitalist project designed to win the coffee oligarchy's support. The political support dilemmas faced by the modernizing regime in Chiapas helped explain the governor's choice of this reregulation project. In all three cases, we saw how reregulation generated divisible benefits and targetable rewards, thus serving as a potent tool for helping governors forge new alliances.

Although this chapter has focused on governors' top-down efforts to impose new institutions on regional coffee economies, the degree to which these elites were able to realize their authoritarian visions of post–INMECAFÉ policy making depended on the strengths and strategies of grassroots producer organizations.[68] These organizations opposed governors' reregulation projects in varied ways, and they frequently had an important impact on the kinds of new institutions for market governance that resulted. For example, in Chiapas and Oaxaca, local producer organizations launched their own reregulation projects "from below," seeking to construct new institutional arrangements (for example, collective marketing cooperatives) through which small producers themselves controlled processing and marketing. Although federal institutional arrangements can benefit subnational authoritarian elites by allowing them to cultivate autonomous support bases, these examples suggest that federalism may also create opportunities for *non-elite* groups in local civil society to organize and defend their interests.

It therefore bears emphasis that governors and state governments are not necessarily the only important actors in Mexico's subnational policy jurisdictions. Scholars seeking to understand the new institutions for economic governance emerging to replace those destroyed by neoliberal reforms would thus do well to study the strategic interactions between the elites who launch reregulation projects and the

---

[67] Although beyond the scope of this analysis, it could be a valuable undertaking to explore the implications of these different regime types for democratization processes at the subnational level.

[68] See Snyder (1997, 1999) on how strategic interactions between governors and grassroots producer organizations resulted in varied new institutions for economic governance across Mexico's coffee-producing states.

societal actors who may respond to them. Explanatory perspectives that combine a focus on actors "from above" (that is, elites, leaders, and incumbent politicians) with a focus on actors "from below" (that is, "subaltern" groups such as grassroots organizations and social movements) should greatly facilitate this task.

To conclude, an additional methodological point should be made. This study has employed a "comparative state politics" approach, which combines the search for causal regularities through case comparisons with sensitivity to case material grounded in extensive field research. Although such an approach has proven fruitful in work on other countries with federal systems, students of Mexican politics have made surprisingly few efforts to engage in systematic comparative analysis of state-level political institutions and processes.[69] Given the findings of this study that subnational regimes with distinct dynamics exist at the state level, the comparative analysis of state politics should prove an indispensable methodological tool for understanding Mexico's ongoing political and economic transformation.

References

Albarrán de Alba, Gerardo. 1994. "Preguntas en la permanente: ¿ajuste de cuentas, venganza política, 'quinazo' financiero?" *Proceso* 932 (September 12).

Aranda Bezaury, Josefina. 1992. "Camino andado, retos y propuestas: la Coordinadora Estatal de Productores de Café de Oaxaca," *Cuadernos del Sur* 1 (2): 89–112.

Bates, Robert H. 1983. "The Nature and Origins of Agricultural Policies in Africa." In *Essays on the Political Economy of Rural Africa*, by Robert H. Bates. New York: Cambridge University Press.

Calderón Mólgora, Marco Antonio. 1994. *Violencia política y elecciones municipales*. Zamora: El Colegio de Michoacán.

Camp, Roderic Ai. 1995. *Mexican Political Biographies, 1935–1993*. 3d ed. Austin: University of Texas Press.

Cantú Peña, Fausto. 1989. "Proyecto de ley para el fomento y desarrollo integral de la cafeticultura en el estado de Oaxaca." In *Primer encuentro estatal de estudio, analisis y capacitación sobre cafeticultura*. Gobierno del Estado de Oaxaca. Oaxaca: Secretaría de Desarrollo Rural.

Carbot, Alberto. 1989. *Fausto Cantú Peña: café para todos*. Mexico City: Grijalbo.

Castro Aguilar, José Luis. 1995. *Marco historico-juridico de los procesos electorales de Chiapas, 1825–1995*. Tuxtla Gutiérrez, Chiapas: Centro de Estudios Profesionales de Chiapas "Fray Bartolomé de Las Casas."

---

[69] Examples of comparative studies of subnational politics in other federal systems include Kohli 1987; Putnam 1993; Hagopian 1996. See Rubin 1996 for an analysis of the Mexican case, which employs a subnational comparative approach that emphasizes varied regional histories. The classic statement on comparative subnational analysis remains Linz and de Miguel 1966.

Ceceña, Ana Esther, and Andrés Barreda. 1995. "Notas para comprender el origen de la rebelión zapatista." In *Chiapas*. Vol. 1. Mexico City: Era.

Cobo, Rosario, and Lorena Paz Paredes. 1991. "El curso de la organización cafetalera en la costa grande de Guerrero," *Cuadernos Agrarios* 3 (September–December): 51–70.

Collier, Ruth Berins. 1992. *The Contradictory Alliance: State-Labor Relations and Regime Change in Mexico*. Berkeley: Institute for International and Area Studies, University of California, Berkeley.

CEPCO (Coordinadora Estatal de Productores de Café de Oaxaca). 1989. *El Cosechero* 1 (1).

Consejo Consultivo del Programa Nacional de Solidaridad. 1994. *El programa nacional de solidaridad*. Mexico City: Fondo de Cultura Económica.

Cornelius, Wayne A., Ann L. Craig, and Jonathan Fox, eds. 1994a. *Transforming State-Society Relations in Mexico: The National Solidarity Strategy*. La Jolla: Center for U.S.–Mexican Studies, University of California, San Diego.

Cornelius, Wayne A., Ann L. Craig, and Jonathan Fox. 1994b. "Mexico's National Solidarity Program: An Overview." In *Transforming State-Society Relations in Mexico: The National Solidarity Strategy*, edited by Wayne A. Cornelius, Ann L. Craig, and Jonathan Fox. La Jolla: Center for U.S.–Mexican Studies, University of California, San Diego.

Díaz Cárdenas, Salvador, et al. 1991. "El sistema agroindustrial café y sus perspectivas." In *Memoria del II seminario nacional sobre la agroindustria en México: alternativa para el desarrollo agroindustrial*. Vol. 1. Chapingo, Mexico: Universidad Autónoma Chapingo.

Díaz Cayeros, Alberto. 1995. *Desarrollo económico e inequidad regional: hacia un nuevo pacto federal en México*. Mexico City: Centro de Investigación para el Desarrollo, A.C.

Elizalde, Triunfo. 1995. "Han occurido 222 homicidios en Guerrero en 6 años," *La Jornada*, July 8.

Estrada Castañón, Alba Teresa. 1994a. *Guerrero: sociedad, economía, política, cultura*. Mexico City: Centro de Investigaciones Interdisciplinarias en Humanidades, Universidad Nacional Autónoma de México.

———. 1994b. "Guerrero." In *La república mexicana: modernización y democracia de Aguascalientes a Zacatecas*, edited by Pablo González Casanova and Jorge Cadena Roa. Vol. 2. Mexico City: Centro de Investigaciones Interdisciplinarias en Humanidades, Universidad Nacional Autónoma de México.

Extra de Oaxaca. 1990. "Faltaron por ejercer 3 mil MDP del pronasol, dice SPP," January 8.

Fox, Jonathan. 1993. *The Politics of Food in Mexico: State Power and Social Mobilization*. Ithaca, N.Y.: Cornell University Press.

———. 1994a. "The Difficult Transition from Clientelism to Citizenship: Lessons from Mexico," *World Politics* 46 (2).

———. 1994b. "Latin America's Emerging Local Politics," *Journal of Democracy* 5 (2).

———. 1996. "How Does Civil Society Thicken? The Political Construction of Social Capital in Rural Mexico," *World Development* 24 (6): 1089–1103.

Fox, Jonathan, and Josefina Aranda. 1996. *Decentralization and Rural Development in Mexico: Community Participation in Oaxaca's Munipal Funds Program.* Monograph Series, no 42. La Jolla: Center for U.S.–Mexican Studies, University of California, San Diego.

Fox, Jonathan, and Gustavo Gordillo. 1989. "Between State and Market: The Campesinos' Quest for Autonomy." In *Mexico's Alternative Political Futures*, edited by Wayne A. Cornelius, Judith Gentleman, and Peter H. Smith. La Jolla: Center for U.S.–Mexican Studies, University of California, San Diego.

García de León, Antonio. 1985. *Resistencia y Utopía: memorial de agravios y crónica de revueltas y profecías acaecidas en la provinica de Chiapas durante los últimos quinientos años de su historia.* Vol. 2. Mexico City: Era.

Gil Olmos, José. 1995. "Ha sido principalmente contra el PRD la violencia política del gobierno de Figueroa," *La Jornada,* July 13.

Gobierno del Estado de Oaxaca. 1989. *Primer encuentro estatal de estudio, análisis y capacitación sobre cafeticultura.* Oaxaca: Secretaría de Desarrollo Rural.

———. 1992a. *Del Oaxaca mágico al encuentro con la modernidad: seis años de transformación y desarrollo, 1986–1992, resumen estadístico.* Oaxaca: Gobierno.

———. 1992b. *Del Oaxaca mágico al encuentro con la modernidad: seis años de transformación y desarrollo, 1986–1992, marco legislativo.* Oaxaca: Gobierno.

———.1992c. *Del Oaxaca mágico al encuentro con la modernidad: seis años de transformación y desarrollo, 1986–1992, resumen general.* Oaxaca: Gobierno.

González Casanova, Pablo, and Jorge Cadena Roa, eds. 1994. *La república mexicana: modernización y democracia de Aguascalientes a Zacatecas.* 3 vols. Mexico City: Centro de Investigaciones Interdisciplinarias en Humanidades, Universidad Nacional Autónoma de México.

González Esponda, Juan, and Pólito Barrios, Elizabeth. 1995. "Notas para comprender el origen de la rebelión zapatista." In *Chiapas.* Vol. 1. Mexico City: Era.

González Oropeza, Manuel. 1987. *La intervención federal an la desaparición de poderes.* 2d ed. Mexico City: Instituto de Investigaciones Jurídicas, Universidad Nacional Autónoma de México.

Guerrero Anaya, Francisco Javier. n.d. "Campesino Organizations in Western Mexico: Four Responses to Deregulation." In *Institutional Adaptation and Innovation in Rural Mexico*, edited by Richard Snyder. La Jolla: Center for U.S.–Mexican Studies, University of California, San Diego. Forthcoming.

Guillén López, Tonatiuh. 1993. *Baja California, 1989–1992. Balance de la transición democrática.* Mexico City: El Colegio de la Frontera Norte/Fundación Friedrich Ebert.

Hagopian, Frances. 1996. *Traditional Politics and Regime Change in Brazil.* New York : Cambridge University Press.

Harvey, Neil. 1994. *Rebellion in Chiapas: Rural Reforms, Campesino Radicalism, and the Limits to Salinismo.* Rev. ed. Transformation of Rural Mexico Series, no. 5. La Jolla: Center for U.S.–Mexican Studies, University of California, San Diego.

Hernández Navarro, Luis. 1994. "The Chiapas Uprising." In *Rebellion in Chiapas*, by Neil Harvey, Luis Hernández Navarro, and Jeffrey W. Rubin. La Jolla: Center for U.S.–Mexican Studies, University of California, San Diego.

Hernández Navarro, Luis, and Fernando Célis Callejas. 1994. "Solidarity and the New Campesino Movements: The Case of Coffee Production." In *Transforming State-Society Relations in Mexico: The National Solidarity Strategy*, edited by Wayne A. Cornelius, Ann L. Craig, and Jonathan Fox. La Jolla: Center for U.S.–Mexican Studies, University of California, San Diego.

Huntington, Samuel 1991. *The Third Wave: Democratization in the Late Twentieth Century*. Norman: University of Oklahoma Press.

INEGI (Instituto Nacional de Estadística, Geografía e Informatica). 1994. *El ingreso y el gasto público en México, Edición 1994*. Mexico City: INEGI.

INI–Solidaridad. 1994. "La reforma del estado, cafeticultores en solidaridad." Mexico: Dirección del Programa de Apoyo a Productores de Café.

Kohli, Atul. 1987. *The State and Poverty in India: The Politics of Reform*. New York: Cambridge University Press.

Legorreta Díaz, María del Carmen. 1994. "Chiapas." In *La república mexicana: modernización y democracia de Aguascalientes a Zacatecas*, edited by Pablo González Casanova and Jorge Cadena Roa. Vol. 1. Mexico City: Centro de Investigaciones Interdisciplinarias en Humanidades, Universidad Nacional Autónoma de México.

———. 1995. "Chiapas." In *Marginación y pobreza en México*, edited by Gloria Vázquez Rangel and Jesús Ramírez López. Mexico City: Ariel.

Linz, Juan J. 1996. "Democratization and Types of Democracies: New Tasks for Comparativists." Paper presented at the Annual Conference of the Political Science Association, University of Glasgow, April 10–12.

Linz, Juan J., and Amando de Miguel. 1966. "Within-Nation Differences and Comparisons: The Eight Spains." In *Comparing Nations: The Use of Quantitiative Data in Cross-National Research*, edited by Richard L. Merritt and Stein Rokkan. New Haven, Conn.: Yale University Press.

Linz, Juan J., and Alfred Stepan. 1996. *Problems of Democratic Transition and Consolidation: Southern Europe, South America, and Post-Communist Europe*. Baltimore, Md.: Johns Hopkins University Press.

López Hernández, Max Arturo. 1988. *Proyecto político y planeacón estatal, 1984–1987. Caso estado de Guerrero*. Chilpancingo, Guerrero: Universidad Autónoma de Guerrero.

López Monjardín, Adriana. 1986. *La lucha por los ayuntamientos, una utopía viable*. Mexico City: Siglo Veintiuno.

Lujambio, Alonso. 1994. "Régimen presidencial, democracia mayoritaria y los dilemas de la transición a la democracia en México." In *Presidencialismo y sistema político: México y los Estados Unidos*, edited by Alicia Hernández Chávez. Mexico City: El Colegio de México.

Mackinlay, Horacio. 1996. "La CNC y el 'nuevo movimiento campesino' (1989–1994)." In *Neoliberalismo y organización social en el campo mexicano*, edited by Hubert C. de Grammont. Mexico City: Instituto de Investigaciones Sociales, Universidad Nacional Autónoma de México.

Martínez Assad, Carlos, and Álvaro Arreola Ayala. 1987. "El poder de los gobernadores." In *La vida política mexicana en la crisis,* edited by Soledad Loaeza and Rafael Segovia. Mexico City: El Colegio de México.

Martínez Vásquez, Víctor Raúl. 1990. *Movimiento popular y política en Oaxaca: 1968–1986.* Mexico City: Consejo Nacional para la Cultura y las Artes.

Moguel, Julio, and Josefina Aranda. 1992. "Los nuevos caminos en la construcción de la autonomía: La experiencia de la la Coordinadora Estatal de Productores de Café de Oaxaca." In *Autonomía y nuevos sujetos sociales en el desarrollo rural,* edited by Julio Moguel, Carlota Botey, and Luis Hernández. Mexico City: Siglo Veintiuno.

Mota Marín, Sergio. 1994. "Estructura económica de Chiapas." In *Chiapas, una radiografía,* edited by María Luisa Armendáriz. Mexico City: Fondo de Cultura Económica.

Munck, Gerardo L. 1998. *Authoritarianism and Democratization: Soldiers and Workers in Argentina, 1976–1983.* University Park, Penn.: Pennsylvania State University Press.

Paz Paredes, Lorena, and Rosario Cobo. 1992. "El proyecto cafetalero de la Coalición de Ejidos de la Costa Grande de Guerrero." In *Autonomía y nuevos sujetos sociales en el desarrollo rural,* edited by Julio Moguel, Carlota Botey, and Luis Hernández. Mexico City: Siglo Veintiuno.

Pólito, Elizabeth, and Juan González Esponda. 1996. "Cronología. Veinte años de conflictos en el campo: 1974–1993." In *Chiapas.* Vol. 2. Mexico City: Era.

Puig, Carlos. 1994. "Cabal contó en el extranjero con apoyo de funcionarios e institutionciones gubernamentales; según Salinas, era un ejemplo," *Proceso* 932 (September 12): 6–14.

Purcell, Susan Kaufman, and John F.H. Purcell. 1980. "State and Society in Mexico: Must a Stable Polity be Institutionalized?" *World Politics* 32 (2): 194–227.

Putnam, Robert. 1993. *Making Democracy Work: Civic Traditions in Modern Italy.* Princeton, N.J.: Princeton University Press.

Ravelo, Ricardo. 1994. "Cabal en Veracruz: un corredor de puertos, con apoyo de comunicaciones y transportes," *Proceso* 932 (September 12): 17.

Rodríguez, Victoria E., and Peter M. Ward. 1994. *Political Change in Baja California: Democracy in the Making?* Monograph Series, no. 40. La Jolla: Center for U.S.–Mexican Studies, University of California, San Diego.

Rodríguez, Victoria E., and Peter M. Ward, eds. 1995. *Opposition Government in Mexico.* Albuquerque: University of New Mexico Press.

Rodríguez Saldaña, Marcial. 1992. *La desaparición de poderes en el estado de Guerrero.* Chilpancingo, Guerrero: Universidad Autónoma de Guerrero.

Rojas, Rosa. 1995. *Chiapas: la paz violenta.* Mexico City: La Jornada/Ediciones.

Rubin, Jeffrey W. 1996. "Decentering the Regime: Culture and Regional Politics in Mexico," *Latin American Research Review* 31 (3): 85–126.

Santoyo Cortés, V. Horacio, Salvador Díaz Cárdenas, and Benigno Rodríguez Padrón. 1994. *Sistema agroindustrial café en México: diagnóstico, problemática y alternativas.* Chapingo: Universidad Autónoma Chapingo.

Snyder, Richard. 1997. "After the State Withdraws: Neoliberalism and the Politics of Reregulation in Mexico." Ph.D. dissertation, University of California, Berkeley.

————. 1999. "After Neoliberalism: The Politics of Reregulation in Mexico," *World Politics* 51 (2).

————. n.d. "Reconstructing Institutions for Market Governance: Participatory Policy Regimes in Mexico's Coffee Sector." In *Institutional Adaptation and Innovation in Rural Mexico*, edited by Richard Snyder. La Jolla: Center for U.S.–Mexican Studies, University of California, San Diego. Forthcoming.

Snyder, Richard, and James Mahoney. n.d. "The Missing Variable: Institutions and the Study of Regime Change," *Comparative Politics*, forthcoming.

Subcomité Especial de Producción y Comercialización del Café. 1989a. "1a. reunión del Subcomité Especial de Producción y Comercialización del Café: minuta de trabajo." March 7.

————. 1989b. Letter to C. Lic. José Patrocinio González Garrido, Governor of Chiapas. April 11.

————. 1989c. "2a. reunion del Subcomité Especial de Producción y Comercialización del Café: aprobación y contenido del programa de trabajo." March 28.

————. 1989d. "Chiapas: sector cafetalero." September.

————. 1990. Letter from Lic. Esteban Figueroa Aramoni, Coordinador General del Sub-Comité to C. Lic. Norberto de Gives C., Treasurer of the State of Chiapas. January 16.

————. n.d. "Puntos y sugerencias planteadas al Lic. Esteban Figueroa A., Coordinador del Sub-Comité Especial de Producción y Comercialización del Café."

Thompson, Mark R. 1996. "Off the Endangered List: Philippine Democratization in Comparative Perspective," *Comparative Politics* 28 (2): 179–205.

Torres, Gabriel. 1998. "The Agave War: Toward an Agenda for the Post–NAFTA Ejido.". In *The Future Role of the Ejido in Rural Mexico*, edited by Richard Snyder and Gabriel Torres. La Jolla: Center for U.S.–Mexican Studies, University of California, San Diego.

Villarreal, René. 1993. *Liberalismo social y reforma del estado: México en la era del capitalismo posmoderno*. Mexico City: Fondo de Cultura Económica.

Vogel, Steven K. 1996. *Freer Markets, More Rules: Regulatory Reform in Advanced Industrial Countries*. Ithaca, N.Y.: Cornell University Press.

Weber, Max. 1968. *Economy and Society*. Berkeley: University of California Press.

Yescas Martínez, Isidoro. 1991. *Política y poder en Oaxaca: la sucesión gubernamental de 1986*. Oaxaca: Dirección de Comunicación Social del Gobierno del Estado de Oaxaca.

14

State Electoral Conflicts and National Interparty Relations in Mexico, 1988–1994

Jean-François Prud'homme

An atypical form of electoral competition for Mexico's state governorships emerged during the presidency of Carlos Salinas de Gortari (1988–1994). This atypical form was most evident in gubernatorial elections held in the states of San Luis Potosí (1991), Guanajuato (1991), Michoacán (1992), Yucatán (1993), and Tabasco (1994). All were resolved (or almost resolved) through a process popularly known as *"concertacesión."* This term, a play on the words *concertación* and *cesión*, conveys the sense of ceding power through negotiation. For broad sectors of Mexico's ruling Institutional Revolutionary Party (PRI), in each of these disputed elections the federal government capitulated unnecessarily to the pressure of intensive opposition postelectoral mobilizations, effectively negotiating away victories duly won by the PRI at the polls. In contrast, from the perspective of the opposition, these negotiated electoral outcomes were interpreted as partial and inadequate solutions to the PRI's continuing practice of electoral fraud.

Each of these highly contested state elections followed a similar, dramatic trajectory. Opposition parties held sufficient evidence that the ruling party had violated the rules of free and fair competition to sustain mass protests against victorious PRI candidates. These demonstrations of the opposition's mobilizational capacities put into question the ability of PRI candidates to govern once they assumed

Translation by Tim Goodman.

office, and they eventually forced the federal government to enter into negotiations. The outcome of these negotiations between the opposition and the federal authorities was that winning PRI candidates were removed. In every case, the search for a resolution to post-electoral conflict took place outside of the designated judicial framework—that is, the state-level electoral institutions.

Quite apart from any judgments that can be made about the justice and validity of these resolutions to state-level post-electoral conflicts, the way such conflicts unfolded and were resolved highlights some of the particularities of the Mexican hegemonic party system during the period of the Salinas presidency. The settlements reveal a shift from one form of institutionalization to another. As Mainwaring and Scully assert, an increase in electoral competitiveness contributes to weakening the institutionalized features of hegemonic party systems (1996: 21).

The argument in this chapter is that the manner in which state post-electoral conflicts were resolved during the Salinas presidency is characteristic of a party system with a low degree of institutionalization. The need to preserve fragile agreements between parties at the national level made it necessary to resolve these state contests and their derivative conflicts outside of the designated normative framework. The type of solution that predominated involved recourse to a traditional defining feature of the Mexican political system: the president's metaconstitutional powers, which give him the political control to compel obedience from members of his own party.[1] Beyond their explicit function of renewing state officeholders, the elections under discussion here served the implicit function of ratifying good faith among the main political parties involved in negotiating changes to the rules of the electoral game at the national level. Hence the need to maintain the fragile equilibrium of the national political system directly influenced the form and dynamic of political struggles in the state subsystems.

The first of the following sections considers the strategic dimensions of change in a hegemonic party system, as well as the impact on local politics. The second examines four cases of highly contested state elections (San Luis Potosí, Guanajuato, Michoacán, and Chihuahua) in order to identify the key factors that influenced their outcomes. The Chihuahua case, which did not give rise to post-electoral conflict, has been included so as to highlight the implicit function of state elections in maintaining national party equilibriums.

---

[1] The means by which the president exercises metaconstitutional control over local politics are well documented in Casar 1996: 160–67. Also see Weldon 1997.

Change in a Hegemonic Party System

In its classic form, the Mexican party system has been defined as the prototype of a hegemonic-pragmatic party system (Sartori 1976).[2] Noncompetitive elections as defined by Hermet (Hermet, Rouquié, and Linz 1982) are the ruling party's principal hegemonic instrument.[3] The organization and supervision of elections constitute part of the functional political guardianship that underpins the authoritarianism of the regime. "Hegemony," understood in its etymological sense as "supremacy" or "management," continues to be the most apt term for describing the way the PRI used "institutional engineering" to maintain its predominance in the political system during the Salinas presidency. In the three electoral reforms that took place under Salinas (in 1989–1990, 1993, and 1994), the government's determination to retain partisan management of the electoral process was at the center of interparty negotiations. The ruling party's reluctance to abandon the logic of hegemony was exemplified by its stance during negotiations over electoral formulas and the management of the national electoral agency.

However, the hegemonic party system that was consolidated in 1946 has been submitted to change. The 1977 political reform marked the start of a period of intensified change in Mexico's party system and electoral politics (Middlebrook 1986). The electoral arena gradually came to occupy a fundamental place both in the system of interest representation and for the expression of political conflict. The increase in competitiveness within the system can be explained by a number of factors: the influence of the reform itself, the consolidation of opposition parties' electoral presence, the weakening of corporate mediations, and changes in the political culture (Crespo 1992: 21ff).

Defining the Mexican system as a hegemonic party system, and at the same time recognizing the existence of factors of change that necessarily bring about further change within it, begs the following question: how is change manifested within this hegemonic party system? Recently, the application of Sartori's model to the Mexican case has been critiqued on a number of grounds. One critique relates to the role of subordinate parties: the perspective from which Sartori elaborated his model overemphasizes the system legitimation function of

---

[2] According to Giovanni Sartori (1976: 230): "The hegemonic party neither allows for a formal nor a de facto competition for power. Other parties are permitted to exist, but as second class, licensed parties; for they are not permitted to compete with the hegemonic party in antagonistic terms and on an equal basis. Not only does alternation not occur in fact; it cannot occur, since the possibility of a rotation in power is not even envisaged."

[3] The institutional engineering of electoral reforms during the Salinas presidency is described in Molinar 1996: 137–59, and Prud'homme 1996.

subordinate parties and minimizes their anti-systemic behavior. Therefore, the model cannot adequately explain the historical behavior of an opposition party like the National Action Party (PAN), for example (see Lujambio 1991: 16–18). A second critique, based on an overly narrow interpretation of Sartori's text, associates hegemony with "election fraud" and the absence of competitiveness. Hence the conclusion that increased interparty competition and relatively clean elections in 1994 and 1995 demonstrate that the hegemonic dimension of PRI predominance had become defunct.

In this connection, it is worth recapturing the spirit of Sartori's model. Despite its imprecisions, the conceptual premise from which his hegemonic party system model (and his whole typology) is constructed is the notion of competition, understood as a structure that makes competitiveness possible. It was precisely change in this unequal structure of competition that was at the center of the three rounds of negotiations over the electoral regime during the Salinas administration, and which underpinned the continued need to think of a "definitive" reform.

From this perspective, the Mexican party system during Salinas's term can be characterized as a hegemonic party system under pressure to change. The functional problems in the system were associated with the tension between, on the one hand, the survival of hegemonic control mechanisms and, on the other, a real increase in competitiveness between parties. The disputed gubernatorial elections examined in this chapter have to be explained in terms of this context. To understand the dynamics of change occurring in the Mexican party system during this period, it is important to emphasize the following tendencies:

- Unequal conditions of competition do not prevent opposition parties from winning political ground. Notwithstanding unequal conditions of competition, transfers of power can occur.

- Political parties can monitor the system. They are not simply victims of circumstances beyond their control. They can select and implement strategies to augment their political capital, and some strategies will obviously be more successful than others.

- In Mexico, institutions have a high capacity to channel processes of change. Thus change continues to be part of the institutional political game, and legislative reform prevails over pacts as an instrument for producing agreement between actors.

- This situation produces a system of transactions in which actors negotiate the asymmetrical positions the electoral system assigns to them. In such negotiations, actors adopt strategies directed as much toward cooperation as confrontation. In turn, discriminating use of such strategies contributes to defining alignments in the party system.

As mentioned above, the history of interparty relations during the Salinas presidency demonstrates problems of institutional deficit in the party system. There are two identifiable phases in the consolidation of the system of interparty interaction during this period. The first phase was characterized by relations of limited cooperation between the PRI and the PAN, and relations of confrontation between the PRI and the Party of the Democratic Revolution (PRD). The second, which began in January 1994, was defined by relations of limited cooperation among all three political forces. This chapter argues that during the first phase, the system of interparty interaction did not succeed in generating the incentives necessary for obtaining consensual agreement among the principal political forces. There are four main reasons why this was the case.

First, there was a problem of incompatibility between cooperation and the maximization of electoral gain among actors (see North 1993: chap. 2). In effect, the political parties as rational competitors were not in conditions to acknowledge the important difference between the acceptance of procedures and the acceptance of the results of those procedures (see Przeworski 1991: 37–40). In the course of events, this became translated into confusion between strategies directed at negotiating the rules of the game and strategies for accumulating political power.

In this context, the Mexican party system produced incentives that led the main political forces to suppose that as much, if not more, could be gained without reaching a consensual agreement about the rules of the game (or about observing those rules) as by reaching such an agreement (or observing the rules). Thus the impossibility of reaching an agreement acceptable to all parties became one more factor in the parties' strategies for winning power. In many instances, as the cases examined below demonstrate, the parties developed an interest in resolving political conflict outside the agreed system of rules. It was only an external threat to the party system and institutional politics (in the form of the January 1994 Chiapas rebellion) that increased incentives for cooperation and the search for consensus on the production and observance of the rules of competition. It is this shift in the incentive structure that makes it possible to talk about the creation of a system of limited cooperation in relation to the 1994 electoral reform.

The second factor contributing to the weakness of incentives for consensus was that the rules of the game agreed among some of the actors seemed to resemble ephemeral guarantees confirming the state of political relations among their signatories, rather than norms underpinning formal and efficient institutional arrangements.[4] The fact that they seemed neither destined to last nor to be effective for the resolution of conflict encouraged adversaries to process political conflict outside these rules.[5]

Third, every legislature since 1986 has produced its own electoral reform; indeed, the last legislature of the Salinas administration produced two. This cycle of reform–elections–reform functioned according to a principle of trial and error, and gave rise to recurring patterns of interaction between the main political forces. In this cycle, elections constituted one instance for assessing correlations of forces between political groups; negotiations over reforms also represented opportunities for comparing forces. The importance of these reforms resided not only in their contents but also in the fact that they endorsed agreement among adversaries.

Fourth, in the context of this cycle of reforms, the process of trial and error involved the totality of relations of cooperation among parties. The consolidation of trust between adversaries emerged within a multilevel system of negotiation. This system encompassed legislative collaboration and involved negotiation over, and respect for, electoral rules at the national, state, and local levels. These levels, though constituting separate spheres with specific dynamics within federalist arrangements, were closely linked in terms of the horizontal diffusion of trust within the party system.[6]

In sum, during most of the Salinas presidency the dynamic of change within the Mexican party system did not, on its own, provide internal incentives to overcome differences between parties. Nor did it permit the consolidation of functional norms that would ensure the resolution of post-electoral conflicts. Relations of cooperation among political parties functioned in a partial manner; asymmetries were

---

[4] One should distinguish here between rules of equilibrium and rules of functioning. The former confirm existing relations between adversaries but do not serve to manage conflicts. When conflicts arise, other means must be found to resolve them and/or to renegotiate the rules. Rules of functioning presuppose the existence of accepted norms that allow the resolution of conflict regardless of its nature. In this author's judgment, until nearly the end of the Salinas administration, Mexico's electoral legislation operated more as rules of equilibrium than as rules of functioning.

[5] In the three cases of post-electoral conflict examined in the second part of this chapter, for example, the deficiencies of the state-level electoral agencies were due not only to their characteristics and means of integration and functioning, but also to the fact that the opposition parties could not judicially prove their allegations of fraud in a satisfactory manner. Eisenstadt (1994) has examined this problem in the federal elections.

[6] In strict terms, the states have independent authority to promulgate their own election laws, which consequently differ from those of the federal government. However, for reasons related to the presidentialist and virtually unitary nature of Mexican federalism, in practice rulings in the states tend to be closely linked to those at the federal level.

negotiated and centrifugal tendencies favored. The limited cooperation achieved regarding electoral reform and legislative collaboration
still had to be ratified in practice; this is how the relations of limited
cooperation established between the PRI and the PAN in the course of
Salinas's term should be understood (see Craig and Cornelius 1996:
288–90; Molinar 1996: 149–55). Constituted in this way, the system of
interaction encouraged polarization and the exclusion of other political forces, as the relationship between the PRI and the PRD demonstrates. It seemed that the only possible way change could occur from
within the party system was if one of the forces polarizing negotiations were to collapse—an unlikely eventuality given their strong
bases of electoral support.

The disputed state elections discussed below occurred in the context of a party system characterized by a low degree of institutionalization and by centrifugal tendencies created by relations of limited
cooperation between the PRI and the PAN and the polarization of the
PRI and the PRD. In light of the party system's low level of institutionalization, it is not surprising that President Salinas's interventions
as an arbiter and guarantor of agreements proved crucial to the outcomes of these contested elections: informal political channels came to
the rescue of institutions incapable of preserving interparty equilibriums.

Four Contested Elections

Throughout the Salinas presidency, state and local elections took
place in an atmosphere of high political tension. In a number of cases,
these elections sparked protest movements that channeled their demands outside formal institutional mechanisms. The segmentation of
competitiveness within the national electoral system, along with the
federal government's determination to divert democratic challenges
toward state and local subsystems, helps explain the regionalization
of electoral conflict. This regionalization of conflict was reinforced by
a series of elections that, in addition to fulfilling the explicit function
of renewing officeholders, also implicitly served to confirm the existence of good faith and respect for established agreements between
political parties at the national level.

In this type of elections, formal and informal negotiations among
contending parties were a constant, a fact that underscores both the
low levels of trust between political parties and the limited capacity of
the legal framework as a channel for resolving electoral conflict. In
practice, the real rules were altered: electoral outcomes were determined not only by majority principle but also by the ability of con-

tending parties to make their multiple political resource capabilities count.[7]

In addition to the federal and local authorities' immediate need to preserve governability, it is possible to identify a number of key factors that contributed to shaping electoral outcomes in each case. These include the history of political conflict in each state, the configuration of local political forces, the vote-winning capacity of the main political organizations, the correlation of political forces nationally, the availability of negotiating channels, and the opposition parties' capacity for post-electoral mobilizations and territorial control.[8] The following sections examine four state elections in which opposition forces played an important role: the elections held in San Luis Potosí and Guanajuato on August 18, 1991, and those that took place in Chihuahua and Michoacán on July 12, 1992.[9]

San Luis Potosí

The August 1991 gubernatorial elections in San Luis Potosí took place in the context of a state with a strong tradition of opposition struggles for clean elections. This tradition dates back to the Navista movement in the 1950s and was reinvigorated in the course of opposition mobilizations against PRI fraud during the 1982 and 1986 municipal elections in the state capital (also named San Luis Potosí).[10] In terms of local political forces, the 1991 elections pitched a state PRI machine fractured by ten years of internal factional struggles against a coalition of autonomous opposition forces that came together under the banner of the Potosí Civic Front (Frente Cívica Postosino)—the Navista movement's civic organization. This broad coalition brought together the National Action Party, the Party of the Democratic Revolution, the Mexican Democratic Party (PDM), and the Civic Front itself behind the candidacy of the charismatic Dr. Salvador Nava. The coalition campaign emphasized both the local character of the contest and Nava's willingness to cooperate with the PRI federal government once in power.

---

[7] The notion of "multiple political resources" includes both those resources that allow fraudulent victories and those that allow the overturning of electoral outcomes through successful post-electoral mobilization—resources that do not form part of the normal electoral game in democratic political systems.

[8] These observations develop ideas discussed in an earlier work; see Prud'homme 1994: 93–94.

[9] Information about these cases was obtained primarily from national and local newspapers. For the first three cases, newspaper reports were complemented by direct observation and personal interviews with the main local political leaders.

[10] See Calvillo, this volume, for a detailed examination of this case. It is discussed here for the purposes of comparison.

For most of the campaign period, relations between the contending forces were characterized by limited cooperation: the two candidates signed a "civility pact," and both sides maintained an ongoing dialogue with the federal authorities. But these relations ruptured when the pact broke down one week before election day. Following the vote count, the PRI candidate was declared the winner by a margin of two to one; the Civic Front had easily carried the capital while the ruling party had triumphed in the countryside. However, with evidence of widespread fraud, the Navista movement refused to recognize the official election results. Rejecting the option of presenting their evidence of fraud to the relevant state electoral authorities, the Navistas launched mass protests and began what was to prove a long post-electoral campaign.

Initially, the correlation of forces at the national level was not favorable to the Navista movement. From the perspective of the federal government, the very existence of a broad coalition of opposition forces represented a dangerous precedent. The national leadership of the PAN, prioritizing the struggle of its own gubernatorial candidate in the post-electoral conflict unfolding in Guanajuato, gave the Navista movement only lukewarm support. The national leadership of the PRD actively supported the Navistas but, due to the party's ongoing standoff with the PRI, lacked informal channels for negotiating with the federal government. The most effective informal channels for negotiating the movement's demands were those commanded by Dr. Nava himself.

Nonetheless, the Navistas demonstrated substantial mobilizational capabilities, especially in the state capital; and after the newly elected PRI governor in Guanajuato was forced to resign following mass protests by the PAN, Nava's campaign got a second wind. Thereafter, reinforced by the backing of the national PAN as well as the PRD, and with grassroots supporters occupying the state capital, Dr. Nava embarked on a "Dignity March" in order to present the movement's demands to the authorities in Mexico City. After more than a month of mass mobilization, and as the political significance of their campaign escalated and threatened to acquire national importance, the Navistas finally forced the resignation of the newly installed PRI governor of San Luis Potosí, Fausto Zapata.

It is impossible to know what outcome the 1991 gubernatorial contest in San Luis Potosí might have had if the elections had been clean. Likewise, we can never know the actual extent and nature of the fraud perpetrated by the PRI. What is clear, though, is that both Zapata's resignation and the appointment of an interim governor committed to holding fresh elections within a short space of time were the result of presidential decisions enforced through informal mechanisms within the system. For a brief moment, through their capacity to sustain mobilization, to undermine local governability, and to project their demands into the national political system, the Navistas succeeded in reversing the conditions of semi-competitiveness that characterized the elections. It is evident, moreover, that the option of influencing presidential decisions was included among the Civic Front's campaign strategies from the start.

Guanajuato

Prior to the 1991 gubernatorial elections, Guanajuato did not have a reputation for being a state with a strong tradition of opposition struggle and electoral contestation. Nonetheless, a tradition did exist: the right-wing Catholic Sinarquista movement had contested elections back in the 1940s, and both the PAN and the PDM had won municipal election victories during the 1980s.

Whatever the state's imputed reputation, it quickly became evident that the 1991 governor's race would be hotly disputed. The first sign to this effect came at the start of the campaign period when the state electoral authorities refused Porfirio Muñoz Ledo permission to register as the PRD's candidate—though this matter was eventually resolved after recourse to nonelectoral legal channels. Notwithstanding the initial controversy surrounding the PRD candidate, the gubernatorial race showed all the characteristics of a classic two-party contest. The PAN, with strong bases of support in the León-Celaya corridor, was a strong contender against a local PRI force that had been weakened by internal divisions following the imposition of an outside candidate by the central party. Vicente Fox Quesada, the PAN's gubernatorial candidate, was a charismatic local businessman; Ramón Aguirre, the PRI's candidate, meanwhile, was former regent of Mexico City.

The campaign period witnessed no civility pacts and was characterized by acrimonious relations between the contending parties. The election day results gave the PRI a wide margin of victory (200,000 votes), but instances of direct and indirect electoral fraud were well documented (Cano 1995: 21). The PAN challenged the validity of the election results through the relevant state legal channels and simultaneously launched intensive mass mobilizations. Although the PAN presented evidence that electoral irregularities had occurred in over seven hundred polling stations, the State Electoral Commission annulled the voting returns from just thirty, not nearly enough to modify the outcome (*Proceso*, September 2, 1991).

At the national level, the results of the federal congressional elections (held the same day as the Guanajuato elections) were far from encouraging for the "gradualist" strategy of democratic transition that the PAN national leadership had pursued since the start of Salinas's term. Discontent with this gradualist policy among the party's grassroots supporters was inflamed by events in Guanajuato, which in turn threatened the viability of limited cooperation between the PAN and the PRI in negotiating new rules of electoral competition. Eleven days after the elections, as a result of intensive mass mobilizations in the state and the ongoing dialogue pursued by PAN leaders with high-ranking federal government representatives, governor-elect Aguirre was forced to resign. Aguirre's resignation came just hours after the PRI–dominated state legislature had formally ratified his electoral victory. Subsequently, the state legislature endorsed the PAN municipal president of León, Carlos Medina Placencia, as interim governor with instructions to organize fresh elections in the near future.[11] Once again, the electoral outcome was determined by a high-level political decision and the opposition's capacity to mobilize its political resources; juridical rules proved incapable of processing the electoral conflict.

Chihuahua

Throughout the 1980s, the PAN's electoral mobilizations in Chihuahua had important demonstration effects on the opposition protests against electoral fraud in other states. The outstanding case was the PAN's sustained protest and civil resistance campaign against fraud in the 1986 gubernatorial elections, a campaign that was led by PAN gubernatorial candidate Francisco Barrio and supported by other opposition forces.

In 1992, two-party competition was more firmly established in Chihuahua than in any other state in Mexico. On the one hand, the PAN had a well-consolidated presence throughout the state and counted on a broad base of political support. On the other, departing PRI governor Fernando Baeza had succeeded in reforming the power structure of the local PRI and, in particular, reducing the influence of the corporate sectors. Indeed, the August 1992 gubernatorial campaign was seen as a trial by fire for the PRI's new electoral strategy which depended on intensive vote mobilization.[12]

---

[11] In fact, this interim period lasted almost four years. The next gubernatorial election, held in May 1995, was won by PAN candidate Vicente Fox. See Shirk, this volume.

[12] The PRI's campaign director in Chihuahua was Leonel Reyes, who was identified as one of the authors of the renovation of the party's electoral mobilization strategies following the 1988 federal elections. Instead of relying primarily on the corporate sectors, as it had previously, the PRI opted to "territorialize" its vote-winning effort and make greater use of local-level "ward heelers." In practice, this still entailed using traditional techniques to identify the geographical location of potential voters

The relationship between the two contenders, Francisco Barrio for the PAN and Jesús Macías for the PRI, reveals that negotiations were focused on the conditions of electoral competitiveness rather than electoral outcomes per se. In practice, the state's new election law was passed with the consensus of all parties, and subsequent conflicts about the administration of elections were resolved through the designated legal channels.[13] Even so, the PAN used its direct and indirect contacts with the highest levels of the federal government to keep the local PRI under constant pressure.[14] Significantly, throughout the campaign the PAN candidate insisted that his program was highly compatible with that being pursued by President Salinas nationally (see Fernández Menéndez 1992: 73).

In the event, the PAN won both the gubernatorial and state legislative elections, obtaining 51 percent of the vote against the PRI's 47 percent, and the majority principle determined the outcome. Thus Chihuahua constituted an exceptional case: negotiation focused on and effectively shaped the conditions of electoral competitiveness. The fact that state elections were held on the same day in Michoacán, where the PRD was the main opposition contender, may well have been an added guarantee that the Chihuahua elections would be conducted in an exemplary fashion.

Michoacán

Michoacán has been a stronghold of the left-wing Party of the Democratic Revolution since 1988. Manipulation of the electoral process by the PRI in the 1989 municipal and state legislative elections provoked intense protest and mobilization. By 1992, the electoral profile of the state was clearly bipartisan: between them, the PRI and the PRD commanded the support of over 90 percent of the electorate. The local PRI, with the help of massive federal aid for public investment in the state, had largely recovered from the collapse that had resulted from the defection of the Democratic Current (CD) in 1988. For its part, the PRD had consolidated a strong presence and grassroots support base, despite internal divisions: it governed 52 of the state's 113 municipalities.

Perhaps to an even greater extent than in Chihuahua, much more than local concerns were at stake in the 1991 elections in Michoacán.

---

and to make them turn out to vote on election day. Author interview with Leonel Reyes, July 1992.

[13] Author interview with Professor Tarrango, president of the PRI in Chihuahua, July 1992.

[14] Author interview with Jorge Manzanera, president of the PAN in Chihuahua, July 1992.

Key national factors that came into play in the state contest were the relative positions of the PRD and the PRI in the national political system, as well as their strategies regarding the transition to democracy and the possibility of forging broad agreement on the new rules of the political game.

The fact that the new state election law, which was to regulate the August 1992 elections, was approved by all political forces constituted an encouraging start to the contest. But from this point onward, relations between the parties deteriorated rapidly, and national political imperatives came to dominate the campaigns for the Michoacán governorship. The PRD candidate, Cristóbal Arias, modified his initial conciliatory discourse and increasingly adopted the rhetoric of anticipated fraud, denouncing the irregularities in the official electoral roll. For his part, the PRI candidate, Eduardo Villaseñor, used all the political resources at his disposal in his attempt to wipe out his adversary.[15] The two sides became increasingly polarized as the campaigns proceeded and the possibilities for political cooperation evaporated.

Although voting took place in a very tense atmosphere, contrary to widespread expectations the election day concluded without violent incident. According to the official results, the PRI obtained over a third more votes than the PRD (52 percent to 34 percent) (*Voz y Voto*, October 1995, p. 14). The PRD responded by repudiating the PRI victory and launched protests through both legal channels and street demonstrations. Attempts to find a political solution to the conflict between the two parties by way of a public examination of the electoral acts failed. Then on September 15, 1992, the state legislature, in a session held clandestinely without the PRD deputies, declared PRI candidate Villaseñor the governor-elect (*GEA Político* 1992b: 6). Confrontations continued for nearly two months. During this time Villaseñor attempted to prove the strength of his popular support and his capacity to govern despite PRD attempts to prove the contrary, until he finally relinquished office on October 6, 1992. The imminence of the December municipal elections and the possibility that the conflict might escalate had forced the government to yield to PRD pressure. Ausencio Chávez, a member of the PRI, was named interim governor, a post he was to occupy for three years.

Whatever moral judgments may be made regarding the contenders' behavior, the Michoacán case demonstrated the fragility of partial agreements on political rules in the context of low mutual trust among the main protagonists. Electoral competition took place on the fringes of—rather than within—the established judicial framework.

---

[15] See CEPNA 1992: 5. According to some estimates, the PRI candidate spent approximately 32 million pesos in the campaign, against some 650,000 pesos spent by the PRD candidate (*GEA Político* 1992a: 6).

The unequalness of the overall conditions of competition, which in this case included the PRI's massive campaign expenditure, overshadowed the existence or not of irregularities as defined by the rules regulating the electoral process. The outcome of the post-electoral conflict was determined by the opposition's mobilizational capacity and its ability to undermine governability. The absence of informal channels for negotiation between the government and the national PRD made resolution of the conflict much more difficult.

Negotiation and Conflict Resolution in the Four Elections

Three of the four cases summarized above illustrate the extremely transitory nature of agreements on the rules regulating state-level electoral competition during the Salinas presidency. Although state election laws are distinct from the Federal Code of Electoral Institutions and Procedures (COFIPE), they nonetheless reflect the spirit of the federal law.[16] In the most highly disputed cases, the elements that sustained the semi-competitiveness of the system rendered the laws and institutions governing the elections ineffective. Conflicts became channeled into demonstrations of forces in which the majority principle was supplanted by the principle of governability, understood in both its positive and negative senses—a fact that obviously did nothing to encourage civic practices. In other words, elected PRI officials attempted to show that they could control the political situation in the state and reestablish political stability, while the opposition sought to demonstrate the contrary.

Thus political negotiation—when channels of communication between opposition and government existed—became the only means of resolving conflict. In local elections, negotiations were channeled toward the president, who exercised his decision-making powers through the informal political procedures of the political system. Even in the case of Chihuahua, where elections took place squarely within the legal framework, continuous contact between the opposition and the federal authorities was essential for guaranteeing the legality of the local process. The fact that President Salinas's famous telephone call congratulating PANista Francisco Barrio on his victory occurred before Barrio had been formally declared governor-elect through the legal process underscores the president's role as arbiter of electoral outcomes.

Although the elections contested and resolved outside the legal channels introduced an element of arbitrariness into the process of political conflict resolution, they also served two latent (and unde-

---

[16] For a comparison of state election laws, see Crespo 1996.

sired) functions. They facilitated the establishment of new parameters for negotiating political rules acceptable to all parties, and they helped lay new informal bases for negotiations between political adversaries, a prerequisite for the consolidation of trust between parties. The objective of the post-electoral conflict resolutions that emerged (or might have emerged) from such disputed elections was to maintain the precarious national equilibrium in a weakly institutionalized system of party interaction.

The Salinas presidency witnessed a number of disputed state elections in addition to the cases described above. State elections in Yucatán (November 1993), Chiapas (August 1994), and Tabasco (November 1994) were all hotly contested and followed by post-electoral conflicts. In both Yucatán and Chiapas, post-electoral disputes were resolved outside legal channels, a fact that was closely linked to the need to preserve political equilibrium at the national level. In the case of Yucatán, elections were held just nine months before the August 1994 federal presidential and congressional elections, a time when it was essential to preserve relations of cooperation between the PRI and the PAN. In Chiapas, the resignation of PRI governor Eduardo Robledo Rincón was part of a package of conciliation measures that followed the military offensive against the Zapatista Army of National Liberation (EZLN) in February 1995. Finally, the Tabasco conflict followed a different course, marking a strategic shift between the Salinas administration and that of Ernesto Zedillo Ponce de León (1994–2000) (see Eisenstadt, this volume).

Conclusion

Both the particular features of the state electoral conflicts that erupted during the Salinas presidency and the manner in which they were resolved are characteristic of a party system with a low degree of institutionalization. During the period examined, the Mexican case demonstrates the coexistence of institutional features associated with the hegemonic dimension of the party system and characteristics associated with the increase in interparty competitiveness. The features associated with the hegemonic dimension were of little utility for resolving conflict through institutional channels, while norms of competition effectively adapted to the increase in interparty competitiveness had yet to be developed.

In this context, the rules negotiated between political parties resembled inoperative rules that ratified the good faith between adversaries, rather than efficient norms that would ensure effective conflict resolution. Thus, prior to the 1994 electoral reform, which established limited relations of cooperation between the main parties, the party system did not offer sufficient incentives to channel political action within the explicit norms. Parties could expect to gain as much from channeling their electoral demands outside the legal framework as from channeling such demands within it. Put differently, the odds were such that the PRI could still bet on winning through fraud or the inappropriate use of public resources, and the opposition parties could bet on preventing the PRI from winning (and even obtaining public offices) through post-electoral mobilization.

Equilibrium within the system was fragile and depended upon a series of events that either facilitated or inhibited the horizontal diffusion of trust among opponents. Such trust circulated (or failed to circulate) through multilevel networks of party transactions in which national electoral affairs, state and local electoral politics, and legislative collaboration in congress were closely interconnected. The interrelations between these three levels are crucial to understanding interparty relations during the Salinas presidency.

In this context, beyond their overt function of renewing political authorities, contested state elections acquired the latent function of ratifying the parties' degree of good (or bad) will in relation to agreements reached at the national level. However, in the context of a weakly institutionalized party system, in which the agreed norms are ineffective for processing conflict, the demonstration of trust is problematic for two reasons. First, the dynamic of political conflict departs from the classic realm of electoral competition and becomes a struggle about governability, thereby introducing a distinct political logic—the policy of the fait accompli. Second, in the absence of effective formal institutions of conflict resolution, conflicts are resolved by means of the system's informal political channels and resources. In the cases examined above, resolutions were obtained through recourse to the de facto resources accorded the Mexican president.

It is likely that this particular form of resolving contested state elections will decline with the consolidation of relations of limited cooperation among Mexico's main national political parties and with the progression toward electoral rules that operate as effective norms for resolving post-electoral conflicts. The introduction of federal penalties for electoral crimes committed at the local and state levels would constitute an important step in this direction. It would allow the federal judiciary to assume, in an institutionalized form, powers that until now have been exercised in an informal and arbitrary manner by the nation's president.

References

Cano, Arturo. 1995. "Guanajuato: cuando la revancha los alcance," *Voz y Voto* 26 (April).

Casar, María Amparo. 1996. "The Sources of Presidential Authority in Post-Revolutionary Mexico." Mexico City: Centro de Investigación y Docencia Económicas.

CEPNA. 1992. "El porvenir de la democracia: Michoacán y Chihuahua," *Este País* 16 (July).

Craig, Ann L., and Wayne A. Cornelius. 1996. "Houses Divided: Parties and Political Reform in Mexico." In *Building Democratic Institutions: Party Systems in Latin America*, edited by Scott Mainwaring and Timothy R. Scully. Stanford, Calif.: Stanford University Press.

Crespo, José Antonio. 1992. "Crisis económica: crisis de legitimidad." In *México: auge, crisis y ajuste*, edited by Carlos Bazdresch et al. Mexico City: Fondo de Cultura Económica.

———. 1996. *Votar en los estados: análisis comparado de las legislaciones electorales estatales en México*. Mexico City: Miguel Angel Porrúa.

Eisenstadt, Todd. 1994. "Evaluating Formal and Informal Constraints on the Independence of Mexico's Federal Electoral Tribunal." Paper presented at the Eighteenth International Congress of the Latin American Studies Association, Atlanta, Georgia, March 10–12.

Fernández Menéndez, Jorge. 1992. "Chihuahua y Michoacán; un día después," *Nexos* 176 (August).

GEA Político. 1992a. "La gubernatura de Michoacán," vol. 48 (July 14).

———. 1992b. "Michoacán," vol. 53 (September 23).

Hermet, Guy, Alain Rouquié, and Juan Linz. 1982. *¿Para qué sirven las elecciones?* Mexico City: Fondo de Cultura Económica.

Lujambio, Alonso. 1991. "Towards an Ambiguous Democracy: Electoral Laws and Democratization Process in Mexico." Mimeo.

Mainwaring, Scott, and Timothy R. Scully, eds. 1996. *Building Democratic Institutions: Party Systems in Latin America*. Stanford, Calif.: Stanford University Press.

Middlebrook, Kevin J. 1986. "Political Liberalization in an Authoritarian Regime: The Case of Mexico." In *Latin America*. Vol. 2 of *Transitions from Authoritarian Rule: Prospects for Democracy*, edited by Guillermo O'Donnell, Philippe C. Schmitter, and Laurence Whitehead. Baltimore, Md.: Johns Hopkins University Press.

Molinar, Juan. 1996. "Changing the Balance of Power in a Hegemonic Party System: The Case of Mexico." In *Institutional Design in New Democracies: Eastern Europe and Latin America*, edited by Arend Lijphart and Carlos H. Waisman. Boulder, Colo.: Westview.

North, Douglas C. 1993. *Instituciones, cambio institucional y desempeño económico*. Mexico City: Fondo de Cultura Económica.

Prud'homme, Jean-François. 1994. "Elecciones, partidos y democracia." In *La construcción de la democracia en México*. Mexico City: ILET/Siglo Veintiuno.

———. 1996. "La negociación de las reglas del juego: tres reformas electorales (1988–1994)," *Política y Gobierno* 3 (2): 93–128.

Przeworski, Adam. 1991. *Democracy and the Market: Political and Economic Reform in Eastern Europe and Latin America.* Cambridge: Cambridge University Press.

Sartori, Giovanni. 1976. *Parties and Party Systems: A Framework for Analysis.* Cambridge: Cambridge University Press.

Weldon, Jeffrey. 1997. "The Logic of Presidentialism in Mexico." In *Presidentialism and Democracy in Latin America*, edited by Scott Mainwaring and Matthew Soberg Shugart. Cambridge: Cambridge University Press.

Acronyms

AEDPCH	Asamblea Estatal Democrática del Pueblo Chiapaneco / Democratic State Assembly of the Chiapanecan People
AMDH	Academia Mexicana de Derechos Humanos / Mexican Human Rights Academy
ANIPA	Asamblea Nacional Indígena Plural por la Autonomía / National Indigenous Assembly for Autonomy
ARDF	Asamblea de Representantes del Distrito Federal / Assembly of Federal District Representatives
ARIC	Asociación Rural de Interés Colectivo / Rural Collective Interest Association
BANAMEX	Banco Nacional de México / National Bank of Mexico
BANRURAL	Banco Nacional de Crédito Rural / National Rural Credit Bank
CCE	Consejo Coordinador Empresarial / Private-Sector Coordinating Council
CD	Corriente Democrática / Democratic Current
CDP	Coalición Democrática Potosina / Potosí Democratic Coalition
CDP	Comité de Defensa Popular / Popular Defense Committee
CECCAM	Centro de Estudios para el Cambio en el Campo Mexicano / Center for Studies to Promote Change in Rural Mexico
CECODES	Centro de Ecodesarrollo / Center for Ecodevelopment
CEE	Comisión Electoral Estatal / State Electoral Commission
CEN	Consejo Ejecutivo Nacional / National Executive Council

CEOIC	Consejo Estatal de Organizaciones Indígenas y Campesinas / State Council of Indigenous and Peasant Organizations
CEPCO	Coordinadora Estatal de Productores de Café de Oaxaca / Oaxaca State Coffee Producers' Network
CFE	Código Federal Electoral / Federal Electoral Code
CFE	Comisión Federal de Electricidad / Federal Electricity Commission
CIOAC	Central Independiente de Obreros Agrícolas y Campesinos / Independent Confederation of Agricultural Workers and Peasants
CM500ARI	Consejo Mexicano de Quinientos Años de Resistencia India y Popular / Mexican Council of Five Hundred Years of Indigenous and Popular Resistance
CNC	Confederación Nacional Campesina / National Peasants' Confederation
CNDH	Comisión Nacional de Derechos Humanos / National Human Rights Commission
CNOC	Coordinadora Nacional de Organizaciones Cafetaleras / National Coordinating Committee for Coffee Producers' Organizations
CNPI	Coordinadora Nacional de Pueblos Indígenas / National Coordinating Committee of Indigenous Peoples
CNPP	Confederación Nacional de Pequeños Propietarios / National Confederation of Small Property Owners
COCEI	Coalición Obrero Campesina Estudiantil del Istmo / Coalition of Workers, Peasants, and Students of the Isthmus
COCEO	Coalición Obrero Campesina Estudiantil de Oaxaca / Coalition of Workers, Peasants, and Students of Oaxaca
COFIPE	Código Federal de Instituciones y Procedimientos Electorales / Federal Code of Electoral Institutions and Procedures
CONAPO	Consejo Nacional de Población / National Population Council
COPARMEX	Confederación Patronal de la República Mexicana / Mexican Employers' Confederation
COPLADE	Comité de Planeación para el Desarrollo Estatal / Planning Committee for State Development
CORFO	Corporación Forestal / Chiapas Forestry Corporation

CPNAB	Consejo de Pueblos Nahuas del Alto Balsas / Council of Nahua Communities of the Upper Balsas
CROC	Confederación Revolucionaria de Obreros y Campesinos / Revolutionary Confederation of Workers and Peasants
CROM	Confederación Regional Obrera Mexicana / Mexican Regional Labor Confederation
CUD	Coordinadora Única de Damnificados / Earthquake Victims' Coordinating Committee
EPR	Ejército Popular Revolucionario / Popular Revolutionary Army
EZLN	Ejército Zapatista de Liberación Nacional / Zapatista Army of National Liberation
FCT	Frente Cívico Tabasqueño / Tabasco Civic Front
FDN	Frente Democrático Nacional / National Democratic Front
FEPADE	Fiscalía Especial para la Atención de Delitos Electorales / Special Prosecutor for Electoral Crimes
FIPI	Frente Independiente de Pueblos Indios en Chiapas / Independent Front of Indigenous Peoples of Chiapas
FSTSE	Federación de Sindicatos de los Trabajadores al Servicio del Estado / Federation of Public Service Workers' Unions
GATT	General Agreement on Tariffs and Trade
GEA	Gestión y Estudios Ambientales / Environmental Studies Group
GNGO	governmental nongovernmental organization
ICA	International Coffee Agreement
IEPES	Instituto de Estudios Políticos, Económicos y Sociales / Institute of Economic, Political, and Social Studies
IFE	Instituto Federal Electoral / Federal Electoral Institute
IMF	International Monetary Fund
INAH	Instituto Nacional de Antropología e Historia / National Institute of Anthropology and History
INI	Instituto Nacional Indigenista / National Indigenous Institute
INMECAFÉ	Instituto Mexicano del Café / Mexican Coffee Institute
MCD	Movimiento Ciudadano por la Democracia / Citizens' Movement for Democracy

MIPRI	Movimiento Integrado del Partido Revolucionario Institucional / Integrated PRI Movement
MOCRI	Movimiento Campesino Regional Independiente / Independent Regional Peasant Movement
NAFIN	Nacional Financiera / National Credit Bank
NAFTA	North American Free Trade Agreement
NGO	nongovernmental organization
OCEZ	Organización Campesina Emiliano Zapata / Emiliano Zapata Peasant Organization
PAN	Partido Acción Nacional / National Action Party
PARM	Partido Auténtico de la Revolución Mexicana / Authentic Party of the Mexican Revolution
PCM	Partido Comunista Mexicano / Mexican Communist Party
PDM	Partido Demócrata Mexicano / Mexican Democratic Party
PEMEX	Petróleos Mexicanos / Mexican Petroleum Company
PFCRN	Partido del Frente Cardenista de Reconstrucción Nacional / Party of the Cardenista Front for National Reconstruction
PGJDF	Procuraduría General de Justicia del Distrito Federal / Attorney General of the Federal District
PMS	Partido Mexicano Socialista / Mexican Socialist Party
PPS	Partido Popular Socialista / Socialist Popular Party
PRD	Partido de la Revolución Democrática / Party of the Democratic Revolution
PRI	Partido Revolucionario Institucional / Institutional Revolutionary Party
PRM	Partido de la Revolución Mexicana / Party of the Mexican Revolution
PRONASOL	Programa Nacional de Solidaridad / National Solidarity Program
PRT	Partido Revolucionario de los Trabajadores / Revolutionary Workers' Party
PST	Partido Socialista de los Trabajadores / Socialist Workers' Party
PSUM	Partido Socialista Unificado de México / Mexican Unified Socialist Party
PT	Partido del Trabajo / Labor Party
PT	Partido dos Trabalhadores / Workers' Party (Brazil)

PVEM	Partido Verde Ecologista de México / Mexican Green Party
SARH	Secretaría de Agricultura y Recursos Hidráulicos / Ministry of Agriculture and Water Resources
SCT	Secretaría de Comunicaciones y Transportes / Ministry of Transportation
SEDESOL	Secretaría de Desarrollo Social / Ministry of Social Development
SER	Servicios del Pueblo Mixe / Services of the Mixe People
SHCP	Secretaría de Hacienda y Crédito Público / Ministry of Finance
SNTE	Sindicato Nacional de Trabajadores de la Educación / National Education Workers' Union
SPP	Secretaría de Programación y Presupuesto / Ministry of Planning and Budget
SRA	Secretaría de la Reforma Agraria / Ministry of Agrarian Reform
SSA	Secretaría de Salubridad y Asistencia / Ministry of Health and Welfare
SUTERM	Sindicato Único de Trabajadores Electricistas de la República Mexicana / General Union of Mexican Electrical Workers
TEE	Tribunal Electoral Estatal / State Electoral Tribunal
UCD	Unión Campesina Democrática / Democratic Campesino Union
UCIRI	Unión de Comunidades Indígenas de la Región del Istmo / Union of Indigenous Communities of the Isthmus
UCL	Unión Cívica Leonesa / Civic Union of León
UE	Unión de Ejidos / Union of Ejidos
UGOCEP	Unión General Obrera Campesina Popular / Popular Union of Workers and Peasants
UNAM	Universidad Nacional Autónoma de México / National Autonomous University of Mexico
UNOSJO	Unión de Organizaciones de la Sierra de Juárez / Union of Organizations of the Sierra Juárez
UNS	Unión Nacional Sinarquista / National Sinarquist Union
UU	Unión de Uniones Ejidales (y Grupos Campesinos Solidarios de Chiapas) / Union of Ejido Unions (and Solidary Peasant Groups of Chiapas)

About the Contributors

Kathleen Bruhn is Assistant Professor of political science at the University of California, Santa Barbara. Her research has focused primarily on the Mexican Left. She is the author of *Taking on Goliath: The Emergence of a New Left Party and the Struggle for Democracy in Mexico*, about the creation of the Partido de la Revolución Democrática (PRD) (Pennsylvania State University Press, 1996). She has also written about welfare spending and campaigns in Mexico, as well as the Zapatista movement.

Tomás Calvillo Unna, a historian, is President of El Colegio de San Luis in San Luis Potosí. His academic research focuses on the regional political history in Mexico, especially the political history of Navismo in San Luis Potosí. He has published several articles on this subject.

Wayne A. Cornelius is the Gildred Professor of Political Science and founding Director of the Center for U.S.–Mexican Studies at UCSD. He now serves as the Center's Director of Studies and Programs. A specialist on Mexican politics and international migration, his most recent books include *The Transformation of Rural Mexico: Reforming the Ejido Sector* (coedited with David Myhre; Center for U.S.–Mexican Studies, 1998) and *Mexican Politics in Transition*, 5th ed. (Center for U.S.–Mexican Studies, 1999).

Todd A. Eisenstadt is a visiting professor of public administration at El Colegio de México, where he is researching democratization in Mexico and other protracted transitions, political party behavior, and judicial politics. He received his doctorate in political science in 1998 from the University of California, San Diego, for the dissertation "Courting Democracy in Mexico: Party Strategies, Electoral Institution-Building, and Political Opening." He is currently revising his dissertation for publication.

Víctor Alejandro Espinoza Valle is Academic Director of El Colegio de la Frontera Norte in Tijuana. He holds doctorates in political sociology (Universidad Complutense de Madrid) and political science

(Universidad Nacional Autónoma de México). His most recent publications are *Alternancia política y gestión pública: el Partido Acción Nacional en el gobierno de Baja California* (El Colegio de la Frontera Norte, 1988) and "El Congreso de Estado en Baja California," in the *Revista Mexicana de Sociología* (1998).

Neil Harvey is Assistant Professor in the Department of Government at New Mexico State University. He has carried out extensive research on campesino movements and rural policy reforms in Chiapas and is the author of *The Chiapas Rebellion: The Struggle for Land and Democracy* (Duke University Press, 1998) and *Rebellion in Chiapas: Rural Reforms, Campesino Radicalism, and the Limits to Salinismo* (Center for U.S.–Mexican Studies, 1994).

Luis Hernández Navarro, a social anthropologist, is a consultant to the Coordinadora Nacional de Organizaciones Cafetaleras (CNOC) and a researcher at the Centro de Estudios para el Cambio en el Campo Mexicano (CECCAM) in Mexico City. He has written widely on rural issues and social and peasant movements in Mexico. Among his recent publications are *Chiapas: la guerra y la paz* (ADN Editores, 1995) and *Chiapas: la nueva lucha india* (Talasa, 1998).

Jane Hindley is a lecturer in the Department of Sociology at the University of Essex, UK, where she teaches courses on comparative development, Latin American politics, ethnicity and gender. She has written a number of articles on indigenous politics in Mexico, including "Towards a Pluricultural Nation: The Limits of Indigenismo and Article 4," in *Dismantling the Mexican State?* (St. Martin's Press, 1996). She is currently completing a book based on her doctoral thesis, "Indigenous Mobilization, Development and Political Reform in Mexico" (University of Essex, 1997).

Jean-François Prud'homme received his doctorate in Political Science from York University, Canada. He has written extensively on the Mexican political system in journals and edited books, and is also a regular contributor to *Nexos* and *Voz y Voto*. He was formerly a research professor at El Colegio de México and is currently a researcher in the División de Estudios Políticos of the Centro de Investigación y Docencia Económicas en Mexico City.

Jeffrey W. Rubin, a political scientist, is a Fellow at the Center for the Critical Analysis of Contemporary Culture at Rutgers University. His research focuses on radical grassroots movements, and he has written on the cultural and political contradictions within the COCEI and on interpretations of postrevolutionary Mexican politics. He is currently conducting research on democracy and grassroots innovation in Mexico and Brazil. His most recent publication is *Decentering the Regime: Ethnicity, Radicalism, and Democracy in Juchitán, Mexico* (Duke University Press, 1997).

David Shirk is a Ph.D. candidate in the Department of Political Science at the University of California, San Diego. His dissertation, "The Growing PAiNs of Mexico's Partido Acción Nacional," focuses on the processes of the party's professionalization, growth, and internal cleavage in three PAN strongholds: Tijuana, Baja California; León, Guanajuato; and Mérida, Yucatán.

Richard Snyder is Assistant Professor of Political Science at the University of Illinois, Urbana-Champaign. His work on comparative political economy and the study of regime change has appeared in journals such as *World Politics, Comparative Politics,* and *Studies in Comparative International Development.* He is the co-editor of *The Future Role of the Ejido in Rural Mexico* (Center for U.S.–Mexican Studies, 1998) and the editor of *Institutional Adaptation and Innovation in Rural Mexico* (Center for U.S.–Mexican Studies, forthcoming). Snyder is currently completing a book manuscript entitled *Politics after Neoliberalism: Reregulation in Mexico.*

Ligia Tavera-Fenollosa, a sociologist, is a Professor and Researcher at the Facultad Latinoamericana de Ciencias Sociales (FLACSO) in Mexico City. She recently completed her dissertation, "Social Movements and Civil Society: The Mexico City 1985 Earthquake Victim Movement," for Yale University. Her research interests include the ideational dimension of social movements, particularly in relation to democratization processes, and the relationship between movements and civil society, especially their embeddedness in preexisting associational networks and organizations. Her publications include "Movimientos sociales," in *Léxico de la política* (forthcoming).

Gabriel Torres holds a doctorate in agricultural and environmental science from the University of Wageningen and is a Researcher and Professor at the Centro de Investigaciones y Estudios Superiores en Antropología Social de Occidente. His research interests include social movements and local power structures in rural Mexico. Among his recent publications are "The Agave War: Toward an Agenda for the Post–NAFTA Ejido," in *The Future Role of the Ejido in Rural Mexico* (Center for U.S.–Mexican Studies, 1998) and "El discurso modernizante y las estrategias de las organizaciones campesinas emergentes," in *Las disputas por el México rural* (El Colegio de Michoacán, 1997).

Publication of important new research on Mexico and U.S.–Mexican relations is a major activity of the Center for U.S.–Mexican Studies. Statements of fact and opinion appearing in Center publications are the responsibility of the authors alone and do not imply endorsement by the Center for U.S.–Mexican Studies, the International Advisory Council, or the University of California.

For a list of all Center publications and ordering information, please contact:

Publications Sales Office
Center for U.S.–Mexican Studies
University of California, San Diego
9500 Gilman Drive, DEPT 0510
La Jolla, CA 92093-0510
Phone (619) 534-1160   Fax (619) 534-6447
e-mail: usmpubs@weber.ucsd.edu